'This study offers a fresh interpretation of queenship and the ways in which queens wielded power in late Medieval and early modern society. Jewellery is often dismissed as a trivial topic when in fact it is at the heart of politics. Tallis remarkably reveals its true importance in defining and challenging power – especially when it came to queens. Thoroughly researched and with an accessible prose, this book is undeniably a significant contribution to the field and is going to be a great resource for students, scholars, and members of the public alike who have an interest in queens and power.'

Estelle Paranque, *New College of the Humanities, UK*

'This exciting new work is an excellent example of innovative new work in queenship studies, tracing the evolution of the queen's jewel collection during a particularly turbulent period from the Wars of the Roses to the last of Henry VIII's six wives. This engaging read demonstrates the importance of the queen's jewels in underpinning her role by projecting majesty as well as enhancing her networks through gift exchange.'

Elena Woodacre, *University of Winchester, UK*

'This study of the jewel collections of the queens consort of England between 1445 and 1548 offers a fluent, engaging, and very informative account of an important aspect of female royalty. Nicola Tallis's book contributes original research to a generation of scholarship into the material history of late-medieval European queenship, drawing on evidence from inventories, wills, portraiture, commissions to artisans, and correspondence. The book presents a comprehensive account of the production, acquisition and care of the queens' jewels and their use as personal adornment and gifts in a wide range of contexts. It ably demonstrates how the deployment of the queens' jewels was an integral part of the magnificence of Plantagenet and Tudor monarchy.'

Glenn Richardson, *St Mary's University, UK*

All the Queen's Jewels, 1445–1548

From Margaret of Anjou to Kateryn Parr, *All the Queen's Jewels* examines the jewellery collections of the ten queen consorts of England between 1445 and 1548 and investigates the collections of jewels a queen had access to, as well as the varying contexts in which queens used and wore jewels.

The jewellery worn by queens reflected both their gender and their status as the first lady of the realm. Jewels were more than decorative adornments; they were an explicit display of wealth, majesty and authority. They were often given to queens by those who wished to seek her favour or influence and were also associated with key moments in their lifecycle. These included courtship and marriage, successfully negotiating childbirth (and thus providing dynastic continuity) and their elevation to queenly status or coronation. This book explores the way that queens acquired jewels, whether via their predecessor, their own commission or through gift giving. It underscores that jewels were a vital tool that enabled queens to shape their identities as consorts and to fashion images of power that could be seen by their households, court and contemporaries.

This book is perfect for anyone interested in medieval and Tudor history, queenship, jewellery and the history of material culture.

Nicola Tallis is an independent historian, whose interests are sixteenth-century queenship and jewellery. She is the author of *Crown of Blood: The Deadly Inheritance of Lady Jane Grey* (2016), *Elizabeth's Rival: The Tumultuous Tale of Lettice Knollys, Countess of Leicester* (2017) and *Uncrowned Queen: The Fateful Life of Margaret Beaufort, Tudor Matriarch* (2019).

All the Queen's Jewels, 1445–1548

Power, Majesty and Display

Nicola Tallis

LONDON AND NEW YORK

Designed cover image: Portrait of the sixth wife of King Henry VIII of England, Catherine Parr (1512–1548) by unknown artist, oil on panel, late 16th century © IanDagnall Computing/ Alamy Stock Photo

First published 2023
by Routledge
4 Park Square, Milton Park, Abingdon, Oxon OX14 4RN

and by Routledge
605 Third Avenue, New York, NY 10158

Routledge is an imprint of the Taylor & Francis Group, an informa business

British Library Cataloguing-in-Publication Data
A catalogue record for this book is available from the British Library

Library of Congress Cataloging-in-Publication Data
Names: Tallis, Nicola, author.
Title: All the queen's jewels, 1445-1548 : power, majesty and display / Nicola Tallis.
Description: Abingdon, Oxon : Routledge, 2023. | Includes bibliographical references and index.
Identifiers: LCCN 2022025184 (print) | LCCN 2022025185 (ebook) | ISBN 9781032065014 (hardback) | ISBN 9781032065021 (paperback) | ISBN 9781003202592 (ebook)
Subjects: LCSH: Jewelry—Great Britain—History—To 1500. | Jewelry—Great Britain—History—16th century. | Queens—Great Britain—History. | Great Britain—History—Tudors, 1485-1603.
Classification: LCC NK7343 .T35 2023 (print) | LCC NK7343 (ebook) | DDC 739.270941—dc23/eng/20220719
LC record available at https://lccn.loc.gov/2022025184
LC ebook record available at https://lccn.loc.gov/2022025185

ISBN: 978-1-032-06501-4 (hbk)
ISBN: 978-1-032-06502-1 (pbk)
ISBN: 978-1-003-20259-2 (ebk)

DOI: 10.4324/9781003202592

Typeset in Sabon
by Apex CoVantage, LLC

All the Queen's Jewels, 1445–1548 is dedicated to my Dad, who inspired my love of jewels in the first place. With much love and gratitude.

Contents

Figures

Tables

Acknowledgements

Writing this book has been both my passion and a privilege, and my research in this field is something that I hope to nurture for many years to come. It has also brought me into contact with many wonderful scholars, historians and jewel enthusiasts, and to all of them I am extremely grateful. First and foremost, I must begin by thanking the truly inspirational Dr Elena Woodacre, without whom this work would never have begun – or, indeed, made into book form. Thank you for always championing me.

Huge thanks also go to Laura Pilsworth at Routledge, for commissioning the book and showing such enthusiasm for the project. I would also like to thank Isabel Voice for sourcing most of the images and for answering my endless questions so patiently. My agent, Donald Winchester, deserves the same thanks for his never-ending patience and support.

There have been so many people who have selflessly given up their time to read chapters of the book and offer feedback, and to them I offer my heartfelt thanks. These include my dear friend the late Christopher Warwick, Linda Porter, Marguerite Lipscomb, Gabby Storey, Natasha Awais-Dean and Joanna Laynesmith. Thank you so much for sharing references and for your suggestions, which I feel sure have infinitely improved the book. I would also like to sincerely thank Joanne Paul, James Ross, Estelle Paranque and Glenn Richardson.

Last but by no means least, thanks to my friends and family for standing by me on this journey. My parents have – as ever – supported me every step of the way, and without my husband, Matthew, I may have given up a long time ago. I love you all from the bottom of my heart.

Abbreviations

Add MS	Additional Manuscript
BJRL	*Bulletin of the John Rylands Library*
BL	British Library
BM	*Burlington Magazine*
CPR	*Calendar of the Patent Rolls Preserved in the Public Record Office, 1476–1509*, 3 vols. (London, 1901–1916)
CSPD	*Calendar of State Papers, Domestic: Edward VI, Mary and Elizabeth*, R. Lemon (ed.) (London, 1856)
CSPM	*Calendar of State Papers and Manuscripts in the Archives and Collections of Milan 1385–1618*, A.B. Hinds (ed.), 1 vol (London, 1912)
CSPS	*Calendar of State Papers, Spain*, G.A. Bergenroth et al. (ed.), 13 vols. (London, 1862–1954)
CSPV	*Calendar of State Papers, Venice*, R. Brown et al. (ed.), 38 vols. (London, 1864–1947)
EHR	*English Historical Review*
GC	Goldsmiths' Company
HLQ	*Huntingdon Library Quarterly*
L & P	*Letters and Papers, Foreign and Domestic, of the Reign of Henry VIII, 1509–1547*, J. Brewer et al. (ed.), 21 vols. (London, 1862–1932)
NPG	National Portrait Gallery
ODNB	*Oxford Dictionary of National Biography*, online edition (2004)

RCT	Royal Collection Trust
SoA	Society of Antiquaries
SP	State Papers
TNA	The National Archives

Explanatory Notes

This book features two queens called Elizabeth, three named Anne, and three named Katherine. Although each queen is generally referred to by her full title, for clarity it has been necessary in some instances to adapt the spellings of their names in order to differentiate them. Elizabeth Wydeville and Elizabeth of York are always referred to in terms of their surname and title, as stated here. The name 'Wydeville' is spelt in several different ways by scholars, and the variation most commonly adopted is 'Woodville'. However, 'Wydeville' is the contemporary spelling that is often adopted, and has thus been used here. In the same manner as the two Elizabeths, Anne Neville and Anne Boleyn are always referenced by their surnames, while Anne of Cleves is referred to as Anna of Cleves, Anna being the name she used when signing her name. Catherine of Aragon is spelt with a 'C' throughout, in reference to the fact that she was christened Catalina. Katherine Howard appears as it is spelt here, while Kateryn Parr refers to the way in which Kateryn herself often spelt her name.

A summary of the pieces and stones used in the jewel inventories included in this book can be seen in several tables in Chapter 3. Since at least the middle of the third millennium BC, gold was the most popular choice of metal for jewellery and remained so in the fifteenth and sixteenth centuries. In all cases hereafter the metal used was gold unless otherwise stipulated. There are also various points when an unspecified amount of stones are listed. For example, several objects are described as being garnished ‘with dyamountes’ or ‘with rubies’. When this occurs, a + sign is used in the table to indicate that there are more than the number stated.

Introduction

As she entered Canterbury Cathedral in the spring of 1520 alongside her husband and her nephew, the Emperor Charles V, the Venetian ambassador was struck by the Queen's appearance. Catherine of Aragon, he reported, 'wore a necklace of very large pearls, from which hung a very valuable diamond cross. Her head gear was of black velvet striped with gold lama, and powdered with jewels and pearls'.[1] Twelve years later in September 1532, Anne Boleyn was made Marquess of Pembroke, an occasion on which she was 'completely covered with the most costly jewels', as the Venetian ambassador observed.[2] Just months later Eustace Chapuys, the Imperial ambassador, noted that Anne attended Mass on the eve of Easter, 'loaded with diamonds and other precious stones'.[3] These references highlight the impact that a queen's jewels created in enhancing her visibility, for they not only were noticed by contemporaries but also drew enough attention for them to remark upon their opulence. This was completely intentional, for throughout history jewels have been viewed as the ultimate symbol of wealth and power: a visual statement of portable riches and a vital part of the projection of majesty.[4] Jewels were 'among the most splendid of the status symbols of the period' and were used to full and dazzling effect by monarchs and their consorts.[5]

In the 102 years from 1445 to 1547, six kings who formed a part of the Plantagenet and Tudor dynasties ruled England.[6] Between them they had ten consorts: Margaret of Anjou,

DOI: 10.4324/9781003202592-1

Elizabeth Wydeville, Anne Neville, Elizabeth of York, Catherine of Aragon, Anne Boleyn, Jane Seymour, Anna of Cleves, Katherine Howard and Kateryn Parr, and it is these women, as well as the jewels they owned, wore and used as part of their royal duties, who are at the core of this book. These consorts played an essential role in royal life: they were wives, mothers, patrons, intercessors and political players. Within this framework, jewels were an imperative tool, underpinning the queen's regality and supporting her in the fulfilment of her responsibilities.[7] Throughout the course of this book, these roles will be explored in various contexts, in order to demonstrate the significance of jewels as an integral element of the exercise of the queen's role. Given that the 'adornment of the queen's body was a vital means of projecting her status as queen', jewels were a pivotal feature of the backdrop of late medieval and early Tudor queenship.[8] They provided queens with tangible sources of wealth and power, which in turn allowed them to shape their own identities as consorts.

The period between 1445, when Margaret of Anjou married Henry VI, and 1548, when Kateryn Parr died, was both a unique and turbulent time of English queenship, and Joanna Laynesmith argued that during this era 'dynastic strife and changing political ideologies constantly reshaped and reinvented the rituals of queenship'.[9] Queens normally acquired their role through political and foreign alliances, but during this period personal reasons also influenced the king's selection for a consort, creating controversy in more than one instance. Similarly, the way in which queens relinquished their roles varied considerably during this period: while natural death – either their own or their husband's – was the normal mode through which a queen's reign ended, at this time we also see annulment, execution and the overthrow of monarchs bringing the tenures of consort to an unorthodox end.[10] The development of queenship and the changing roles of queen consorts in this period were both remarkable and unprecedented: both Margaret of Anjou and Elizabeth Wydeville's reigns were exceptional, for both were queens during a period of civil war that witnessed the deposition and reinstallation of their husbands at various points. The political turbulence of the period inevitably impacted upon them as individuals, queens, and consequently on their jewel collections and the transitions between them. Anne Neville also underwent an extraordinary shift between the opposing sides of the Wars of the Roses, as her first marriage was to Edward of Lancaster, the only son of Henry VI and Margaret of Anjou, yet her second marriage to the future Richard III transferred her to the house of York, through which she was ultimately elevated to queenship. The tussle for power between the rival houses of Lancaster and York did not end there, and arguably it was not until after 1509 that England began to experience a period of dynastic stability.

The turbulent nature of queenship, however, continued during the reign of Henry VIII. Both Catherine of Aragon and Kateryn Parr were given the power to act briefly as regents on the King's behalf while he was absent in 1513 and 1544, respectively – a dramatic contrast to Catherine of Aragon's fall from grace following her husband's decision to end their marriage in order to marry Anne Boleyn. Anne, in turn, wielded influence over Henry in a personal capacity, which materialised into her elevation as Queen of England. However, her fall in 1536 was both swift and unprecedented – she was the first queen of England to be executed, a fate that was later meted out to Katherine Howard, Henry's fifth wife and Anne's cousin. Though successful in dynastic terms through the production of a male heir, Jane Seymour's experience of queenship was cut short by her untimely death, and her successor Anna of Cleves held no sway with Henry during her short tenure as queen. Anna did, though, manage to retain an amicable relationship with him following the breakdown of their brief marriage. Considering the fates of her predecessors, the task that lay ahead of Kateryn Parr following her royal marriage in 1543 was an unenviable one. Yet it was a role that she performed admirably, taking the opportunity to establish herself firmly as Henry's consort and fashioning her own royal identity through a variety of means which included the considered use of jewels. Fundamentally, therefore, the combined turmoil of the Wars of the Roses that witnessed a transition between dynasties, the blending of the medieval period with the Renaissance and early modern, and the unusual experiences of Henry VIII's wives emphasise that this was a unique and distinctive period of English queenship. Moreover, the impact that this turbulent period had on the queens' collection of jewels – including the ways in which they were accumulated, dispersed and used – was profound.

Numerous works have demonstrated the ways in which queens used fashion to project their status, and the studies of Maria Hayward, Eleri Lynn and Evelyn S. Welch's edited collection are particularly relevant to the queens in this period.[11] Also important is Janet Cox-Rearick's article examining the dress of French consort queens and the Medici duchesses, and Erin Griffey's edited collection about fashioning women in Early Modern Europe.[12] When it comes to jewels, records and inventories relating to earlier medieval English queens survive, including those of Isabella of France, Philippa of Hainault, and Isabella of Valois, some of which have been the subject of previous research.[13] Likewise, work has also been done on the jewellery collection of Elizabeth I, but the period 1445–1548 has yet to be covered.[14] The only example of scholarship on the queens' jewels in this period comes from A.R. Myers, whose article considered Margaret of Anjou's use of jewels.[15] A comparative study of the jewel collections of these particular queens has never been undertaken, and this book therefore provides a new and essential strand of scholarly research to the field. Not only does it add a significant element to our understanding of queenship but also to English history and our knowledge of jewellery and material culture during this period. A broad range of sources have been used in this study in order to thoroughly examine this aspect of queenship, and on occasion contemporary European queens and English noblewomen have been incorporated as points of comparison. Documentary sources, variable in both quantity and quality, are analysed alongside portraits and material culture. Inevitably there are gaps, for there are no surviving documents that make reference to the jewel collections of Anne Neville, for example, and the only evidence of her ceremonial use of jewels refers to her coronation.[16] By contrast, there are several surviving accounts made by Margaret of Anjou's Keeper of the Jewels as well as the Queen's Book of expenses for the last year of

Elizabeth of York's life and inventories of the jewels of several of Henry VIII's wives.[17] This rich variety of both primary and secondary sources will be used in order to unpick and document the collections of the queens in this period.

The Development of Queenship

Theresa Earenfight asserted that queenship was a 'complex historical process that took shape over a considerable span of time', and the development of research on the subject has evolved considerably in recent years.[18] Research on queenship gathered pace in the 1960s, and, as a serious discipline, began to develop following the important work of Marion Facinger in 1968.[19] Facinger's seminal article, which used Capetian France as a case study, highlighted the importance and influence of queen consorts in relation to their husbands. This was in keeping with Pauline Stafford's assertion that both court and family gave queens 'legitimate authority and power'.[20]

In the 1980s academic interest in queens began to take further shape, with a significant amount of consequent work on queenship focused on both early medieval queens and their early modern successors. Following on from Facinger, Lois Huneycutt's contribution to the field has been invaluable. Huneycutt's article about medieval queenship explored some of the key themes, which were later expanded in her biography of Matilda of Scotland.[21] In this work, Huneycutt argued that a queen's political influence overlapped with the role that she was expected to play in the domestic sphere. Indeed, Elena Woodacre claimed that a consort's role was defined by her marriage to the sovereign, but the power she wielded was based on the strength of their personal relationship or the need of the king for his wife to be involved in the affairs of the kingdom.[22]

It is interesting to consider how queens have been seen through the prism of their husbands, and several scholars have explored the balance between kingship and queenship. Janet Nelson contended that queenship was fashioned 'by men and women in particular times and places', so that a queen's subjects understood her role: chiefly supporting her husband.[23] Marty Williams and

Anne Echols underlined that queens were expected to be discreet and subservient to their husbands, thereby reinforcing Nelson's view.[24] These opinions were in keeping with those expressed by Jacobus de Cessolis in his 1474 text, *The Game and Playe of the Chesse*, in which he claimed that 'a quene ought to be chaste, wyse, of honest lyf, wel manerd'.[25] In her important introduction to queens and queenship, Woodacre also supported this view, rightly asserting that while chastity was 'a prized quality for women generally for queens it was absolutely essential'.[26]

John Carmi Parsons, whose edited collection, *Medieval Queenship*, covered a broad chronological and geographical framework, claimed that there has long been an interest in queens.[27] He too presented arguments about the relationship between queens and their husbands, remarking that the queenship of Elizabeth Wydeville was grounded 'in her carnality' and Edward IV's passion for her.[28] Nelson expressed similar views, claiming that an astute queen exploited her sexuality – partially by her jewels and dress – in order to secure power.[29] Parsons believed that queens should be studied as individuals, and his study of Eleanor of Castile analysed her power as a consort, and the negative perception that her contemporaries had of such influence.[30] Margaret Howell's study of Eleanor of Provence also demonstrated the power and sway of a queen consort and provides a useful point of comparison when addressing the relationship between a husband and wife as a royal couple.[31]

In spite of the fruitful studies of individual rulers and their consorts (both male and female), Theresa Earenfight's 2007 article expressed the belief that queenship ought to be studied alongside kingship, rather than as an individual discipline, to understand how rulers and their consorts functioned as a unit.[32] Earenfight acknowledged that each office was important in its own right: kingship for its association with public authority, and queenship for its connection with 'private power' but argued that both roles should be studied as a pair in order to understand them fully.[33] Earenfight's contribution to queenship studies has been significant, and her article also emphasised that 'Queens are not born, they "become"'.[34] She expanded this concept further by asserting that 'One becomes a queen by living as a queen, changing the category as one incorporates and inspires it'.[35] Earenfight's work has also stressed that while queens were visible as the foremost women in the realm, the historical record has often obscured their actions.[36] This underlined the need for more studies, and Earenfight's 2013 book explored the themes of queenship in a European context.[37] Here she argued that a queen's authority depended on her proximity to the king, and this in turn had a profound impact on the influence she wielded. A consort, Earenfight asserted, was 'situated both inside and outside official power'.[38]

Thanks to the developments in portraiture, Earenfight observed that in a physical sense later medieval queens were more visible than their predecessors, which in turn had an effect upon their queenship.[39] This is certainly a valid point, and the rise of portraiture at the end of the fifteenth century will be analysed in Chapter 4. Earenfight claimed that the development of portraiture meant that for the first time, queens were depicted as 'an individual woman, not just an iconic image of an ideal queen'.[40] The representation of queens formed the basis of Kavita Mudan Finn's 2012 work. Incorporating all of the consorts in this book, Finn examined these queens in the context of contemporary culture, exploring the ways in which they have been depicted over time by chroniclers, poets and playwrights, providing a different perspective of queenship in this period.[41]

The role of the queen as a mother has been a popular theme among scholars, with Elena Woodacre suggesting that it was arguably the most vital aspect of queenship.[42] This element of queenship was not only important for securing the future of the dynasty, but 'it ensured a royal woman's future as well'.[43] Indeed, Helen Maurer argued that 'Motherhood was the defining moment for a queen consort', and recent work in the field has further considered this central element of queenship.[44] It was one of the themes explored by Liza Benz St John, whose work examined queenship in fourteenth-century England.[45] Benz argued that a queen immediately received power by virtue of her position as queen but acknowledged that when she produced an heir her symbolic power automatically increased.[46] Another excellent example of work in queenship studies, which follows on chronologically from Benz, is that of Joanna Laynesmith.[47] Rather than providing individual character studies, Laynesmith's work on the queens of the late fifteenth century concentrated on a number of themes that were relevant to the queens in their roles as consorts. Her focus was firmly on queenship and its development, and she discussed the expected roles of queens as mothers, intercessors and patrons, as well as their relationships with their husbands and courts. Laynesmith was also one of the first recent historians to dispute the traditional view of Elizabeth Wydeville as greedy and grasping and convincingly argued that Elizabeth would not have been able to promote the interests of her family without Edward IV's connivance.[48] She suggested that many of Edward IV's nobles were happy to ally themselves with Elizabeth's family by marriage, and viewed these matches as a sign of the queen's favour as opposed to her rapacity. Laynesmith's work covered intercession, the queen's household and patronage, and these themes also feature prominently in recent scholarly work.[49]

Academic studies on the lives of fifteenth-century queens have been plentiful. A.R. Myers not only wrote about Margaret of Anjou's jewels but also produced an article about her household, in which he compared Margaret's expenses with those of Joan of Navarre and Elizabeth Wydeville.[50] Helen Maurer drew on some of Myers' scholarship in her biography of Margaret, in which she examined Margaret's queenship and the extraordinary challenges she faced.[51] Thanks largely to the work of William Shakespeare, Margaret has earned a reputation as a domineering queen who broke with the expected conventions of a consort and ruled her husband.[52] Margaret was doubtless of strong character, but Maurer argued that during the early years of her queenship she conformed with the expected behaviour of a consort and was subservient to her husband. Maurer contended that it was Henry VI's descent into mental illness and the Wars of the Roses that forced Margaret's hand, propelling her into becoming a leading political force. Maurer's work enhanced many of the ideas expressed in Patricia-Ann Lee's 1986 article about Margaret's queenship, which also went some way to restoring Margaret's reputation alongside the later work of Laynesmith.[53]

In the same manner as her predecessor, Elizabeth Wydeville has earned an unfavourable reputation over the centuries.[54] David MacGibbon provided a balanced and thoroughly researched account of Elizabeth's life, presenting a sympathetic view of her and concluding that her reputation is largely undeserved.[55] Anne Sutton and Livia Visser-Fuchs also considered Elizabeth's reputation but did so in the context of her piety and her book collection.[56] These aspects of Elizabeth's personality and her scholarly interests are frequently overlooked, and Sutton and Visser-Fuchs' work therefore filled a vital gap.

Due to a lack of surviving source material, scholarship on Anne Neville has been restricted. The most thorough academic biography is that of Michael Hicks.[57] Hicks' task was an unenviable one, given the fragmentary nature of the sources, but the resulting book provided a well-researched and convincing picture of Anne's life. Fortunately, there is more evidence to help document the life of Anne's successor, Elizabeth of York. Elizabeth was the subject of Arlene Okerlund's biography and was also included in Laynesmith's study in the context of queenship.[58] Alison Weir's 2013 biography of Elizabeth is also important, and was based on sound academic research which offered many new insights into the life of the first Tudor queen.[59] Elizabeth also formed an integral part of Retha Warnicke's study of the queen and her six daughters-in-law.[60] This interesting work compared the seven queens in a variety of areas, including their religiosity and the structure of their households.

Garrett Mattingly's biography of Catherine of Aragon is widely regarded as the best in the field.[61] However, Theresa Earenfight's new biography with an emphasis on material culture has made a significant contribution to our knowledge and understanding of Catherine, both as a woman and as a queen.[62] Earenfight asserted that on her journey to England in 1501, 'infanta Catalina was transformed into Catherine, Princess of Wales', yet her Spanish heritage remained of the utmost importance to Catherine throughout her life.[63] Catherine was also the subject of Michelle Beer's research, which compared Catherine's queenship with that of her sister-in-law, Margaret Tudor.[64] Beer made a convincing case for Catherine as a successful and important consort, concluding that she was always a politically active queen whose advice Henry VIII relied upon.[65] An article by J. Dewhurst examined the failed pregnancies of both Catherine and her successor, Anne Boleyn.[66] As in all historical cases, it is difficult to draw accurate conclusions on scholarship of this nature, but Dewhurst effectively summarised the evidence and various arguments which have been made about the reproductive difficulties of both queens.

Anne Boleyn has attracted a great deal of scholarly interest, with Eric Ives' 2004 biography providing a comprehensive and analytical account of her life.[67] Using numerous examples of Anne's own scholarship, Ives was successfully able to demonstrate that Anne was a highly intelligent woman and important patroness. He also emphasised Anne's ability to use her learning to her advantage in engaging the attention of Henry VIII. As well as underlining Anne's achievements, Ives portrayed her vulnerability at the time of her fall. In addition to a book, Ives wrote a number of articles about Anne in which he examined her role in the English Reformation and her demise.[68] He was not alone in his interest on the latter topic, for Anne's disgrace has been the subject of many academic articles.[69] Like Ives, George Bernard's book provided an opportunity to reiterate the arguments expressed in his article about Henry VIII's second queen: that Anne was guilty of the crimes of which she was accused.[70] Bernard is unique among modern historians in this respect, for most are now in agreement that Anne was framed, and thus guilty of neither adultery nor incest.[71]

Aside from her collective work on Elizabeth of York and the six wives of Henry VIII, Retha M. Warnicke wrote extensively about Anne as an individual. In a number of articles, Warnicke examined Anne's childhood and her relationship with Sir Thomas Wyatt and placed her into the context of sixteenth-century queenship.[72] These all underlined the significance of Anne's role in sixteenth-century politics, and much of Warnicke's research was incorporated in her book about Anne's rise and fall.[73] In another context, Warnicke used Anne as a case study in her book about Tudor women who have acquired a poor reputation.[74]

Academic work on both Jane Seymour and Anna of Cleves has been limited. This may be partially explained by reason of their short reigns, though Jane did feature in an article by Richard L. DeMolen about the birth of her son and the controversy surrounding a Caesarean section.[75] Warnicke attempted to resolve the lack of scholarship around Anna of Cleves with the production of both an article and a book, which examined Anna's marriage and royal protocol in the sixteenth century.[76] In this she noted Henry VIII's disappointment upon discovering that – in his opinion – Holbein's portrait of Anna bore little resemblance to the woman herself.

Katherine Howard was represented in Warnicke's book about 'wicked' Tudor women.[77] In a similar manner to her cousin Anne Boleyn, Warnicke dealt with the origins of Katherine's poor reputation and sought to redress this. She concluded, though, by acknowledging that 'By her society's standards, Katherine led a wicked life' and was therefore more deserving of her reputation than Anne had been.[78] Gareth Russell's 2017 biography of Katherine is also excellent.[79] Russell's work not only gives the trajectory of Katherine's brief life and reign as queen but also demonstrates his extensive research on Katherine's household.

Kateryn Parr is arguably the best represented of the six wives, and Susan James presented her findings in her 2008 biography of the queen.[80] James's work concentrated on Kateryn's tenure as queen, emphasising her role as a royal patron of the arts and learning. In 1996 it was James who was responsible for the re-identification of a portrait of Kateryn, previously thought to have been Lady Jane Grey. James revealed that it was the sitter's jewellery that led her to conclude that the portrait was Kateryn.[81] Linda Porter's biography of Kateryn has also shed some much-needed light on the life of Henry VIII's sixth wife, affirming Kateryn's importance as a consort.[82] Additionally, Janel Mueller was responsible for compiling an edited collection of Kateryn's books and letters, in which she included a thorough analysis of their contents.[83]

The examples of scholarship cited throughout this section reveal the nature and extent of some of the existing work in the field of queenship on the consorts featured in this book. They also show the varying degrees in which contributions have been made to our knowledge of queens in the period 1445–1548. This book, however, will add a new dimension to our understanding of these important women and queenship in the period through an examination of the composition and use of the queens' jewel collections. It seeks to build upon the ideas presented by Joanna Laynesmith and Theresa Earenfight by examining another aspect of queenship and showcasing queens in the late medieval and early Tudor period as women who were able to craft their own personas through the prism of their jewels.

Aims

A key aim of this book is to build as complete a picture as possible of the jewellery collections of the queens between 1445 and 1548. Queens had access to two separate collections of jewels: ceremonial jewels that were Crown property and used to assist the queen in her role as consort, and personal jewels that were her own property and could be used to adorn the queen in her everyday life. Though two separate collections, these jewels fall into three different categories, and as such can sometimes be difficult to define. For the purpose of this book, they have been categorised as follows: the Crown Jewels (the jewels used to adorn the queen on ceremonial occasions, for example her coronation), the queen's jewels (those belonging to the queen/Crown and worn as part of the role in daily ceremonial and court life) and the queen's personal collection, which she may have brought into the role and could in theory take with her if she was widowed. Each of these collections will be analysed throughout the course of the book and will show that jewels were frequently recycled, broken down or re-fashioned. This can make determining their use and ownership more challenging to establish with certainty.

Of equal importance is examining some of the ways in which queens acquired jewels. There were many ways in which a queen could obtain jewels, including directly from foreign merchants. In 1546, for example, Christopher Haller, a merchant from Antwerp, was licenced by Henry VIII to 'resort into England with jewellery, goldsmiths' work, etc, for the pleasure of the King, Queen, nobles, gentlemen and others'.[84] This book, however, concentrates on the commissioning of jewels and gift giving as the primary means through which queens obtained, created and gave jewels to others. Gift giving overlaps with the final aim, which seeks to determine how queens used jewels, whether as demonstrations of power to enhance their own image or as gifts and rewards with a view to expanding and consolidating their networks. Exploring jewels in this context exemplifies the way in which these decorative objects provided queens with a tangible way of fashioning their identities, both as individuals and consorts, and allows us to learn more about their relationships with their husbands, families, household and court.

Considering the way in which queens used jewels in order to fulfil their roles as consorts is also paramount. This will be examined chiefly in the context of coronations and ceremonial occasions but also seeks to analyse jewels that were chosen for both decorative and more functional purposes.

Structure

The book has been structured thematically with a view to addressing each of its aims, and with this in mind Chapter 1 provides an introduction to jewellery in the period and the queenly use of jewels. To establish the nature of the queen's collections, the following three chapters discuss the key sources which give us an insight into their composition; Chapter 2 focuses on wills, while Chapter 3 analyses inventories. Surviving portraits can also be useful in terms of tracking specific pieces and visualising how queens used jewels in order to demonstrate power, and portraiture is therefore the subject of Chapter 4. The focus of Chapters 5 and 6 is the acquisition of jewels, beginning with the role of the goldsmith and the commissioning of jewels. The importance of gifts of jewels will be considered in Chapter 6, given that 'the visual language of objects conveyed the majesty of monarchy' and that gift giving was a vital means for queens to create and maintain networks at court and beyond.[85] Finally, Chapter 7 explores the Crown Jewels, used primarily for coronations and state occasions. They were stored separately from the other jewels used by queens in their roles as consorts and were worn less frequently. Likewise, they were unlike any other form of jewel available to the rest of society and were made to fulfil a specific purpose.[86] Taken together, these seven chapters will illuminate contemporary jewellery, the composition of the queen's jewel collections, and demonstrate how the wearing, use and gift giving of jewels were a vital aspect of fifteenth- and sixteenth-century queenship.

Notes

1 *CSPV*, iii, no. 50.
2 *CSPV*, iv, no. 802.
3 *CSPS*, iv, part 2, no. 1061.
4 J. Hollis (ed.), *Princely Magnificence: Court Jewels of the Renaissance, 1500–1630* (London, 1980), p. 3; D. Hinton, *Medieval Jewellery* (Aylesbury, 1982), pp. 20–1.
5 Hollis (ed.), *Princely Magnificence*, p. 9.
6 Henry VI, r. 1422–1461, 1470–1471. Edward IV, r. 1461–1470, 1471–1483. Edward V, r. 1483. Richard III, r. 1483–1485. Henry VII, r. 1485–1509. Henry VIII, r. 1509–1547.
7 B.J. Harris, 'The View from My Lady's Chamber: New Perspectives on the Early Tudor Monarchy', *HLQ*, 60 (1997), p. 216; M. Howell, *Eleanor of Provence: Queenship in Thirteenth Century England* (Oxford, 1998), p. 75.
8 E. Woodacre, *Queens and Queenship* (Leeds, 2021), p. 97.
9 J. Laynesmith, *The Last Medieval Queens* (Oxford, 2004), p. 129.
10 Ibid.
11 M. Hayward, *Dress at the Court of King Henry VIII* (Leeds, 2007); M. Hayward, *Rich Apparel: Clothing and the Law in Henry VIII's England* (Farnham, 2009); E. Lynn, *Tudor Fashion* (London, 2017); E. Welch, *Fashioning the Early Modern: Dress, Textiles, and Innovation in Europe 1500–1800* (Oxford, 2017).
12 J. Cox-Rearick, 'Power-Dressing at the Courts of Cosimo de'Medici and François I: The "moda alla spagnola" of Spanish Consorts Eléonore d'Autriche and Eleanora di Toledo', *Artibus et Historiae*,

30:60 (2009), pp. 39–69; E. Griffey (ed.), *Sartorial Politics in Early Modern Europe: Fashioning Women* (Amsterdam, 2019).

13 E 101/361/7; E 101/398/19; E 101/393/4; W.E. Rhodes, 'The Inventory of the Jewels and Wardrobe of Queen Isabella (1307–8)', *EHR*, 12 (1897), pp. 517–21; J. Cherry, 'Late Fourteenth-Century Jewellery: The Inventory of November 1399', *BM*, 130 (1988), pp. 137–40.

14 A.J. Collins (ed.), *Jewels and Plate of Queen Elizabeth I: The Inventory of 1574* (London, 1955).

15 A.R. Myers, 'The Jewels of Queen Margaret of Anjou', *BJRL*, 42 (1959), pp. 113–31.

16 See A.F. Sutton and R.W. Hammond (eds), *The Coronation of Richard III: The Extant Documents* (London, 1984).

17 E 101/409/14; E 101/409/17; E 101/410/2; E 101/410/8; E 101/410/11; E 36/210; BL, Royal MS 7 C XVI, f. 18r-31r; BL, Stowe MS 559, f. 55r-68r; SoA, MS 129, f. 178r-183v.

18 T. Earenfight, *Queenship in Medieval Europe* (Basingstoke, 2013), p. 31; See also R. Gibbons, 'Medieval Queenship: An Overview', *Reading Medieval Studies*, 21 (1995), pp. 97–107.

19 L. Benz St John, *Three Medieval Queens: Queenship and the Crown in Fourteenth-Century England* (Basingstoke, 2012), p. 24; M.F. Facinger, 'A Study of Medieval Queenship: Capetian France, 987–1237', *Studies in Medieval and Renaissance History*, 5 (1968), pp. 3–47.

20 P. Stafford, 'The Portrayal of Royal Women in England, Mid-Tenth to Mid-Twelfth Centuries', in J.C. Parsons (ed.), *Medieval Queenship* (Stroud, 1993), p. 146.

21 L.L. Huneycutt, 'Medieval Queenship', *History Today*, 39 (1989), pp. 16–22; L. Huneycutt, *Matilda of Scotland: A Study in Medieval Queenship* (London, 2003).

22 E. Woodacre, 'Introduction', in E. Woodacre (ed.), *Queenship in the Mediterranean: Negotiating the Role of the Queen in the Medieval and Early Modern Eras* (Basingstoke, 2016), p. 3.

23 J.L. Nelson, 'Medieval Queenship', in L.E. Mitchell (ed.), *Women in Medieval Western European Culture* (London, 1999), p. 179.

24 M. Williams and A. Echols, *Between Pit and Pedestal: Women in the Middle Ages* (Princeton, 1994), pp. 184–5.

25 J. de Cessolis, *The Game and Playe of the Chesse*, ed. J. Adams (Kalamazoo, 2009), p. 26.

26 Woodacre, *Queens and Queenship*, p. 14.

27 J.C. Parsons, 'Family, Sex and Power: The Rhythms of Medieval Queenship', in J.C. Parsons (ed.), *Medieval Queenship*, p. 1.

28 Ibid, p. 6.

29 Nelson, 'Medieval Queenship', p. 192.

30 J.C. Parsons, *Eleanor of Castile: Queen and Society in Thirteenth-Century England* (London, 1995).
31 Howell, *Eleanor of Provence*.
32 T. Earenfight, 'Without the Persona of the Prince: Kings, Queens and the Idea of Monarchy in Late Medieval Europe', *Gender and History*, 19 (2007), p. 2.
33 Ibid, p. 10.
34 Ibid, p. 14.
35 Ibid.
36 T. Earenfight, 'Highly Visible, Often Obscured: The Difficulty of Seeing Queens and Noble Women', *Medieval Feminist Forum: A Journal of Gender and Sexuality*, 44 (2008), pp. 86–90.
37 Earenfight, *Queenship*.
38 Ibid, p. 6.
39 Ibid, p. 185; See also Earenfight, 'Highly Visible', pp. 86–90.
40 Earenfight, *Queenship*, p. 185.
41 K. Mudan Finn, *The Last Plantagenet Consorts* (Basingstoke, 2012). See also K. Mudan, ' "So Mutable Is That Sexe": Queen Elizabeth Woodville in Polydore Vergil's *Anglica historia* and Sir Thomas More's *History of King Richard III*', in L. Oakley-Brown and L.J. Wilkinson (eds), *The Rituals and Rhetoric of Queenship: Medieval to Early Modern* (Dublin, 2009), pp. 104–17.
42 E. Woodacre and C. Fleiner (eds), *Royal Mothers and their Ruling Children: Wielding Political Authority from Antiquity to the Early Modern Era* (Basingstoke, 2015), p. 1.
43 Woodacre, *Queens and Queenship*, p. 44.
44 H.E. Maurer, *Margaret of Anjou: Queenship and Power in Late Medieval England* (Woodbridge, 2003), p. 39; J.C. Parsons, 'Mothers, Daughters, Marriage, Power: Some Plantagenet Evidence, 1150–1500', in J.C. Parsons (ed.), *Medieval Queenship*, pp. 63–78; Woodacre and Fleiner (eds), *Royal Mothers*; E. Woodacre and C. Fleiner (eds), *Virtuous or Villainous? The Image of the Royal Mother from the Early Medieval to the Early Modern Era* (Basingstoke, 2016).
45 L. Benz, 'Queen Consort, Queen Mother: The Power and Authority of Fourteenth Century Plantagenet Queens', unpublished PhD thesis, University of York, 2009; Benz, *Three Medieval Queens*.
46 Benz, 'Queen Consort', p. 23.
47 J.L. Chamberlayne, 'English Queenship 1445–1503', unpublished PhD thesis, University of York, 1999; Laynesmith, *Last Medieval Queens*.
48 Laynesmith, *Last Medieval Queens*; See M. Hicks, 'The Changing Role of the Wydevilles in Yorkist Politics to 1483', in C. Ross (ed.) *Patronage, Pedigree, and Power in Later Medieval England* (Gloucester, 1979), pp. 60–86 and J.R. Lander, 'Marriage and

Politics in the Fifteenth Century: The Nevilles and the Wydevilles', in *Crown and Nobility 1450–1509* (Montreal, 1976), pp. 94–126.

49 Benz, *Three Medieval Queens*; C. Campbell Orr (ed.), *Queenship in Britain, 1660–1837: Royal Patronage, Court Culture, and Dynastic Politics* (Manchester, 2002); R.M. Warnicke, *Elizabeth of York and Her Six Daughters-in-Law* (Basingstoke, 2017).

50 A.R. Myers, 'The Household of Queen Margaret of Anjou, 1452–3', *BJRL*, 50 (1957–8), pp. 79–113; A.R. Myers, 'The Captivity of a Royal Witch: The Household Accounts of Queen Joan of Navarre, 1419–21', *BJRL*, 24 (1940), pp. 263–84; A.R. Myers, 'The Household of Queen Elizabeth Woodville, 1466–7', *BJRL*, 50 (1967–8), pp. 207–15.

51 Maurer, *Margaret of Anjou*.

52 W. Shakespeare, *Henry VI, Part One*, ed. M. Taylor (Oxford, 2003); W. Shakespeare, *Henry VI, Part Two*, ed. R. Warren (Oxford, 2002); W. Shakespeare, *Henry VI, Part Three*, ed. R. Martin (Oxford, 2001). See also M.L. Stapleton, ' "I of Old Contemptes Complayne": Margaret of Anjou and English Seneca, *Comparative Literature Studies*, 43 (2000), pp. 100–33; S. Logan, 'Margaret and the Ban: Resistances to Sovereign Authority in Henry VI 1, 2, & 3 and Richard III', in S. Logan (ed.), *Shakespeare's Foreign Queens: Drama, Politics and the Enemy Within* (Basingstoke, 2018), pp. 209–60.

53 P.A. Lee, 'Reflections of Power: Margaret of Anjou and the Dark Side of Queenship', *Renaissance Quarterly*, 39 (1986), pp. 183–217; Laynesmith, *Last Medieval Queens*. See also D. Dunn, 'Margaret of Anjou, Queen Consort of Henry VI: A Reassessment of her Role, 1445–53', in R. Archer (ed.), *Crown, Government and People in the Fifteenth Century* (New York, 1995), pp. 107–43; D. Dunn, 'The Queen at War: The Role of Margaret of Anjou in the Wars of the Roses', in D. Dunn (ed.), *War and Society in Medieval and Early Modern Britain* (Liverpool, 2000), pp. 141–61.

54 See D. Mancini, *The Usurpation of Richard III*, trans. C.A.J. Armstrong (London, 1984).

55 D. MacGibbon, *Elizabeth Woodville: A Life* (London, 1938).

56 A. Sutton and L. Visser-Fuchs, 'A *'Most Benevolent Queen'*: Queen Elizabeth Woodville's Reputation, Her Piety and Her Books', *The Ricardian*, 10 (1995), pp. 214–45.

57 M. Hicks, *Anne Neville: Queen to Richard III* (Stroud, 2007).

58 A. Okerlund, *Elizabeth of York* (Basingstoke, 2009); Laynesmith, *Last Medieval Queens*.

59 A. Weir, *Elizabeth of York: The First Tudor Queen* (London, 2013).

60 Warnicke, *Elizabeth of York*.

61 G. Mattingly, *Catherine of Aragon* (London, 1942).

62 T. Earenfight, *Catherine of Aragon: Infanta of Spain, Queen of England* (Pennsylvania, 2021).

63 Ibid, p. 49. Earenfight's research on Catherine has also formed the basis of several other scholarly works. See T. Earenfight, 'A Precarious Household: Catherine of Aragon in England, 1501–1504', in T. Earenfight (ed.), *Royal and Elite Households in Medieval and Early Modern Europe* (Leiden, 2018), pp. 338–56; T.M. Earenfight, 'Raising *Infanta* Catalina de Aragón to be Catherine, Queen of England', *Anuario de estudios medievales*, 46 (2016), pp. 417–43; T. Earenfight, 'Regarding Catherine of Aragon', in C. Levin and C. Stewart-Nuñez (eds), *Scholars and Poets Talk about Queens* (New York, 2015), pp. 137–57.

64 M.L. Beer, 'Practices and Performances of Queenship: Catherine of Aragon and Margaret Tudor, 1503–1533', unpublished PhD thesis, University of Illinois, 2014; M.L. Beer, 'Between Kings and Emperors: Catherine of Aragon as Counsellor and Mediator', in H. Matheson-Pollock, J. Paul and C. Fletcher (eds), *Queenship and Counsel in Early Modern Europe* (Basingstoke, 2018), pp. 35–58; M.L. Beer, *Queenship at the Renaissance Courts of Britain: Catherine of Aragon and Margaret Tudor, 1503–1533* (Fakenham, 2018).

65 Beer, *Queenship*, p. 1.

66 J. Dewhurst, 'The Alleged Miscarriages of Catherine of Aragon and Anne Boleyn', *Medical History*, 28 (1984), pp. 49–56.

67 E.W. Ives, *The Life and Death of Anne Boleyn* (Oxford, 2004).

68 E.W. Ives, 'Anne Boleyn and the Early Reformation in England: The Contemporary Evidence', *Historical Journal*, 37 (1994), pp. 389–400; E.W. Ives, 'Faction at the Court of Henry VIII: The Fall of Anne Boleyn', *History,* 57 (1972), pp. 169–88; E.W. Ives, 'The Fall of Anne Boleyn Reconsidered', *EHR*, 107 (1992), pp. 651–64; E.W. Ives, 'Anne Boleyn on Trial Again', *Journal of Ecclesiastical History*, 62 (2011), pp. 763–77.

69 G.W. Bernard, 'The Fall of Anne Boleyn', *EHR*, 106 (1991), pp. 584–610; G.W. Bernard, 'The Fall of Anne Boleyn: A Rejoinder', *EHR*, 107 (1992), pp. 665–74; G. Walker, 'Rethinking the Fall of Anne Boleyn', *Historical Journal*, 45 (2002), pp. 1–29; R.M. Warnicke, 'The Fall of Anne Boleyn: A Reassessment', *History,* 70 (1985), pp. 1–15; R.M. Warnicke, 'The Fall of Anne Boleyn Revisited', *EHR*, 108 (1993), pp. 653–65; S. Lipscomb, 'The Fall of Anne Boleyn: A Crisis in Gender Relations?', in S. Lipscomb and T. Betteridge (eds), *Henry VIII and the Court: Art, Politics and Performance* (Farnham, 2013), pp. 287–305.

70 G.W. Bernard, 'Anne Boleyn's Religion', *Historical Journal,* 36 (1993), pp. 1–20; G.W. Bernard, *Anne Boleyn: Fatal Attractions* (London, 2010).

71 Ives, *Life and Death*, p. 345; Lipscomb, 'Fall of Anne Boleyn', p. 288.

72 R.M. Warnicke, 'Anne Boleyn's Childhood and Adolescence', *Historical Journal,* 28 (1985), pp. 939–52; R.M. Warnicke, 'The Eternal Triangle and Court Politics: Henry VIII: Anne Boleyn, and Sir Thomas Wyatt', *Albion,* 18 (1986), pp. 565–79; R.M. Warnicke, 'Anne Boleyn Revisited', *Historical Journal,* 34 (1991), pp. 953–4.
73 R. Warnicke, *The Rise and Fall of Anne Boleyn* (Cambridge, 1989).
74 R. Warnicke, *Wicked Women of Tudor England: Queens, Aristocrats, Commoners* (New York, 2012).
75 R.L. DeMolen, 'The Birth of Edward VI and the Death of Queen Jane: The Arguments for and Against Caesarean Section', *Renaissance Studies*, 4 (1990), pp. 359–91.
76 R.M. Warnicke, 'Henry VIII's Greeting of Anne of Cleves and Early Modern Court Protocol', *Albion,* 28 (1996), pp. 565–85; R.M. Warnicke, *The Marrying of Anne of Cleves: Royal Protocol in Tudor England* (Cambridge, 2004).
77 See Warnicke, *Wicked Women*, pp. 45–76.
78 Ibid, p. 75.
79 G. Russell, *Young and Damned and Fair: The Life and Tragedy of Catherine Howard at the Court of Henry VIII* (London, 2017).
80 S.E. James, *Catherine Parr: Henry VIII's Last Love* (Stroud, 2008).
81 S. James, 'Lady Jane Grey or Queen Kateryn Parr?', *BM,* 138 (1996), pp. 20–4.
82 L. Porter, *Katherine the Queen: The Remarkable Life of Katherine Parr* (London, 2011).
83 J. Mueller (ed.), *Katherine Parr: Complete Works and Correspondence* (Chicago, 2011).
84 *L & P*, xxi, part 2, no. 90.
85 Earenfight, *Queenship*, p. 86.
86 H. Tait (ed.), *7000 Years of Jewellery* (London, 1986), p. 20.

References

Manuscript Sources

Kew, The National Archives

EXCHEQUER

E 36 Treasury of Receipt, Miscellaneous Books.
E 101 King's Remembrancer, Various Accounts.
E 315 Court of Augmentations and Predecessors, Miscellaneous Books.

LONDON, BRITISH LIBRARY

Royal Manuscripts 7 C XVI.
Stowe Manuscripts 559.

LONDON, SOCIETY OF ANTIQUARIES

MS 129 Inventory of King Henry VIII.

Printed Primary Sources

Bergenroth, G.A., Mattingly, G., de Gayangos, P., Hume, M.A.S., and Tyler, R., (eds), *Calendar of State Papers, Spain*, 13 vols (London, 1862–1954).

Brewer, J., et al., (ed.), *Letters and Papers, Foreign and Domestic, of the Reign of Henry VIII, 1509–1547*, 21 vols (London, 1862–1932).

Brown, R., et al., (ed.), *Calendar of State Papers, Venice*, 38 vols (London, 1864–1947).

Collins, A.J., (ed.), *Jewels and Plate of Queen Elizabeth I: The Inventory of 1574* (London, 1955).

De Cessolis, J., *The Game and Playe of the Chesse*, ed. Adams, J. (Kalamazoo, 2009).

Mancini, D., *Usurpation of Richard III*, ed. and trans. Armstrong, C.A.J. (Sutton, 1984).

Mueller, J., (ed.), *Katherine Parr: Complete Works and Correspondence* (Chicago, 2011).

Shakespeare, W., *Henry VI, Part One*, ed. Taylor, M. (Oxford, 2003).

Shakespeare, W., *Henry VI, Part Two*, ed. Warren, R. (Oxford, 2002).

Shakespeare, W., *Henry VI, Part Three*, ed. Martin, R. (Oxford, 2001).

Sutton, A.F., and Hammond, P.W., (eds), *The Coronation of Richard III: The Extant Documents* (London, 1983).

Secondary Sources

Beer, M.L., 'Between Kings and Emperors: Catherine of Aragon as Counsellor and Mediator', in Matheson-Pollock, H., Paul, J., and Fletcher, C. (eds), *Queenship and Counsel in Early Modern Europe* (Basingstoke, 2018), pp. 35–58.

Beer, M.L., *Queenship at the Renaissance Courts of Britain: Catherine of Aragon and Margaret Tudor, 1503–1533* (Fakenham, 2018).

Beer, M.L., 'Practices and Performances of Queenship: Catherine of Aragon and Margaret Tudor, 1503–1533', unpublished PhD thesis, University of Illinois, 2014.

Benz, L., 'Queen Consort, Queen Mother: The Power and Authority of Fourteenth Century Plantagenet Queens', unpublished PhD thesis, University of York, 2009.

Benz St John, L., *Three Medieval Queens: Queenship and the Crown in Fourteenth-Century England* (Basingstoke, 2012).

Bernard, G.W., *Anne Boleyn: Fatal Attractions* (London, 2010).

Bernard, G.W., 'Anne Boleyn's Religion', *Historical Journal*, 36 (1993), pp. 1–20.

Bernard, G.W., 'The Fall of Anne Boleyn', *EHR*, 106 (1991), pp. 584–610.

Bernard, G.W., 'The Fall of Anne Boleyn: A Rejoinder', *EHR*, 107 (1992), pp. 665–74.

Campbell Orr, C., (ed.), *Queenship in Britain, 1660–1837: Royal Patronage, Court Culture, and Dynastic Politics* (Manchester, 2002).

Chamberlayne, J.L., 'English Queenship 1445–1503', unpublished PhD thesis, University of York, 1999.

Cherry, J., 'Late Fourteenth-Century Jewellery: The Inventory of November 1399', *BM*, 130 (1988), pp. 137–40.

Cox-Rearick, J., 'Power-Dressing at the Courts of Cosimo de'Medici and François I: The "Moda Alla Spagnola" of Spanish Consorts Eléonore d'Autriche and Eleanora di Toledo', *Artibus et Historiae*, 30:60 (2009), pp. 39–69.

DeMolen, R.L., 'The Birth of Edward VI and the Death of Queen Jane: The Arguments for and against Caesarean Section', *Renaissance Studies*, 4 (1990), pp. 359–91.

Dewhurst, J., 'The Alleged Miscarriages of Catherine of Aragon and Anne Boleyn', *Medical History*, 28 (1984), pp. 49–56.

Dunn, D., 'Margaret of Anjou, Queen Consort of Henry VI: A Reassessment of Her Role, 1445–53', in Archer, R. (ed.), *Crown, Government and People in the Fifteenth Century* (New York, 1995), pp. 107–43.

Dunn, D., 'The Queen at War: The Role of Margaret of Anjou in the Wars of the Roses', in Dunn, D. (ed.), *War and Society in Medieval and Early Modern Britain* (Liverpool, 2000), pp. 141–61.

Earenfight, T.M., 'A Precarious Household: Catherine of Aragon in England, 1501–1504', in Earenfight, T. (ed.), *Royal and Elite Households in Medieval and Early Modern Europe* (Leiden, 2018), pp. 338–56.

Earenfight, T.M., *Catherine of Aragon: Infanta of Spain, Queen of England* (Pennsylvania, 2021).

Earenfight, T.M., 'Highly Visible, Often Obscured: The Difficulty of Seeing Queens and Noble Women', *Medieval Feminist Forum: A Journal of Gender and Sexuality*, 44 (2008), pp. 86–90.

Earenfight, T.M., 'Raising *Infanta* Catalina de Aragón to be Catherine, Queen of England', *Anuario de estudios medievales*, 46 (2016), pp. 417–43.

Earenfight, T.M., 'Regarding Catherine of Aragon', in Levin, C., and Stewart-Nuñez, C. (eds), *Scholars and Poets Talk about Queens* (New York, 2015), pp. 137–57.

Earenfight, T.M., *Queenship in Medieval Europe* (Basingstoke, 2013).

Earenfight, T.M., 'Without the Persona of the Prince: Kings, Queens and the Idea of Monarchy in Late Medieval Europe', *Gender and History*, 19 (2007), pp. 1–21.

Facinger, M.F., 'A Study of Medieval Queenship: Capetian France, 987–1237', *Studies in Medieval and Renaissance History*, 5 (1968), pp. 3–47.

Fahy, C., 'The Marriage of Edward IV and Elizabeth Woodville: A New Italian Source', *EHR*, 76 (1961), pp. 660–72.

Gibbons, R., 'Medieval Queenship: An Overview', *Reading Medieval Studies*, 21 (1995), pp. 97–107.

Griffey, E. (ed.), *Sartorial Politics in Early Modern Europe: Fashioning Women* (Amsterdam, 2019).

Harris, B.J., 'The View from My Lady's Chamber: New Perspectives on the Early Tudor Monarchy', *HLQ*, 60 (1997), pp. 215–47.

Hayward, M., *Dress at the Court of King Henry VIII* (Leeds, 2007).

Hayward, M., *Rich Apparel: Clothing and the Law in Henry VIII's England* (Farnham, 2009).

Hicks, M., *Anne Neville: Queen to Richard III* (Stroud, 2007).

Hicks, M., 'The Changing Role of the Wydevilles in Yorkist Politics to 1483', in Ross, C. (ed.), *Patronage, Pedigree, and Power in Later Medieval England* (Gloucester, 1979), pp. 60–86.

Hinton, D., *Medieval Jewellery* (Aylesbury, 1982).

Hollis, J., (ed.), *Princely Magnificence: Court Jewels of the Renaissance, 1500–1630* (London, 1980).

Howell, M., *Eleanor of Provence: Queenship in Thirteenth Century England* (Oxford, 1998).

Huneycutt, L.L., *Matilda of Scotland: A Study in Medieval Queenship* (London, 2003).

Huneycutt, L.L., 'Medieval Queenship', *History Today*, 39 (1989), pp. 16–22.

Ives, E.W., 'Anne Boleyn and the Early Reformation in England: The Contemporary Evidence', *Historical Journal*, 37 (1994), pp. 389–400.

Ives, E.W., 'Anne Boleyn on Trial Again', *Journal of Ecclesiastical History*, 62 (2011), pp. 763–77.

Ives, E.W., 'Faction at the Court of Henry VIII: The Fall of Anne Boleyn', *History*, 57 (1972), pp. 169–88.

Ives, E.W., 'The Fall of Anne Boleyn Reconsidered', *EHR*, 107 (1992), pp. 651–64.

Ives, E.W., *The Life and Death of Anne Boleyn* (Oxford, 2004).

James, S.E., *Catherine Parr: Henry VIII's Last Love* (Stroud, 2008).

James, S.E., 'Lady Jane Grey or Queen Kateryn Parr?' *BM*, 138 (1996), pp. 20–4.

Lander, J.R., 'Marriage and Politics in the Fifteenth Century: The Nevilles and the Wydevilles', in *Crown and Nobility 1450–1509* (Montreal, 1976), pp. 94–126.

Laynesmith, J., *The Last Medieval Queens* (Oxford, 2004).

Lee, P.A., 'Reflections of Power: Margaret of Anjou and the Dark Side of Queenship', *Renaissance Quarterly*, 39 (1986), pp. 183–217.

Lipscomb, S., 'The Fall of Anne Boleyn: A Crisis in Gender Relations?', in Lipscomb, S. and Betteridge, T. (eds), *Henry VIII and the Court: Art, Politics and Performance* (Farnham, 2013), pp. 287–305.

Logan, S., 'Margaret and the Ban: Resistances to Sovereign Authority in Henry VI 1, 2, & 3 and Richard III', in Logan, S. (ed.), *Shakespeare's Foreign Queens: Drama, Politics and the Enemy Within* (Basingstoke, 2018), pp. 209–60.

Lynn, E., *Tudor Fashion* (London, 2017).

MacGibbon, D., *Elizabeth Woodville: A Life* (London, 1938).

Mattingly, G., *Catherine of Aragon* (London, 1942).

Maurer, H.E., *Margaret of Anjou: Queenship and Power in Late Medieval England* (Woodbridge, 2003).

Mudan, K., '"So mutable is that sexe": Queen Elizabeth Woodville in Polydore Vergil's *Anglica historia* and Sir Thomas More's *History of King Richard III*', in Oakley-Brown, L., and Wilkinson, L.J. (eds), *The Rituals and Rhetoric of Queenship: Medieval to Early Modern* (Dublin, 2009), pp. 104–17.

Mudan Finn, K., *The Last Plantagenet Consorts* (Basingstoke, 2012).

Mueller, J., 'Devotion as Difference: Intertextuality in Queen Katherine Parr's "Prayers or Meditations" (1545)', *HLQ*, 53 (1990), pp. 171–97.

Myers, A.R., 'The Captivity of a Royal Witch: The Household Accounts of Queen Joan of Navarre, 1419–21', *BJRL*, 24 (1940), pp. 263–84.

Myers, A.R., 'The Household of Queen Elizabeth Woodville, 1466–7', *BJRL*, 50 (1967–8), pp. 207–15.

Myers, A.R., 'The Household of Queen Margaret of Anjou, 1452–3', *BJRL*, 50 (1957–8), pp. 79–113.

Myers, A.R., 'The Jewels of Queen Margaret of Anjou', *BJRL*, 42 (1959), pp. 113–31.

Nelson, J.L., 'Medieval Queenship', in Mitchell, L.E. (ed.), *Women in Medieval Western European Culture* (London, 1999), pp. 179–207.

Okerlund, A., *Elizabeth: England's Slandered Queen* (Stroud, 2005).

Okerlund, A., *Elizabeth of York* (Basingstoke, 2009).

Parsons, J.C., *Eleanor of Castile: Queen and Society in Thirteenth-Century England* (London, 1995).

Parsons, J.C., 'Family, Sex and Power: The Rhythms of Medieval Queenship', in Parsons, J.C. (ed.), *Medieval Queenship* (Stroud, 1993), pp. 1–12.

Parsons, J.C., 'Mothers, Daughters, Marriage, Power: Some Plantagenet Evidence, 1150–1500', in Parsons, J.C. (ed.), *Medieval Queenship* (Stroud, 1993), pp. 63–78.

Parsons, J.C., (ed.), *Medieval Queenship* (Stroud, 1993).

Porter, L., *Katherine the Queen: The Remarkable Life of Katherine Parr* (London, 2011).

Rhodes, W.E., 'The Inventory of the Jewels and Wardrobe of Queen Isabella (1307–8)', *EHR*, 12 (1897), pp. 517–21.

Russell, G., *Young and Damned and Fair: The Life and Tragedy of Catherine Howard at the Court of Henry VIII* (London, 2017).

Stafford, P., 'The Portrayal of Royal Women in England, Mid-Tenth to Mid-Twelfth Centuries', in Parsons, J.C. (ed.), *Medieval Queenship* (Stroud, 1993), pp. 143–67.

Stapleton, M.L., '"I of Old Contemptes Complayne": Margaret of Anjou and English Seneca', *Comparative Literature Studies*, 43 (2000), pp. 100–33.

Sutton, A., and Visser-Fuchs, L., 'A *'Most Benevolent Queen'*: Queen Elizabeth Woodville's Reputation, Her Piety and Her Books', *The Ricardian*, 10 (1995), pp. 214–45.

Tait, H. (ed.), *7000 Years of Jewellery* (London, 1986).

Walker, G., 'Rethinking the Fall of Anne Boleyn', *Historical Journal*, 45 (2002), pp. 1–29.

Warnicke, R.M., 'Anne Boleyn Revisited', *Historical Journal*, 34 (1991), pp. 953–4.

Warnicke, R.M., 'Anne Boleyn's Childhood and Adolescence', *Historical Journal*, 28 (1985), pp. 939–52.

Warnicke, R.M., *Elizabeth of York and Her Six Daughters-in-Law* (Basingstoke, 2017).

Warnicke, R.M., 'Henry VIII's Greeting of Anne of Cleves and Early Modern Court Protocol', *Albion*, 28 (1996), pp. 565–85.

Warnicke, R.M., 'The Eternal Triangle and Court Politics: Henry VIII: Anne Boleyn, and Sir Thomas Wyatt', *Albion*, 18 (1986), pp. 565–79.

Warnicke, R.M., 'The Fall of Anne Boleyn: A Reassessment', *History*, 70 (1985), pp. 1–15.

Warnicke, R.M., 'The Fall of Anne Boleyn Revisited', *EHR*, 108 (1993), pp. 653–65.

Warnicke, R.M., *The Marrying of Anne of Cleves: Royal Protocol in Tudor England* (Cambridge, 2004).

Warnicke, R.M., *The Rise and Fall of Anne Boleyn* (Cambridge, 1989).

Warnicke, R.M., *Wicked Women of Tudor England: Queens, Aristocrats, Commoners* (New York, 2012).

Weir, A., *Elizabeth of York: The First Tudor Queen* (London, 2013).

Welch, E., *Fashioning the Early Modern: Dress, Textiles, and Innovation in Europe 1500–1800* (Oxford, 2017).

Williams, M., and Echols, A., *Between Pit and Pedestal: Women in the Middle Ages* (Princeton, 1994).

Woodacre, E., *Queens and Queenship* (Leeds, 2021).

Woodacre, E., 'Introduction', in Woodacre, E. (ed.), *Queenship in the Mediterranean: Negotiating the Role of the Queen in the Medieval and Early Modern Eras* (Basingstoke, 2016), pp. 1–7.

Woodacre, E., and Fleiner, C. (eds), *Royal Mothers and Their Ruling Children: Wielding Political Authority from Antiquity to the Early Modern Era* (Basingstoke, 2015).

Woodacre, E., and Fleiner, C. (eds), *Virtuous or Villainess? The Image of the Royal Mother from the Early Medieval to the Early Modern Era* (Basingstoke, 2016).

1 An Introduction to Jewellery and the Queenly Use of Jewels

Rulers across Europe and beyond have adopted jewels as an expression of magnificence and a way of upholding their authority for centuries. 'Magnificence sent messages: it presented the court as a centre of patronage and power; it demonstrated the king's wealth', and this was prevalent at the fifteenth- and early sixteenth-century English court.[1] Some jewels were so valuable and famous that they were given individual names in order to identify them: the Three Brothers, the Mirror of Naples, the Great Harry and the Lennox Jewel were notable fifteenth- and sixteenth-century examples.[2] Jewels were the most personal of the decorative arts, often giving an insight into an individual and their tastes, as well as providing vital clues about the society in which they lived.[3] Due to the rapidity of changing fashions, few of the jewels that were owned by the queens in this period survive. Following Jane Seymour's death, for example, three of her pieces were passed to Alard, almost certainly Alard Plomer or Plomyer, a French jeweller who was in Henry VIII's service.[4] These items were undoubtedly broken down and recast, and such examples show the regularity with which jewels were refashioned. Fortunately, there are enough high-status pieces to allow us to understand the way in which jewels were made and worn by queens. Many of these pieces can be found in the British Museum and the Victoria and Albert Museum, and they aid our practical understanding of the form and style of jewels of the period. The Dunstable Swan Jewel and the Middleham Jewel provide two significant examples.[5] As Diana Scarisbrick stated,

DOI: 10.4324/9781003202592-2

however, 'almost as much can be learnt about the role of jewellery in Britain from the documents, the designs and the pictorial evidence' as from the pieces themselves.[6]

Jewels could appear in various forms, shapes and sizes, and after a brief summary of the existing scholarship relating to jewellery history, this chapter aims to provide a short history of the genres of elite and courtly jewellery that were available in the late fifteenth and early sixteenth centuries.[7] This includes the stones that were incorporated into these pieces, which were chiefly fashioned from gold and often featured enamelled decoration in keeping with contemporary fashions. It highlights some of the jewels that were popular among the English queens in this period and their uses, drawing on some of their European counterparts when there are comparisons to be made: some favoured particular genres for decorative purposes, while other pieces – although also often highly ornamented – were chosen for more practical reasons. This chapter ultimately aims to provide an introduction for some of the themes that follow in the subsequent chapters and demonstrates the opulence to which queens at the English court would have become accustomed.

Jewellery Literature

The history of jewellery has and continues to attract a plethora of scholars. Between the 1950s and 1970s, Joan Evans was a significant contributor to the field, producing several works that charted the history of jewellery, the development of English jewellery, and the superstitions surrounding jewels in the medieval period.[8] Evans' work also examined the role of jewellery from the viewpoint of social status, in a similar manner to the work of Marion Campbell and David Hinton, both of whose books concentrated on medieval jewellery.[9] These works are useful for placing the history of jewellery into a European perspective, as is the work of Ronald Lightbown, whose extensive research provides an ideal starting point for those working on jewels.[10]

From a practical standpoint, Philippa Glanville's contribution to our knowledge of Tudor and Stuart silver offers a useful grounding for understanding the materials that were used in the construction of jewels.[11] In a slightly different context, Timothy Schroder's work about gold and silver at the court of Henry VIII explores not only the physicalities of these high-status pieces of material culture but also the ways in which they were used throughout Henry's reign. In so doing, Schroder shows how, for kings, 'power and visible wealth went hand in hand and to be secure it was essential to be seen to be rich'.[12] Additionally, Natasha Awais-Dean's work on Tudor and Jacobean jewellery from a male perspective has made an important contribution to our knowledge of the material culture owned and used by men from all levels of society.[13] Diana Scarisbrick has written extensively about many aspects of jewellery, but her work on Tudor and Jacobean jewellery specifically discussed jewellery in relation to portraiture.[14] Scarisbrick effectively explored symbolism in jewels and analysed examples of rare surviving jewels from the period. As such, she is deservedly one of the leading contributors in this field. The work of Maria Hayward on various aspects of material culture has made an invaluable contribution to jewellery scholarship. Not only did Hayward's thesis on Henry VIII's inventories incorporate her research about the King's jewels and those of his wives but so too has much of her subsequent work.[15]

Genres of Jewellery

Throughout history, the ring has been the most continuous form of jewellery in use, being always highly prized and worn by people from all levels of society.[16] It is therefore unsurprising that rings feature more than any other type of jewel in contemporary accounts and were often purchased in large quantities.[17] Joan Evans claimed that it was Margaret of Anjou who introduced the trend of wearing rings on many different joints and fingers, but evidence of this can be seen in many fifteenth-century portraits, and it is feasible that this was an artistic style rather than truly representative.[18] Rings served multiple purposes: they expressed loyalty and devotion, conveyed messages, rewarded good service, and were also a token of love and friendship. Signet rings, which served a practical as well as a decorative purpose, were also popular, being both symbols of authority and authentication. During the Renaissance, they would be worn on either the thumb or index finger, where they would be ready to use if needed.[19] Kateryn Parr is known to have owned such a ring, which was listed in Henry VIII's inventory as 'one ring of golde being sometime Quene Katherynes Signet'.[20]

The most personal form of ring that was owned by all of the queens in this period and beyond was a wedding ring. As there was no codified form, wedding rings could appear in a variety of styles, but as the sixteenth century progressed one of the preferred designs for this most personal of pieces was the plain gold band, often containing an inscription.[21] It is likely that this style was adopted by Jane Seymour, whose possible wedding ring can be seen in her portrait by Hans Holbein.[22] Although these were special possessions that 'carried the aura of family history as well as the mark of individual identity' and appear frequently in women's wills of this period, none of the queens or women in this book made any mention of their wedding rings in their wills.[23] It is possible that women were buried wearing them or that they had been bequeathed orally rather than by written word. Alternatively, they may have been broken up and refashioned. The fifteenth and sixteenth centuries were periods of rapidly changing fashions, and this partially explains why there are so few surviving examples of jewels from this period.

From 1100 until 1400, the brooch was the most popular form of jewel, and this is likely to have been the way in which the Dunstable Swan Jewel was worn.[24] Excavated in 1965, the swan is symbolic of the house of Lancaster, and as John Cherry asserted, was evidently a high-status jewel because of the rare enamel decoration.[25] This was thanks to a technique of enamelling known as *émail en ronde bosse* developed in the late fourteenth century by French and Burgundian goldsmiths, which meant that rich jewels could be fashioned in a multitude of colours.[26] Brooches served a dual purpose, for not only were they decorative, but they were also used to fasten clothes. The popularity of brooches was superseded by the trend for necklaces and collars, as the fashion for low-cut gowns increased.[27] Nevertheless, items described as brooches appear in the inventories of Henry VIII and his wives, demonstrating that such pieces still held their appeal.[28] Brooches were unisex items, and among Henry VIII's collection was a piece that the initial suggests may have belonged to his mother, Elizabeth of York: 'A brooch with E enamelled red'.[29] If this was the case then it may have been one of the few surviving items that had been owned by Elizabeth, for following her death in 1503 Henry VII's Chamber Books record the 'plegging of certain of the quenes Juelles'.[30]

Necklaces and pendants were favoured throughout the fifteenth and sixteenth centuries, and the visual evidence discussed in Chapter 4 illustrates how fashions for these particular pieces changed in a short space of time. During the fifteenth century, devotional pendants peaked in popularity.[31] Their importance was stressed by the Burgundian courtier Olivier de la Marche in 1490, who is cited by Scarisbrook: 'Its property is a safeguard, protecting the wearer from broken bones and death. You cannot pay too much for one'.[32] The Middleham Jewel is one such example, and the arguments surrounding its commission and significance will be considered in Chapter 5.[33] The trend for religious-themed necklaces persisted into the sixteenth century, and the inventories of both Katherine Howard and Kateryn Parr contain three identical 'Jesuses'.[34] These may have been the IHS brooches/pendants that can be seen adorning portraits of both Catherine of Aragon and Jane Seymour, which will be analysed in Chapter 4.[35] Certainly, Jane Seymour's matches the descriptions of pieces found in both inventories: 'a Jehus of golde conteignyng xxxij diamondes hauyng thre peerlles hanging at the same', and 'a Ihesus furnysshed with xxxij Dyamountes and three perles pendaunt'.[36] A jewel found in Henry VIII's 1519 and 1530 jewel inventories also fits: 'A diamond Jhs with three hanging pearls'.[37] Necklaces that featured a medallion and heart-shaped pendants also grew in popularity during the sixteenth century.[38]

Gold collars provided another form of adornment that could be worn in a number of contexts, and large collars of this nature were usually symbolic and displayed some sign of the wearer's allegiance.[39] They could also be used as signs of friendship to allies and ambassadors.[40] Many of Europe's medieval rulers used collars in these ways, including Piero di Cosimo de Medici and Charles the Bold.[41] In 1506, Henry VII's Chamber Books record that he paid a London goldsmith for 'a Coller of garters' for the King's use, and another for Philip of Castile who was his guest.[42] The description clearly indicates that both pieces were designed to reflect the Order of the Garter that Philip was invested with during his stay.[43] These collars were often extremely valuable, as is suggested by the Venetian ambassador's reference to one worn by Henry VIII in 1520: this one was so lavish, it was 'said to be worth more than 10,000 ducats'.[44] Queens also wore collars, and by the mid-fifteenth century the precedent had already been set. Anne of Bohemia, consort of Richard II, seems to have owned several, and Joan of Navarre's tomb effigy in Canterbury Cathedral shows her wearing the SS collar associated with the house of Lancaster.[45] The following century, Margaret Tudor, Queen of Scots, had several collars in her possession, while Katherine Howard's inventory notes that she owned a 'Partelet or collor conteignyng xvj diamondes xx Rubyes/and lxv peerles/all set in Goldesmythesworke ennamuled hauyng a verey small Cheyne of golde upon thedge of the same'.[46] Interestingly, to this piece Katherine added 'x of the same diamondes set in a Sipher by the quene'.[47] This could provide evidence of the recycling of something that had possibly become unfashionable or reflect Katherine's desire to put her own stamp on the piece. A collar owned by Catherine of Aragon will be discussed in Chapter 2.

Initial jewellery came into fashion throughout Europe during the latter part of the fourteenth century, reflected in Richard II's inventory, and this continued through the sixteenth century.[48] A ring associated with Mary of Burgundy, said to have been a wedding gift from her new husband Maximilian in 1477, features a diamond 'M', and the couple's daughter Margaret of Austria also appears to have been fond of these pieces.[49] Among Margaret's inventory was a sumptuous jewel described as 'vne M de sept bonnes pieces de dyamens' ('an M of seven good pieces of diamonds').[50] Henry VIII inherited several items featuring the initials of his parents, and it is not unreasonable to suppose that some of these had once belonged to his mother, Elizabeth of York.[51] In the 1520s initial pendants became popular, peaking in the 1530s and 1540s – indeed, Janet Arnold argued that such pieces never lost their appeal, and this is largely true.[52] Both men and women wore initial jewels and other pendants attached to collars or necklaces. The most notable owner of initial jewellery remains Anne Boleyn, and her pieces will be analysed in greater depth in subsequent chapters. It is, though, important to note that the trend did not begin with Anne, and neither did it end with her.

Although Theresa Earenfight pointed out that Catherine of Aragon was responsible for introducing the fashion for wearing earrings in England, a trend that she had brought with her from Spain, there are few examples of queens in this period adopting them.[53] Indeed, Diana Scarisbrick underlined that while ears were covered by the hair or a headdress, there was little need for them, and they did not appear with greater frequency until later in the sixteenth century – even then they were rare.[54] Both Elizabeth I and Gabrielle d'Estrées can be seen wearing earrings in portraits, and they were also adorned by men.[55]

Bracelets were popular with both men and women in fifteenth-century Europe, and Ronald Lightbown pointed out that in 1452–1453 Margaret of Anjou spent £19 3s 6d on 43 gold bracelets, which she gave to members of her household.[56] Although this trend was retained during the Tudor period, they feature rarely among the collections of the English queens.[57] This is likely to be accounted for by the fashion for long sleeves in the earlier part of the sixteenth century, which rendered them unnecessary.[58] Circular in form and often appearing in pairs, like rings bracelets symbolised neverending affection.[59] Jane Seymour and Kateryn Parr were evidently fond of them, as four pairs appear in Jane's inventory, while not only are four pairs listed in Kateryn's queenly collection, but a pair were also to be found in her personal inventory.[60] Kateryn also used them as gifts.

Precious Stones and Their Properties

Throughout the medieval period, it was widely believed that stones had various magical and medicinal properties, a belief that was reinforced by the eleventh-century *Liber Lapidum*

(Book of Stones), written by the Bishop of Rennes.[61] The *Liber Lapidum* described 60 individual stones and their meanings, and this heavily influenced the jewellery choices people made. For example, it was widely believed that sapphires protected from poison and promoted peace and reconciliation, as well as healing ulcers, eye conditions and headaches.[62] Rubies were thought to aid reconciliation and combat lust, while pearls were symbolic of purity, power and authority.[63] Even the Reformation did not serve to alter these longstanding beliefs.[64]

By the fifteenth century, sapphires, rubies and pearls were the predominant stones used in jewellery making among the nobility.[65] It was also not unusual for royalty to use counterfeit stones in less important pieces, and surviving recipes for artificial stones and pearls from the fourteenth century serve as evidence of such practice.[66] Several such stones were noted among Kateryn Parr's effects during her term as Queen Dowager, perhaps a reflection of her reduced need to impress.[67] They were also to be found among a later inventory of jewels belonging to Mary, Queen of Scots.[68] The lower value of such stones would have rendered them more suitable for everyday use.

Although diamonds had been known in Europe since the Roman period, prior to the last quarter of the fifteenth century they only appeared in small numbers.[69] As they were highly prized for their lustre and as emblems of constancy, innocence and fortitude, it is little wonder that diamonds were so popular.[70] The rulers of sixteenth-century Europe competed to obtain the best diamonds possible, and after 1498 they became slightly easier to source.[71] Ultimately, it was the French king François I who gained fame for acquiring the Great Table of François I, the largest diamond then known in Europe.[72] Conversely in terms of their availability, diamonds appear frequently in the jewel inventory of Margaret of Austria.[73] As is shown in Chapter 3, they also featured in large quantities among the items of jewellery owned by both Katherine Howard and Kateryn Parr, a testament to the high quality of material wealth that was available to queens. Additionally, diamonds worn close to the heart, on the finger and next to the skin were considered to provide the best means of imparting their qualities to the wearer.[74] Surviving portraits, discussed in Chapter 4, show that Jane Seymour, Katherine Howard and Kateryn Parr all wore diamonds in this way.

By the fifteenth century, Bruges had become the main diamond cutting centre in Europe, though its prominence was later replaced by Antwerp.[75] Nevertheless, cutting techniques were still in their infancy in the sixteenth century and thus diamonds could sometimes appear black. On some occasions, though, they were deliberately set on black backgrounds within pieces of jewellery in order to show the lustre of the diamond.[76] This seems to be the case in pieces worn by Kateryn Parr in a seventeenth-century copy portrait of a lost original.[77] The most fashionable cut was the table-cut, and examples of diamonds cut in this way appeared in the 1467 inventory of Charles the Bold.[78] Both Katherine Howard and Kateryn Parr also owned pieces featuring the table-cut.[79] Point cuts were desirable, and Charlotte of Savoy, consort of Louis XI of France, had items cut in this fashion.[80] Similarly, Kateryn Parr owned 'a Ringe of golde with a pointed Diamounte'.[81] The rose cut also came into being in the first half of the sixteenth century, and the lozenge and triangle cuts were popular.[82] It is possible that many of the diamonds used in the pieces that appear in Katherine Howard and Kateryn Parr's inventories were cut and polished abroad before they were imported to England.[83] There were, however, also those in England who had the ability to do so, for in 1499 Henry VII's Chamber Books recorded a payment to John Shaa for 'setting and polishing of stones'.[84]

The voyages of discovery that came with the end of the fifteenth century had a profound impact on the gem trade, ensuring that, among others, pearls became more readily and easily available.[85] In the cases of both Katherine Howard and Kateryn Parr, these stones were by far the most common material used to decorate the queens' jewellery. Pearls sourced from the Far East or the Americas were popular (they were known for many centuries as 'the Queen of Gems') and were believed to be symbolic of purity.[86] Nevertheless, they remained expensive. Alice Perrers, mistress of Edward III, had 20,000 pearls, and she was not alone.[87] Margaret of Austria seems to have been particularly fond of pearls, for among her collection was a string containing 762 medium pearls, and a headdress containing 58 medium pearls.[88] Eleanor of Austria, consort of Manuel I of Portugal and later François I, also owned strands of pearls.[89]

Rubies were primarily sourced from India and Sri Lanka.[90] They were more readily available than some other forms of gems and thus were also cheaper, being second in value to both emeralds and diamonds.[91] South American emeralds were generally well favoured during the first half of the sixteenth century, as were sapphires from Sri Lanka and opals from the Czech Republic.[92] It is therefore noteworthy that these stones feature far less frequently than diamonds and rubies in the inventories of Henry VIII's wives. The emeralds that appear in Jane Seymour's inventory were attached to a single piece – 'a Tabelet of golde anticke worke sett with x emerades with lytle white childrin'.[93] This same piece may later have been owned and altered by Katherine Howard.[94] Unsurprisingly, examples of pieces that incorporated greater quantities of emeralds can be found in the queenly inventories of Katherine Howard and Kateryn Parr.[95] Amethysts hailed from Germany, and an inventory of jewels belonging to Isabella of Austria, consort of Christian II of Denmark, shows that she owned pieces of amethyst jewellery, but generally rings set with amethysts were uncommon.[96] It is significant that the only example of an amethyst ring found among the possessions of Henry VIII's wives – in fact of amethyst being used at all – belonged to Kateryn Parr.[97]

Turquoises largely from Persia and the Sinai Peninsula were a popular gem and were often referred to as 'Turkeys' in inventories.[98] Charlotte of Savoy had several set in rings, and they also appeared in large quantities in Katherine Howard's collection.[99] Jane Seymour had two separate pairs of 'beydes of turquisses gauded with golde', as well as another pair featuring the stones, while their appearance in Kateryn Parr's list of possessions could be an indication of both queens' beliefs in their qualities; they were thought to turn pale as soon as the wearer was in any kind of danger.[100]

Despite the Reformation, there is evidence that Kateryn Parr believed in the properties and supposed powers of certain objects. Among an inventory of her possessions, 'xij Cram-pringes of gold' were listed.[101] In a similar manner to the belief in the magical properties of stones, cramp rings were thought to cure ailments, and were often worn by women during pregnancy. Likewise, rings engraved with inscriptions were thought to protect the wearer from harm.[102] The origins of cramp rings are unclear, but their healing powers were traditionally ascribed to Edward the Confessor, who was buried wearing a ring. When the ring was removed from the dead king's hand in 1163, it was said that miracles began to happen.[103] Cramp rings were part of an important ceremony at the Tudor court, whereby the monarch blessed the rings each Good Friday, and their healing powers were still rated in the 1540s.[104] Regular payments and receipts for cramp rings can be found among Henry VIII's expenses, made from both gold and silver, and it is likely that at least some of these were for the use of his wives.[105] As such, they served a practical rather than simply decorative purpose. Kateryn's belief would explain the presence of some of the other objects found in her inventory, including 'a pece of an vnicornes horne', which was thought to protect against poison.[106] It is also possible that an ouche owned by Jane Seymour, Katherine Howard and Kateryn Parr may have had similar qualities, and this will be analysed in Chapter 4 in relation to portraiture.

The Queenly Use of Jewels

Jewels could serve many purposes, and their greatest advantage was their status as luxury goods. This meant that they provided queens with valuable material assets, and the precious materials from which they were fashioned ensured that they were always likely to retain a high value in monetary terms. This was something that Catherine of Aragon was forced to make use of in the aftermath of the death of her first husband, Prince Arthur. By 1506, the treatment Catherine was receiving from her father-in-law, Henry VII, and her father, Ferdinand of Aragon, was so poor that she was driven to desperation. She wrote to her father, informing him that 'I have now sold some bracelets to get a dress of black velvet, for I was all but naked'.[107] That Catherine was forced to take such a measure is a testament to the extreme circumstances in which she found herself. Her situation, though, was far from unique, and selling or pawning jewels was a strategy that had been employed by numerous of her contemporaries and predecessors, including the Duke of Anjou in 1380.[108]

As well as displaying status, jewels were a source of personal pleasure that could be enjoyed by both kings and queens. They could also be used to illustrate political preferences, cultural interests and religious faith. There are numerous examples of queens throughout this period using jewels in such a way, many of which can be seen in their surviving portraits. When her nephew, the Emperor Charles V, visited England in May 1520, Catherine of Aragon used her jewels to make a statement. This was evident when one day she appeared sumptuously arrayed, and around her neck wore 'five large strings of pearls, with a pendent St. George on horseback slaying the dragon, all in diamonds'.[109] Including the figure of St George in her jewels provided Catherine with a tangible way of showcasing her loyalty to her husband and her marital country, in spite of her Spanish roots. Similarly, in 1525 Catherine and Henry's daughter, Mary, was painted by the miniaturist Lucas Horenbout. In this image, Mary wears a brooch labelled 'The Emperor' in a declaration of her engagement to Charles V, contracted in 1522.[110] Using jewels in such a clear, visual proclamation of the family's intended political alliance suggests that the miniature was intended to be seen and left the viewer in no doubt of the hoped-for union.

Not only did jewels serve to decorate the queen's person, but some were also more functional and were used to fulfil a slightly different purpose. For example, the whistle pendant that by family tradition was Henry VIII's first gift to Anne Boleyn.[111] Although there is no firm evidence to link this piece to Anne, she would certainly have been familiar with this sort of jewel, which would have been worn attached to a masquing costume. It also reflects the multiple functions served by some jewels, for not only was it a pendant, but it also contained two toothpicks and an ear-spoon. James IV of Scotland also owned toothpicks of gold.[112]

Practical items owned by Jane Seymour included 'a litle coffer of golde with a Diamonde in it and iiij truloves of pirles', perhaps a gift from Henry VIII. The same is likely to be true of a piece that was probably a mirror, described as 'a glasse with the Hymag of the Kinges Hyghnes his father and others as aperith with two Lambes of the owt syde'. The reference to the lambs may indicate that it was also some form of Agnus Dei. There was also 'a litle coffer of golde with iij King of Collen' – the Three Kings of Cologne, better known as the Magi who presented gifts to Christ.[113] The Magi had an important role to play in medieval pageantry, and they not only helped to explain 'the roots of legitimate monarchy' but also 'reaffirmed the sense that monarchs' high temporal status extended to some sort of precedence in spiritual matters'.[114] This piece may therefore have been a further gift from Henry to Jane, and a reminder of his role as Head of the Church of England. This and the other coffer may have been used to store Jane's jewels.

Other forms of more practical jewels included belts, jewels on headdresses – known as billiments – jewels stitched around a neckline – referred to as squares – girdles and pomanders, which often contained fragrant herbs with which to sweeten the air. Examples of all of these items will be cited throughout the course of this book. Jane Seymour and Katherine Howard even had books decorated with jewels, while Jane and Kateryn Parr also owned jewelled buttons.[115] Details in Jane's inventory allow us to see how these were worn, such as the 18 buttons of gold which had been 'sett of a gowne of cremsen satten', while 18 pillars of gold were 'sett uppon a gowne of blacke velvet'.[116] Buttons were particularly versatile, having the ability to be transferrable between items of clothing.

Gold and silver plate could serve both a decorative and a more practical purpose, offering the potential to be used to serve food and drink. The inventory of James V of Scotland lists several gold cups, and a similar surviving piece can be linked to Anne Boleyn.[117] Known as the Boleyn Cup, this beautiful silver-gilt goblet is hallmarked 1535–1536 and is now on display in the Church of St John the Baptist, Cirencester.[118] Timothy Schroder argued that the goblet was probably owned by Anne too, and its most significant feature is the Queen's personal falcon badge, a design element often employed by Anne.[119] Richard Martin, physician to Anne's daughter Elizabeth I, traditionally gave the cup to the church, although this tale is impossible to corroborate.[120] What is more certain though are the goblet's associations with one of England's most notorious queens.

Conclusion

This brief history of the genres of jewellery available to queens in the fifteenth and sixteenth centuries, coupled with the summary of some of their uses, provides a contextual introduction to the chapters that follow, in which many of these elements will be analysed in greater depth. It forms an integral part of the themes that are explored in relation to the collections of the queens of England during this period and is crucial in allowing us to understand some of the key pieces – and their composition – that were owned by queens.

Notes

1 T. Schroder, *'A Marvel to Behold': Gold and Silver at the Court of Henry VIII* (Woodbridge, 2020), pp. 7–8.
2 D. Scarisbrick, *Diamond Jewelry: 700 Years of Glory and Glamour* (London, 2019), p. 30; Unknown Maker, 'Lennox Jewel', c. 1571–78, gold, enamel, rubies, emerald, RCT, RCIN 28181. See K. Piacenti and J. Boardman, *Ancient and Modern Gems and Jewels in the Collection of Her Majesty The Queen* (London, 2008); A. Reynolds, *In Fine Style: The Art of Tudor and Stuart Fashion* (London, 2013).
3 M. Campbell, *Medieval Jewellery* (London, 2009), p. 8.
4 BL, Royal MS 7 C XVI, f. 20r; *L & P*, xxi, part 2, no. 199.
5 Unknown Maker, 'Dunstable Swan Jewel', fifteenth century, gold and enamel, British Museum, 1966,0703.1; Unknown Maker, 'Middleham Jewel', fifteenth century, gold and sapphire, Yorkshire Museum, YORYM: 1991.43.
6 D. Scarisbrick, *Jewellery in Britain 1066–1837* (Norwich, 1994), p. xix.
7 Theresa Earenfight noted that while she was a Spanish Infanta, Catherine of Aragon's shoes contained jewels. See *Catherine of Aragon*, p. 57.

8 J. Evans, *A History of Jewellery 1100–1870* (New York, 1953); J. Evans, *English Jewellery: From the Fifth Century A.D. to 1800* (London, 1921); J. Evans, *Magical Jewels of the Middle Ages and the Renaissance* (New York, 1976).
9 Campbell, *Medieval Jewellery*; Hinton, *Medieval Jewellery*.
10 R.W. Lightbown, *Medieval European Jewellery* (London, 1992).
11 W.M. Milliken, 'The Art of the Goldsmith', *Journal of Aesthetics and Art Criticism*, 6 (1948), p. 311; P. Glanville, *Silver in Tudor and Early Stuart England* (London, 1990).
12 Schroder, 'A Marvel to Behold', p. 34.
13 N. Awais-Dean, *Bejewelled: Men and Jewellery in Tudor and Jacobean England* (London, 2017).
14 D. Scarisbrick, *Tudor and Jacobean Jewellery* (London, 1995); D. Scarisbrick and M. Henig, *Finger Rings* (Oxford, 2003); Scarisbrick, *Jewellery in Britain*; D. Scarisbrick, *Historic Rings: Four Thousand Years of Craftmanship* (Tokyo, 2004); D. Scarisbrick, *Rings: Jewelry of Power, Love and Loyalty* (London, 2007); D. Scarisbrick, *Portrait Jewels: Opulence and Intimacy from the Medici to the Romanovs* (London, 2011); D. Scarisbrick, C. Vachaudez, and J. Walgrave (eds), *Brilliant Europe: Jewels from European Courts* (Brussels, 2007); Scarisbrick, *Diamonds*.
15 M. Hayward, 'The Possessions of Henry VIII: A Study of Inventories', unpublished PhD thesis, London School of Economics and Political Science, University of London, 1998; M. Hayward, 'Gift Giving at the Court of Henry VIII: The 1539 New Year's Gift Roll in Context', *Antiquaries Journal*, 85 (2005), pp. 125–75; Hayward, *Dress*.
16 Scarisbrick, *Rings*, p. 9; S. Bury, *Rings* (London, 1984), p. 9.
17 H. Forsyth, *The Cheapside Hoard: London's Lost Jewels* (London, 2013), p. 204.
18 Evans, *English Jewellery*, p. 64.
19 Scarisbrick, *Rings*, p. 70.
20 D. Starkey (ed.), *The Inventory of King Henry VIII: The Transcript*, trans. P. Ward (London, 1998), p. 87.
21 Tait (ed.), *7000 Years*, p. 239.
22 Hans Holbein, 'Jane Seymour', 1536–37, Kunsthistorisches Museum, Vienna, Inv. No. 881.
23 S. James, *Women's Voices in Tudor Wills, 1485–1603: Authority, Influence and Material Culture* (Farnham, 2015), p. 91.
24 Unknown Maker, 'Dunstable Swan Jewel', fifteenth century, gold and enamel, British Museum, 1966,0703.1.
25 J. Cherry, 'The Dunstable Swan Jewel', *Journal of the British Archaeological Association*, 32 (1969), pp. 38–9.
26 A. Somers Cocks, *An Introduction to Courtly Jewellery* (London, 1982), p. 14.
27 Campbell, *Medieval Jewellery*, p. 36.

28 See *L & P*, iv, no. 6789; BL, Royal MS 7 C XVI, f. 27r-v; BL, Stowe MS 559, f. 57v.
29 *L & P*, iv, no. 6789.
30 BL, Add MS 59899, f. 23v.
31 Evans, *History of Jewellery*, p. 74.
32 Scarisbrick, *Diamonds*, p. 31.
33 Unknown Maker, 'Middleham Jewel', 1475–1499, gold and sapphire, Yorkshire Museum, YORYM: 1991.43.
34 BL, Stowe MS 559, f. 59v-60r; SoA, MS 129, f. 178v.
35 Lucas Horenbout, 'Katherine of Aragon', c. 1525–6, NPG, NPG L244; Holbein, 'Jane Seymour', Kunsthistorisches Museum.
36 BL, Stowe MS 559, f. 60r; SoA, MS 129, f. 178v.
37 *L & P*, iv, no. 6789.
38 Y. Hackenbroch, *Renaissance Jewellery* (London, 1979), p. 276; Scarisbrick, *Diamonds*, p. 31.
39 C. Phillips, *Jewelry: From Antiquity to Present* (London, 1996), p. 71
40 Scarisbrick, *Diamonds*, p. 28.
41 Ibid, pp. 28–9.
42 E 36/214, f. 19r.
43 *CSPS*, i, p. 379.
44 *CSPV*, iii, no. 50.
45 See J. Stratford (ed.), *Richard II and the English Royal Treasure* (Woodbridge, 2012), p. 52, 63, 76, 80, 84; M. Duffy, *Royal Tombs of Medieval England* (Stroud, 2011), p. 202; Campbell, *Medieval Jewellery*, p. 101.
46 T. Thomson (ed.), *A Collection of Inventories and Other Records of the Royal Wardrobe and Jewelhouse, and of the Artillery and Munition in Some of the Royal Castles, 1488–1606* (Edinburgh, 1815), p. 24; BL, Stowe MS 559, f. 56v.
47 BL, Stowe MS 559, f. 56v.
48 See Stratford (ed.), *Richard II*, p. 186 for examples; Lightbown, *European Jewellery*, p. 218.
49 Unknown Maker, 'Ring of Mary of Burgundy', c. 1477, gold and diamond, Kunsthistorisches Museum, Vienna, Inv: P 1 131; Scarisbrick, *Diamonds*, p. 16.
50 F.C. Cremades (ed.), *Los Inventarios de Carlos V y la Familia Imperial*, iii (Madrid, 2010), p. 2365.
51 *L & P*, iv, no. 6789. Examples include a ring and buttons with the initials 'H and E'.
52 J. Arnold (ed.), *Queen Elizabeth's Wardrobe Unlock'd* (Leeds, 1988), p. 70.
53 Earenfight, *Catherine of Aragon*, p. 128.
54 Scarisbrick, *Diamonds*, p. 60.
55 Ibid.
56 Lightbown, *Medieval European Jewellery*, p. 296.

57 Tait (ed.), *7000 Years*, p. 151.
58 Scarisbrick, *Tudor and Jacobean Jewellery*, p. 88.
59 Scarisbrick, *Diamonds*, p. 35.
60 BL, Royal MS 7 C XVI, f. 28r; SoA, MS 129, f. 217v.
61 Campbell, *Medieval Jewellery*, p. 33.
62 Forsyth, *Cheapside Hoard*, p. 122.
63 Campbell, *Medieval Jewellery*, p. 33; B. Chadour-Sampson and H. Bari, *Pearls* (London, 2013), p. 10.
64 Scarisbrick, *Tudor and Jacobean Jewellery*, p. 51.
65 Stratford (ed.), *Richard II*, p. 18.
66 Campbell, *Medieval Jewellery*, p. 16.
67 Phillips, *Jewelry*, p. 78.
68 Thomson (ed.), *Collection of Inventories*, p. 266.
69 Phillips, *Jewels and Jewellery*, p. 16.
70 Forsyth, *Cheapside Hoard*, p. 166; Phillips, *Jewelry*, p. 78.
71 Scarisbrick, *Diamonds*, p. 40.
72 Ibid, p. 44.
73 Cremades (ed.), *Inventarios*, iii, p. 365 for example.
74 Forsyth, *Cheapside Hoard*, p. 166.
75 Phillips, *Jewelry*, p. 58, 78.
76 Reynolds, *Fine Style*, p. 73; Scarisbrick, *Diamonds*, p. 41.
77 After Master John, 'Queen Catherine Parr (1512–1548)', 1600–1770, Seaton Delaval Hall, Northumberland, National Trust, NT 1276906.
78 Scarisbrick, *Diamonds*, p. 16.
79 Forsyth, *Cheapside Hoard*, p. 160.
80 H. Tillander, *Diamond Cuts in Historic Jewellery 1381–1910* (London, 1995), pp. 99–105; P.A. Tuetey (ed.), *Inventaire des Biens de Charlotte de Savoie, Reine de France, (1483)* (Paris, 1865), p 47.
81 SoA, MS 129, f. 218r.
82 Scarisbrick, *Diamonds*, p. 40.
83 Phillips, *Jewelry*, p. 78.
84 E 101/414/16, f. 53v.
85 Phillips, *Jewelry*, p. 77.
86 Ibid, p. 78.
87 J. Anderson Black, *A History of Jewels* (London, 1974), p. 134.
88 Cremades (ed.), *Inventarios*, iii, p. 2372.
89 Ibid, p. 2598.
90 Scarisbrick, Vachaudez and Walgrave, *Brilliant Europe*, p. 32.
91 G. Hughes, *A Pictorial History of Gems and Jewellery* (Oxford, 1978), p. 25.
92 Scarisbrick, *Tudor and Jacobean Jewellery*, p. 38. Opals do not feature in any of these inventories.
93 BL, Royal MS 7 C XVI, f. 22r.

94 BL, Stowe MS 559, f. 67r. The tablet in Katherine Howard's collection is similar and was described as 'oone Tablette of Golde with a border of antiques abought the same hauyng x Emeraldes'. The theme, though, was different, having 'upon thonesyde thereof is an antiqueman standing in red and upon thothersyde an antiqueman rydyng upon alyan hauyng also oone peerll hangyng at the same'. If it had once been owned by Jane Seymour, Katherine had evidently had it altered.
95 BL, Stowe MS 559, f. 56r; SoA, MS 129, f. 178r-183v.
96 Campbell, *Medieval Jewellery*, p. 28; Cremades (ed.), *Inventarios*, iii, p. 2625; Forsyth, *Cheapside Hoard*, p. 204.
97 SoA, MS 129, f. 218r.
98 Scarisbrick, *Tudor and Jacobean Jewellery*, p. 38.
99 Tuetey (ed.), *Charlotte de Savoie*, p. 48; BL, Royal MS 7 C XVI, f. 18v-19r.
100 Scarisbrick, *Historic Rings*, p. 64.
101 SoA, MS 129, f. 218r.
102 Campbell, *Medieval Jewellery*, p. 90.
103 Evans, *Magical Jewels*, p. 137.
104 F. Kisby, '"When the King Goeth a Procession": Chapel Ceremonies and Services, the Ritual Year, and Religious Reforms at the Early Tudor Court, 1485–1547', *Journal of British Studies*, 40 (2001), p. 63; Scarisbrick, *Tudor and Jacobean Jewellery*, p. 52.
105 *L & P*, iv, no. 5341; *L & P*, xviii, part 1, no. 436.
106 SoA, MS 129, f. 217v; Evans, *Magical Jewels*, p. 176.
107 M.A.E. Wood, *Letters of Royal and Illustrious Ladies of Great Britain*, I (London, 1846), p. 139.
108 Campbell, *Medieval Jewellery*, pp. 9–10.
109 *CSPV*, iii, no. 50.
110 Lucas Horenbout, 'Queen Mary I', c. 1525, NPG, NPG 6453.
111 Unknown Maker, 'Miniature Whistle Pendant', 1525–1530, gold, Victoria & Albert Museum, LOAN:MET ANON.1–1984.
112 T. Dickson and J. Paul Balfour (eds), *Accounts of the Lord High Treasurer of Scotland*, I (Edinburgh, 1877–1916), p. 81.
113 BL, Royal MS 7 C XVI, f. 21v-22r.
114 M.C. Brown, 'The "Three Kings of Cologne" and Plantagenet Political Theology', *Mediaevistik*, 30 (2017), p. 64.
115 BL, Royal MS 7 C XVI, f. 21r-v; BL, Stowe MS 559, f. 68r; BL, Royal MS 7 C XVI, f. 29r; SoA, MS 129, f. 181r.
116 BL, Royal MS 7 C XVI, f. 29r.
117 Thomson (ed.), *Collection of Inventories*, p. 59.
118 Unknown Maker, 'Boleyn Cup', 1535–6, silver-gilt, Church of St John the Baptist, Cirencester.
119 Schroder, '*A Marvel to Behold*', p. 220.

120 Ibid, pp. 220–1; Collins (ed.), *Jewels and Plate of Queen Elizabeth I*, p. 197.

References

Manuscript Sources

Kew, The National Archives

EXCHEQUER

E 36 Treasury of Receipt, Miscellaneous Books.
E 101 King's Remembrancer, Various Accounts.

LONDON, THE BRITISH LIBRARY

Additional Manuscripts 59899.
Royal Manuscripts 7 C XVI.
Stowe Manuscripts 559.

LONDON, SOCIETY OF ANTIQUARIES

MS 129 Inventory of King Henry VIII.

Portraits

After Master John, 'Queen Catherine Parr (1512–1548)', 1600–1770, Seaton Delaval Hall, Northumberland, National Trust, NT 1276906.
Hans Holbein, 'Jane Seymour', 1536–37, Kunsthistorisches Museum, Vienna, Inv. No. 881.
Lucas Horenbout, 'Katherine of Aragon', c. 1525–6, NPG, NPG L244.
Lucas Horenbout, 'Queen Mary I', c. 1525, NPG, NPG 6453.

Physical Objects

Unknown Maker, 'Boleyn Cup', 1535–6, silver-gilt, Church of St John the Baptist, Cirencester.
Unknown Maker, 'Dunstable Swan Jewel', fifteenth century, gold and enamel, British Museum, 1966,0703.1.
Unknown Maker, 'Lennox Jewel', c. 1571–78, gold, enamel, rubies, emerald, RCT, RCIN 28181.

Unknown Maker, 'Middleham Jewel', fifteenth century, gold and sapphire, Yorkshire Museum, YORYM: 1991.43.
Unknown Maker, 'Miniature Whistle Pendant', 1525–1530, gold, Victoria & Albert Museum, LOAN:MET ANON.1–1984.
Unknown Maker, 'Pendant reliquary cross', c. 1450–1475, silver, silver gilt, ruby, sapphire, garnet, pearl, Victoria & Albert Museum, 4561–1858.
Unknown Maker, 'Ring of Mary of Burgundy', c. 1477, gold and diamond, Kunsthistorisches Museum, Vienna, Inv: P 1 131.

Printed Primary Sources

Arnold, J. (ed.), *Queen Elizabeth's Wardrobe Unlock'd* (Leeds, 1988).
Bergenroth, G.A., et al., (ed.), *Calendar of State Papers, Spain*, 13 vols (London, 1862–1954).
Brewer, J., et al., (ed.), *Letters and Papers, Foreign and Domestic, of the Reign of Henry VIII, 1509–1547*, 21 vols (London, 1862–1932).
Brown, R., et al., (ed.), *Calendar of State Papers, Venice*, 38 vols (London, 1864–1947).
Collins, A.J., (ed.), *Jewels and Plate of Queen Elizabeth I: The Inventory of 1574* (London, 1955).
Cremades, F.C., (ed.), *Los inventarios de Carlos V y la familia imperial*, 3 vols (Madrid, 2010).
Dickson, T., and Balfour Paul, J., (eds), *Accounts of the Lord High Treasurer of Scotland*, 13 vols (Edinburgh, 1877–1916).
Starkey, D., (ed.), *The Inventory of King Henry VIII: The Transcript*, trans. Ward, P. (London, 1998).
Stratford, J., (ed.), *Richard II and the English Royal Treasure* (Woodbridge, 2012).
Thomson, T., (ed.), *A Collection of Inventories and Other Records of the Royal Wardrobe and Jewelhouse, and of the Artillery and Munition in Some of the Royal Castles, 1488–1606* (Edinburgh, 1815).
Tuetey, P.A., (ed.), *Inventaire des biens de Charlotte de Savoie, reine de France, (1483)* (Paris, 1865).
Wood, M.A.E, *Letters of Royal and Illustrious Ladies of Great Britain*, 3 vols (London, 1846).

Secondary Sources

Anderson Black, J., *A History of Jewels* (London, 1974).

Awais-Dean, N., *Bejewelled: Men and Jewellery in Tudor and Jacobean England* (London, 2017).

Brown, M.C., 'The "Three Kings of Cologne" and Plantagenet Political Theology', *Mediaevistik*, 30 (2017), pp. 61–85.

Bury, S., *Rings* (London, 1984).

Campbell, M., *Medieval Jewellery* (London, 2009).

Chadour-Sampson, B., and Bari, H., *Pearls* (London, 2013).

Cherry, J., 'The Dunstable Swan Jewel', *Journal of the British Archaeological Association*, 32 (1969), pp. 38–53.

Duffy, M., *Royal Tombs of Medieval England* (Stroud, 2011).

Earenfight, T., *Catherine of Aragon: Infanta of Spain, Queen of England* (Pennsylvania, 2021).

Evans, J., *A History of Jewellery 1100–1870* (New York, 1953).

Evans, J., *English Jewellery: From the Fifth Century A.D. to 1800* (London, 1921).

Evans, J., *Magical Jewels of the Middle Ages and the Renaissance* (New York, 1976).

Forsyth, H., *The Cheapside Hoard: London's Lost Jewels* (London, 2013).

Hackenbroch, Y., *Renaissance Jewellery* (London, 1979).

Hayward, M., *Dress at the Court of King Henry VIII* (Leeds, 2007).

Hayward, M., 'Gift Giving at the Court of Henry VIII: The 1539 New Year's Gift Roll in Context', *Antiquaries Journal*, 85 (2005), pp. 125–75.

Hayward, M., 'The Possessions of Henry VIII: A Study of Inventories', unpublished PhD thesis, London School of Economics and Political Science, University of London, 1998.

Hinton, D., *Medieval Jewellery* (Aylesbury, 1982).

Hughes, G., *A Pictorial History of Gems and Jewellery* (Oxford, 1978).

James, S., *Women's Voices in Tudor Wills, 1485–1603: Authority, Influence and Material Culture* (Farnham, 2015).

Kisby, F., '"When the King Goeth a Procession": Chapel Ceremonies and Services, the Ritual Year, and Religious Reforms at the Early Tudor Court, 1485–1547', *Journal of British Studies*, 40 (2001), pp. 44–75.

Lightbown, R.W., *Mediaeval European Jewellery* (London, 1992).

Milliken, W.M., 'The Art of the Goldsmith', *Journal of Aesthetics and Art Criticism*, 6 (1948), pp. 311–22.

Phillips, C., *Jewelry: From Antiquity to the Present* (London, 1996).

Phillips, C., *Jewels and Jewellery* (London, 2000).

Piacenti, K., and Boardman, J., *Ancient and Modern Gems and Jewels in the Collection of Her Majesty the Queen* (London, 2008).

Reynolds, A., *In Fine Style: The Art of Tudor and Stuart Fashion* (London, 2013).

Scarisbrick, D., *Diamond Jewelry: 700 Years of Glory and Glamour* (London, 2019).

Scarisbrick, D., *Historic Rings: Four Thousand Years of Craftsmanship* (Tokyo, 2004).

Scarisbrick, D., *Jewellery in Britain 1066–1837* (Norwich, 1994).

Scarisbrick, D., *Portrait Jewels: Opulence and Intimacy from the Medici to the Romanovs* (London, 2011).

Scarisbrick, D., *Rings: Jewelry of Power, Love and Loyalty* (London, 2007).

Scarisbrick, D., *Tudor and Jacobean Jewellery* (London, 1995).

Scarisbrick, D., and Henig, M., *Finger Rings* (Oxford, 2003).

Scarisbrick, D., Vachaudez, C., and Walgrave, J., (eds), *Brilliant Europe: Jewels from European Courts* (Brussels, 2007).

Schroder, T., *'A Marvel to Behold': Gold and Silver at the Court of Henry VIII* (Woodbridge, 2020).

Somers Cocks, A., *An Introduction to Courtly Jewellery* (London, 1980).

Tait, H., (ed.), *7000 Years of Jewellery* (London, 1986).

Tillander, H., *Diamond Cuts in Historic Jewellery 1381–1910* (London, 1995).

2 The Wills of the Queens of England, 1445–1548

Five of the ten queens in this period made surviving wills: Margaret of Anjou, Elizabeth Wydeville, Catherine of Aragon, Anna of Cleves and Kateryn Parr. In three of these instances, this is unsurprising, given the circumstances in which these women found themselves at the time of their deaths. Anna of Cleves was a single woman with financial independence and full control of her assets, therefore, everything mentioned in her will was hers to bestow where she chose.[1] Margaret of Anjou and Elizabeth Wydeville were widows and were thus at liberty to make wills without seeking the permission of a husband. A husband's consent was required for a married woman to make a will since legally, all property and effects owned by a married couple belonged to the husband.[2] Though it is possible that some of the remaining five queens also made wills, their positions at the time of their deaths make this unlikely. This chapter explores the surviving wills of the queens and their contemporaries during this period, in order to ascertain what jewels and wealth they had at their disposal at the time of their deaths. It then examines the way in which they bequeathed this wealth – specifically their jewels – in order to show how they were able to use this as a way of reinforcing their relationships and networks. In so doing, it shows the quantity and sometimes quality of jewels available to queens, which is in turn a reflection of them as both individuals and as consorts.

The Context of Wills

When studying jewels wills and inventories provide crucial documentary evidence. They provide intricate and often exquisite

DOI: 10.4324/9781003202592-3

details about the nature of an individual's personal belongings, their values and their relationships with their contemporaries. Through the use of the surviving wills, we can see both the material wealth that was amassed, or in the cases of Margaret of Anjou and Elizabeth Wydeville, diminished, and the way in which queens chose to bequeath their remaining jewels.[3] There are limitations though, and in contrast to the inventories discussed in Chapter 3, wills do not necessarily list everything an individual owned. Lucinda M. Becker asserted that 'Final gift giving could begin even before death as part of the ritual of the deathbed', and as such wills do not specify gifts that were made during the giver's lifetime, by means of either a written or a verbal bequest.[4] The approach to death of those making wills was often to provide for loved ones, to make provision for their souls, to recognise the service of their servants and to make a memorial for themselves, and examples of all of these appear in the wills of queens in this period.[5]

Sources written by women during the fifteenth and early sixteenth centuries can be limited, and sources written *about* women are often equally restricted.[6] Women were identified by the relationships they shared with the men in their lives, whether as daughters, wives, or mothers, rather than as individuals, which explains the lack of evidence in some quarters. Nevertheless, women often had an important role to play when it came to wills: it was not uncommon for women to be made the executors of others' wills, including their husbands'. Following the death of her husband in 1425, Joan Beaufort, Countess of Westmorland, was made the executor of his will.[7] Similarly, Elizabeth Catesby was listed as executor following her husband's execution in 1485.[8] However, none of the queens in this period are known to have fulfilled such a role for their husbands.

Wills in a recognisably modern form did not take shape until the late thirteenth century. Prior to 1445 several English medieval queens are known to have made wills, including Margaret of France, second consort of Edward I, and Katherine of Valois, wife of Henry V.[9] Wills made by women accounted for 400,000, or 20%, of all wills recorded between the mid-sixteenth century and the mid-eighteenth century.[10] Nearly 80% of these were made by widows, almost 20% by single women, and less than 1% by wives.[11] Generally married women did not write wills, accounting for their exclusion from these figures. Married women who did make wills required their husband's permission and were relatively unusual.[12] Kateryn Parr was the only queen in this period to do so, but she was not alone among her contemporaries. Frances Grey, Duchess of Suffolk, also made a will, even though her second husband, Adrian Stokes, was alive at the time of her death.[13] This is likely to be because of the Duchess's superior status and the substantial wealth she had to bequeath.[14] Kateryn Parr was in a similar position, and her situation will be discussed later in this chapter. This leads us to consider the circumstances in which queens made wills, and in most of the examples cited there were different reasons surrounding their creation.

Kings and noblemen also made wills, and though these documents were not exclusive to royalty and nobility, they were more likely to be made by those who had more to bequeath. Of the six kings in this period, it is probable that five made wills, the exception being Edward V. Of these, only two have survived: those of Henry VII and Henry VIII.[15] Wills could be written at entirely different points in an individual's life, and in both the surviving instances the wills underwent several drafts throughout the course of the kings' reigns. The same process is known to have been true of Edward IV, although none of his wills have survived.[16] It is probable that Henry VI and Richard III also made wills, but the documents may have been destroyed following their deaths. Final wills were frequently drawn up or amended when the maker was ill or suspected that they were dying, and this was the case in the instances of the three kings who are known with certainty to have made them.[17]

As historical sources, wills can supply information about property ownership, particularly in the case of widows. Evidence for this appears in the wills of Cecily Neville and Anna of Cleves.[18] Likewise, the wills of Lady Katherine Hastings and Lady Maud Parr demonstrate the lands that were in their possession at the times of their deaths.[19] Finally, and perhaps most crucially, wills make a vital contribution to our knowledge of familial relationships and alliances in the complex network of fifteenth- and sixteenth-century society. This is revealing in terms of queens and their jewels, providing clues as to the nature of the relationships they shared with their contemporaries, and how they chose to dispose of their belongings. Wills that mention jewels indicate the high rank of the maker; jewels were a vital enhancement of status and were affordable primarily to those at the top end of the social hierarchy.[20] It is therefore to be expected that jewels should appear in the wills of queens, and their absence in some of those that survive can be invariably explained by circumstances.

Unfortunately, the wills of Margaret of Anjou and Elizabeth Wydeville reveal nothing about their jewellery collections or the fate of their jewels, and it is for this reason that the wills of two of their contemporaries are worthy of consideration. Both Cecily Neville and Margaret Beaufort made extensive and detailed wills, which not only reflect their exalted status at the time of their deaths but also provide clues as to how the wills of Margaret of Anjou and Elizabeth Wydeville could have looked had their circumstances been different.[21] At the time of their deaths, both Margaret of Anjou and Elizabeth had been deprived of their titles as queen and were forced into penury. Therefore, the fact that neither had any jewels left to dispose of and few material goods is unsurprising. This is reflected in the lengths of both of their wills, which are significantly shorter than those of Cecily Neville and Margaret Beaufort. Though neither Cecily nor Margaret enjoyed the position of queen consort, they were both privileged to benefit from the status of the king's mother and were both wealthy in their own right.[22] Their wills reflect this affluence and could ordinarily have been expected in those of Margaret of Anjou and Elizabeth.

The example of Catherine of Aragon provides an interesting and unique contrast. Catherine considered herself to be a married woman rather than a singleton at the time of her death, which makes the fact that she made a will in the first place rather remarkable. Even so, as will be discussed shortly it is evident that her will was not considered as such by either Catherine or her supporters. Instead, it was intended to be a remembrance of her final wishes rather than a legal document.[23]

Kateryn Parr provides an exception to the other four queens, as she alone was married for the fourth time at the time of her death, her husband being Sir Thomas Seymour.[24] In such circumstances, it was unusual for a woman to make a will, but as the document explains,

> being persuaded, and perceiving the extremity of death to approach her; disposed and ordained by the permission, assent, and consent of her most dear, beloved husband, the Lord Seymour aforesaid, a certain disportion, gift, testament, and last will of all her goods, chattel, and debts.[25]

Kateryn was not the only queen who had made a will in spite of a further marriage. Katherine of Valois had done the same, although she was almost certainly married to Owen Tudor.[26] The precedent had, therefore, already been set.

The remaining five queens in this period are unlikely to have made wills, and this can be easily explained by their circumstances. Anne Neville, Elizabeth of York and Jane Seymour all died while they were married – and their husbands were alive – thus rendering the need for them to make a will redundant. All of their property naturally came into the possession of their husbands, and presumably so too did many of their personal belongings. Following Jane Seymour's death, Henry VIII chose to disburse some of her jewels to her relatives and the women who had served her. An inventory of Jane's collection will be discussed in Chapter 3; whether the disbursement of jewels derived from a request made by Jane as she lay dying or was her husband's decision is uncertain.[27] This is, though, the only surviving recorded example we have during this period of a king distributing his deceased wife's property to a named list of recipients. Some of Jane's royal jewels were inherited by her successors, and these examples will be mentioned in the following chapter.

Anne Boleyn and Katherine Howard were exceptional among their contemporary queens. As both were condemned and executed for treason, in keeping with standard procedure neither queen was entitled to make a will. Instead, their property was forfeited to the Crown. Following the death of Anne Boleyn, the King chose to distribute some of her personal belongings to his eldest daughter, Mary, but evidence for the fate of other belongings is obscure. Presumably, either Mary or Henry passed on at least one of Anne's jewels to her daughter, Elizabeth, for she can be seen wearing an 'A' initial necklace in the painting, 'The Family of Henry VIII', which will be analysed in Chapter 4.[28]

Margaret of Anjou and Elizabeth Wydeville

Margaret and Elizabeth's wills were not reflective of those that might have been expected of former queens of England. The circumstances of Margaret's mother-in-law, Katherine of Valois, were in some ways similar to those in which Margaret and Elizabeth found themselves at the times of their deaths, so Margaret and Elizabeth's wills could be said to fit the same pattern.[29]

Both Margaret and Elizabeth claimed to have nothing of value to leave their loved ones.[30] Margaret's surviving jewel accounts reveal that at the height of her power she gave generously to her servants, and therefore her claim to have nothing to bequest in her will is likely to have been a true reflection of the penury in which she found herself.[31] Margaret's depleted finances were confirmed at the time of her death in 1482, when she was not even in possession of her wedding ring. This is unsurprising: by the time Margaret began her captivity in 1471 at the hands of Edward IV she probably had few jewels remaining, and any personal effects she did own were almost certainly seized at this time; this explains how her wedding ring wound up in the royal coffers in 1530, as Chapter 5 reveals.[32] If this was indeed the case, it shows how harshly Edward IV dealt with Margaret. Additionally, before Margaret left England in 1475 for exile in France, she was forced to renounce all her claims to lands and titles in England.[33]

Considering Margaret's circumstances, it is little wonder that her will made no mention of any jewels or bequests of other property. The document confirms that her primary concern was for her soul and burial. This was common, and is demonstrated in all of the wills discussed in this chapter – all save Anna of Cleves and Kateryn Parr stated precisely where they wished to be buried, and Margaret's request that she should be interred in Angers Cathedral was honoured. She further stated, 'My will is

[that] the few goods which God and he [Louis XI] have given and lent to me be used for this purpose and for the paying of my debts as much to my poor servants'.[34] There is no indication as to the nature of the goods to which Margaret referred; however, they were clearly of little monetary value. This is confirmed by Margaret's next sentence; 'And should my few goods be insufficient to do this, as I believe they are, I implore the king [to] meet and pay the outstanding debts'.[35] She named Louis XI, king of France, as the 'sole heir of the wealth which I inherited through my father and mother and my other relatives and ancestors'.[36] As Margaret's biographer Helen Maurer has shown, following Margaret's arrival in France she had been required to sign over her rights of inheritance to Louis, so this would have been fully expected.[37]

Although Edward IV's will has not survived, David Baldwin stressed that according to its terms Elizabeth Wydeville was permitted to keep her jewels after his death.[38] The lack of the original document makes this impossible to corroborate, but it seems probable that Edward would have made some such provision for his widow. It is likely that Elizabeth took most of her jewels with her during her flight into sanctuary in Westminster Abbey in the spring of 1483. The contemporary chronicler Dominic Mancini reported that 'it was commonly believed that the late king's treasure, which had taken such years and pains to gather, was divided between the queen, the marquess [of Dorset, Elizabeth's eldest son by her first marriage], and Edward [V]'.[39] Mancini is, however, the only contemporary source to make any such reference, and Rosemary Horrox demonstrated that it is unlikely that there was much left in the coffers at this time in any case.[40] In March 1486 Elizabeth's son-in-law Henry VII restored her dower lands, but the cost of maintaining a dower queen and his own queen could have been a decisive factor in Elizabeth's withdrawal to Bermondsey Abbey in 1487.[41] She was nevertheless granted a pension of 400 marks, a sum that was later increased.[42] This ensured that Elizabeth did have access to funds, but certainly not on the same scale as she had enjoyed during her tenure as queen consort.

Laynesmith argued that Elizabeth's 'status as a widow meant that she could choose a funeral which was a ritual for a woman, not a queen', and it may be that this was also reflected in the style in which she made her will.[43] After all, Elizabeth Wydeville's funeral was in direct contrast to that of her daughter, Elizabeth of York, whose funeral, analysed in Chapter 4, was a reflection of her position and wealth at the time of her death. Laynesmith has suggested that Elizabeth Wydeville's funeral and her will could have placed a deliberate emphasis on poverty in an underhand attempt to criticise Henry VII.[44] Yet it is highly unlikely that Elizabeth Wydeville had anything of worldly value left to bequeath. Any royal treasure that she had appropriated upon the death of her husband almost certainly found its way into the coffers of Richard III.

Elizabeth's will was made on 10 April 1492, two months prior to her death on 8 June. Significantly, she referred to herself as 'Elisabeth by the grace of God Quene of England', emphasising that she still considered herself to be a queen and was conscious of her exulted status.[45] Elizabeth's primary concern was meeting her maker, as she expressed in her hope that he would accept her soul and 'all the holy company of hevyn, to be good meanes for me'.[46] She also conveyed her desire to be interred next to her husband at Windsor 'without pompes entreing or costlie expensis donne thereabought'.[47] It is difficult to ascertain whether this request for simplicity reflected Elizabeth's finances, or a genuine desire for a quiet burial, as is suggested by Laynesmith.[48]

The crucial point of her will, though, is highlighted next: 'Item, where I have no wordely goodes to do the Quene's Grace, my derest doughter, a pleaser with, nether to reward any of my children, according to my hart and mynde, I besech Almyghty Gode to blisse her Grace'.[49] This must surely be a true reflection that Elizabeth did indeed have nothing of value to leave to her children. Nevertheless, she continued: 'Item, I will that suche smale stufe and goodes that I have be disposed truly in the contentac'on of my dettes and for the helth of my sowle, as farre as they will extende'.[50] There is no indication as to the nature of these goods. It is wholly possible that there were some jewels perceived to be of little value; however, as jewels were considered to be extremely precious commodities, it is more credible that the goods referred to something else entirely. It is possible that some of these goods held some kind of value for the Queen's family, even if only for sentimental reasons, as she continued to state: 'Item, yf any of my bloode will any of my saide stufe or goodes to me perteyning, I will that they have the prefermente before any other'.[51] Perhaps this referred to household items or furniture, but whether any of Elizabeth's family requested these goods is unknown.

Margaret and Elizabeth's wills can be considered a reflection of the circumstances in which they found themselves at the end of their lives, rather than providing a true representation of a queen's will. Had they died during their husband's lifetimes, the nature of their finances and material goods would have borne a greater similarity to those evidenced in the wills of Cecily Neville and Margaret Beaufort.

Cecily Neville and Margaret Beaufort

The wills of Cecily Neville and Margaret Beaufort provide a startling contrast to those of their contemporary queens.[52] They are interesting to consider because although neither woman was a queen, both were still powerful in the context of fifteenth- and early sixteenth-century England. Their wills reveal the kind of material wealth that was available to them and provide interesting points of comparison. Both are notable for their length and the number of bequests that they contain. This significantly reflects the variance with the circumstances of the aforementioned queens in the last section and the positions of Cecily and Margaret in society.

The wills of both Cecily and Margaret are representative of the religiosity of the women who made them, both of whom were considered to be pious by their contemporaries.[53] This is particularly apparent in Margaret Beaufort's will, which concerns itself primarily with her funeral arrangements and bequests to religious foundations.[54] Both wills are also indicative of the amount of material wealth that Cecily and Margaret had access to, and although they are only representative of a proportion of what they owned, they nevertheless serve as evidence of the sort of lifestyle both women enjoyed. Unlike inventories, wills were selective documents that took account of whatever goods the maker chose.

All the money Cecily was owed from a royal grant of customs' duties was left to Henry VII, as well as 'two cuppes of gold'.[55] That Henry VII was listed as the first beneficiary is an indication of courtesy and his social precedence, although Laynesmith has also suggested that Cecily's will is expressive of 'a genuinely positive relationship' between the two.[56] Cecily's granddaughter, Elizabeth of York, naturally followed Henry. She was the only member of Cecily's family to whom she chose to bequeath items of jewellery, and was to receive 'a crosse croslette of diamantes, a sawter [psalter] with claspes of silver and guilte enameled covered with grene clothe of golde, and a pix with the fleshe of Saint Cristofer'.[57] It seems likely that these jewels held some special significance to Cecily that is not mentioned, either because they were particularly valuable in monetary terms, or due to their sentimental value and religious and/or decorative symbolism.[58] It was not uncommon for women to leave their most prized possessions and jewels to their closest female relative. Susan James related that women 'sought to create through personally chosen artefacts vehicles that would carry their memory down the generations', and Cecily could have had this in mind.[59]

Having ensured that her family and religious affairs were in order, Cecily's next thoughts were for her friends and retainers. She left bequests of almost 50 pieces of jewellery to a total of 11 named recipients, and the items she listed contained everything from rings, to tablets, to pendants and pomanders.[60] The most frequently occurring items were Agnus Dei, evidence of Cecily's religious devotion. Such pieces were popular in this period, and several Agnus Dei appear in an inventory of the possessions of Charlotte of Savoy.[61] Laynesmith has observed that all of Cecily's Agnus Dei were bequeathed to either women or married couples within her household.[62] It was not uncommon for women to leave bequests to their friends, or 'gossip networks', and examples also appear in the will of Anna of Cleves.[63] In Cecily's will, Anne Pinchbeke – probably a member of Cecily's household – received the most in terms of quantity, with a total of 11 bequests, while two other couples both received seven jewelled objects each.

With the exception of Sir Henry Heydon, the steward of Cecily's household, all of the recipients received more than one item. This can potentially be explained by the value of the jewel given to Heydon, which was likely more both in monetary terms and sentimentally. He received 'a tablett and a cristall garnesshed with ix stones and xxvij perles, lacking a stone and iij perles'.[64]

Besides the Agnus Dei, many of the jewels listed by Cecily were of a religious nature and were used as expressions of her piety. This indicates that Cecily chose these items as part of a deliberate strategy to leave those close to her a personal memento that encouraged the recipients to pray for her soul and remember her as a woman of immense religiosity. A bequest that conveys this particular point was left to Richard Brocas and his wife Jane. Among other objects they were to have 'a greate Agnus of gold with the Trinite, Saint Erasmus, and the Salutacion of our Lady; an Agnus of gold with our Lady and Saint Barbara'.[65] Further religious jewels were left to Anne Pinchbeke, who received 'all other myne Agnus unbequeithed, that is to say, ten of the Trinite'.[66] As James has shown, the bequest of beads or other religious jewels were a common portable legacy that was almost unique to women during this period.[67] After the Reformation, such bequests rarely appeared, and it is interesting to consider that even though Anna of Cleves died a Catholic in a restored Catholic England in 1557, her will made no mention of any such bequests.[68]

It is improbable that the jewels mentioned in Cecily's will reflect her entire collection. More likely is that they were a selection of those perceived to hold the most value, or that Cecily had chosen as a specific gift to a named person. This theory is supported by the known existence of Cecily's signet ring, which though not accounted for, Cecily made reference to. John Metcalfe and his wife, Alice, were to receive 'all the ringes that I have', with the exception of 'such as hang by my bedes and Agnus, and also except my signet'.[69] The signet ring was probably just one example, and Cecily may have bestowed this more personal jewel elsewhere by means of oral instruction.

Like Cecily Neville, Margaret Beaufort's will demonstrates an extraordinary level of material wealth, and the document reflected only a small part of this.[70] An inventory of Margaret's plate and jewels taken after her death shows the true extent of her belongings, and it is therefore fair to assume that her will can be taken as evidence of where her true priorities lay.[71] Margaret was not a queen, yet in the first line of her will she not only made it apparent that she identified herself with royalty but that she considered herself to be royal too. Initially describing herself as 'Moder to the most excellent Prince King Henry the VIIth, by the grace of God King of Englond', thereafter Margaret consistently referred to herself as 'Princesse'.[72] Such a description confirms Margaret's pride both in her royal blood and in her position as Henry VII's mother.

Margaret's foremost concerns were religious, but in February 1509, four months before her death, she added a schedule of bequests.[73] In this she left her grandson, Henry VIII, several of her books as well as 'v of my best cuppes of gold with theire couers', before turning her attention to her granddaughters and Catherine of Aragon.[74] Her granddaughter and namesake Margaret, Queen of Scotland, was bequeathed 'a gyrdell of gold conteynyng xxix lynckes with a great pomaundere at oonn ende'.[75] Margaret may have considered girdles to be among her best pieces, as she also left one to Catherine of Aragon: 'a gyrdell of gold conteynyng vj flowres', as well as her next best cup after the ones she had bequeathed to her grandson.[76] Margaret's youngest granddaughter, Mary, was the only one of the three women not to receive a girdle, and instead was to be given 'a stonding cuppe of gold couered garnyshed with white hertes perles and stonys', in addition to an elaborate salt covered in costly gems.[77] These gifts to her family were the most noteworthy of Margaret's bequests, demonstrating her affection for them. However, Margaret also left various gifts of plate to her friends and members of her household, probably intended as tokens of remembrance.[78] The numerous bequests she made serve as a testament not only to the remarkably large amount of portable wealth Margaret owned but also to her generous nature in choosing to remember so many.

Catherine of Aragon, Anna of Cleves and Kateryn Parr

When Catherine of Aragon made her will in 1536, she was estranged from her husband and living in relatively stringent conditions at Kimbolton Castle. Catherine had been banished from court in 1531 and was sent to live in a series of uncomfortable houses before finally settling at Kimbolton.[79] On 23 May 1533, Thomas Cranmer, Archbishop of Canterbury, officially declared Catherine's marriage to Henry VIII to be null and void. Of all of the queens in this period, we know more about the circumstances of Catherine's death and in which she made her will, thanks to the detailed reports of the Imperial ambassador, Eustace Chapuys. Although Chapuys was a friend and supporter of Catherine's, the nature of his position as ambassador meant that he had a responsibility to report faithfully to his master, the Holy Roman Emperor, Charles V. From his observances, it is clear that Catherine herself did not consider her will to be her final legal testament. When relating the manner of Catherine's death to Charles V, who was also Catherine's nephew, Chapuys explained that

> Knowing that according to English law a wife can make no will while her husband survives, she would not break the said laws, but by way of request caused her physician to write a little bill, which she commanded to be sent to me immediately, and which was signed by her hand, directing some little reward to be made to certain servants who had remained with her.[80]

It is this 'little bill' that survives, and it is indeed a short document.[81] Because Catherine did not consider it to be a legal document in the same way as a will, she did not appoint any executors. It ought, though, to be treated in a similar manner because it contains a faithful list of the items Catherine wished to bequeath in her final hours. In addition, it reveals that Catherine had more material wealth at her disposal than either Margaret of Anjou or Elizabeth Wydeville, although she was not living in a regal manner at the time of her death. Shortly after Catherine's death, Sir Edmund Bedingfield, who the King had entrusted with her care, wrote to Thomas Cromwell that 'the persons who had the custo[dy of her] jewels, plate, and apparel, have given us a just and plain declaration, containing much more than [we could] see or know before'.[82] Catherine had evidently been eager to conceal her goods from those who might have cause to report to the King, perhaps leading to their disposal.

Few examples of jewels are found in Catherine's will, and this is unsurprising. In September 1532, Catherine had been forced to renounce her custody of the royal jewels, and initially refused to do so, claiming that 'I would consider it a sin and a load upon my conscience if I were persuaded to give up my jewels for such a wicked purpose as that of ornamenting a person who is the scandal of Christendom'.[83] The person to whom she referred was Anne Boleyn. In the event Catherine had no choice: in February 1533 a disgusted Chapuys reported that Anne 'still keeps in her possession the Queen's rings and jewels, and there is no talk for the present of her restoring them to their legitimate owner'.[84] His statement provides confirmation that Catherine's collection had been passed to her replacement, but she did manage to retain some jewels which later appeared in her will, presumably because they were her own personal property.[85]

Catherine's primary bequests were of small sums of money to her servants, including one to 'Mrs Margery' – later Lady Lister who was charged with the care of Jane Seymour's jewels.[86] However, she also requested that 'my goldsmyth be paid of his wage [missing words] year coming. And beside that all that is due [missing word]'.[87] Such a reference does not necessarily indicate that Catherine had been commissioning jewels from the goldsmith and is instead likely to refer to the purchase of plate or other household items. Goldsmiths received frequent commissions for plate, and this together with their role at the royal court will be discussed in Chapter 5. This does show though, that although Catherine was no longer queen and was living on a reduced income, her financial circumstances contrasted drastically with those of Margaret of Anjou and Elizabeth Wydeville. This is also supported by the brief reference she made to the 'goods whiche I do holde as well in gold and sylver as other thyngs'.[88]

Catherine made two gifts of jewels, both for her daughter, Mary. The first was a cross necklace, followed by the more significant bequest: 'the colar of gold whiche I brought [missing words] Spayne be to my doughter'.[89] Gold collars were popular during this period but would soon go out of fashion.[90] The importance of the jewellery though, lies in its sentimentality, for it was a treasured piece of Catherine's that she had owned prior to her arrival in England. It was almost certainly an heirloom, perhaps inherited from her own mother Isabel of Castile, who had also gifted one to her daughter-in-law Margaret of Austria.[91] Catherine intended to pass hers on to her own daughter, and such bequests appear frequently in women's wills. Dagmar Eichberger's study of Margaret of Austria's 1499 jewel inventory has shown that at the time of her marriage to Prince Juan, Margaret was given large numbers of jewels from Isabel of Castile, and some from her father-in-law, Ferdinand of Aragon, and the same may have been true in Catherine's case.[92] By passing on such a piece of jewellery to her daughter, Catherine could have intended the collar to serve as a more personal reminder to Mary of her mother and her heritage.

Catherine only referred to two pieces of jewellery, but that does not mean that these were the only two that she owned. It is more likely that they were the items that held the most significance to her. Like Cecily Neville before her, it is probable that Catherine had been selective in her choices, and for reasons that were personal to her. The importance of the cross necklace lay in its religious associations, for Chapuys noted that 'there are not 10 crowns worth of gold in the said cross nor any jewellery, but within is a portion of the true Cross'.[93] To this, Mary felt 'great devotion', confirming that it was intended to offer her comfort.[94]

Although Catherine did not name executors, she did ensure that there were those about her who knew of her wishes. In his report to the Emperor, Chapuys confirmed that 'the furs should be reserved for the Princess, her daughter, to whom she likewise desired to be given a collar with a cross which she had brought from Spain', as well as relating Catherine's requests for her final interment.[95] These final wishes were ignored, and when she was buried at Peterborough it was with the rights afforded to a princess dowager rather than a queen – confirmation that Henry VIII firmly believed Catherine to have been no more than his sister-in-law.[96]

All the arrangements regarding Catherine's will were entrusted to Thomas Cromwell, who had confirmed to Chapuys that 'everything would be done as regards the Princess and the servants as honourably and magnificently as I could demand'.[97] Presumably he was referring to the delivery of the jewels Catherine had bequeathed to her daughter, but a day later the circumstances had changed. It is unclear what prompted this, but Chapuys explained that Cromwell had said that 'if the Princess wished to have what had been given her she must first show herself obedient to her father, and that I ought to urge her to be so'.[98] Henry had evidently attempted to use Catherine's dying bequests to her daughter as a way of manipulating Mary into acknowledging that she was illegitimate. Clearly, he later changed his mind, as on 25 February Chapuys confirmed that Mary had received the cross.[99]

Mary later featured in the will of her stepmother, Anna of Cleves. Anna's will provides yet another unique example to those of her predecessors and contemporaries. It is important to note that, unlike any of Anna's predecessors or her later successor Kateryn Parr, when she made her will, just a few days before her death in July 1557, she made it clear that it was not made from the perspective of one who was or had been a queen of England. Referring to herself as 'Anne the Daughter of John late Duke of Cleves and Sister to the Excellent Prynce Will[ia]m nowe reignynge', Anna clearly identified herself with her German family and her position within it.[100] She made no reference to her former status, or indeed her unofficial title of 'King's sister' that Henry VIII had bestowed upon her following the annulment of her marriage.[101] Instead, Anna made only one reference to her former husband. Identifying him solely in his capacity as Queen Mary's father, she addressed him as 'hir Majesties Late Father of moste famous memory Kinge Henry the Eight'.[102]

Anna's relationship with Mary at the time of her death was evidently still a relatively close one, as is demonstrated by Anna's request that

> our moste Dearest and entierlie belovyd soveraign Lady Quene Mary we earnestlie Desier to be our overseer of this

> our saied Laste Will and Testament with moste humble request to see the same performed as to hir Highnes shall seame best for the healthe of our soule.[103]

That she had asked Mary to oversee her final wishes is a testament to the high regard in which she held her former stepdaughter, who she also asked to choose her place of burial – Mary selected Westminster Abbey. By way of thanks and 'in token of our especiall truste and affyannce', as well as a mark of Mary's status as queen, Anna proceeded to make Mary a bequest. Her 'moste Excellent Majestie' was 'for a remembringe', to receive 'our bet [best] Juell'.[104] Frustratingly, there is no further description or indication of what this jewel may have been, although Anna must have left verbal instructions to ensure that Mary received it. That it was given for a remembering, however, shows that it was intended as a personal memento. The same is true of the bequest that followed. Anna's 'seconde beste Jewell' was left to her younger former stepdaughter, 'the Lady Elizabeths grace'.[105] Presumably Anna had left clearer directions to identify these pieces to those who witnessed the will or to her executors. Her bequest to Elizabeth also reveals that she had remained on good terms with her younger stepdaughter and wished to leave her a personal reminder.

Anna was financially provided for during the reign of her late husband, and part of the agreement for her annulment stated that she would be allowed to keep her personal jewels.[106] Presumably most of these had been brought with her from Cleves, with the possible addition of some that were provided for her by the King and those that she commissioned during her brief reign. A contemporary source supports this theory, stating that Henry sent several of his officials to Anna 'to see her household fully established and present certain jewels and other things of great value' which the King gave her.[107] But the circumstances changed during the reign of her former stepson, Edward VI, who took two of her manors from her and replaced them with two of lesser value in Kent.[108] This could have had some effect on her will and the property that she had available to her at the time of creating her final testament. Anna's will is similar to that of Cecily Neville in terms of the thorough distribution of her goods. It is striking though, for one other reason. Although all of the other queens, and indeed Cecily and Margaret Beaufort, expressed concern for the welfare of their servants, in Anna's will this was her foremost and primary interest. It superseded even religious considerations, and she continually stressed that their well-being was a priority.

Seven named recipients were left jewels. What is interesting is that each of them received a ring, and rings that were described in detail. Rings were highly personal and often used as tokens of friendship.[109] This suggests that Anna had chosen each of them for a specific purpose, either as a reflection of her relationship with the wearer, or perhaps for some other personal reason known only to the recipient. James emphasised that such bequests were reiterations of friendship and affection, endorsers of personal memory and 'engaging the recipients as personally designated rememberers'.[110]

Anna's bequests are revealing in terms of her relationships with her family and friends. Foremost among the recipients were her family, all listed in order of precedence. Naturally, the first among these was her brother, the Duke of Cleves, who was to receive 'a rynge of golde with a fayre dyamonde like unto a harte with sundrie square Cutt[es] in the same'.[111] The heart-shaped diamond was probably a deliberate choice of Anna's and intended to underline the familial relationship between the two, which was to be symbolised in this tangible reminder. Next, to 'the Duches of Cleaves his wife a rynge havinge thereon a grete Rocke Rubye and the ringe beinge blacke enamelid'.[112] The language suggests that this could have been chosen as it was the next valuable in monetary terms and was therefore a mark of the status of Anna's sister-in-law, Maria of Austria, as Duchess of Cleves. The bequests to Anna's family ended with her sister, 'the Ladie Emely', who was to receive 'a ringe of golde havinge therein a fayre poynted Dyamond'.[113] The description of this ring is of a far less personal nature than that which Anna left to their brother, although the report of the diamond as 'fayre' intimates that it was precious.

Those to her friends followed the bequests to Anna's three family members. Foremost among them was 'Ladie Katheryne

Duches of Suffolke', who was to receive 'a ringe of golde havinge therein a faire table Dyamond some what longe'.[114] This is worthy of further comment. Not only was Katherine Willoughby, Duchess of Suffolk, a fervent Protestant with views completely at odds with Anna's own at the time of her death, but in 1557 when Anna's will was made, the Duchess was in self-imposed exile in Europe to avoid persecution in England.[115] Despite their religious differences, the two women were still able to maintain a friendship, and Anna evidently trusted Queen Mary to ensure that her bequest was honoured. Whether or not the Duchess ever received the ring is unknown, for she did not return to England until 1559, following the accession of Elizabeth I.[116]

Following the Duchess of Suffolk, three further bequests of rings followed. Mary Arundell, Countess of Arundel, was given 'a ringe of golde with a faire table Dyamonde havynge an Hand in it of golde set under the stone'.[117] The significance of the hand is unclear, but such a description indicates that, like the other rings, it had been chosen especially for the recipient. The inclusion of the Countess is unsurprising, as she had served in Anna's household during her short term as queen, and therefore confirms that the two women had remained friends.[118] Anna's will shows that, like Cecily Neville, she was at pains to materially reward those who had shown her good service. It also sheds light on her relationships with her contemporaries and family members, whom she was eager to leave some tangible reminder to.

In contrast to all of the examples cited, the will of Kateryn Parr was verbally dictated during the dying queen's final hours, and as such is remarkably brief and very general.[119] Following the delivery of her first child on 30 August 1548, Kateryn was initially expected to make a full recovery, but died days later of puerperal fever.[120] The rapid decline in her health therefore meant that there was no time for the former queen to make a thorough account of her dying wishes. The circumstances of Kateryn's death were unexpected, yet in some respects it is surprising that she did not make some provision of her final wishes at an earlier time. The risks involved in childbirth in the sixteenth century were well known, and at 36 Kateryn was considered old by contemporary standards to be bearing her first child.[121] It is therefore difficult to comprehend why she chose not to prepare herself should the worst happen and can perhaps only be explained by a sense of optimism. This also explains why Kateryn did not make any bequests to any of her friends or family and instead entrusted all of her assets to her husband, Sir Thomas Seymour. As her will was verbally dictated, however, there is a possibility that Kateryn did leave some small material bequests, but if this was the case then no record of them has survived.

Unlike Anna of Cleves, though Henry VIII was dead at the time that Kateryn made her will, she still chose to identify herself in her former role as his consort, as well as of the wife of Sir Thomas Seymour. Kateryn described herself as 'The moste noble and excellent Princesse, Dame Kathryn, Quene of England, Fraunce, and Irelande; late the wyfe of the moste excellent prince of famous memory, king henry theight, late kinge of England; and then wyfe to the right honourable Sir Thomas Seymour'.[122] Such an identification shows that although Kateryn was evidently proud of her position as Seymour's wife, she still considered herself to be royal. She also had greater reason to emphasise her status than Anna would later have, for her background lacked the same prestige that Anna's ducal ties to her homeland of Cleves provided her with. Kateryn's short will, witnessed by her physician, Robert Huicke, and her chaplain, John Parkhurst, simply stated that 'with all hir harte and desire, frankely and freely', Kateryn gave all of her 'goodes, chattels, and debtes that she than hadd, or of ryght ought to have in all the world, wisshing them to be a thousand tymes more in value than they were or been', to Seymour.[123] Though her will is brief, one point that is worthy of comment is Kateryn's statement about the goods she 'of ryght ought to have'. It is likely that this was a reference to her royal and personal jewels, which were appropriated by the Duke of Somerset following the death of Henry VIII – including the wedding ring that Henry VIII had bestowed on her.[124] Kateryn's struggles to regain custody of her jewels are well documented, but such a reference could signify that she perceived that Seymour would continue this fight after her death – as indeed he did – in which case her wishes were that he should be able to keep them.[125] Like Kateryn, Seymour was also unsuccessful in his attempt to regain the jewel collection.

Conclusion

The surviving wills of the queens and noblewomen examined in this chapter demonstrate how much emphasis was placed on jewels at the end of their lives, and how they could be given as personal memorials. The wills provide a variety of contrasts, thereby reinforcing the extraordinary nature of queenship in this period. Although Becker is quite correct in saying that wills 'were rarely written by the testatrix herself', a statement that is almost certainly true in all of the examples cited here, they are nevertheless invaluable sources.[126] While those of Margaret of Anjou and Elizabeth Wydeville signify the decline in material wealth following the downward spiral in their circumstances, that of Cecily Neville provides a stark contrast and is a more accurate reflection of what one might expect to find in a queen's will. By the same token, the wills of Cecily, Margaret Beaufort, and Anna of Cleves offer some detailed descriptions of material culture and are a reflection of the comfortable circumstances in which these three women found themselves at the times of their deaths. The wills of Catherine of Aragon and Kateryn Parr provide yet more contrasts. Though Catherine of Aragon considered her will to be a written record of her final wishes, it reveals that though she was estranged from her husband at the time of her death, she did still have access to money and material goods which she chose to bequeath. The example of Kateryn Parr illustrates that the queen was unprepared for death and was perhaps unable to bestow her property as she may have wished had the circumstances been different. Her will is no reflection of her personality and provides little evidence as to the nature and quantity of her goods at the time of her death, or how she would have chosen to distribute them. For the most part though, each of the wills offers 'not only a glimpse into an individual life but a new voice commenting on the feminine condition in a rapidly changing society'.[127]

Notes

1 PROB 11/39/368, f. 261v-263r.
2 James, *Women's Voices*, p. 7.
3 Cited in J.J. Bagley, *Margaret of Anjou* (London, 1948), p. 240; PROB 11/9/207.
4 L.M. Becker, *Death and the Early Modern Englishwoman* (Aldershot, 2003), p. 160.
5 Ibid, p. 13.
6 J. Eales, *Women in Early Modern England, 1500–1700* (London, 1998), p. 16.
7 SC 8/26/1295.
8 PROB 11/7/290.
9 *CPR*, 1317–1321, p. 139; J. Nichols (ed.), *A Collection of All the Wills, Now Known to be Extant, of the Kings and Queens of England* (London, 1780), pp. 244–9.
10 Eales, *Women*, p. 20.
11 Ibid.
12 Ibid.
13 PROB 11/42B/688.
14 See B.J. Harris, *English Aristocratic Women 1450–1550: Marriage and Family, Property and Careers* (Oxford, 2002).
15 E 23/3; E 23/4. See also T. Astle (ed.), *The Will of Henry VII* (London, 1775).
16 See C. Ross, *Edward IV* (London, 1974), pp. 417–18 for further details.
17 Warnicke, *Wicked Women*, p. 165.
18 PROB 11/10/447; PROB 11/39/368.
19 PROB 11/14/93; J.G. Nichols and J. Bruce (eds), *Wills from Doctors' Commons: A Selection from the Wills of Eminent Persons Proved in the Prerogative Court of Canterbury, 1495–1695* (London, 1863) pp. 9–20.
20 Hollis (ed.), *Princely Magnificence*, p. 3.
21 PROB 11/10/447; PROB 11/16/419. See also Nichols and Bruce (eds), *Doctors' Commons*, pp. 1–8; Nichols (ed.), *Collection of All the Wills*, pp. 356–403.
22 See J.L. Laynesmith, *Cecily Duchess of York* (London, 2017), pp. 95–113; M. Jones and M.G. Underwood, *The King's Mother: Lady Margaret Beaufort Countess of Richmond and Derby* (Cambridge, 1992), pp. 66–92.
23 BL, Cotton MS Otho C X, f. 216r-v.
24 G.W. Bernard, 'Seymour, Thomas, Baron Seymour of Sudeley', *ODNB*.
25 PROB 11/32/19, f. 142v.
26 Nichols (ed.), *Collection of all the Wills*, pp. 244–9. There is no surviving evidence that Katherine and Tudor were married, but most

modern historians generally believe this to have been the case. See M. Jones, 'Catherine [Catherine of Valois]', *ODNB*.

27 BL, Royal MS 7 C XVI, f. 18r-31r.
28 Unknown Artist, 'The Family of Henry VIII', c. 1545, RCT, RCIN 405796.
29 See Nichols (ed.), *Collection of All the Wills*, pp. 244–9.
30 Cited in Bagley, *Margaret of Anjou*, p. 240; PROB 11/9/207.
31 E101/409/14; E101/409/17; E101/410/2; E101/410/8; E101/410/11. See also Myers, 'Jewels of Queen Margaret'.
32 See Hayward, 'Possessions', p. 50; *L & P*, iv, no. 6789.
33 Laynesmith, *Last Medieval Queens*, p. 172.
34 Cited in Bagley, *Margaret of Anjou*, p. 240. It has been impossible to track down the original will, and most scholars now cite the one used by Bagley.
35 Ibid.
36 Ibid.
37 Maurer, *Margaret of Anjou*, p. 208.
38 D. Baldwin, *Elizabeth Woodville: Mother of the Princes in the Tower* (Stroud, 2002), p. 62.
39 Mancini, *Usurpation*, p. 23.
40 R. Horrox, 'Financial Memoranda of the Reign of Edward V', *Camden Miscellany XXIX*, 34 (Camden Fourth Series, 1987), p. 211.
41 See Ross, *Edward IV*, pp. 201–3.
42 M. Hicks, 'Elizabeth', *ODNB*.
43 Laynesmith, *Last Medieval Queens*, p. 129.
44 Ibid.
45 PROB 11/9/207, f. 74r.
46 Ibid.
47 Ibid.
48 Laynesmith, *Last Medieval Queens*, p. 129.
49 PROB 11/9/207, f. 74r.
50 Ibid.
51 Ibid.
52 PROB 11/10/447; PROB 11/16/419.
53 See Laynesmith, *Cecily*, pp. 136–40 for Cecily's religious patronage; Jones and Underwood, *King's Mother*, pp. 193–8 for Margaret's.
54 PROB 11/16/419.
55 PROB 11/10/447, f. 195r.
56 Laynesmith, *Cecily*, p. 169.
57 PROB 11/10/447, f. 195r.
58 Laynesmith, *Cecily*, p. 141.
59 James, *Women's Voices*, p. 94.
60 PROB 11/10/447.
61 Tuetey (ed.), *Charlotte de Savoie*, pp. 39–40.
62 Laynesmith, *Cecily*, p. 141.

63 James, *Women's Voices*, p. 77.
64 PROB 11/10/447, f. 196r.
65 Ibid.
66 Ibid.
67 James, *Women's Voices*, p. 80.
68 PROB 11/39/368, f. 361v-363r. In *Women's Voices* James stated that even during Mary's reign, such bequests were a rarity, and when they did appear it was often because they were family heirlooms, p. 80.
69 PROB 11/10/447, f. 196r.
70 PROB 11/16/419.
71 E 101/417/1.
72 PROB 11/16/419, f. 238r.
73 Jones and Underwood, *King's Mother*, pp. 240–1.
74 St John's College Quatercentenary publication, *Collegium Divi Johannis Evangelistae, 1511–1911* (Cambridge, 1911), p. 121.
75 Ibid.
76 Ibid.
77 Ibid.
78 Ibid, pp. 121–3.
79 Mattingly, *Catherine of Aragon*, p. 242, 280.
80 *L & P*, x, no. 141.
81 BL, Cotton MS Otho C X, f. 216r-v.
82 Ibid, f. 219v.
83 *L & P*, v, no. 1377.
84 *CSPS*, iv, part 2, no. 1047.
85 BL, Cotton MS Otho C X, f. 216r-v.
86 Ibid, f. 216v.
87 Ibid.
88 Ibid, f. 216r.
89 Ibid.
90 Phillips, *Jewelry*, p. 71.
91 Cremades (ed.), *Inventarios*, iii, p. 2371.
92 D. Eichberger, 'A Courtly Phenomenon from a Female Perspective', in D. Eichberger (ed.), *Women of Distinction* (Leuven, 2008), p. 288.
93 *L & P*, x, no. 351.
94 Ibid.
95 BL, Cotton MS Otho C X, f. 216r.
96 Mattingly, *Catherine of Aragon*, p. 308.
97 *L & P*, x, no. 141.
98 Ibid.
99 *L & P*, x, no. 351.
100 PROB 11/39/368, f. 261v.
101 *L & P*, xv, no. 899.

102 PROB 11/39/368, f. 262v.
103 Ibid.
104 Ibid.
105 Ibid.
106 *L & P*, xv, no. 899.
107 *L & P*, xv, no. 925.
108 Warnicke, *Marrying of Anne of Cleves*, p. 252.
109 Tait (ed.), *7000 Years*, p. 140.
110 James, *Women's Voices*, p. 78.
111 PROB 11/39/368, f. 262r.
112 Ibid.
113 Ibid.
114 Ibid.
115 See S.A. Kujawa-Holbrook, 'Katherine Parr and Reformed Religion', *Anglican and Episcopal History*, 72 (2003), p. 66.
116 S. Wabuda, 'Bertie [*née* Willoughby; *other married name* Brandon], Katherine, Duchess of Suffolk', *ODNB*.
117 PROB 11/39/368, f. 262r.
118 *L & P*, xv, no. 21.
119 PROB 11/32/283.
120 See SP 10/5/2, f. 3r, a letter dated 1 September from Kateryn's brother-in-law, the Duke of Somerset, in which he congratulates Kateryn and her husband on the birth of their daughter and remarks on Kateryn 'escapyng all daunger'.
121 James, *Catherine Parr*, p. 284.
122 PROB 11/32/283, f. 19r.
123 Ibid.
124 James, *Catherine Parr*, p. 273; SP 10/6/24.
125 See SP 10/6/72; SP 10/6/24; S. Haynes (ed.), *A Collection of State Papers Relating to the Affairs in the Reigns of King Henry VIII, King Edward VI, Queen Mary and Queen Elizabeth From the Year 1542 to 1570* (London, 1740), pp. 71, 84.
126 Becker, *Death*, p. 152.
127 James, *Women's Voices*, p. 1.

References

Manuscript Sources

Kew, The National Archives

EXCHEQUER

E 23 Treasury of Receipt, Royal Wills.
E 101 King's Remembrancer, Various Accounts.

PREROGATIVE COURT OF CANTERBURY

PROB 11 Registered Copy Wills.

SPECIAL COLLECTIONS

SC 8/26/1295 Ancient Petitions

STATE PAPERS

SP State Papers

LONDON, BRITISH LIBRARY

Cotton Manuscripts	MS Otho C X.
Royal Manuscripts	7 C XVI.

Portraits

Unknown Artist, 'The Family of Henry VIII', c. 1545, RCT, RCIN 405796.

Printed Primary Sources

Astle, T., (ed.), *The Will of Henry VII* (London, 1775).

Bergenroth, G.A., et al., (ed.), *Calendar of State Papers, Spain*, 13 vols (London, 1862–1954).

Brewer, J.S., Gairdner, J., and Brodie, R.H., (eds), *Letters and Papers, Foreign and Domestic, of the Reign of Henry VIII, 1509–47*, 21 vols. and addenda (London, 1862–1932).

Brodie, R.H., Black, J.G., and Maxwell Lyte, H.C., (eds), *Calendar of the Patent Rolls Preserved in the Public Record Office, 1476–1509*, 3 vols. (London, 1901–16).

Cremades, F.C., (ed.), *Los inventarios de Carlos V y la familia imperial*, 3 vols (Madrid, 2010).

Haynes, S., (ed.), *A Collection of State Papers Relating to the Affairs in the Reigns of King Henry VIII, King Edward VI, Queen Mary and Queen Elizabeth from the Year 1542 to 1570* (London, 1740).

Knighton, C.S., (ed.), *Calendar of State Papers Domestic Series of the Reign of Edward VI 1547–1553* (London, 1992).

Mancini, D., *Usurpation of Richard III*, ed. and trans. Armstrong, C.A.J. (Stroud, 1984).

Nichols, J.G., (ed.), *A Collection of All the Wills, Now Known to Be Extant, of the Kings and Queens of England* (London, 1780).

Nichols, J.G., and Bruce, J., (eds), *Wills from Doctors' Commons: A Selection from the Wills of Eminent Persons Proved in the Prerogative Court of Canterbury, 1495–1695* (London, 1863).

St John's College Quatercentenary Publication, *Collegium Divi Johannis Evangelistae, 1511–1911* (Cambridge, 1911).

Tuetey, P.A., (ed.), *Inventaire des biens de Charlotte de Savoie, reine de France, (1483)* (Paris, 1865).

Secondary Sources

Bagley, J.J., *Margaret of Anjou* (London, 1948).

Baldwin, D., *Elizabeth Woodville: Mother of the Princes in the Tower* (Stroud, 2002).

Becker, L.M., *Death and the Early Modern Englishwoman* (Aldershot, 2003).

Bernard, G.W., 'Seymour, Thomas, Baron Seymour of Sudeley', *ODNB*, https://doi.org/10.1093/ref:odnb/25181

Eales, J., *Women in Early Modern England, 1500–1700* (London, 1998).

Earenfight, T., *Queenship in Medieval Europe* (Basingstoke, 2013).

Eichberger, D., 'A Courtly Phenomenon from a Female Perspective', in Eichberger, D. (ed.), *Women of Distinction* (Leuven, 2008), pp. 286–95.

Harris, B.J., *English Aristocratic Women 1450–1550: Marriage and Family, Property and Careers* (Oxford, 2002).

Hayward, M., 'The Possessions of Henry VIII: A Study of Inventories', unpublished PhD thesis, London School of Economics and Political Science, University of London, 1998.

Hicks, M., 'Elizabeth', *ODNB*, https://doi.org/10.1093/ref:odnb/8634

Hollis, J., (ed.), *Princely Magnificence: Court Jewels of the Renaissance, 1500–1630* (London, 1980).

Horrox, R., 'Financial Memoranda of the Reign of Edward V', *Camden Miscellany XXIX*, 34 (Camden Fourth Series, 1987), pp. 200–44.

James, S., *Catherine Parr: Henry VIII's Last Love* (Stroud, 2008).

James, S., *Women's Voices in Tudor Wills, 1485–1603: Authority, Influence and Material Culture* (Farnham, 2015).

Jones, M., 'Catherine [Catherine of Valois]', *ODNB*, https://doi.org/10.1093/ref:odnb/4890

Jones, M., and Underwood, M.G., *The King's Mother: Lady Margaret Beaufort Countess of Richmond and Derby* (Cambridge, 1992).

Kujawa-Holbrook, S.A., 'Katherine Parr and Reformed Religion', *Anglican and Episcopal History*, 72 (2003), pp. 55–78.
Laynesmith, J.L., *Cecily Duchess of York* (London, 2017).
Laynesmith, J.L., *The Last Medieval Queens* (Oxford, 2004).
Mattingly, G., *Catherine of Aragon* (London, 1942).
Maurer, H.E., *Margaret of Anjou: Queenship and Power in Late Medieval England* (Woodbridge, 2003).
Myers, A.R., 'The Household of Queen Elizabeth Woodville, 1466–7', *BJRL*, 50 (1967–8), pp. 207–15.
Myers, A.R., 'The Household of Queen Margaret of Anjou, 1452–3', *BJRL*, 50 (1957–8), pp. 79–113.
Myers, A.R., 'The Jewels of Queen Margaret of Anjou', *BJRL*, 42 (1959), pp. 113–31.
Phillips, C., *Jewelry: From Antiquity to the Present* (London, 1996).
Ross, C., *Edward IV* (London, 1974).
Tait, H., (ed.), *7000 Years of Jewellery* (London, 1986).
Wabuda, S., 'Bertie [*née* Willoughby; *other married name* Brandon], Katherine, duchess of Suffolk', *ODNB*, https://doi.org/10.1093/ref:odnb/2273
Warnicke, R.M., *The Marrying of Anne of Cleves: Royal Protocol in Tudor England* (Cambridge, 2004).
Warnicke, R.M., *Wicked Women of Tudor England: Queens, Aristocrats, Commoners* (New York, 2012).

3 The Jewel Inventories of Jane Seymour, Katherine Howard and Kateryn Parr

An inventory could be drawn up at various times in an individual's life and provided an efficient way of recording their own possessions or those of others.[1] Following the execution of Anne Boleyn for example, the King ordered Sir William Kingston to draw up 'a composition for such jewels and apparel as the late Queen had in the Tower'.[2] Unfortunately, this list is no longer extant; however, four inventories relating to the jewels of Henry VIII's third, fifth and sixth wives survive: for Jane Seymour, an inventory of her personal jewellery, composed in 1537; for Katherine Howard, an inventory of her queenly jewels – those that were Crown property – drawn up in 1541; and two inventories concerning Kateryn Parr.[3] The first contains her queenly jewels, while the second was made up of her personal effects. The first dates from 1547/8, and the second was recorded in 1549. All of the inventories are variable in length and detail, and they were all organised according to the genre of jewel.

This chapter will contextualise the jewel inventories of Jane Seymour (Table 3.1), Katherine Howard (Table 3.2) and Kateryn Parr (Tables 3.3 and 3.4) before analysing their contents. It will track individual pieces, where the evidence permits, thereby confirming that a number of items were owned by both Katherine Howard and Kateryn Parr. It then provides a brief analysis of some of the materials that were used to create these pieces, before unpicking the designs and descriptions of the contents of the inventories. This chapter therefore demonstrates the amount of material wealth that Henry VIII's queens had available to

DOI: 10.4324/9781003202592-4

them, its quality and varied designs. Collectively this reinforces the level of splendour that surrounded them.

The Context of the Inventories of Henry VIII's Queens

The Tudor inventories began in 1521, but prior to this several medieval royal inventories survive, most notably that of Richard II.[4] Containing 1,206 entries, the inventory lists the jewels and plate belonging to the King and his two queens. The Bedford inventories, a record of the belongings of John, Duke of Bedford, also survive, supplying further points of comparison.[5] Aside from these English examples, several foreign inventories are extant. These include the jewel inventory of Clemence of Hungary, composed in 1328, the Hapsburg inventories, and the inventory of Jeanne de Boulogne to name just a few.[6]

In contrast to wills, inventories only account for moveable goods and do not consider other possessions, such as land. Neither do they provide emotional context in the way that wills demonstrate the human value associated with objects.[7] They are nonetheless useful sources because they provide a more complete picture of an individual's belongings, albeit at a single point in time and in consideration only of those goods that were available to the appraiser. The inventory of Lettice Knollys, Countess of Leicester, made following her death in 1634, was an attempt to supply a complete account of all of her assets to establish their value, while the jewel inventory of Katherine Howard was intended to provide a record of the former queen's possessions before some of them were returned to her husband.[8] The 1447 Holland Inventory, meanwhile, was composed in order to ascertain which pieces of John Holland's plate and jewels had been sold off to pay debts.[9]

Shortly after Jane Seymour's premature death on 24 October 1537, an inventory of her jewels was drawn up.[10] As Chapter 4 will demonstrate, pieces that Jane is known to have owned were later used by both Katherine Howard and Kateryn Parr, yet they are not listed in the inventory. The magnificent ouche, for example, that Jane can be seen wearing in Hans Holbein's masterpiece, is not among the items detailed in the inventory.[11] After her death, many of Jane's jewels were given as gifts to members of her household in reward for their service. This is almost certainly because they were pieces of lesser monetary value, indicating that the inventory is primarily representative of Jane's personal collection rather than her queenly one.

On 7 November 1541, Katherine Howard's queenly jewels were seized from her in a very public display of her disgrace, a tangible sign that she was no longer entitled to wear the trappings of a queen. Katherine's biographer Joanna Denny confirmed that 'There could be no greater indication that her term was over'.[12] This was reinforced when, while under house arrest at Syon, Sir Ralph Sadler issued orders that all of her apparel should be 'without stone or pearl'.[13] A thorough account of the jewels was made, to provide a record of the material wealth that had been bestowed on Katherine. The bulk were then entrusted to the safekeeping of Anne Parr, the younger sister of Katherine's successor.[14] Six of these pieces were then 'Taken by the kyng wholy into his owne handes', for his own personal use.[15]

The circumstances surrounding the creation of Kateryn Parr's queenly jewel inventory contrasted with those of both of her predecessors, for it was a small part of a far larger project that served a different purpose.[16] In September 1547, eight months after the death of Henry VIII, commissioners were appointed on the orders of his successor, Edward VI, to compile an inventory of all of the late King's goods, a task that took 18 months.[17] Its purpose was to create a record of all of Henry VIII's possessions, or more accurately, those of the Crown. Containing everything from clothes to jewels, books and items purchased for the royal pets, the inventory provides a detailed and intimate insight into the life of the sixteenth-century royal family.[18] Not only does it offer glimpses of the King's lifestyle but also those of his queens, particularly Kateryn Parr. Over 17,000 objects are listed, and while some entries contain multiple items, many are individual.[19] This gives a staggering indication of the material wealth accumulated by Henry and of the splendour that surrounded him and his wives. Prominent among the list of possessions are the jewels and precious metals owned by the King, of which there are more than 3,500 items. Foremost among these are the Crown Jewels, used by Henry and his predecessors on ceremonial occasions – most notably coronations.[20] These will be examined fully in Chapter 7, but they account for a mere 18 of the total objects listed among the jewels, providing tangible evidence of the King's penchant for jewels and rich objects.

Among the inventory, which is divided into multiple sections, is a list headed 'The Quenes Jewelles' (Table 3.3).[21] These were contained in a sealed coffer that, like the Crown Jewels, had been kept in the Jewel House at the Tower of London for safekeeping. This alone reinforces the high monetary value that was placed on them. 'The Quenes Jewelles' refers to the jewels that were Crown property but were reserved for the use of the queen consort. At the time of Henry's death, this right was bestowed on Kateryn Parr, who was entitled to utilise them in order to fulfil her role as Henry's consort – they were a tool that enabled her to enhance her royal image.

The queenly jewels inventoried for Katherine Howard and Kateryn Parr were not considered to be their personal property but that of the Crown. It is also evident that the additional jewels bestowed upon the two queens by Henry after their marriages were considered to be a part of the queen's collection, rather than the personal property of the individual queen. Following Katherine Howard's fall, this was confirmed when all of her jewels were taken from her, and the French ambassador heard that they had been inventoried in a visible demonstration of her disgrace.[22] Similarly, the jewels that Kateryn Parr later ordered were to become a part of the queen's collection, rather than her own property, and pieces can be identified in the collections of her successors.[23]

Yet there is good reason to suspect that Kateryn did not believe this to be the case. By the terms of Henry VIII's will, she had been gifted 'plate Iewelz and Stuff of household' to the value of £3,000.[24] It seems reasonable to assume that the pieces that the King was giving to his wife were indeed the 'The Quenes Jewelles' and that Kateryn expected to be able to retain their use after she was widowed. Arguably they were not

Henry's to bestow, and this was the belief of the new regime who refused to return them to Kateryn.[25] This caused her great anguish, likely to have been exacerbated because some of the jewels that she had owned prior to her royal marriage were among the queen's jewels. This may reveal nothing more than the sentimental value that Kateryn placed on these pieces by allowing them to be stored with her more monetarily valuable royal jewels. This appears to be somewhat confirmed in a letter from her fourth husband, Sir Thomas Seymour, in which he referred to 'your mothers geffte'; a diamond cross and a cache of loose pearls which Kateryn was desperate to have returned to her.[26]

Another collection of Kateryn's belongings was later added to the inventory. Taken in 1549, a year after her death in September 1548, it was described as a 'Parcell of the Quenes Juelles and other stuff, which come from the late Admyralles howse of Sudeley, in the countie of Gloucestre'.[27] Presumably many of these items would have been in Kateryn's possession during her term as queen, yet they were completely different from those that formed her queenly inventory and were primarily dissimilar from those used by her predecessor (Table 3.4).[28] This confirms that queens had access to different sets of jewels, pieces that they adorned in order to fulfil their ceremonial role, and jewels and items that were intended for everyday use, but the line between these collections was not always clear.

Content of the Inventories

Table 3.1 Jewels listed in Jane Seymour's Inventory: BL, Royal MS 7 C XVI, f. 18r-31r

Jewel	*Quantity*	*Pearls*	*Diamonds*	*Rubies*	*Emeralds*	*Other*
Beads	54	15 +	1 +	2 +	0	2 +Agates 3 +Turquoise
Books	8	6	4	20	0	
Pomanders	5	0	0	0	0	1 Garnettes 1 +Agate
Tablets	12	0	0	0	10	1 Agate
Coffers	2	4	1	0	0	

Jewel	*Quantity*	*Pearls*	*Diamonds*	*Rubies*	*Emeralds*	*Other*
Glass	1	0	0	0	0	
Girdles	24	0	0	0	0	
Borders	66	0	0	0	0	
Brooches	27	1 +	1 +	1 +	0	1 + Turquoise
Pairs of Bracelets	4	0	0	0	0	
Needles & Thimbles	3	0	0	0	0	
Buttons	170	0	0	0	0	
Aglettes	121 pairs +	0	0	0	0	
Chains	11	60	0	0	0	
TOTAL:	508	86 +	7 +	23 +	10	9 +

Source: Total number of stones: 135+

Table 3.2 Jewels listed in Katherine Howard's Inventory: BL, Stowe MS 559, f. 55r-68r

Jewel	*Quantity*	*Pearls*	*Diamonds*	*Rubies*	*Emeralds*	*Other*
Habille-ments	9	439	81	181	0	6 Machistes
Squares	6	469	60	89	0	
Carcanets	6	110	32	23	3	
Brooches	7	0	62	47	6	
Ouches	11	13	8	9	7	
Crosses	4	8	27	0	0	
Haches	2	4	6	0	2	
Jesuses	3	6	90	1	3	
Flowers	5	10	60	1	1	
Collar/ Partelet	1	65	16	20	0	
Rings	16	0	11	4	1	
Ship	1	1	29	1	0	
Girdles	17	476+	109+	252+	0	93 Tur-quoises
Beads	25	180+	+	+	0	+ Turquoises & Lapis Lazarus
Chains	8	223	122	157	0	
Tablets	7	36	69+	46+	10	

(*Continued*)

Table 3.2 (Continued)

Jewel	*Quantity*	*Pearls*	*Diamonds*	*Rubies*	*Emeralds*	*Other*
Pomanders	1	32	0	23	0	16 Turquoises
Books	5	43	15	86	0	4 Turquoises & 1 Sapphire
Purses	2	0	15	0	0	
Mufflers	1	207	0	38	0	
Laces	15	1,028	36	31	0	
Goldsmith's Work	23	87	25	10	0	
TOTAL:	175	3,437+	873+	1,019	32	120+

Source: Total number of stones: 5,481+

Table 3.3 'The Quenes Jewelles': SoA, MS 129, f. 178r-183v

Jewel	*Quantity*	*Pearls*	*Diamonds*	*Rubies*	*Emeralds*
Ouches	13	15	11+	10	9
Crosses	6	14	42	4	1
Jesuses	3	6	90	1	3
Ship	1	1	2+	1	0
Initials	2	4	7	0	1
Brooches	7	0	36+	4+	1
Tablets	11	2	104+	70+	1 Also 1 Sapphire
Books	1	0	12	2+	0
Clasps	4	0	5+	1	1
Chains	10	580	200	232	0
Carcanets	7	85	28	58+	4+
Buttons	4	0	13	36	0
Necklaces	4	327	33	29	0
Habillements	24	1349	157	114	0
Girdles	11	893+	160	122	0
Pairs of Bracelets	4	0	26	58	6
Beads	8	1	0	0	0
Rings	10	0	7	3	0
Aglettes	28	0	14	14	0
Partlet	1	2116	25	47	6

Jewel	*Quantity*	*Pearls*	*Diamonds*	*Rubies*	*Emeralds*
Loose Stones	5	95	11	7	0
TOTAL:	164	5,488+	983+	813+	33+ 1 Sapphire

Source: Total number of stones: 7,318+

Table 3.4 Jewels and items found in the inventory of Kateryn Parr's personal effects: SoA, MS 129, f. 216v-220v

Jewel	*Number*	*Pearls*	*Diamonds*	*Rubies*	*Emeralds*	*Other*
Rings	56	0	10	8	3	1 Turquoise 1 Sapphire 1 Amethyst
Buttons	34	17	0	0	0	0
Clasps	2	4	0	0	1	1 Sapphire
Brooches	1	0	1	2	0	0
Purses	4	0	0	0	0	0
Aglettes	53 pairs 1 single	0	0	0	0	0
Books	23	0	2	29	0	0
Mufflers	1	2+	0	20	0	0
Habille-ments	4	0	0	0	0	0
Tablets	1	0	2	0	0	0
Chains	1	0	0	0	0	0
Girdles	7	1+	2+	0	0	1+ red stones
Pairs of beads	5	50+	2+	0	0	1+ white stones
Brooches, aglettes & buttons attached to velvet caps	223	4+	1	0	0	0
Other	89	81+	4	7	0	2 Turquoises 4+ Other 6 fake stones
Total:	**505**	**159+**	**24+**	**66**	**4**	**18+**

Source: Total number of stones: 271+

Tracking the Contents of the Inventories

The tables reveal that with a total of 508 pieces, Jane Seymour's collection was significantly larger than that of either of her successors. As mentioned previously, it is likely to be a personal inventory consisting of jewels of lesser value. The make-up of the jewels themselves supports this, as it contained far fewer precious stones than those found in the queenly inventories of her two successors. However, there are several pieces in Jane's inventory that potentially match those found in Katherine Howard and Kateryn Parr's, showing that it may have included items that were deemed worthy of the queenly collection. Containing a total of 175 pieces, Katherine Howard's inventory consisted of more items than that of the queenly inventory of her successor, Kateryn Parr, which listed 164 pieces.[29] A comparison of the two queenly inventories shows that 24 items match, which given the proximity of Katherine Howard and Kateryn Parr's reigns is unsurprising (see Appendix). These include, for example, an ouche 'wherin is averey ffeir diamond holden by two antiquez personz with averey ffeir peerle hangyng at the same' (see Appendix for the remainder).[30] While there are a further 27 potential matches, the lack of detail in the descriptions prevents confirmation. Rings, for example, that were listed among Katherine Howard's possessions as 'Item xvj Rynges of golde in xj whereof be set xj diamondes in iiij, be set iiij Rubyes/and in one of them is an Emeralde' are likely to match some of those described in Kateryn Parr's queenly inventory in the following three listings: 'Item vij Ringes of golde in euery of them a Dyamounte'; 'Item an other Ring of golde set with a rubie'; 'Item twoo other ringes of golde with rubies in them'.[31]

The matching items found among Katherine Howard and Kateryn Parr's queenly jewels confirm that both queens had access to the belongings of their predecessors, and thus that jewels were frequently recycled. It is likely that their predecessors had also used many of these pieces in order to fulfil their roles as Henry VIII's consorts, although the nature of Jane Seymour's inventory does not permit confirmation of this.

None of the pieces listed in Kateryn Parr's later inventory match those in her queenly one, although it is possible that 'a Mowfler of black vellat garneshed with twentie Rubes course and fullie furneshed with peerle with a small cheyne hanging at it of golde and peerle' may have once belonged to Katherine Howard.[32] In Katherine Howard's inventory the potential match is described as 'a mufler of black veluet furred with Sabilles conteignyng xxxviij rubyes/and vclxxij peerlles/betwixt euery rowe certeyn small cheynes of golde/with also a cheyne to hang the same mufler by conteignyng xxx peerlles'.[33] Generally, however, the items found in Kateryn Parr's final inventory were of a far more functional nature than the decorative jewels in her queenly collection and reveal the sort of objects she used in her everyday life. For example, the 'two dogges collers of crimsen vellat embraudred with damaske golde tirrettes gilt silver', and 'paire of sheeres in a case of crimsen vellat garneshed withe silver and gilt', served a practical purpose.[34] In many ways, Kateryn's inventory accurately reflects Earenfight's assertion that these documents can be seen as 'mirrors of a woman's personality'.[35]

When seeking to track the transition of jewels from queen to queen, Katherine Howard's inventory provides valuable details. Marginal notes next to the 'Jesus of golde conteignyng xxxij diamondes hauyng thre peerlles hanging at the same', for example, show that this piece was 'Gyven by the kyng at Hamptoncourte at Cristmasse anno xxxijdo'.[36] This thereby establishes that it was one of the more recent pieces that may have been purchased especially for Katherine. It also appears in Kateryn Parr's collection.[37] Not all of Katherine Howard's jewels were newly commissioned though, and another piece in her collection is likely to have originated with the King's first wife, Catherine of Aragon. This was the 'Gurdell of golde whereof parte ar pomegarnettes parte pillors squared and parte ragged staves fully furnesshed with small rubyes and small diamondes hauyng a Tassell of peerlles'.[38] As the pomegranate was the symbol of the former Spanish princess and a design she favoured in her jewels, it is highly plausible that this object originated with her.[39] It does not appear in Jane Seymour's personal inventory – although it may have been among her queenly collection – but neither does it feature in Kateryn Parr's queenly possessions.[40] This suggests that it either became absorbed into the King's collection following Katherine Howard's fall or was refashioned by Kateryn Parr.

In some instances, the inventories also record when pieces left the collection altogether. Following Jane Seymour's death, her stepdaughter Mary received several items of her jewellery, and it is also possible that Mary appropriated some of Katherine Howard's jewels. In the aftermath of Katherine's fall, Mary received several large parcels of jewels as gifts from her father, and while many of them do not tally with those found in Mary's inventory, there are several potential matches.[41] For example, there is a strong possibility that the New Year's gift of 'a Broche of thistory of Noyes [Noah's] floode set with litle Diamondes and Rubies' that Mary received in 1543, could be the 'one broche of golde conteignyng xxxv small diamondes and xviij rubyes with thre persones and two horses in the same being the story of Noye [Noah]' that had formerly been owned by Katherine.[42] Its description underscores the importance of detail in terms of identifying pieces in inventories.

The fates of several of Kateryn Parr's pieces are recorded in her final inventory. Of nine diamond rings, one that was 'sett with a longe diamount cutt full of squares was gyven by the king to the ladie Elizabeth doughter of Fraunce', while another set with 'a fayer table diamount was given by the king to the skotysh Quene'.[43] Both of these provide further examples of the recycling of jewels, as well as their use as diplomatic gifts that incurred no additional costs to the monarch. A further entry of two rings set with emeralds was returned to its owner: 'One Emerade was deliuered 20 November 1549 by commaundement of the counsaill to sir William Herbert as his owne being sent to the quene for a tokin and nott otherwise gyven to her grace'. Evidently jewels could be returned to the giver – Kateryn's brother-in-law in this instance – in the case of a recipient's death.[44] In the same manner, a ruby was returned to Kateryn's brother, the Marquess of Northampton. These are, though, the only mentions of the fates of specific jewels in the inventory. The rest were 'deliuered into the kinges Secret Juellehowse in t[he] Towre', where they were added to Edward VI's jewels.[45, 46]

Materials in the Inventories

Table 3.5 Quantity of stones found in the four queenly inventories: BL, Royal MS 7 C XVI, f. 18r-31r, BL, Stowe MS 559, f. 55r-68r, SoA, MS 129, f. 178r-183v, SoA, MS 129, f. 216v-220v

Type of Stone	*Jane Seymour*	*Katherine Howard*	*Kateryn Parr f. 178r-183v*	*Kateryn Parr f. 216v-220v*
Pearls	28 +	3,437+	5,488+	161+
Diamonds	7 +	873+	983+	22+
Rubies	21 +	1,019	813+	66
Emeralds	10	32	33+	4
Sapphires	0	1	2	2
Other	7 + Agates 4 + Turquoises	6 Machistes, 113+ Turquoises, 1+ Lapis Lazarus	0	6 fake stones, 1+ red stone, 1+ white stone, 3 Turquoises, 1 Amethyst

In terms of the queenly collections, Katherine Howard owned more individual pieces of jewellery, but Kateryn Parr surpassed her predecessor in terms of the quantity of stones with which they were adorned. Jane Seymour's inventory shows a distinct lack of stones, even in comparison with Kateryn Parr's later inventory. It is possible that more of her pieces did contain stones and that they were not detailed when her inventory was compiled. A note added to the listing of a pair of bracelets supports this, which referred to 'the settyng of the stonys'.[47] Instead, many of the items were made up of beads manufactured from a variety of materials that included coral and turquoises, and goldsmith's work – many had also been enamelled – which may have been considered to be sufficient in terms of decoration.[48] Featuring approximately 267 stones, Kateryn Parr's personal inventory reveals the startling contrast in the quantity and quality of stones that she had access to in the aftermath of Henry VIII's death, as opposed to the 7,319 stones that were attached to her queenly jewels.

The stones listed in the inventories varied in size. On several occasions 'one small rubie' or 'foure very small dyamountes' were noted, while when a stone was either large or a particularly fine example – which only appears in Katherine Howard and Kateryn Parr's inventories – it was often referred to as being 'faire'.[49] This is a possible indication of the varying quality of the stones in use; some of the smaller ones may have been cheaper to acquire, hence why there were more of them.

Rubies were the most popular form of gemstone used in the decoration of Jane Seymour's jewels, a trend that was echoed by Katherine Howard's collection. Among Kateryn Parr's queenly pieces diamonds superseded rubies, and while the quantities of rubies may reflect a personal preference on both Jane Seymour and Katherine Howard's part, rubies were more readily available than diamonds, as noted in Chapter 1.[50] Kateryn Parr's penchant for diamonds, therefore, was a visual proclamation of wealth and status that she – who was acutely conscious of the importance of the royal image – would have been eager to express.

Gem engraving, intaglios and cameos had been extremely popular in Ancient Greece and Rome, and fifteenth-century Italy witnessed a revival of cameos engraved into gemstones, particularly admired by Lorenzo 'the Magnificent' de Medici.[51] This trend spread into England during the Renaissance, where jewels featuring cameos were well favoured – some ancient cameo gemstones were placed within sixteenth-century settings – but were both rare and valuable.[52] The designs of cameos were influenced by the antique style that grew in popularity during the Tudor period.[53] Given their rarity, it is unsurprising that only one example appears in Katherine Howard's inventory, a piece that she gave to the Countess of Surrey as a gift.[54] Neither Jane Seymour nor Kateryn Parr's queenly inventories feature any pieces described as cameos, although evidence, which will be discussed in Chapter 5, shows that Kateryn did commission them. Given their value and rarity, it is therefore curious that there was a piece featuring cameos among her personal possessions: 'a paire of Beades of Camewes garneshed with gold with a Tassell of veanice golde'.[55] Although cameos themselves were rare, the classical themes that they often presented were a popular form of decoration for other pieces of jewellery. Numerous examples, frequently referred to as 'antique', appear in both queenly inventories, as well as in Jane Seymour's.[56] These include an 'ooche of golde wherin is averey ffeir diamond holden by two antiquez personz with averey ffeir peerle hangyng at the same' owned by Katherine Howard, that later passed to Kateryn Parr.[57] Such pieces often featured mythological stories in their design, reflecting contemporary interests and providing an alternative to biblical subjects.[58] Their appearance in all three inventories shows that this was an interest that was shared by queens.

It is interesting to consider that four of Jane Seymour's pieces are described as being broken in some way. For example, a collection of broken aglettes, a pair of beads 'sett with Rubies and turquisses Lacking a Rubie and a turquis', and 'iij litle borders of golde broken by the Quenes comandement'.[59] For the most part, this is likely to be reflective of the wear and tear that was inflicted upon everyday pieces, although in a further example of recycling, the inventory records that the three borders were 'putt into Dressing of cappis Ageynst newers daie'.[60] Presumably Jane gave these recycled items as gifts. Broken pieces were also to be found among Kateryn Parr's personal effects, including the 'litell pece of a broken ringe of golde' and 'three frenche Crownes wherof one broken'.[61] The eight broken items listed could indicate that Kateryn had less access to both funds and resources with which to pay for repairs during her term as Queen Dowager, but given that in the aftermath of her royal marriage her 'house was termed "a second court" of right' – in other words, it was functioning on an almost royal scale – this seems unlikely.[62] The Lady Mary's jewel inventory confirms that it was not unusual for items to become broken; it mentions two pieces that she had ordered to be 'put to broken golde'.[63]

Description and Design

The inventories all feature different genres of jewellery, a possible reflection of both fashion and personal taste. Joan Evans emphasised that Renaissance jewels became more personal and individual, something that all of the inventories convey.[64] For example, Katherine Howard owned six squares, while none are listed in Jane Seymour and Kateryn Parr's inventories.[65] Jane Seymour could have chosen not to wear such pieces on an everyday basis, though they may have appeared in her queenly collection, but in Kateryn Parr's case this could be reflective of the changing styles of dress that were becoming fashionable. This can be seen in the high-necked dresses worn by Kateryn in several of her portraits, rendering the need for squares almost redundant.[66] It is therefore possible that some of the loose stones noted in Kateryn's inventory were the product of squares and other surplus jewels that had been broken down.[67]

Habillements or billiments were items that could be worn every day to adorn clothing, as were aglettes; however, the fact that habillements appear only in the queenly inventories of Katherine Howard and Kateryn Parr indicates that they were primarily worn on more formal occasions.[68] Clearly, however, Jane Seymour also owned decorative habillements, for her portrait by Holbein shows her wearing one.[69] She was, though, known to favour the English gable hood, rather than the fashionable French hood worn by Katherine Howard and Kateryn Parr, and such decorations may have seemed unnecessary in her everyday life.[70] Jane did make use of aglettes, and large quantities can be found in her inventory as well as in both of Kateryn Parr's.[71] The lack of aglettes in Katherine Howard's collection suggests that either there were none, which seems unlikely, given their practicality, or that they were deemed to be too small to consider including in her inventory.[72]

This could also have been the case with buttons, which do not appear among Katherine Howard's possessions despite being one of the most common items of sixteenth-century jewellery.[73] This is attested to in Jane Seymour's inventory and both of Kateryn Parr's, whose personal collection contained a particularly fine set: 'vj Buttons of golde made like katherin wheles'.[74] These were almost certainly made to Kateryn's specifications, for later examples show that she was particularly fond of jewels that harboured a personal meaning. Jane Seymour's buttons contained nothing so personal, but they did include 'xij buttons lyke faces enameled' – possibly cameos – showing an alternative style of decoration that was in keeping with contemporary fashions.[75] Later in the century, Catherine de Medici was known to have had a set of buttons depicting faithful friendship.[76]

Girdles were jewels that combined fashion with practicality and could be used to attach smaller items, and appear in all four inventories. They had long been popular, and in the previous century Charlotte of Savoy had owned one that was elaborately decorated with diamonds.[77] This was not uncommon, and their style meant that they frequently used a large quantity of precious stones. In one of Katherine Howard's girdles alone, 24 diamonds and 24 pearls were used.[78] It was unnecessary to use precious stones in everyday wear in such a way, and this is reflected in the make-up of Jane Seymour's girdles. Although many of them contained goldsmith's work, none of them mentioned precious stones in their descriptions. Instead, examples such as 'a gurdell of golde enameled with blacke', and 'a gurdell of golde enameled with blacke and blewe' appear.[79]

In many respects, the two queenly inventories of Katherine Howard and Kateryn Parr are evenly matched. Highly prized were the ouches, an elaborate type of jewel that could be used as a brooch or as a pendant. Specific ouches in the collection will be analysed in greater depth in relation to portraiture in Chapter 4. Unsurprisingly, no ouches are listed in either Jane Seymour or Kateryn Parr's personal inventories, confirming that they were extremely valuable objects that were not intended for everyday use. Ten out of the eleven owned by Katherine Howard were almost certainly the same as those owned by Kateryn Parr (five pieces match exactly), who added a further two to the collection. One of these was the crown ouche, which will feature more fully in Chapter 5, but is so distinctive that it is easily identifiable.[80] The other is described as 'an Ouche of golde conteyning a very faire table dyamount a faire rounde Emerode and a perle pendaunt'.[81] Katherine Howard also owned three 'flowers', which were a similar type of jewel that often hung from a collar, chain, or could be attached to a bodice.[82]

All of the ouches contained pearls, while nine had at least one diamond, eight used a minimum of one ruby, and six featured at least one emerald. In both inventories, almost all of the ouches were described in only the vaguest of terms, providing little clue as to their overall appearance or design. For example, 'one ouche or flower with a Rubie and a Dyamounte and a perle pendaunt'.[83] This makes it difficult to definitively identify specific pieces worn by the queens in portraits. However, it is likely that the ouche that Jane Seymour and Katherine Howard wore for their respective portraits by Holbein is that described in Katherine's inventory as 'oone other ooche of golde hauyng averey ffeir table diamond and a verey feir ruby with a long peerle hangyng at the same'.[84]

Another jewel that features in both Katherine Howard and Kateryn Parr's queenly inventories is a ship, probably worn as either a pendant or a brooch. Described in Kateryn Parr's inventory as 'Item a Shipp garnysshed fullie with Dyamountes lacking ij small Dyamountes and set with one Rubie and a perle pendaunt', from the added detail in Katherine Howard's it is possible to glean that the same jewel was 'Item a Ship of golde saylyng conteignyng one feir rubye in two ffysshes mouthes/and xxix diamondes greate and small in the same Ship with affeir peerle hanging at the same'.[85] As symbols of happiness, ships were a popular theme for jewels in this period, and this piece is therefore reflective of contemporary fashions.[86]

Several genres of jewels in both queenly inventories have a religious theme, some of which were noted in Chapter 1. The most easily identifiable are the crosses, 'the most powerful Christian symbol'.[87] As the most apparent symbol of piety, throughout the fifteenth and sixteenth centuries crosses were adopted by both men and women across Europe and appeared in various forms. Both Charlotte of Savoy and Margaret of Austria owned such jewels, and among Margaret's collection were several elaborately decorated cross jewels, including one that contained six diamonds.[88] Similarly, all six of Henry VIII's wives owned crosses, and Kateryn Parr later inherited all four of those owned by Katherine Howard, with the addition of two more. One of the crosses owned by both queens was made of 'xij dyamountes onelye' and was probably particularly valuable for this reason – it may have been inherited by Anna of Denmark, together with another cross.[89] Kateryn also added 'a Crosse of fyve Dyamountes iiij rubies one Emerode and three perles pendaunte' and 'a Crosse of golde conteyng x fair dyamountes of sundry making and three faire perles pendaunte' to the collection.[90] This last cross could have been the one left to Kateryn in her mother's will.[91] Kateryn seems to have been particularly fond of necklaces in all forms, as in almost all genres in her queenly inventory she owned more neck jewellery than her predecessor. Her collection reveals that ornamental necklaces, known as carcanets, could be extremely elaborate. Six carcanets and numerous necklaces were listed, including 'a Carcanet set with a faire poynted dyamounte viij large Rubies and xx faire perles by cooples betwixt euery Rubie and one lardge perle pendaunt' which may have been made especially for the Queen.[92] By contrast, Jane Seymour's inventory contained no such elaborate pieces but did list 11 chains, which were probably worn as necklaces, a smaller number than those found in Kateryn's.[93]

The beads that feature in all four inventories were probably also religious: they were almost certainly paternoster beads made from materials which included agate.[94] These were popular among women in the fifteenth and sixteenth centuries, and such pieces appear in the inventories of both Margaret of Austria and Isabella of Austria.[95] Jane Seymour had the largest collection in an assortment of colours and designs, perhaps a reflection of her religiosity. Katherine Howard also appears to have been fond of them, and they may have served to emphasise that she came from a fervently Catholic family.[96]

Religiously themed pieces appear more frequently in Katherine Howard's inventory than in that of both her predecessor and her successor. This could be seen as evidence of Katherine's Catholic piety, but it seems more likely to have been influenced by her predecessors. The lack of Jane Seymour's queenly inventory for comparison prevents confirmation. However, the Lady Mary's inventory is heavily laden with religious pieces, a tangible sign of her devotion to Catholicism.[97] The firmly Protestant Kateryn Parr would have found at least one of the pieces that she inherited from Katherine Howard to her taste. This was the anti-Roman Catholic

> Tablet of Golde conteignyng on thonesyde a goodly diamonde lozenged with divers other small rubyes and diamondes two naked boyes and a litle boy with a crosse in his hand and divers other persones one with a sawe/and scripture under the said diamonde/and on thothersyde a ffeyer Ballas and the pycture of the busshopp of Rome comyng awey lamentyng/and divers other persones one settyng his sole upon the busshop ouerthowen.[98]

The very theme of the jewel allows us to date its creation to between 1533 and 1541, when it appears in Katherine Howard's inventory. Although a fictional scene, it is possible that it was made for either Henry VIII or Anne Boleyn in order to mark the King's break from Rome, and its fashioning demonstrates the impact that the Reformation had on jewellery design.

Tablets and brooches are listed in all four of the inventories.[99] Their queenly inventories show that Katherine Howard and Kateryn Parr owned seven and 11 tablets, respectively, while

Kateryn's later collection contained one and Jane Seymour's referred to 11.[100] As part of court dress, tablets were considered to be decorative items that played little role in everyday life but were popular objects that were not gendered in their use: numerous examples appear in the inventories of Henry VI and Henry VIII.[101] Pieces such as these that allowed more space for decoration often reflected the interests of the owner, and the design of one of Jane Seymour's tablets was more sentimental. This featured 'the Kinges pictu[re] in it' and was perhaps a gift.[102] It is possible, although by no means certain, that this was the same tablet that later appears in the queenly inventory of Kateryn Parr, described as

> a Tablet of golde hauing on thone side the kinges Picture peynted and on thesame side is a roose of Dyamountes and Rubies conteyning therein v dyamountes and sixe rubies on the border thereof is v verye small Dyamountes and one Rubie in the toppe thereof and an other vnderneth and in the border thereof is foure very small dyamountes on the other side is ij men lifting of a Stone being a Dyamounte conteyning in that side xxij Dyamountes ij rubies and a faire Emerode.[103]

The piece does not appear in Katherine Howard's possessions, so if this was the same jewel then the King had clearly chosen not to bestow it upon his fifth wife.[104] If Jane and Kateryn Parr both owned the tablet, it shows that it was possible for pieces to be moved between a queen's personal and queenly collection. It is equally feasible that the piece that appears in Kateryn Parr's inventory was a different jewel, commissioned either by herself or by her husband as a gift. In the same manner as objects such as small books and pomanders, both of which were also owned by Jane, tablets could hang from girdles.[105]

All of the tablets in the two queenly inventories were richly garnished with a variety of stones and were fashioned in assorted shapes and designs. Some of Katherine Howard's tablets may have been inherited and embellished by Kateryn Parr, and this seems plausible in the instance of at least one. Recorded in Katherine Howard's inventory as

> Item one Tablet of Golde on thonesyde thereof is set a litle Roose of diamondes being vj small diamondes/with h.k. of diamondes being xiij diamondes in them bothe and an E of diamondes being v diamondes/and on thothersyde one greate Table diamonde with ij lettres in the ffoyle/and iiij other diamondes in the same with certeyn persones,

this item may be the same as that in Kateryn Parr's described as a tablet with 'H and K a Roose and E all of dyamountes and Osystryche Fethers and fyve small Rubies and on thother side a faire Dyamounte holden by an Image with iiij other dyamountes'.[106] If this was the case, then the rubies and ostrich feathers were a later addition. The inclusion of three initials in the design of the tablet made it quite distinct, and it therefore seems possible that it was the same piece.[107]

Tablets were among some of the most creative pieces in the collections of Katherine Howard and Kateryn Parr. Unfortunately, many of those listed in Jane Seymour's inventory are simply described as 'a Tabelet of golde', which prevents further analysis.[108] One however, featured the passion of Christ, while another included 'toow Angelles', signs of Jane's piety.[109] Designs for tablets among Kateryn Parr's queenly possessions included 'a Clock fasshioned like an Harte', while another was described as 'a whistell of gold'.[110] Both Katherine Howard and Kateryn Parr owned pieces that featured clocks, representing the dual function of jewels and the ability to combine practicality with style and an element of novelty.[111] Kateryn Parr is known to have had a particular interest in clocks.[112]

Katherine Howard and Kateryn Parr's queenly possessions listed seven brooches apiece, while Kateryn Parr's final inventory shows that she had three others in her possession at the time of her death. Jane Seymour had 27. Two of the brooches in the queenly inventories could be the same, and there are relatively detailed descriptions of both.[113] Their style may partially account for this, but primarily they all related a story. Examples from Katherine Howard's inventory include a brooch of gold enamelled black 'hauyng iij persones one of them being a woman with a bowe and an arrowe', an enamelled brooch 'wherein is a woman and a naked boy with a verey ffeir diamond' and another enamelled example 'hauyng iiij naked men and a child stering a pott'.[114] Many of these stories were based on the classical themes that were popular in the sixteenth century.[115]

Royalty was the predominant theme in the design of Kateryn Parr's brooches. This is demonstrated by two items in her collection, which were the

> 'Brouche conteyning the Image of king henry the eight with the Quene having a Crowne of dyamountes ouer them and a Rose of dyamountes vnder them and of eche side a man of dyamountes', and 'a brouche of Imagerie one being a king sitting vpon an Emerode with certeyne pottes of dyamountes and furnysshed otherwise with dyamountes'.[116]

These pieces could have been commissioned by Kateryn, or given to her as a gift – both passed into the hands of Mary I, who gave the latter to her cousin, Lady Margaret Clifford.[117] The image of a king was popular; in these instances it served to emphasise Kateryn's loyalty to her husband, and her determination to convey her royal status in a tangible form. Katherine Howard's inventory lists several pieces that featured a king but are not as numerous or as prolific as those owned by her successor. Another that is likely to have been made especially for Kateryn Parr is described as 'a brouche wrought therin a Castell furnysshed with Dyamountes and the Image of a damsell within thesame hauing at the foote therof a faire rubie'.[118] The design was probably based on the emblem that Kateryn adopted on becoming queen: that of a maiden rising out of a Tudor rose.[119] That these designs were intended both to be seen and to underscore royalty is supported by the style of those found in Jane Seymour's inventory. The vagueness with which most of the brooches are described prevents a definitive conclusion, but the few that are recorded in more detail confirm that they served as decorative pieces. For example, 'a grene brouche of golde sett with ony litle Diamons and with small perll', and 'a nother brouche sett with lytle Rocke Rubies and litle turquis'.[120] There are no elaborate designs in the same manner as those that appear among Katherine Howard and Kateryn Parr's queenly jewels, confirming that such symbolism was rendered unnecessary in everyday life.

Two jewels of a very personal nature appear in Kateryn Parr's queenly inventory, which were worn as either pendants or brooches as they are listed between the two. These are initial jewels, one of which was an 'H and K with a large Emerode and one large perle pendaunt'. The other was an 'H with vij Dyamountes and iij perles pendaunte'.[121] These were almost certainly either commissioned by Kateryn or given to her as gifts; neither appears in the inventory of her predecessor. Chapter 1 highlighted the popularity of initial jewellery, and Kateryn was especially fond of this more personal kind of jewel.[122] The latter jewel was probably the same as that which appears in Anna of Denmark's inventory, described as 'A Jewell of gold in forme of a Romane H hauing vij faire Diamondes, v table and two pointed; with iij faire Peare pearles pendant, hauing iiij knottes of carnation riband'.[123] If so then it was an extraordinary survival, for jewels of this personal nature were usually broken up and recast for this very reason. The 'haches' listed in Katherine Howard's inventory were also initial jewels, the 'hache' representing 'H' for Henry.[124] They are listed alongside the pendant jewels, indicating that they were intended as a neck adornment. The only comparable piece in Jane Seymour's inventory is the 'greate pomander of golde with H and J and a Crouer' that was either commissioned by Jane or given to her.[125] Although this too was a personal jewel, its function meant that it could not be worn with the same kind of intimacy as those owned by Kateryn Parr, which could have been worn as necklaces.

There were five books in Katherine Howard's possession, one of which was later acquired by the King.[126] By contrast, the first of Kateryn Parr's inventories shows only one book, while her later one lists 20.[127] Although Katherine Howard had received an education, none of her contemporaries remarked upon her scholarly abilities.[128] The books may therefore reflect a greater degree of interest from Katherine than she has hitherto been credited with. Alternatively, they could have been inherited from her predecessors or were collected for their decorative appeal. Although Jane Seymour's inventory lists her personal belongings, the same could also be true of her, who like her successor, was not referenced by her contemporaries in terms of her academic credentials.[129] Judging by the decoration of some of the seven books in Jane's inventory, they were clearly of some value. The 'Booke of golde with viij Rooke Rubies and toow Saveou's' and the 'primer of golde enameled with Redde and eight Roock Rubies in it' are likely to have been prized as much for their appearance as for their contents.[130] By contrast, Kateryn Parr was widely renowned for her academic interests and ability as her later inventory reinforces.[131] Evidence in her accounts shows that she was interested in the appearance of her books, making payments for them to be 'gorgiousely bound'.[132] That only one book appears in her earlier inventory is likely to be a sign that she considered her books to be necessary everyday items that were in frequent use, hence why they were not stored with the bulk of her queenly jewels.

Conclusion

The inventories of Jane Seymour, Katherine Howard and Kateryn Parr offer us a tantalising glimpse of the vast assortment of jewels and everyday objects that were used by queen consorts. They also provide compelling details as to the number and variety of stones that were used to create them. Certainly, they do not compare with the volume of jewels amassed by Henry VIII, but this is to be expected. Not only because Henry was the reigning monarch, but the queenly inventories of Katherine Howard and Kateryn Parr also show that their collections were not static, with pieces entering and leaving between queens.

The jewels in the queenly collections underscore the level of splendour that both queens became accustomed to, providing an insight into the quantity and quality of jewellery that was available to a consort. That many of the pieces in the two queenly inventories match shows that queens were expected to handle second-hand jewels and reuse and recycle them for their own needs. This is in keeping with the assertion of Eric Ives that 'the taste of one generation is raw material to the next'.[133] The evidence strongly suggests that Kateryn Parr added jewels to the collection that were commissioned on her own orders. Many of these pieces had a royal theme which demonstrated both her taste and the importance that she placed on using jewels as a tool to project the royal image. By contrast, both Jane Seymour's and Kateryn Parr's later inventories show a different side of queenship. Though primarily consisting of jewels, Jane's collection contained pieces of lower value that she would have worn on an everyday basis. It was markedly different from Kateryn Parr's, which though also containing jewellery for everyday use, consisted of more practical items that were used by the consort regularly, thereby showcasing the functionality of life in the queen's household. The contents of these two inventories combined confirm the vast contrast to the jewels that were provided to assist the queen in her visual representation of majesty.

The inventories of Jane Seymour, Katherine Howard and Kateryn Parr are the most detailed to survive during this period and provide the most in terms of documentary evidence for comparison. They act as 'a form of documentary archaeology' and are invaluable sources that reinforce the material wealth of Henry VIII's queens.[134] This, in turn, provides a reflection of the riches of the Tudor monarch himself.

Notes

1 M. Hayward, 'Rich Pickings: Henry VIII's Use of Confiscation and Its Significance for the Development of the Royal Collection', in Lipscomb and Betteridge (eds), *Henry VIII and the Court*, p. 43.
2 *L & P*, xi, no. 381.
3 BL, Royal MS 7 C XVI, f. 18r-31r; BL, Stowe MS 559, f. 55r-68r.
4 E 101/411/9. See Stratford (ed.), *Richard II*.
5 J. Stratford (ed.), *The Bedford Inventories: The Worldly Goods of John, Duke of Bedford, Regent of France (1389–1435)* (London, 1993).

6 L. Douet-D'Arcq (ed.), *Nouveau recueil de comptes de l'argenterie des rois de France* (Paris, 1874); M. Proctor-Tiffany, *Portrait of a Medieval Patron: The Inventory and Gift Giving of Clemence of Hungary* (Providence, 2007); Cremades (ed.), *Inventarios*; L. Douet-D'Arcq (ed.), 'Inventaire des meubles de la reine Jeanne de Boulogne, 1360', *Bibliotheque de 'Ecole des Chartes*, XL (1879).
7 Becker, *Death*, p. 231.
8 BL, Add MS 18985; BL, Stowe MS 559, f. 55r-68r.
9 Holland Inventory, 1447, Plate and jewels of John Holland, late Duke of Exeter, taken 8 September 1447, Westminster Abbey Muniments 6643.
10 BL, Royal MS 7 C XVI, f. 18r-31r.
11 Holbein, 'Jane Seymour', Kunsthistorisches Museum.
12 J. Denny, *Katherine Howard: A Tudor Conspiracy* (London, 2005), p. 234.
13 *L & P*, xvi, no. 1333.
14 BL, Stowe MS 559, f. 55r.
15 Ibid, f. 67r.
16 SoA, MS 129, f. 178r-183v.
17 SoA, MS 129; BL, Add MS 46348. See also Starkey (ed.), *Inventory*; M. Hayward and P. Ward (eds), *The Inventory of King Henry VIII: Textiles and Dress* (London, 2012).
18 Hayward and Ward (eds), *Textiles and Dress*; SoA, MS 129; BL, Add MS 46348.
19 SoA, MS 129; BL, Add MS 46348.
20 SoA, MS 129, f. 7r-8v.
21 Ibid, f. 178r-183v.
22 *L & P*, xvi, no. 1332.
23 See D. Scarisbrick, 'Anna of Denmark's Jewellery Inventory', *Archaeologica*, CIX (1991), pp. 193–237.
24 E 23/4, f. 15r.
25 See SP 10/4 for a collection of letters relating to this argument.
26 Ibid, f. 35r-36r.
27 SoA, MS 129, f. 216v.
28 Ibid, f. 216v-220v.
29 Ibid, f. 55r-68r; Ibid, f. 178r-183v.
30 BL, Stowe MS 559, r. 59r.
31 Ibid, f. 59v; SoA, MS 129, f. 183v.
32 SoA, MS 129, f. 217v.
33 BL, Stowe MS 559, f. 57v.
34 SoA, MS 129, f. 217v.
35 Earenfight, *Queenship*, p. 179.
36 BL, Stowe MS 559, f. 60r.
37 SoA, MS 129, f. 178v.
38 BL, Stowe MS 559, f. 62r.

39 Scarisbrick, *Tudor and Jacobean Jewellery*, p. 10.
40 BL, Royal MS 7 C XVI, f. 18r-31r; SoA, MS 129, f. 178r-183v.
41 See F. Madden (ed.), *Privy Purse Expenses of the Princess Mary* (London, 1831), pp. 175–201. See also BL, Royal MS B XXVIII; E 101/419/15; E 101/419/19; E 101/420/2; E 101/420/6; E 101/421/4.
42 Madden (ed.), *Privy Purse Expenses*, p. 183; BL, Stowe MS 559, f. 60r.
43 The King was Edward VI. The Princess Elisabeth was at one time proposed as a marriage candidate for Edward VI. The Scottish queen was the dowager, Marie de Guise, and the occasion of the gift was her visit to England in 1551.
44 The note that it was given for a token 'and nott otherwise gyven' is puzzling and suggests that Herbert expected to have the emerald back.
45 SoA, MS 129, f. 220v.
46 BL, Harley MS 7376.
47 BL, Royal MS 7 C XVI, f. 28r.
48 Ibid, f. 18r-19v.
49 See BL, Stowe MS 559, f. 55r-68r & SoA, MS 129, f. 178r-183v for numerous examples.
50 Hinton, *Medieval Jewellery*, p. 11.
51 Campbell, *Medieval Jewellery*, p. 18; Scarisbrick, *Portrait Jewels*, p. 10, 18.
52 Hinton, *Medieval Jewellery*, p. 12.
53 Evans, *History of Jewellery*, p. 82.
54 Phillips, *Jewelry*, p. 78; BL, Stowe MS 559, f. 57v.
55 SoA, MS 129, f. 218v.
56 Scarisbrick, *Tudor and Jacobean Jewellery*, p. 56; See BL, MS Stowe 559, f. 55r-68r, SoA, MS 129, f. 178r-183r; BL, Royal MS 7 C XVI, f. 18r-31r.
57 BL, Stowe MS 559 f. 59r; SoA, MS 129, f. 178r.
58 Phillips, *Jewels and Jewellery*, p. 34.
59 BL, Royal MS 7 C XVI, f. 30r, 18v, 26r.
60 Ibid, f. 26r.
61 SoA, MS 129, f. 216v, 217v.
62 Mueller (ed.), *Katherine Parr*, p. 192.
63 Madden (ed.), *Privy Purse Expenses*, p. 189.
64 Evans, *English Jewellery*, p. 77.
65 BL, Stowe MS 559, f. 56r-v; BL, Royal MS 7 C XVI, f. 18r-31r; SoA, MS 129, f. 178r-183v.
66 See William Scrots, 'Katherine Parr', late sixteenth century, NPG, NPG 4618 for an example of contemporary fashions.
67 SoA, MS 129, f. 183v.
68 BL, Stowe MS 559 f. 55r-v; SoA, MS 129, f. 181v-182v.

69 Holbein, 'Jane Seymour', Kunsthistorisches Museum.
70 Hayward, *Dress*, p. 171.
71 See SoA, MS 129, f. 178r-183v, 216v-220v.
72 After Hans Holbein the Younger, 'Unknown woman, formerly known as Catherine Howard', late seventeenth century, NPG, NPG 1119.
73 Scarisbrick, *Jewellery in Britain*, p. 141.
74 SoA, MS 129, f. 217r.
75 BL, Royal MS 7 C XVI, f. 29r.
76 Scarisbrick, *Diamonds*, p. 72.
77 Ibid, p. 35.
78 BL, Stowe MS 559, f. 62r.
79 BL, Royal MS 7 C XVI, f. 23r.
80 SoA, MS 129, f. 178r.
81 Ibid, f. 179v.
82 BL, Stowe MS 559, f. 59v; Scarisbrick, *Diamonds*, p. 70.
83 BL, Stowe MS 559, f. 178v.
84 Holbein, 'Jane Seymour', Kunsthistorisches Museum; Hans Holbein, 'Portrait of a Lady, perhaps Katherine Howard', c. 1540, RCT, RCIN 422293; BL, Stowe MS 559, f. 58v. The alternative is 'one other ooche of Golde hauyng a verey feir table diamond and a ruby with a feir lose peerle to hange at the same'. In Kateryn Parr's inventory the same ouche could be one of several.
85 SoA, MS 129, f. 178v; BL, Stowe MS 559, f. 59v.
86 Scarisbrick, *Diamonds*, p. 71; S. James, *The Feminine Dynamic in English Art, 1485–1603: Women as Consumers, Patrons and Painters* (Abingdon, 2009), p. 105.
87 Scarisbrick, *Diamonds*, p. 66.
88 Tuetey (ed.), *Charlotte de Savoie*, p. 40; Cremades (ed.), *Inventarios*, iii, p. 2365. Listed as 'Item vne croix de six gros dyamans'.
89 SoA, MS 129, f. 178v; The fact that the same number of diamonds are listed lends itself to the possibility that the cross may have been Anna's. Scarisbrick, 'Anna of Denmark's Jewellery', no. 160, p. 208, no. 183, p. 211.
90 SoA, MS 129, f. 178v; Ibid, f. 179v.
91 Cited in James, *Catherine Parr*, p. 55.
92 SoA, MS 129, f. 181r.
93 BL, Royal MS 7 C XVI, f. 31r.
94 From the mid-sixteenth century, they came to be known as rosary beads. Scarisbrick, *Tudor and Jacobean Jewellery*, p. 42; See BL, Stowe 559, f. 63r for example. Beads made from other materials also appear across the inventories.
95 Cremades (ed.), *Inventarios*, iii, p. 2515, 2627.
96 See BL, Stowe MS 559, f. 63r-65r.

97 See Madden (ed.), *Privy Purse Expenses*, pp. 191–5 for examples.
98 BL, Stowe 559, f. 68r.
99 Hollis (ed.), *Princely Magnificence*, p. 36.
100 BL, Stowe 559, f. 67r-68r; SoA, MS 129, f. 179r-180r; Ibid, f. 218r; BL, Royal MS 7 C XVI, f. 21r-22r.
101 Scarisbrick, *Diamonds*, p. 68; E 36/84, p. 9, 33; SoA, MS 129, f. 155r.
102 BL, Royal MS 7 C XVI, f. 21v.
103 SoA, MS 129, f. 179v.
104 BL, Stowe MS 559, f. 55r-68r.
105 Scarisbrick, *Tudor and Jacobean Jewellery*, p. 84; BL, Royal MS 7 C XVI, f. 21r.
106 BL, Stowe MS 559, f. 68r; SoA, MS 129, f. 179r.
107 The 'E' stood for Elizabeth, in reference to either the King's mother or his daughter. The former is more likely.
108 BL, Royal MS 7 C XVI, f. 22r.
109 Ibid, f. 21v.
110 SoA, MS 129, f. 179v.
111 BL, Stowe MS 559 f. 64v, 67r-v records that Katherine Howard owned beads, a tablet, pomander, and a book that featured a clock. SoA, MS 129, f. 179v shows that Kateryn Parr had two tablets featuring clocks.
112 James, *Catherine Parr*, p. 105.
113 BL, Stowe MS 559, f. 57v; SoA, MS 129, f. 178v-179r; Ibid, f. 217r, 219r.
114 BL, Stowe MS 559, f. 57v.
115 Scarisbrick, *Historic Rings*, p. 75.
116 SoA, MS 129, f. 179r.
117 BL, Harley MS 7376, f. 2v.
118 Ibid.
119 See Starkey, *Six Wives: The Queens of Henry VIII (London, 2004)*, p. 731.
120 BL, Royal MS 7 C XVI, f. 27r.
121 SoA, MS 129, f. 178v.
122 Scarisbrick, *Tudor and Jacobean Jewellery*, p. 83.
123 Scarisbrick, 'Anna of Denmark's Jewellery', pp. 208–9.
124 BL, Stowe MS 559, f. 59r.
125 BL, Royal MS 7 C XVI, f. 21r.
126 BL, Stowe MS 559, f. 67v-68r.
127 SoA, MS 129, f. 179r; Ibid, f. 216v-220v.
128 Russell, *Young and Damned*, pp. 51–3.
129 See B.L. Beer, 'Jane [*née* Jane Seymour]', *ODNB*.
130 BL, Royal MS 7 C XVI, f. 21r.
131 See James, *Catherine Parr*, pp. 23–36.

132 E 315/161, f. 46r; Theresa Earenfight has noted that payments appear in the Castilian treasurer's accounts for gold and silver decorations and bindings for books for Catherine of Aragon prior to her arrival in England. See *Catherine of Aragon*, p. 144.
133 Ives, *Life and Death*, p. 252.
134 Earenfight, *Catherine of Aragon*, p. 16.

References

Manuscript Sources

Kew, The National Archives

EXCHEQUER

E 23 Treasury of Receipt, Royal Wills.
E 36 Treasury of Receipt, Miscellaneous Books.
E 101 King's Remembrancer, Various Accounts.
E 315 Court of Augmentations and Predecessors Miscellaneous Books.
SP State Papers

LONDON, THE BRITISH LIBRARY

Additional Manuscripts 18985, 46348.
Harley Manuscripts 7376.
Royal Manuscripts B XXVIII, 7 C XVI.
Stowe Manuscripts 559.

LONDON, WESTMINSTER ABBEY MUNIMENTS

6643 Holland Inventory, 1447, Plate and jewels of John Holland, late Duke of Exeter, taken 8 September 1447.

LONDON, SOCIETY OF ANTIQUARIES

MS 129 Inventory of King Henry VIII.

Portraits

After Hans Holbein the Younger, 'Unknown woman, formerly known as Catherine Howard', late seventeenth century, NPG, NPG 1119.

Hans Holbein, 'Jane Seymour', 1536–7, Kunsthistorisches Museum, Vienna, Inv. No. 881.

Hans Holbein, 'Portrait of a Lady, perhaps Katherine Howard', c. 1540, RCT, RCIN 422293.

Levina Teerlinc, 'Katherine Parr', c. 1544–5, Sudeley Castle.

Lucas Horenbout, 'Katherine of Aragon', c. 1525, NPG, NPG 4682.

Lucas Horenbout, 'Katherine of Aragon', c. 1525–6, NPG, NPG L244.

Possibly Lucas Horenbout, 'Jane Seymour', sixteenth century, Sudeley Castle.

William Scrots, 'Katherine Parr', late sixteenth century, NPG, NPG 4618.

Printed Primary Sources

Brewer, J., et al., (ed.), *Letters and Papers, Foreign and Domestic, of the Reign of Henry VIII, 1509–1547*, 21 vols (London, 1862–1932).

Cremades, F.C. (ed.), *Los inventarios de Carlos V y la familia imperial*, 3 vols (Madrid, 2010).

Douet-D'Arcq, L. (ed.), 'Inventaire des meubles de la reine Jeanne de Boulogne, 1360', *Bibliotheque de 'Ecole des Chartes*, XL (1879).

Douet-D'Arcq, L. (ed.), *Nouveau recueil de comptes de l'argenterie des rois de France* (Paris, 1874).

Hayward, M., and Ward, P., (eds), *The Inventory of King Henry VIII: Textiles and Dress* (London, 2012).

Hume, M.A.S. trans., *The Chronicle of King Henry VIII of England* (London, 1889).

Knighton, C.S., (ed.), *Calendar of State Papers Domestic Series of the Reign of Edward VI 1547–1553* (London, 1992).

Madden, F., (ed.), *Privy Purse Expenses of the Princess Mary* (London, 1831).

Mueller, J., (ed.), *Katherine Parr: Complete Works and Correspondence* (Chicago, 2011).

Proctor-Tiffany, M., *Portrait of a Medieval Patron: The Inventory and Gift Giving of Clemence of Hungary* (Providence, 2007).

Starkey, D., (ed.), *The Inventory of King Henry VIII: The Transcript*, trans. Ward, P. (London, 1998).

Stratford, J., (ed.), *Richard II and the English Royal Treasure* (Woodbridge, 2012).

Stratford, J., (ed.), *The Bedford Inventories: The Worldly Goods of John, Duke of Bedford, Regent of France (1389–1435)* (London, 1993).

Tuetey, P.A., (ed.), *Inventaire des Biens de Charlotte de Savoie, Reine de France*, (*1483*) (Paris, 1865).

Secondary Sources

Becker, L.M., *Death and the Early Modern Englishwoman* (Aldershot, 2003).

Beer, B.L., 'Jane [*née* Jane Seymour]', *ODNB*, https://doi.org/10.1093/ref:odnb/14647

Campbell, M., *Medieval Jewellery* (London, 2009).

Denny, J., *Katherine Howard: A Tudor Conspiracy* (London, 2005).

Earenfight, T., *Catherine of Aragon: Infanta of Spain, Queen of England* (Pennsylvania, 2021).

Earenfight, T., *Queenship in Medieval Europe* (Basingstoke, 2013).

Evans, J., *A History of Jewellery 1100–1870* (New York, 1953).

Evans, J., *English Jewellery: From the Fifth Century A.D. to 1800* (London, 1921).

Forsyth, H., *The Cheapside Hoard: London's Lost Jewels* (London, 2013).

Hayward, M., *Dress at the Court of King Henry VIII* (Leeds, 2007).

Hayward, M., 'Rich Pickings: Henry VIII's Use of Confiscation and Its Significance for the Development of the Royal Collection', in Lipscomb, S., and Betteridge, T. (eds), *Henry VIII and the Court: Art, Politics and Performance* (Farnham, 2013), pp. 29–4.

Hinton, D., *Medieval Jewellery* (Aylesbury, 1982).

Hollis, J., (ed.), *Princely Magnificence: Court Jewels of the Renaissance, 1500–1630* (London, 1980).

Ives, E., *The Life and Death of Anne Boleyn* (Oxford, 2004).

James, S.E., *Catherine Parr: Henry VIII's Last Love* (Stroud, 2008).

James, S.E., *The Feminine Dynamic in English Art, 1485–1603: Women as Consumers, Patrons and Painters* (Abingdon, 2009).

Phillips, C., *Jewels and Jewellery* (London, 2000).

Phillips, C., *Jewellery: From Antiquity to the Present* (London, 1996).

Russell, G., *Young and Damned and Fair: The Life and Tragedy of Catherine Howard at the Court of Henry VIII* (London, 2017).

Scarisbrick, D., 'Anna of Denmark's Jewellery Inventory', *Archaeologica*, CIX (1991), pp. 193–237.

Scarisbrick, D., *Diamond Jewelry: 700 Years of Glory and Glamour* (London, 2019).
Scarisbrick, D., *Historic Rings: Four Thousand Years of Craftsmanship* (Tokyo, 2004).
Scarisbrick, D., *Jewellery in Britain 1066–1837* (Norwich, 1994).
Scarisbrick, D., *Portrait Jewels: Opulence and Intimacy from the Medici to the Romanovs* (London, 2011).
Scarisbrick, D., *Tudor and Jacobean Jewellery* (London, 1995).
Starkey, D., *Six Wives: The Queens of Henry VIII* (London, 2004).

4 Portraiture

Susan James observed that 'Royal portraits were the concrete iconography of divinely authorised rule', a concept that applied to female consorts.[1] Portraits provided monarchs and their consorts with an opportunity to showcase their image to their greatest advantage, using jewels as a way of emphasising their magnificence, power, ideals of queenship, or to convey a message. In an age in which outward display meant everything, portraiture provided an ideal medium not only for ensuring that that image was projected among contemporaries but also for posterity. It therefore served a very serious function, and this explains why both monarchs and their consorts often wore their finest clothes when sitting for artists.

Jewels made a significant contribution to the splendour of queenship, projecting the majesty and wealth of queens, their husbands and the dynasties of which they were a part. By the same token, portraiture highlighted rank, and aside from royalty few sitters sat for their portrait more than once in a lifetime.[2] It was a service primarily available to only the highest ranks of society, which is reflected in many of the surviving examples. Portraits were symbolic of both wealth and power and could be commissioned and used for a variety of reasons.[3] The observation of Anna Reynolds that 'it was customary for a portrait to show a sitter in formal attire' that consisted of 'the most expensive highly decorated fabrics' confirms this.[4] This in turn was reflected in the jewellery a sitter wore, on which both men and women placed great emphasis: kings and queens often chose the

DOI: 10.4324/9781003202592-5

best pieces in their collections.[5] This is apparent in several of the surviving examples of portraits of queens from the period 1445 to 1548, and these will be discussed throughout the course of this chapter.

Portraits reveal a number of things about the way in which queens wished to project their images, both as individuals and as consorts. Stephen Greenblatt, who used Holbein's 'The Ambassadors' as an example of the way in which the symbolism in portraiture was constructed, explored this notion of self-fashioning, and many of the principles about which he wrote were applicable to queens.[6] This is particularly clear with Kateryn Parr, who exploited the powers of portraiture in order to build her image. She in turn is likely to have influenced the future Elizabeth I, who would seek to control her image through portraiture.[7] Though there are over 100 surviving images of Elizabeth, it is evident that the trend of using portraiture to project a persona began earlier.[8]

Wills and inventories are both crucial documentary sources in terms of jewels for this period, but much of our understanding also derives from portraits.[9] During the Renaissance, both men and women wore more jewellery than ever before, as the portraits and accounts of Henry VII and Henry VIII bear testimony.[10] This in turn is reflected in the portraits of queens. Portraits of fifteenth-century queens are sparse, and even in the sixteenth century not all portraits of queens were contemporary. Additionally, many portraits have either been mislabelled or remain unidentified. There may, therefore, be more surviving portraits of these queens of which we are as yet unaware. There are also limitations when using portraits as sources. Though they provide visual evidence of the genres of jewels and the way in which they were worn, in some instances we have no way of knowing if the pieces painted were genuine items or if the artist employed some artistic licence. When we have the ability to combine portraits with sources such as inventories, therefore, we can determine the authenticity of specific jewels with greater accuracy.

Portraits not only demonstrate how jewels were worn but in some cases mark the transition from queen to queen. They also show how swiftly fashions changed during this short period. For example, the lozenge-shaped jewel worn by Isabel Neville in the Rous Roll in the last quarter of the fifteenth century was quickly replaced with more elaborately designed pendants within the next 25 years.[11] In the sixteenth century, the fashion changed from simple pieces to those that were intricate and elaborate.[12] Even in the two decades between the reigns of Catherine of Aragon and Kateryn Parr, surviving portraits show how greatly jewellery designs had altered. During the Elizabethan era when portraits became 'biography not merely a likeness', portraiture was particularly emblematic, yet there is earlier evidence for this too.[13]

This chapter will explore the rise and development of portraiture and its function in relation to the queen consorts of England, in order to emphasise its importance as a historical source when studying jewels. In a similar manner to the previous chapter, it seeks to use surviving portraits as a way of tracking pieces in the royal jewel collection from queen to queen. It will then examine the various mediums in which portraits of queens appeared, analysing the way in which they wore their jewels. Portraits of queens were not restricted to those painted on wooden panels but appeared in a variety of forms. These include manuscripts, books, medals, funeral effigies and jewels: manuscript portrayals, although unlikely to have been any genuine attempt at portraiture, provide the only contemporary visual representations we have of Anne Neville. Many images of the queens in this period survive from later eras, especially the nineteenth century when history entered a period of heightened romanticism.[14] However, this chapter will only examine original portraiture or that which appears to have been based on lost originals. In some cases, there are numerous examples, but only those that render the most significance or demonstrate specific points with relation to the queen's jewel collection will be analysed. This will all convey how queens employed portraiture as an effective tool which showcased their jewels and allowed them to promote their royal image. In so doing, the chapter concludes by signifying how portraits provide visual evidence that supports the documentary sources in showcasing the wealth of the queens in this period.

The Rise of Portraiture

Until the turn of the sixteenth century, many of the surviving contemporary images of English queens had been created in order to depict and promote the expected ideals of queenship. In keeping with the ideas expressed by Jacobus de Cessolis in *The Game and Playe of the Chesse*, this meant being seen as the king's partner and mother to his children, rather than an individual.[15] We see an example of this in a fifteenth-century manuscript, which shows Edward IV being presented with a book, flanked by his son and heir, and his queen, Elizabeth Wydeville in the background.[16] Queens were also portrayed carrying out their duties, evidence of which can be found on surviving seals (demonstrating their administrative role), in manuscripts, which in the case of Philippa of Hainault highlight her success as her husband's regent in 1346, and in images depicting marriages.[17] It was not unusual for queens to be portrayed like the Virgin Mary in an association with the Queen of Heaven, and Chapter 7 will consider Elizabeth Wydeville's representation in this way.[18] For Elizabeth, this is likely to have been an attempt to accentuate her royal status following her marriage to Edward IV.

Richard II was the first English monarch of whom a contemporary painted likeness survives, and the execution confirms that portraiture in England was still in its infancy.[19] In fact, sculpture appears to have been more advanced than painting, for though there are no surviving examples of contemporary portraits of queens, we have the tomb effigy of Philippa of Hainault, which appears to have been an attempt at a genuine likeness.[20] The funeral effigy of Katherine of Valois may have been trying to provide the same.[21] As the fifteenth century progressed, more accurate likenesses of queens began to emerge, although in the case of Margaret of Anjou the only image we have which may be an attempted likeness is a medal analysed in Chapter 7.[22] The changes in portraiture and the greater interest in recording the appearance of an individual ensured that late medieval queens were depicted more as individuals than as the iconic image of an ideal queen, and their likenesses were more widely circulated.[23] Portraits instead started to be valued as they 'recorded the physical presence of a person'.[24] However, Erin Barrett argued that in most instances queens wanted to be associated with their husbands and used their images as ways of highlighting this.[25] It will shortly become apparent that there are some cases where this could be said to be true, but by the reign of Henry VIII at least one of his wives, Kateryn Parr, used her image as a way of communicating her own majesty. By 1500 techniques and styles of portraiture in England had changed very little, and this is apparent in the contemporary and near-contemporary portraits of Elizabeth Wydeville and Elizabeth of York in the Royal Collection.[26] Both women appear two-dimensional, but what is more striking is the remarkable similarities between the two portraits. They show a lack of the sophistication that was displayed by artists such as Michelangelo in Italy, and it is possible that the same artist painted both women.[27] In John Fletcher's 1974 article, he argued that tree-ring analysis dated Elizabeth Wydeville's portrait firmly to the 1470s, but more recent research has shown that it probably dates to the 1520s.[28] It is likely that the portrait of Elizabeth of York, which Fletcher also analysed, although over-painted, dates to the early sixteenth century and could have been painted during her lifetime.[29]

The onset of the sixteenth century witnessed the rise of portraiture in England, but elsewhere in Europe the trend had begun much earlier. The contribution to portraiture made by artists from the Low Countries was significant, and both Isabel of Castile and Catherine of Aragon were known to have owned Flemish works.[30] In Bruges Jan van Eyck is generally considered to have been one of the great early portraitists, who earned the patronage of Philip the Good and managed to achieve three dimensions in two-dimensional painting.[31] In fifteenth-century Italy, the popularity and sophistication of portraiture truly developed. Sandro Botticelli became renowned for displaying the 'kernel of the personality' in his portraits, which was important as John Pope-Hennessy stressed that Renaissance painting 'reflects the reawakening interest in human motives and the human character'.[32] Profile portraits were a popular way of depicting women as it was believed to present the most flattering view, but in England the presentation was very different.[33] Paola Tinagli asserted that the choice of finery by women who sat for their portraits was 'not an empty gesture of vanity' but instead a deliberate strategy through which 'women made their position visible to the eyes of society'.[34] The examples cited throughout this chapter show that the same was also true of many English portraits.

The beginning of the sixteenth century witnessed the peak in the careers of Italian artists such as Leonardo da Vinci, Raphael and Michelangelo.[35] What was more, these artists began to travel elsewhere in Europe: the Florentine Pietro Torrigiano brought his skills to England, where the royal family employed them, while Da Vinci travelled to France, where he enjoyed the patronage of François I.[36] His consort, Eleanor of Austria, was also an enthusiastic patron of portraiture.[37] The developments in portraiture in France and England largely coincided with one another, and the work of Jean Clouet, François's court painter from 1516, is a useful point of comparison, for he was the contemporary of Henry VIII's court painter, Hans Holbein, whom Clouet is likely to have met and may have influenced.[38]

The reign of Henry VIII witnessed a huge advancement in portraiture techniques and the representation of monarchs in England, combining old forms with recent developments in Renaissance art in a similar manner to the style Clouet had adopted in France.[39] The arrival of the German artist Hans Holbein at Henry VIII's court in the 1530s signalled a turning point in English portraiture, for as Robert Tittler summarised, 'Holbein arrived at a time when England was ready for his skills and experience'.[40] Precisely when the artist entered the King's service is unclear, as he does not appear in accounts before 1536.[41] What is evident though is that Holbein had travelled widely and had been influenced by Italian artists, including Leonardo da Vinci.[42] He was able to employ these influences when he began working in England, doing so with great skill and, thanks to his fondness for detail, conveying a greater sense of realism in his portraits.[43] His work was not unparalleled, but from an English perspective it was impressive.

Holbein was not alone among the artists who found patronage at the English court, but his work is undoubtedly the most famous in this period.[44] Patronage was an important aspect of queenship, and building relationships with artists provided a way of enlarging a queen's network through supporting those who could aid her with the means to create her own image. It was also a demonstration of power and cultural influence.[45] Henry's consorts are known to have patronised several artists, and it was the belief of John Rowlands and David Starkey that Anne Boleyn was responsible for Holbein's patronage.[46] They argued that Holbein created a likeness of Anne, although he did not achieve recognition at court until after her fall.[47] Such evidence is subjective, but Holbein certainly designed jewellery for Anne, demonstrating a direct link between the patronage of artists and queens.[48] His role in doing so forms part of the discussion in Chapter 5. In terms of portraiture, what is more certain is that Holbein painted at least two, and probably three of Anne's successors, evidence of his success at court.[49]

Functions of Portraiture

Portraits were needed as truthful records of the appearance of persons, something that was of particular importance in connection with royal marriages.[50] The first example of this in this period is in 1442, when Henry VI sent an artist to paint the daughters of a French count.[51] In this instance, portraiture was used to serve a personal role that could potentially impact upon influencing a public choice. Henry VI was by no means unique, for portraits were often exchanged between the royal courts of various countries, and it became an accepted part of marriage negotiations.[52] This trend continued in the reign of Henry VII, who sent for portraits of both Margaret of Austria and Joanna of Naples following the death of Elizabeth of York in 1503, and likewise arranged for his own portrait to be painted.[53] Similarly, examples of portraits of Eleanor of Austria that were used for this purpose also survive.[54] Jewels were an integral part of such portraits, as they served as visual evidence of the wealth of the family from which the potential bride or bridegroom hailed. As such, they reinforced their magnificence.

The importance of portraiture becomes apparent when studying the marriage negotiations of Anna of Cleves.[55] Following the death of Jane Seymour in October 1537, Holbein was sent abroad, charged with capturing the likenesses of several European princesses, including Christina of Denmark, Duchess of Milan, Anna of Cleves and her sister, Amelia.[56] That the court painter was tasked with such a crucial assignment signifies the faith Henry VIII had in his ability, and underlines the way in which artists could become intimately involved in politics.[57] In August 1539 Nicholas Wotton, the King's ambassador in Cleves, was able to inform his master, 'Your Grace's servant Hanze Albein hathe taken th'effigies of my ladye Anne and the ladye Amelye and hath expressyd theyr imaiges verye lyvelye', and the result of Holbein's portrait was pleasing to Henry.[58] The decisive factor in securing the marriage treaty was political, but on a personal level Anna's portrait set the King's expectations with disastrous consequences.

Anna's portrait shows her wearing two gold chains and an elaborately jewelled necklace to which is attached a cross pendant (Figure 4.1). This could have been intended to reflect her religiosity, and her costume is adorned with a number of pearls that represent her purity.[59] She also wears five rings displaying diamonds and a ruby. Lorne Campbell has suggested that Holbein may not have had time to complete the entirety of Anna's portrait from life, and thus could have added the jewels at a later time.[60] This brings us back to the limitations of using portraits as sources, for as such there is no way of knowing whether the jewels in Anna's portrait were genuine items, or if Holbein employed some artistic licence.[61] When the King was confronted with Anna in person, he was unimpressed.[62] Yet there is no evidence to suggest that Holbein was criticised for his role in the creation of an image that Henry had admired.[63]

Aside from marriage negotiations, portraiture served as a useful tool for royal propaganda. Both Henry VII and Henry VIII were particularly aware of the importance of the royal image and ordered the creation of several portraits to highlight the power of their dynasty. The first of these was painted between 1503 and 1509 and shows Henry VII and Elizabeth of York with their seven children and St George and the Dragon.[64] Completed after Elizabeth's death, it was never intended to present an accurate

Figure 4.1 Anna of Cleves by Hans Holbein

Source: Getty Museum Collection. Public Domain. www.getty.edu/art/collection/object/107QBT

likeness of the deceased queen but was instead full of symbolism. The inclusion of St George as patron saint of England and protector of the royal family is highly significant, for the purpose of the painting was to stress the progeny of the Tudor dynasty as a result of Henry and Elizabeth's union.[65]

As the heiress of the House of York, the image of Elizabeth of York was essential in establishing the new identity of the Tudor dynasty and was played to full effect.[66] Yet Jacqueline Johnson pointed out that Elizabeth was always shown both as Henry VII's consort whose position depended on him and in her role as a mother.[67] It was thus made glaringly apparent to the King's subjects that from Henry's perspective, Elizabeth had earned her position as queen solely through her marriage to him. Tellingly, her coronation did not take place until after the couple's first son was born. Image making was not only a way of showcasing the power of the Tudor dynasty, underlining its claim to the throne and the continuation of its line, but of persuading their subjects of their right to rule in the first place.[68] Kevin Sharpe asserted that Henry VII's concern with public display was related to his dynastic insecurity, and thus such display also served as a visual reminder of royal descent.[69]

While Henry VIII's parents provided a way of underlining his lineage, his children were a means of demonstrating the future of the dynasty. This was important, as Sydney Anglo observed, because it was necessary for 'rulers to make themselves, their dynasty and their possessions instantly recognizable'.[70] This can be seen in a portrait dating from around 1545: 'The Family of Henry VIII'.[71] Intended to emphasise the solidity and strength of the Tudors, Henry is shown with his three children – his heirs – and Jane Seymour.[72] Jane's inclusion is interesting, given that at the time the portrait was painted she had been dead for eight years, but it was a way of emphasising that she was the mother of the King's male heir. That Jane, along with her son Edward, was depicted in closer proximity to the King than his daughters accentuated her role in creating the next – and most important – generation of the dynasty. Jane's portrait was based on previous likenesses of her painted during her lifetime and provides a further example of the way in which the royal image could be used for propaganda purposes.[73] In the same way as Elizabeth of York, Jane's image was exploited posthumously. It was used more than any of her predecessors or successors for the sole reason that it was she alone who had succeeded in providing her husband with his longed-for male heir. The jewels that Jane wears are either the same or similar to those worn in her portrait by Holbein, analysed later in this chapter. Their inclusion was therefore only significant in terms of accentuating Jane's role as queen, rather than providing an accurate representation of specific pieces.

Manuscripts

Four contemporary manuscripts provide likenesses of Margaret of Anjou, one of which will be considered in Chapter 7. All, however, are problematic in terms of assessing both Margaret's appearance and analysing her jewels. The first dates from 1445, the year of Margaret's marriage, and appears in the Talbot Shrewsbury Book.[74] It stresses Margaret's role as her husband's consort and their royal union, as is in evidence by her clasping his hand. This is in keeping with the traditional expectations of queens, who were expected to act as their husband's chief supporters.[75] De Cessolis's *The Game and Playe of the Chesse*, which appeared in the 1470s, had emphasised many of these assumptions, stating that the queen ought to sit on the king's left side, as Margaret is shown, for 'In that she is sette on his lifte syde is by the grace gevyn to the kynge by nature and of right'.[76]

By contrast, the second image shows Margaret's marriage to Henry VI and was produced almost 40 years after the event.[77] This image is also likely to have been based on contemporary ideals of matrimony rather than conveying an accurate likeness. In both images Margaret is shown with blonde hair, a fashionable feature for queens at the time – this may therefore have been nothing more than a compliance with contemporary fashions.[78] Indeed, Margaret's depiction as blonde is at odds with the Milanese ambassador's description of her as 'somewhat dark', although it is important to note that he had not seen her personally, and was writing to flatter his mistress by extolling her own beauty.[79] In both images Margaret wears her crown in a symbol of her exalted status, and her wedding ring can also be seen in the Talbot Shrewsbury Book. A similar image of Margaret appears in a prayer roll in the Bodleian Library, but this will be considered in Chapter 7 in relation to coronations.[80] It is important to note, however, that in the prayer roll Margaret can be seen wearing not only her crown but several rings and gold chains, which accentuate her majestic appearance.[81]

One other contemporary manuscript image provides an interesting point of comparison with those that represent Margaret as a reigning consort. This is the illumination that marked Margaret's entry into the Skinners Company of London in 1475.[82] This likeness is a marked contrast to other images of Margaret, and although she is referred to as 'The Qween Margarete sutyme wyff and Spowse to kyng Harry the sexthe', that she was no longer queen at this time is in evidence. Her crown and sceptre have both been removed and have been placed on the altar at which a black-clad Margaret kneels. She is no longer shown as a queen consort but instead kneels in prayer, her royal apparel and jewels removed. No other jewels are in evidence, and Margaret's appearance is remarkably different from that of her successor, Elizabeth Wydeville, whose likeness appears in the same manuscript and will also be discussed in Chapter 7.

The emphasis on queenship as opposed to queens as individuals is further apparent in the likenesses of Anne Neville as queen. In all three images – those in the Rous Roll, the Beauchamp Pageant and the Salisbury Roll, she is seen carrying items of coronation regalia, although not always accurately represented.[83] Like Margaret of Anjou, these images emphasised Anne's importance as Richard III's consort, rather than capturing a genuine likeness. This makes it difficult to establish their accuracy, and contemporary sources do little to clarify the situation. The only insight into Anne's appearance comes from the Crowland Chronicle, whose author simply asserted that 'Queen Anne and Lady Elizabeth, eldest daughter of the dead king, who were alike in complexion and figure'.[84] If this is true then Anne may have been blonde like her niece, Elizabeth of York. Michael Hicks supported the view that none of these contemporary likenesses can be taken as true evidence of Anne's appearance, claiming that none of them are realistic.[85] Similarly, given that they all show Anne wearing coronation regalia, it is difficult to glean further information as to the nature of her jewellery. In the Rous Roll she can be seen wearing a necklace to which is attached a pendant, the design of which is comparable to those worn in portraits of Elizabeth of York. Although this can by no means be taken as reliable evidence of an accurate portrayal of one of Anne's pieces, it does at least show an adherence by the artist to contemporary fashions.

Medals

The fashion for medals was prevalent among European rulers, who were able to distribute them in order to commemorate specific occasions: examples of medals being used in such a way appeared across Europe.[86] Images of two of the queens survive in the form of medals: one depicting Margaret of Anjou will be discussed in Chapter 7 in relation to the Crown Jewels. A medal of Anne Boleyn was created in 1534, at which time she was believed to be pregnant with a male heir: this explains the inclusion of her motto, 'The Moost Happi'.[87] The face of the medal is badly damaged, but in a similar manner to the medal of Margaret its purpose was never to present a true likeness of Anne. When she miscarried her child, the medal was cancelled, and no further copies were made.[88] This strongly suggests that the circulation of Anne's image as queen to those for whom the medals were intended – possibly her supporters or as rewards for loyalty and good service to those whom the King chose to distribute them to – was completely dependent on her ability to produce a male heir. Maria Hayward has argued that the choice of the English gable hood that Anne is shown wearing was deliberate, for 'the aim was to present her as an English woman with English taste'.[89] A cross is attached to her necklace, and this could also be significant. No other likenesses of Anne portray her wearing a cross, and this may have been a deliberate choice in order to stress her piety.[90]

Portraits of Queens

The most common form of portraiture was the painted likeness that appeared on wooden panels.[91] These had been in production across Europe since at least the fourteenth century, yet Elizabeth Wydeville was the first queen of England who we know was painted from life – her portrait is the first near-contemporary surviving example.[92] In his 1934 article, William Shaw maintained that a portrait of Elizabeth whose whereabouts are now unknown was painted by John Stratford in 1463, representing Elizabeth before her royal marriage (Figure 4.2).[93] This is unlikely to be the case, for there would have been little cause or opportunity for Elizabeth's likeness to have been created prior to her marriage to Edward IV when she was the wife of a mere knight.[94] What is more probable is that the portrait was painted during Elizabeth's term as queen when there would have been a greater demand for it. At least ten versions of the portrait type survive, all dating from after Elizabeth's death and all differing in style and quality.[95] A version painted between 1513 and 1530 referred to briefly earlier in this chapter, and now in the Royal Collection, could be that which appears in Henry VIII's inventory.[96] Although painted after Elizabeth's death, given that it is the earliest version it is likely to be that which is closest to the original. When studying the multiple versions, although all differ in terms of precise details, the style of clothes and jewels are similar. The fifteenth-century fashion for low-cut gowns, which allowed women to wear necklaces, is reflected in Elizabeth's portraits.[97] In a further visible demonstration of her wealth, she wears two necklaces, both of which are richly decorated.

When comparing the style of jewels worn by Elizabeth Wydeville with those of her daughter, Elizabeth of York, we can see that fashions had already begun to change within a brief period. In the same manner as those of her mother's, Elizabeth of York's portraits are of one type, based on a lost original painted in the last years of her life by a Flemish artist, Maynard Waynwyck.[98] However, Henry VIII's inventory provides evidence that several portraits once existed, one of which is likely to survive in the

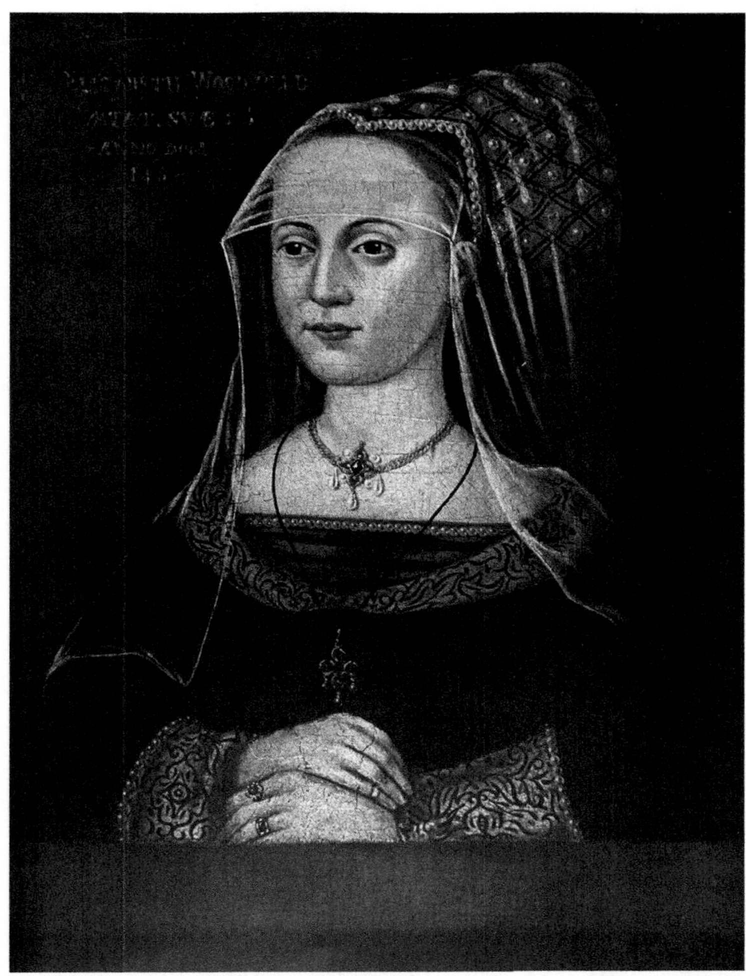

Figure 4.2 A lost portrait of Elizabeth Wydeville

Source: © Timewatch Images/Alamy Stock Photo

Royal Collection and is therefore probably an accurate likeness (Figure 4.3).[99] In this version, Elizabeth's neck jewellery differs from that of her mother, Elizabeth Wydeville, and she is instead

Figure 4.3 A portrait of Elizabeth of York from the Royal Collection

Source: © IanDagnall Computing/Alamy Stock Photo

shown wearing a simple pearl necklace from which individual pearls and rubies are suspended. The style of Elizabeth of York's necklace is unusual, yet rubies were a popular choice of stone for queens and feature regularly in portraits: they were admired not only for their physical qualities but also for their association with marriage.[100] Jewels featuring rubies that were worn by queens reflected not only their status as married women but could have been intended to enhance their image of the embodiment of queenship, for they were also believed to combat lust – de Cessolis continually stressed the importance of a queen's chastity.[101] Elizabeth is also pictured wearing rings on several fingers: her left hand is not fully visible, but it seems that the two rings worn on this hand were on her index and little fingers. Neither, therefore, was her wedding ring, which was made of gold and cost 23s. 4d.[102] Her dress is embroidered with jewels, which contrasts with the simple border of pearls that were the only jewels worn on the clothes of her mother.

The importance of Elizabeth's image in establishing the identity and legitimacy of the Tudor dynasty has already been recognised, but her individual portraits served to stress the role that Henry VII had played in uniting the houses of Lancaster and York. In most of the many copies of the Royal Collection portrait, Elizabeth is shown holding the white rose associated with the house of York, although Jennifer Scott has highlighted that a version that may have belonged to Elizabeth's daughter, Margaret Tudor, Queen of Scots, showed her holding a red rose.[103] The white rose was symbolic of her heritage and is likely to have served as a companion piece to a portrait of Henry VII in the Society of Antiquaries, in which he holds the red rose of Lancaster.[104] Together they signify the union of the two houses. Frederick Hepburn suggested that there may once have been companion portraits of Edward IV and Richard III with their queens, which if true, confirms the popularity of such pairs.[105] Elizabeth of York's image in conjunction with that of Henry VII is particularly important, and in a later version of the same portrait type she is shown wearing a square-shaped pendant made of pearls and rubies.[106]

The differences between the jewels worn by Elizabeth Wydeville and Elizabeth of York become all the more striking when compared with contemporary likenesses of Catherine of Aragon.

Catherine seems to have sat for her portrait on several occasions, which is unsurprising given the length of her reign. Doubt has recently been cast on a portrait once believed to have been of Catherine by Michel Sittow, with Mojmír Frinta suggesting that the sitter may not be royal at all.[107] It is nevertheless clear that while in Spain Catherine did favour Sittow, for having been shown two portraits of the Duchess of Savoy by an unspecified artist in 1505, she expressed the opinion that 'Michel would have made better portraits'.[108] Given that Sittow served as court painter to her mother for ten years, Catherine would have been very familiar with his work, and at the beginning of this chapter it was noted that she was enthusiastic about Flemish art, the style in which Sittow had been trained.[109]

Elsewhere a portrait once thought to have been Kateryn Parr was recently re-identified as Catherine of Aragon.[110] Dating from around 1520, the portrait formed one half of a pair, the other depicting Henry VIII.[111] The royal couple evidently favoured these companion pieces, for they also commissioned miniatures, which will be analysed later in this chapter. After Catherine's death, a pair of portraits was found among her possessions, indicating that they were treasured items.[112] Theresa Earenfight suggested that the 1520 companion pieces may have been created to commemorate an event as 'a visual representation of the power and sophisticated cosmopolitan culture of the Tudor monarchy', and this is certainly feasible.[113] Catherine is shown in full court dress, wearing three strings of pearls from one of which is attached a jewelled pendant. Pendants remained popular during this period as the fashion for necklines on gowns was still low cut, but the shape and design of Catherine's pendant is very different from that worn by Elizabeth Wydeville in the previous century.[114] Fashions were constantly adapting, and Earenfight claimed that the design is similar to the styles that were produced by goldsmiths from Toledo.[115] If this was indeed the case, then it was evidently a sign of Catherine's preference for Spanish designs. Catherine wears jewels and goldsmiths' work around the rim of her headdress, a trend that was adopted by many queens during this period as headdresses became more prominent. She also wears a single ring on her right hand that seems to be studded with a ruby – perhaps a sign of marital fidelity. Overall, Catherine's 'clothing and jewelry are unexceptional for a queen' and reflect Earenfight's assertion that the artist wanted those who saw the portrait to know that her appearance conveyed 'the ordinary attire of a queen consort'.[116]

The fashion for ropes of pearls like those worn by Catherine was continued by her successor, Anne Boleyn. The most famous likeness of Anne postdates her death but is likely to have been a copy of a lost original (Figure 4.4) – there was once at least one full-length portrait, listed in the collection of Lord Lumley until 1773.[117] Like images of her predecessors several copies of this portrait exist, all slightly different but nevertheless confirming a demand for Anne's likeness.[118] The main reason for owning a royal portrait was as an expression of loyalty, which explains the existence of numerous copies of various royal portraits.[119] In this image which is housed in the National Portrait Gallery, Anne wears copious amounts of pearls, both on her headdress and sewn on to her neckline – indicating either a preference for them or a declaration of her chastity. Aside from her pearls, the most notable item among Anne's jewellery is her 'B' initialled necklace. This proclaimed her pride in her Boleyn roots, and she is known to have owned several such jewels. Another appears in a portrait of Anne at Nidd Hall, while her daughter, Elizabeth, can be seen wearing an 'A' pendant in the dynasty piece previously discussed.[120]

That Anne not only owned several of these initial jewels but chose to wear them in more than one portrait shows her determination to be portrayed as a queen who was eager for her identity and her lineage to be remembered. This suggests that she was very conscious of image creation in the same manner as was adopted by several of her predecessors and successors. This is also implied by the choice of jewels she adorned aside from her initial jewel in the Nidd Hall portrait: her rich gold chain studded with rubies and pearls, and the pendant containing three rubies and a pendant pearl are high-status pieces that were intended to make a statement – unfortunately, while the chain potentially matches two items in Katherine Howard's inventory, the pendant is likely to have been recycled or absorbed into the King's

Figure 4.4 Anne Boleyn, probably a copy of a lost original

Source: © IanDagnall Computing/Alamy Stock Photo

collection following Anne's fall.[121] It is interesting that Anne's daughter Elizabeth chose to wear – or was given – the 'A' initial pendant for the family portrait her father commissioned.[122] This implies not only that Elizabeth had probably received some of her mother's jewellery following Anne's death but also underlines her association with Anne – likely a choice made by her father as a way of highlighting her illegitimacy on Anne's account in this significant piece of Tudor propaganda.

There is tangible evidence in the form of jewellery to suggest that Elizabeth felt a resonance with her mother, which can be found in a ring.[123] Inside are images of Elizabeth and a woman who is likely to be Anne Boleyn, although Susan James has suggested that it could represent Elizabeth's stepmother, Kateryn Parr.[124] Elizabeth once owned the ring, and though it does not match with any of the pieces listed in her inventories, Eric Ives convincingly argued that it must have been made for her or given as a gift.[125] While it is plausible that Kateryn Parr gave Elizabeth such a piece, the intimacy of the ring is indicative of an item that served a more personal function, perhaps as a memorial for Elizabeth of Anne.

Anne Boleyn may have been responsible for Holbein's patronage, yet one of his greatest masterpieces was his portrait of her successor, Jane Seymour (Figure 4.5).[126] Not only does Jane's likeness survive, but so too does the preparatory sketch, revealing the way in which Holbein developed her image.[127] This may have been something that Holbein had learned from Clouet, who also prepared drawings of his subjects and to whose work Holbein's drew many parallels.[128] Holbein's portrait of Jane showcases some of the great developments that the artist had introduced to English portraiture: the details such as the richness of her clothes and jewels, and the light and shade of the background contrast sharply with the more two-dimensional images of Elizabeth Wydeville and Elizabeth of York. The message conveyed by the portrait is clear: Jane is dressed in a rich costume with some of the most important jewels in the queen's collection, proclaiming her royal status as Henry's consort. The IHS brooch she wears was a monogram illustrative of a highly

Figure 4.5 Hans Holbein's masterpiece of Jane Seymour
Source: © PAINTING/Alamy Stock Photo

significant marker of Catholic identity that retained its popularity throughout Europe into the seventeenth century, and it certainly made a statement of Jane's piety.[129] Interestingly, the beautiful pearls that adorn her headdress, necklace, dress and around her waist are identical, indicating that they formed a matching set. The beads suspended from Jane's belt match several pairs that appear in her inventory, and serve to further accentuate her costume.[130] None of the other jewels she wears can be identified with those in her inventory.[131] This confirms that those in the portrait were a part of the queenly collection that were reserved for the most splendid occasions. Her clasped hands showcase her left hand on which she wears three rings. One diamond ring is similar to another worn by Kateryn Parr, while it is possible that, in keeping with the point raised in Chapter 1 about the preference for plain gold bands, the one worn on the third finger of Jane's left hand may be her wedding ring.[132] Above it she wears another gold ring containing what could be a ruby.[133] This may be a sign that Jane was demonstrating that she was a married woman, a state on which her status as queen depended. The most significant piece is the ouche she wears suspended from a necklace. It was evidently of value or held particular meaning, for Katherine Howard also chose to wear it in her portrait and it can be identified in both her inventory and that of Kateryn Parr.[134] In both Jane's portrait and that of Katherine Howard, the jewel appears in an open setting which touches the skin. Similarly, Kateryn Parr is portrayed wearing an opulent ouche in two of her portraits in the same manner.[135] That all three queens chose to wear their ouches in such a way could indicate that they were believed to have certain medicinal or healing properties, if the properties of the stone were able to touch the wearer.[136]

Another portrait of Jane served a more personal function and provides a sharp contrast to the magnificence conveyed by Holbein. Possibly commissioned by Jane's family either shortly before her death or shortly after, the image may have been ordered as a memorial.[137] The setting of the portrait supports this, for although Jane is dressed finely her jewels are restricted to two strings of pearls, creating an entirely different image to Holbein's masterpiece. This suggests that the portrait was not intended to impress in the same way as the Holbein likeness, and shows the impact that jewels had on accentuating the royal image and contributing to the aura of magnificence.

Given the duration of the reign of Anna of Cleves, it is unsurprising that no likenesses of her were painted during this period. Similarly, there are no definitive portraits of Katherine Howard, although for many years a portrait by Holbein in the National Portrait Gallery, based on an original in the Toledo Museum of Art, was believed to depict her.[138] In his 1910 article, Lionel Cust offered convincing evidence that Katherine was indeed the sitter, based among other things on the jewellery she wears, including a brooch designed by Holbein.[139] This jewel does not, though, appear in Katherine's inventory and the identification has since been disputed, while other sitters including Elizabeth Seymour and Frances Grey, Duchess of Suffolk have been suggested for this particular piece.[140]

Of all of Henry VIII's queens, it is Kateryn Parr of whom the most portraits survive. Kateryn was extremely fond of portraiture and commissioned more portraits of herself than any of her predecessors.[141] Perhaps more than any of them Kateryn was conscious of building an image, and Linda Porter has highlighted that there were more portraits of her than any other sixteenth-century queen other than her stepdaughter, Elizabeth I.[142] Like her royal husband, Kateryn understood that portraiture could be a tool for royal propaganda and took advantage of it. She was a great patron of artists, and among others patronised John Bettes and William Scrots, whose portrait of her survives.[143] This all serves to convey Kateryn's determination to be seen and remembered as an important consort in spite of the fact that she was not the mother of the King's heir – using her image as a means of showcasing her exalted status following her royal marriage and accentuating both her visibility and her regality.

The most impressive of Kateryn's portraits is the full-length once thought to be Lady Jane Grey, reidentified in 1996 (Figure 4.6).[144] Exemplifying Elena Woodacre's argument of the way in which image fashioning spoke directly to the ideals of

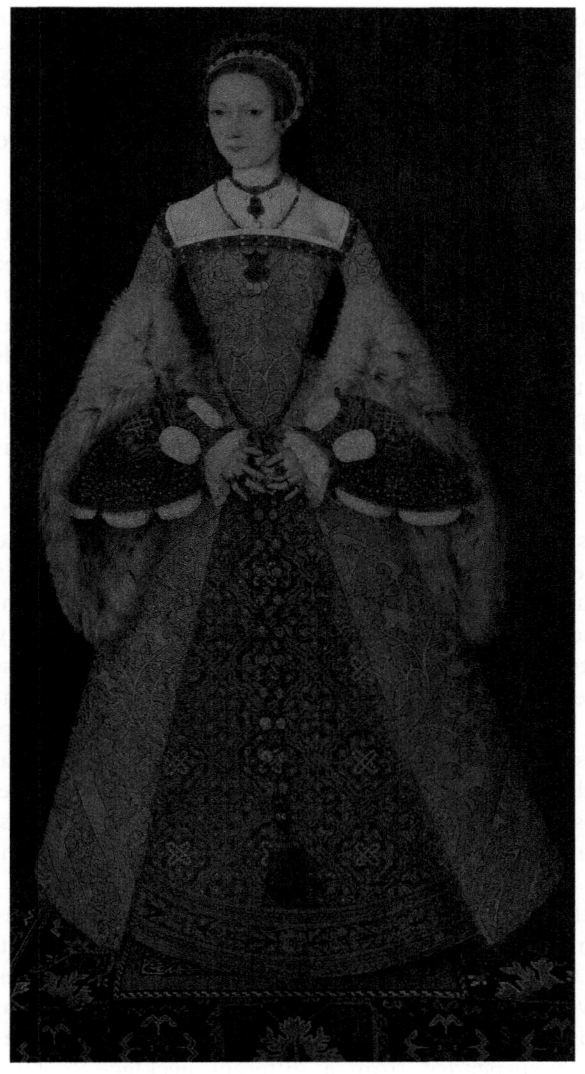

Figure 4.6 Kateryn Parr by Master John

Source: © PRISMA ARCHIVO/Alamy Stock Photo

queenship, whereby each queen sought to create an image that reflected these expectations as well as her own individual success, this is a statement piece in which Kateryn is dressed in the full finery of a queen of England.[145] Painted at the height of her reign in 1544–1545, perhaps to commemorate her regency during her husband's absence in France, Kateryn successfully presented herself as a magnificent queen. This is one of the most iconic and powerful images of a queen of England prior to the reign of Elizabeth I.[146] Retha Warnicke stressed that jewels were so essential to a queen's image that artists were expected to paint the jewels accurately.[147] This portrait provides exacting evidence of this, for the jewels worn by Kateryn exude her sovereignty. Not only are the jewels painted in enough detail to allow us to identify them among Kateryn's collection, but they also epitomise the developments that had taken place both in portraiture techniques and jewellery design since the fifteenth century.

The significance of Kateryn's crown ouche forms part of the discussion in Chapter 5, but there are other splendid pieces from the queenly collection that need to be considered. These include the magnificent beads suspended from her waist, which reveal antique faces reflective of contemporary trends. Kateryn was eager to be at the forefront of fashion, and thus it is no surprise that her jewels and her costume encapsulate this. By the same token, the six diamond rings she wears on her fingers display the latest styles in diamond cutting – Chapter 1 related that these were chiefly the table-cut and the pointed cut, which had evolved as the sixteenth century progressed.[148] Diamonds were also symbolic of fidelity, a particularly poignant message, given the adulterous behaviour of Kateryn's predecessor.[149]

Further evidence of the value Kateryn placed on the jewellery chosen for this image appears in the form of another portrait, in which she displayed many of the same pieces. This suggests that they were highly prized or favourites of hers. The second portrait, by William Scrots, shows Kateryn wearing the same ouche, although suspended from a different necklace.[150] The ouche matches the descriptions of three of those listed in her inventory, making it impossible to identify it further.[151] However, it is almost certainly the same ouche described in Katherine Howard's inventory as 'oone other Ooche of Golde wherin is averey feir large ruby and a rounde diamond with a verey feir peerle hangyng at the same'.[152] The importance that details such as the size, shape and cut of a gemstone have in identifying specific jewels cannot be underestimated.

One of the diamond rings Kateryn wears seems to match one in the Master John portrait, although it is worn on a different finger.[153] Kateryn is also shown wearing two ruby rings, thereby showcasing more pieces from her collection. Her fashion consciousness is exuded in this image, in which the design of her costume is completely different from that of her previous portrait and shows the style of clothing that other extant portraits confirm was popular in the 1540s. This could reflect Kateryn's desire to be seen as fashionable, characterised by her clothes and jewels. The detail with which her jewels have been painted provides a stark contrast to earlier paintings of queens. Not only are the more important pieces – the ouche and her necklace, beautifully painted, but so too are the aiglettes which adorn Kateryn's clothes. These are likely to be those described in her inventory as 'square Aglettes golde enameled blacke whereof xiiij paire euery of them hauing a Dyamounde at thone ende and thother xiiij euery of them a Rubie at thone ende'.[154]

Of all of the queens in this period, it is from Kateryn that the message of magnificence and a consciousness of the need to impress emerge most clearly. James went as far as to describe Kateryn as 'an aggressive patron' of portraiture.[155] With a line of predominantly unsuccessful predecessors before her, this may convey Kateryn's desire to be remembered in a more positive light – particularly following her success as regent in 1544. Moreover, as James has highlighted, with Henry VIII promoting Jane Seymour in his dynastic propaganda, Kateryn needed her own way of establishing herself as consort and thus began building her own 'independent mask of royalty'.[156] Portraiture, coupled with Kateryn's triumphal regency and her close relationship with Prince Edward, led her to hope that in the event of her husband dying while Edward was a minor, she would play a prominent role in his government.[157] Motherhood could consolidate a queen's position not only in her lifetime but also that of the next reign, and though Kateryn was not Edward's biological mother she hoped that this would be the case.[158] To her disappointment this never transpired, as she was not named to join the regency council set up by her husband to govern the young Edward VI in 1547.

The extant jewel inventories of Jane Seymour, Katherine Howard and Kateryn Parr reveal that the genres and quantities of jewels owned by queens were varied. Portraits do not, however, reflect all of the categories of jewels worn by queens, and this could in part be dictated by fashion. For example, pairs of bracelets appear in Kateryn Parr's inventory but are not portrayed on any of the queens during this period, primarily because as previously observed, long sleeves rendered them redundant.[159] Portraits of queens should not be taken as conclusive proof of all of the genres of jewels that were worn, but when coupled with surviving documentary evidence, they can be a useful way of visualising pieces that are described.

Miniatures

Miniatures first appeared at the French and English courts in the 1520s.[160] Unlike panel portraits, they generally served a more personal function as their portability allowed them to be carried around easily, or as Jones and Stallybrass related, actually 'turned the sitters into jewels'.[161] Indeed, it is Catherine of Aragon who is credited with the first known example of a miniature that could be worn as a jewel, appearing in the form of a tablet that featured portraits of the queen and Henry VIII.[162] Miniatures were always treasured objects and came into fashion with the court.[163] Contemporary miniatures of five of Henry VIII's queens survive, a testament to the popularity of this genre of portraiture. It was with the Fleming Lucas Horenbout, who along with his sister Susana, was patronised by Catherine of Aragon, that the tradition of miniatures in England began, and he was commissioned by Henry VIII to complete several miniatures of the royal family.[164] Appropriately these began with his patroness Catherine of Aragon, of whom two contemporary miniatures survive, almost certainly painted from life.[165]

The Latin inscription on the first miniature 'Katherine, his wife', suggests that it was one of a pair, the other one representing Henry VIII (Figure 4.7).[166] Catherine can be seen wearing a border of pearls, gold and diamonds, while the remainder of her jewels represent her piety. The brooch with the letters IHS – a transliteration of the first three letters of the name Jesus in Greek – and the necklace to which a tau cross is attached, were probably a deliberate choice by Catherine to convey her religious devotion and most particularly to the Observant Friars with whom both

Figure 4.7 Catherine of Aragon by Lucas Horenbout

Source: © The Print Collector/Alamy Stock Photo

pieces had associations. It is possible that the tau cross was the same as that which appears in miniatures of Jane Seymour and Kateryn Parr – it is certainly remarkably similar.[167] The crosses worn by the latter two queens show two fewer diamonds, yet they are otherwise identical in design and it has already been noted that it was not uncommon for jewels to be refashioned. Additionally, the same tau crosses worn by Jane Seymour and Kateryn Parr appear in both Kateryn and Katherine Howard's inventories.[168] This confirms that the cross was a part of the collection from at least the reign of Jane Seymour, and Susan James suggested that it may have been owned by Anne Boleyn.[169] It is equally likely that it originated with Catherine of Aragon.[170] If so, then it serves as further visual evidence that queens had access to the belongings of others, and there may be yet a further example of this. Although not identical, the IHS brooch worn by Catherine is similar to the one worn in Holbein's portrait of Jane Seymour.[171] Jane was known to be a great admirer of Catherine, in whose household she had once served.[172] If Jane's jewels had been deliberately chosen for their resemblance, it could reflect a desire to emulate the pious example of queenship that had been set by her former mistress.

Painted at a similar time, Horenbout's second miniature of Catherine portrays her in less elaborate jewellery.[173] She wears a border of pearls around her hood and a necklace of pearls, and is dressed simply in black. This miniature could have been intended to provide a contrast to the brighter, more elaborate costume and jewellery that appear in the first image, for Catherine is demurer in appearance. Horenbout's favour with the royal family was well known, for he painted not only Henry and Catherine but also their daughter Mary.[174] Mary's inclusion in Horenbout's family set indicates that they were intended to serve a more personal function and were perhaps suspended from jewellery. The cross pendant worn by the Princess appears to match the one listed in Mary's inventory, described as a 'Little Crosse wt iiij great Diamonds and oon great perle pendunte'.[175] The cross pendant and her necklace bear a striking resemblance to those she wears in 'The Family of Henry VIII', implying that they held some importance to her.[176]

The surviving miniature of Jane Seymour may have been a more personal piece.[177] This too could have been the work of Horenbout, but its history is unclear. The similarities between the tau crosses have been noted, but Jane also wears a jewelled necklace from which hangs a pendant. The pendant is similar to the one worn by Jane in her magnificent Holbein portrait, and it is possible that this miniature was based on that larger piece.[178] What is certain is that in the same way as the majority of Jane's other portraits, this one too shows her wearing the trappings of a queen of England.

Unlike paintings, it was common for miniatures to be painted in watercolour on vellum and then placed on playing cards.[179] This is the case with a piece by Holbein now in the Royal Collection, believed to be Katherine Howard (Figure 4.8).[180] It has been suggested that Holbein learned this art from Clouet, who also painted miniatures.[181] This is by no means certain, but if true it demonstrates a further link between the two artists. The existence of a copy of the miniature thought to be Katherine in the collection of the Duke of Buccleuch supports its identification, as there was clearly some demand for likenesses of the sitter.[182] As observed earlier in this chapter, portraiture of Katherine is controversial, and this heightens the important role that jewellery can play in aiding the identification of portraits.[183] Other sitters have been suggested, but that the jewellery can be identified with items in Katherine's collection and that of her successor is a strong indication that it is indeed Katherine.[184] Likewise, the richness of the clothes, including the fur sleeves, support this theory, and it has been proposed that this miniature was painted during her first winter as queen.[185] Moreover, some of the jewels also appear in portraits of Jane Seymour and Kateryn Parr. The splendid ouche that was owned by Jane Seymour for example, is seen, while several items in Katherine's inventory match the habillement that adorns her French hood.[186] It is, however, important to note that it was not until the eighteenth century that Katherine was first suggested as the sitter.[187]

Kateryn Parr had a fondness for miniatures, and in 1547 her fourth husband, Sir Thomas Seymour, wrote to her requesting 'one of your small pictures if ye have any left'.[188] It is possible

Figure 4.8 A lady thought to be Katherine Howard, by Hans Holbein
Source: © Art Collection 2/Alamy Stock Photo

that Kateryn was at least partly responsible for the patronage of the female miniaturist Levina Teerlinc, who enjoyed the support of Henry VIII and Elizabeth I.[189] Teerlinc's work is characterised by the small arms of the sitters, and this is apparent in her surviving miniature of Kateryn.[190] According to the miniature, the sitter's age at the time of painting was 32, in which case it dates to around 1544.[191] This is in keeping with the dates of several of Kateryn's portraits, and it is perfectly feasible that her regency could have prompted a flurry of images to mark the height of her reign. The surviving accounts for this period in her life, however, do not bear this out, suggesting that payments were made either by the King or in accounts of Kateryn's that have not survived.[192] This example shows Kateryn dressed sumptuously with splendid jewels. The tau cross was discussed previously, and there is a rich brooch pinned to her dress. Unfortunately, the image makes it difficult to determine whether the brooch matches any of those in Kateryn's inventory.

That Kateryn was active in ordering portraiture is clear, as her 1547 accounts show two items that seem to have been miniatures: first, 'Item to Lucas wife for makynge of the Quenes pykture and the Kynges'.[193] Second, 'to Hewe Hawarde for drawinge of the Kynges pyktures and the Quenes by the Quenes comaundement accordinge to Mr Secretoryes lettre'.[194] Although these pieces were paid for in 1547 after the King's death, they were almost certainly commissioned and received during his lifetime. Further evidence of Kateryn commissioning portrait cameos appears in Chapter 5, but these two examples provide the only direct documentary evidence we have for the patronage of queens and artists during this period. That Kateryn was ordering such items shows not only her great interest in art but also a determination to circulate her image as widely as possible.

Tomb Effigies

Walter Ullmann stated that a dead queen became a 'blank canvas on which to create an official image', and this is certainly true of Elizabeth of York.[195] She is the only queen in this period who has a contemporary tomb effigy. This is partly reflective of the circumstances in which the queens died: for example, as fallen queens found guilty of treason, there was no question of tombs being provided for Anne Boleyn and Katherine Howard, while Margaret of Anjou died in poverty in France. In other instances, like those of Anne Neville and Jane Seymour, it may have been the intention of their husbands to raise monuments to them at a later time.[196] Henry VIII certainly put plans in place for his own tomb, though at that time they included Catherine of Aragon.[197] Although Anna of Cleves was given the privilege of a burial in Westminster Abbey, where her tomb still survives, as a table-top design it never featured a likeness of her. Elsewhere, Kateryn

Parr's original tomb was destroyed during the English Civil War and was later replaced with an effigy designed by Sir George Gilbert Scott.[198] It therefore provides no evidence as to the way in which Kateryn was depicted after her death. By contrast, not only does Elizabeth of York's tomb effigy survive but so too does the head of her funeral effigy. This could have been based on a death mask, in which case it serves as reliable evidence that her surviving portraits do provide a relatively accurate likeness of the queen. The effigy was used in Elizabeth's funeral procession in 1503, but sadly the rest of the body was destroyed in 1941.[199] An account of Elizabeth's funeral relates that it was once adorned with a crown, sceptre and 'her fyngers well garneshed with rynge of gold and presyous stones'.[200] This would have served as a visual reminder of the magnificence of the queen even in death, for Laynesmith asserted that Elizabeth's funeral was a 'huge celebration of the wealth and prestige of Tudor kingship'.[201] This is confirmed by the entry in Henry VII's Chamber Books which notes the payment of £2832 7s. 3d. 'for thentirment of the Quenes grace', as well as other payments for her funeral expenses.[202]

The double tomb in Westminster Abbey that Elizabeth shares with her husband, Henry VII, further supports this image. Sculpted by the Florentine Pietro Torrigiano in the Italian Renaissance style, the tomb was completed by 1518.[203] The intention of the tomb was to highlight Elizabeth's importance as joint founder of the Tudor dynasty.[204] As such, although the effigy did once feature her crown, the emphasis is not on jewels.[205] Thus, it is unsurprising that none are included, and instead Elizabeth and her husband are shown with their hands raised in prayer. As the 'final expression of patronage, display, and ritual', a queen's tomb 'often becomes the most enduring expression of her image', and this is in evidence with Elizabeth.[206]

Conclusion

The surviving examples of portraits of queens – for some of which there are multiple versions – demonstrate a demand for portraits of the royal family that continued even after the death of the sitter, as the examples of Elizabeth of York and Jane Seymour confirm. The examples of the jewels queens wore in their portraits show how these items could be used to convey any message a queen chose, as well as enhancing her image. This would later become more apparent when Elizabeth I chose pearls in order to accentuate her image of virginity.[207] However, when studying the queens of this period, it is clear that they too wanted to convey their own messages. There is more evidence for this in the case of Henry VIII's wives, due to the advances in portraiture that allowed queens to be painted as individuals and in greater detail. For Catherine of Aragon and in some respects Jane Seymour too, the prominent message was that of piety – a crucial element of medieval queenship – while for Anne Boleyn, it was a sense of pride in her individual and familial identity. Finally, Kateryn Parr was eager to identify herself with the royal family into which she was married, and the magnificence of the queen's jewellery collection provided a tangible way for her to do so.

When combined with documentary evidence, portraits provide a powerful historical tool when studying the jewellery of the queens of England during this period, as well as the queens themselves. They not only allow us to track pieces, thereby making connections between individual queens, but provide visual evidence of the trends and the way in which queens wore jewels. They are a crucial source that allow us to witness first-hand the ways in which queens chose to style themselves. For not only did jewels serve to reinforce and accentuate a queen's status, they were also a visible sign of her wealth and splendour, and ultimately her character. As such, they were a fundamental part of her identity as a consort.

Notes

1 James, *Catherine Parr*, p. 119.
2 R. Strong, *Tudor and Jacobean Portraits*, I (London, 1969), p. 9.
3 T. Cooper, *A Guide to Tudor and Jacobean Portraits* (London, 2008), p. 6.
4 Reynolds, *Fine Style*, p. 8.
5 Ibid.
6 S. Greenblatt, *Renaissance Self-Fashioning: From More to Shakespeare* (Chicago, 1980), pp. 20–1.
7 See C.L. Howey, 'Dressing a Virgin Queen: Court Women, Dress, and Fashioning the Image of England's Queen Elizabeth I', *Early Modern Women*, 4 (2009), p. 201.

8 C. Lloyd, *The Royal Collection* (London, 1992), p. 261.

9 I. Wardropper, 'Between Art and Nature: Jewelry in the Renaissance', *Art Institute of Chicago Museum Studies*, 25 (2000), p. 7.

10 After Hans Holbein the Younger, 'Henry VIII', probably seventeenth century based on a work of 1536, NPG, NPG 157; BL, Add MS 7099, f. 4, 26; Starkey (ed.), *Inventory*, pp. 65–77.

11 Unknown Artist, John Rous, 'The Rous Roll', c. 1483–84, BL, Add MS 48976, f. 7cr; J. Cherry, *The Middleham Jewel and Ring* (York, 1994), p. 16.

12 Anderson Black, *History of Jewels*, p. 161.

13 D. Howarth, *Images of Rule* (Basingstoke, 1997), p. 107.

14 See R. Strong, *And When Did You Last See Your Father? The Victorian Painter and British History* (London, 1978).

15 De Cessolis, *Game and Playe*, pp. 26–30.

16 Unknown Artist, 'Edward IV, with Elizabeth Woodville, Edward V and Richard, Duke of Gloucester', c. 1477, Lambeth Palace Library, MS 265, f. 6v.

17 Benz, 'Queen Consort', p. 36; Unknown Artist, 'The Battle of Neville's Cross' in Jean Froissart, *Chroniques*, fourteenth century, Bibliothèque municipale de Besançon, Besançon, MS 864, f. 145v.

18 Unknown Artist, 'Elizabeth Wydeville', c. 1470, Worshipful Company of Skinners' Fraternity, Guildhall Library, MS 31692, f. 32v.

19 Unknown Artist, 'Richard II', c. 1390, Westminster Abbey. See F. Hepburn, *Portraits of the Later Plantagenets* (Woodbridge, 1986), p. 13.

20 Institute of Historical Research, 'Philippa of Hainault (1310/15–1369) and Richard II', https://archives.history.ac.uk/richardII/philippa.html

21 See A. Harvey and R. Mortimer (eds), *The Funeral Effigies of Westminster Abbey* (Woodbridge, 1994), pp. 41–2.

22 Pietro Da Milano, 'Marguerite d'Anjou', fifteenth century, Milan, gilt bronze, Victoria & Albert Museum (A. 182–1910).

23 Earenfight, *Queenship*, p. 185.

24 Earenfight, *Catherine of Aragon*, p. 10.

25 E.G. Barrett, 'Art and the Construction of Early Medieval Queenship: The Iconography of the Join Royal/Imperial Portrait and the visual Representation of the Ruler's Consort', unpublished PhD thesis, Courtauld Institute of Art, University of London, 1997.

26 Unknown Artist, 'Elizabeth Woodville', c. 1513–30, RCT, RCIN 406785; Unknown Artist, 'Elizabeth of York', sixteenth century, RCT, RCIN 403447.

27 See F. Zollner, *Michelangelo: The Complete Paintings, Sculptures and Arch* (Berlin, 2017).

28 J. Fletcher, 'Tree Ring Dates for Some Panel Paintings in England', *BM*, 166 (1974), pp. 250–8; 'Elizabeth Woodville (1437?-1492)',

www.royalcollection.org.uk; J. Scott, 'Painting from Life? Comments on the Date and Function of the Early Portraits of *Elizabeth Woodville* and *Elizabeth of York* in the Royal Collection', in H. Kleineke and C. Steer (eds), *The Yorkist Age* (Donington, 2013), p. 20.

29 Fletcher, 'Tree Ring Dates', p. 256; 'Elizabeth of York (1465–1503)', www.royalcollection.org.uk

30 M. Whinney, *Early Flemish Painting* (London, 1968), p. 23; James, *Feminine Dynamic*, p. 25.

31 Whinney, *Flemish Painting*, pp. 45, 23.

32 J. Pope-Hennessy, *The Portrait in the Renaissance* (London, 1966), pp. 30, 3.

33 Ibid, p. 41.

34 P. Tinagli, *Women in Italian Renaissance Art* (Manchester, 1997), p. 5.

35 P. Mellen, *Jean Clouet: Complete Edition of the Drawings, Miniatures and Paintings* (London, 1971), p. 18.

36 See A. Phipps Darr, 'Pietro Torrigiani and His Sculpture in Henrician England: Sources and Influences', in C.M. Sicca and L.A. Waldman (eds), *The Anglo-Florentine Renaissance: Art for the Early Tudors* (New Haven, 2012), pp. 49–50; A.E. Popham, 'Hans Holbein's Italian Contemporaries in England', *BM*, 84 (1944), pp. 12–15, 17.

37 L. Mansfield, 'Portraits of Eleanor of Austria: From Invisible to Inimitable French Queen Consort', in S. Broomhall (ed.), *Women and Power at the French Court, 1483–1563* (Amsterdam, 2018), p. 190.

38 Pope-Hennessy, *Portrait*, p. 187; Mellen, *Clouet*, pp. 11, 18.

39 Lloyd, *Royal Collection*, p. 257.

40 R. Tittler, *Portraits, Painters, and Publics in Provincial England, 1540–1640* (Oxford, 2012), p. 17.

41 P. Ganz, 'Holbein and Henry VIII', *BM*, 83 (1943), p. 269.

42 Tittler, *Portraits*, p. 31; Pope-Hennessy, *Portrait*, pp. 130–1.

43 There has been an abundance of scholarship about Holbein's work in England, much of which concerns itself with the identification of his portraits. Strong wrote several articles about the artist's presence in England, while Paul Ganz effectively placed Holbein into the context of sixteenth-century court painting, describing his position in Henry VIII's service as 'extraordinary and exceptional'. See Ganz, 'Hobein and Henry VIII', pp. 269–73; P. Ganz, 'Two Unpublished Portraits by Hans Holbein', *BM*, 20 (1911), pp. 31–3; P. Ganz, 'Henry VIII and His Court Painter, Hans Holbein', *BM*, 63 (1933), pp. 144–55; C. Winter, 'Holbein's Miniatures', *BM*, 83 (1943), pp. 266–9.
R. Strong, 'Holbein in England – I and II', *BM*, 109 (1967), pp. 276–81; R. Strong, 'Holbein in England – III to IV', *BM*, 109 (1967), pp. 698–703; Ganz, 'Holbein and Henry VIII', p. 269.

44 T. Cooper, 'Making Art in Tudor Britain: New Research on Paintings in the National Portrait Gallery', *British Art Journal*, 9 (2009), p. 6.
45 Benz, 'Queen Consort', p. 86.
46 J. Rowlands and D. Starkey, 'An Old Tradition Reasserted: Holbein's Portrait of Queen Anne Boleyn', *BM*, 125 (1983), p. 92.
47 Ibid, pp. 91–2. Ives also wrote on the subject of portraiture of Anne. See E. Ives, 'The Queen and the Painters: Anne Boleyn, Holbein and Tudor Royal Portraits', *Apollo*, 140 (1994), pp. 36–45.
48 See Hans Holbein, 'Oval pendant', c. 1532–43, British Museum, SL,5308.107; Hans Holbein, 'Design for a pendant', c. 1536–7, British Museum, SL,5308.117; Hans Holbein, 'Ring with crest', c. 1532–43, British Museum, SL,5308.78 for several examples of Holbein's designs.
49 Holbein, 'Jane Seymour', Kunsthistorisches Museum; Hans Holbein, 'Anne of Cleves', 1538, Louvre Museum, Paris, Inv. 1348; Holbein, 'Portrait of a Lady, perhaps Katherine Howard', RCT.
50 E. Auerbach, *Tudor Artists* (London, 1954), p. 49.
51 Ibid.
52 Ibid, p. 74.
53 F. Heal, *The Power of Gifts: Gift-Exchange in Early Modern England* (Oxford, 2014), pp. 164–5.
54 See Mansfield, 'Eleanor of Austria', in Broomhall (ed.), *Women and Power*, pp. 186–8.
55 P. Hacker and C. Kuhl, 'A Portrait of Anne of Cleves', *BM*, 134 (1992), p. 172.
56 Hans Holbein, 'Christina of Denmark, Duchess of Milan', 1538, National Gallery, NG2475; Holbein, 'Anne of Cleves', Louvre Museum; Amelia's portrait is lost.
57 Howarth, *Images*, p. 96.
58 *L & P*, xiv, part 2, no. 33.
59 Campbell, *Medieval Jewellery*, p. 96.
60 L. Campbell, *Renaissance Portraits: European Portrait-Painting in the 14th, 15th and 16th Centuries* (New Haven and London, 1990), p. 85.
61 Holbein also completed a miniature based on the same portrait. Hans Holbein, 'Box in the form of a rose, with a miniature portrait of Anne of Cleves', c. 1539, Victoria & Albert Museum, P. 153:1, 2–1910. See Hacker & Kuhl, 'A Portrait', pp. 172–5 for another portrait of Anna.
62 Warnicke, *Marrying of Anne of Cleves*, p. 131.
63 Ibid, p. 141.
64 Flemish School, 'The Family of Henry VII with St George and the Dragon', c. 1503–09, RCT, RCIN 401228.
65 J. Scott, *The Royal Portrait: Image and Impact* (London, 2010), p. 13.

66 C. Bolland and T. Cooper, *The Real Tudors: Kings and Queens Rediscovered* (London, 2014), p. 17.
67 J. Johnson, 'Elizabeth of York: Mother of the Tudor Dynasty', in L. Oakley-Brown and L.J. Wilkinson (eds), *The Rituals and Rhetoric of Queenship* (Dublin, 2009), pp. 48, 54.
68 Lloyd, *Royal Collection*, p. 257; K. Sharpe, *Selling the Tudor Monarchy: Authority and Image in Sixteenth-Century England* (London, 2009), p. 6.
69 Sharpe, *Tudor Monarchy*, p. 66; James, *Catherine Parr*, p. 119.
70 S. Anglo, *Images of Tudor Kingship* (London, 1992), p. 5.
71 Unknown Artist, 'Family of Henry VIII', RCT.
72 Lloyd, *Royal Collection*, p. 211.
73 J.M. Richards, 'Mary Tudor as 'Sole Quene?': Gendering Tudor Monarchy', *Historical Journal*, 40 (1997), p. 915.
74 Unknown Artist, 'Talbot Shrewsbury Book', 1445, BL, Royal MS 15 E. vi, f. 2v.
75 Earenfight, *Queenship*, p. 6.
76 De Cessolis, *Game and Playe*, p. 26.
77 Martial d'Auvergne, 'Marriage of Henry VI & Margaret of Anjou', *Vigiles de Charles VII*, c. 1475–1500, Bibliothèque Nationale de France, MS Français 5054, f. 126v.
78 Laynesmith, *Last Medieval Queens*, p. 52.
79 *CSPM*, i, no. 26.
80 Unknown Artist, 'The Prayer Roll of Margaret of Anjou', c. 1445–55, Bodleian Library, Jesus College, MS 124.
81 See S. Drimmer, 'Beyond Private Matter: A Prayer Roll for Queen Margaret of Anjou', *Gesta*, 53 (2014), p. 95.
82 Unknown Artist, 'Margaret of Anjou', c. 1475, Worshipful Company of Skinners' Fraternity, Guildhall Library, MS 31692, f. 34v.
83 Unknown Artist, 'Rous Roll', BL, Add MS 48976, f. 7cr; A. Sinclair (ed.), *The Beauchamp Pageant* (Donnington, 2003); BL, Cotton MS Julius E 1V, f. 28r; Unknown Artist, 'The Salisbury Roll', 1483–5, BL, Loan MS 90, f. 154r.
84 N. Pronay and J. Cox (eds), *The Crowland Chronicle Continuations: 1459–1486* (London, 1986), p. 175.
85 Hicks, *Anne Neville*, p. 21.
86 Scarisbrick, *Portrait Jewels*, p. 48.
87 Unknown Maker, 'Lead medal', 1534, lead, British Museum, M.9010; Rowlands & Starkey, 'Old Tradition', p. 91.
88 A. Fraser, *The Six Wives of Henry VIII* (London, 1992), p. 219.
89 Hayward, *Dress*, p. 48.
90 See Bernard, 'Anne Boleyn's Religion', pp. 1–20.
91 Cooper, 'Making Art', p. 3.
92 Hepburn, *Later Plantagenets*, p. 54.
93 W.A. Shaw, 'Early English School of Portraiture', *BM*, 65 (1934), p. 184.

94 See Baldwin, *Elizabeth Woodville*, p. 5.

95 The following provide a sample: Unknown Artist, 'Elizabeth Woodville', sixteenth century, Queen's College Cambridge, portrait 88; Unknown Artist, 'Elizabeth Woodville', late sixteenth century, RCT, RCIN 404744.

96 Unknown Artist, 'Elizabeth Woodville', RCT; Starkey (ed.), *Inventory*, p. 238.

97 Campbell, *Medieval Jewellery*, p. 36.

98 J. Litten, 'The Funeral Effigy: Its Function and Purpose', in Harvey and Mortimer (eds), *Funeral Effigies*, p. 48; Strong, *Tudor and Jacobean Portraits*, I, p. 34.

99 Starkey (ed.), *Inventory*, pp. 237, 384–5; Unknown Artist, 'Elizabeth of York', RCT, RCIN 403447.

100 Campbell, *Medieval Jewellery*, p. 96.

101 Ibid; De Cessolis, *Game and Playe*, pp. 26–30.

102 Campbell, *Medieval Jewellery*, p. 72; W. Campbell (ed.), *Materials for a History of the Reign of Henry VII from Original Documents Preserved in the Public Record Office*, 2 vols (London, 1873), I, p. 264.

103 Scott, 'Painting from Life?', in Kleineke and Steer (eds), *Yorkist Age*, pp. 24–5.

104 Unknown Artist, 'Henry VII', c. 1500, SoA, LDSAL 332; Bolland & Cooper, *Real Tudors*, pp. 16–17.

105 Hepburn, *Later Plantagenets*, p. 88.

106 Unknown Artist, 'Elizabeth of York', late sixteenth century, based on a work of c. 1500, NPG, NPG 311.

107 Michel Sittow, 'Mary Rose Tudor', c. 1514, Kunsthistorisches Museum, Vienna, Inv. No. 5612; M. Frinta, 'Observation on Michel Sittow, *Artibus et Historiae*, 30 (2009), pp. 147–51. Earenfight agrees that the sitter in the Sittow portrait may not be Catherine. See *Catherine of Aragon*, pp. 10–11.

108 *CSPS*, i, no. 439.

109 Earenfight, *Catherine of Aragon*, p. 8.

110 Unknown Artist, 'Catherine of Aragon', c. 1520, NPG, NPG L246.

111 Ibid.

112 J.G. Nichols, *Inventories of the Wardrobe, Plate, Chapel Stuff, Etc. of Henry Fitzroy, Duke of Richmond, and of the Wardrobe Stuff at Baynard's Castle of Katherine, Princess Dowager* (London, 1855), p. 38.

113 Earenfight, *Catherine of Aragon*, p. 125.

114 Campbell, *Medieval Jewellery*, p. 42.

115 Earenfight, *Catherine of Aragon*, p. 128.

116 Ibid, pp. 128, 127.

117 Unknown Artist, 'Anne Boleyn', late sixteenth century, based on a work of c. 1533–6, NPG, NPG 668; Ives, *Life and Death*, pp. 42–3.
118 Unknown Artist, 'Anne Boleyn' sixteenth century, NPG, NPG 4980(15); Unknown Artist, 'Anne Boleyn', sixteenth century, Hever Castle.
119 Anglo, *Tudor Kingship*, p. 117.
120 Unknown Artist, 'Anne Boleyn', sixteenth century, Nidd Hall; Unknown Artist, 'Family of Henry VIII', RCT.
121 BL, Stowe MS 559, f. 57r: 'two other laces conteignyng xxxi Table Rubyes and vjxx xvi ffeir peerlles'.
122 Unknown Artist, 'Family of Henry VIII', RCT.
123 Unknown Artist, 'Chequers Ring', sixteenth century, mother of pearl, gold, rubies, Chequers, Buckinghamshire.
124 James, *Feminine Dynamic*, p. 109.
125 See Collins (ed.), *Jewels and Plate*; BL, Stowe MS 555; BL, Stowe MS 556; Ives, *Life and Death*, p. 373.
126 Holbein, 'Jane Seymour', Kunsthistorisches Museum.
127 Hans Holbein, 'Queen Jane Seymour', c. 1536, RCT, RCIN 912267.
128 Mellen, *Clouet*, p. 29.
129 Phillips, *Jewels and Jewellery*, p. 36.
130 BL, Royal MS 7 C XVI, f. 18r-20r.
131 Ibid, f. 18r-31r.
132 Master John, 'Katherine Parr', NPG.
133 Tait (ed.), *7000 Years*, p. 239.
134 Holbein, 'Portrait of a Lady, perhaps Katherine Howard', RCT; BL, Stowe MS 559 f. 58v; SoA, MS 129, f. 178r.
135 Master John, 'Katherine Parr', NPG; Scrots, 'Katherine Parr', NPG.
136 Scarisbrick, *Tudor and Jacobean Jewellery*, p. 51.
137 Unknown Artist, 'Jane Seymour', c. 1536–40s, Weiss Gallery, London. See M. Weiss, *Tudor and Stuart Portraits* (London, 2012), pp. 16–18.
138 After Holbein, 'Unknown woman, formerly known as Catherine Howard', NPG; L. Cust, 'A Portrait of Queen Catherine Howard, by Hans Holbein the Younger', *BM*, 17 (1910), pp. 192–5. See also B. Dolman, 'Reading the Portraits of Henry VIII's Queens', in Lipscomb and Betteridge (eds), *Henry VIII and the Court*, p. 125.
139 Cust, 'Portrait of Queen Catherine', pp. 192–9.
140 Strong, *Tudor and Jacobean Portraits*, I, p. 43; Russell, *Young and Damned*, pp. 385–8.
141 James, *Catherine Parr*, p. 13.
142 Porter, *Katherine the Queen*, p. 155.

143 Scrots, 'Katherine Parr', NPG.
144 Master John, 'Katherine Parr', NPG; James, 'Lady Jane Grey or Queen Kateryn Parr?', pp. 20–4.
145 Woodacre, *Queens and Queenship*, p. 87.
146 See D. Starkey, *Elizabeth* (London, 2000), pp. 35–41; Warnicke, *Elizabeth of York*, p. 119.
147 Warnicke, *Elizabeth of York*, p. 85.
148 Campbell, *Medieval Jewellery*, p. 17; Tillander, *Diamond Cuts*, pp. 99–105.
149 Scarisbrick, *Rings*, p. 302.
150 Scrots, 'Katherine Parr', NPG.
151 Ibid.
152 BL, Stowe MS 559, f. 58v.
153 Master John, 'Katherine Parr', NPG; Scrots, 'Katherine Parr', NPG.
154 SoA, MS 129, f. 183v.
155 James, *Feminine Dynamic*, p. 29.
156 Ibid, pp. 143–4.
157 See James, *Catherine Parr*, pp. 256–7.
158 Woodacre, 'Introduction', in Woodacre and Fleiner (eds), *Royal Mothers*, p. 1.
159 SoA, MS 129, f. 183r-v.
160 Bolland and Cooper, *Real Tudors*, p. 45.
161 A.R. Jones and P. Stallybrass, *Renaissance Clothing and the Materials of Memory* (Cambridge, 2000), p. 41.
162 Earenfight, *Catherine of Aragon*, p. 147.
163 R. Strong, *Artists of the Tudor Court: The Portrait Miniature Rediscovered 1520–1620* (London, 1983), p. 9; M. Howard, *The Tudor Image* (London, 1995), p. 65.
164 Earenfight, *Catherine of Aragon*, p. 145; G. Reynolds, *The Sixteenth and Seventeenth Century Miniatures in the Collection of Her Majesty the Queen* (London, 1999), p. 13.
165 Lucas Horenbout, 'Katherine of Aragon', c. 1525, NPG, NPG 4682; Horenbout, 'Katherine of Aragon', NPG L244.
166 Horenbout, 'Katherine of Aragon', NPG 4682; Lucas Horenbout, 'Henry VIII', c. 1525–6, RCT, RCIN 420010.
167 Possibly Horenbout, 'Jane Seymour', sixteenth century, Sudeley Castle; Levina Teerlinc, 'Katherine Parr', c. 1544-5, Sudeley Castle.
168 SoA, MS 129, f. 178v; BL, Stowe MS 559, f. 59r.
169 BL, Royal MS 7 C XVI, f. 18r-31r; James, *Catherine Parr*, p. 104.
170 Lucas Horenbout, 'Katherine of Aragon', c. 1525, NPG, NPG 4682. A portrait of Catherine's daughter, Mary, painted by Hans Eworth in 1554 shows her wearing a tau cross, but the design differs slightly from Catherine's.
171 Holbein, 'Jane Seymour', Kunsthistorisches Museum.

172 Phillips, *Jewels and Jewellery*, p. 36.
173 Horenbout, 'Katherine of Aragon', NPG L244.
174 Lucas Horenbout, 'Queen Mary I', c. 1525, NPG, NPG 6453.
175 Madden (ed.), *Privy Purse Expenses*, p. 176.
176 Unknown Artist, 'Family of Henry VIII', RCT.
177 Possibly Horenbout, 'Jane Seymour', Sudeley Castle.
178 Holbein, 'Jane Seymour', Kunsthistorisches Museum.
179 Reynolds, *Miniatures*, p. 50.
180 Holbein, 'Portrait of a Lady, perhaps Katherine Howard', RCT.
181 Mellen, *Clouet*, p. 42.
182 Reynolds, *Miniatures*, p. 51.
183 See Russell, *Young and Damned*, pp. 383–91.
184 Reynolds, *Miniatures*, p. 52.
185 Denny, *Katherine Howard*, p. 175.
186 BL, Stowe MS 559, f. 58v, 55r-v.
187 J. Roberts (ed.), *Treasures: The Royal Collection* (London, 2008), p. 61.
188 *CSPD*, i, no. 27.
189 K. Coombs, *The Portrait Miniature in England* (London, 1995), p. 15.
190 Teerlinc, 'Katherine Parr', Sudeley Castle.
191 Ibid.
192 E 315/161; E 101/425/15; E 101/423/15.
193 E 315/340, f. 23v.
194 Ibid, f. 30r.
195 W. Ullmann (ed.), *Liber Regie Capelle* (London, 1961), p. 333.
196 See Laynesmith, *Last Medieval Queens*, p. 122.
197 C.M. Sicca, 'Pawns of International Finance and Politics: Florentine Sculptors at the Court of Henry VIII', *Renaissance Studies*, 20 (2006), pp. 1–34; G. Gentilini and T. Mozzatti, '"142 Life-size Figures . . . with the King on Horseback": Baccio Bandinelli's Mausoleum for Henry VIII', in C.M. Sicca and L.A. Waldman (eds), *The Anglo-Florentine Renaissance: Art for the Early Tudors* (New Haven, 2012), p. 214.
198 Porter, *Katherine the Queen*, p. 343.
199 Litten, 'The Funeral Effigy', p. 6.
200 College of Arms, MS I.ii, f. 27r-32r.
201 Laynesmith, *Last Medieval Queens*, p. 127.
202 BL, Add MS 7099, f. 82; BL, Add MS 59899, f. 15r.
203 Phipps Darr, 'Pietro Torrigiani', pp. 49–51.
204 Howarth, *Images of Rule*, p. 156.
205 F. Sandford, *A Genealogical History of the Kings and Queens of England, and Monarchs of Great Britain, &c. from the Conquest, Anno 1066, to the Year 1677* (London, 1677), no page number.
206 Woodacre, *Queens and Queenship*, p. 116.
207 See Howey, 'Dressing a Virgin Queen', p. 203.

References

Manuscript Sources

Kew, The National Archives

EXCHEQUER

E 101 King's Remembrancer, Various Accounts.
E 315 Court of Augmentations and Predecessors, Miscellaneous Books.

LONDON, THE BRITISH LIBRARY

Additional Manuscripts	7099, 59899.
Cotton Manuscripts	Julius E 1V.
Royal Manuscripts	7 C XVI.
Stowe Manuscripts	555, 556, 559.

LONDON, COLLEGE OF ARMS

MS I. ii Account of the Funeral of Elizabeth of York.

LONDON, SOCIETY OF ANTIQUARIES

MS 129 Inventory of King Henry VIII.

Portraits

After Hans Holbein the Younger, 'Henry VIII', probably seventeenth century based on a work of 1536, NPG, NPG 157.

After Hans Holbein the Younger, 'Unknown woman, formerly known as Catherine Howard', late seventeenth century, NPG, NPG 1119.

Flemish School, 'The Family of Henry VII with St George and the Dragon', c. 1503–9, RCT, RCIN 401228.

Hans Holbein, 'Anne of Cleves', 1538, Louvre Museum, Paris, Inv. 1348.

Hans Holbein, 'Box in the form of a rose, with a miniature portrait of Anne of Cleves', c. 1539, Victoria & Albert Museum, P. 153:1, 2–1910.

Hans Holbein, 'Christina of Denmark, Duchess of Milan', 1538, National Gallery, NG2475.

Hans Holbein, 'Design for a pendant', c. 1536–7, British Museum, SL,5308.117.

Hans Holbein, 'Jane Seymour', 1536–7, Kunsthistorisches Museum, Vienna, Inv. No. 881.

Hans Holbein, 'Oval pendant', c. 1532–43, British Museum, SL,5308.107.

Hans Holbein, 'Portrait of a Lady, perhaps Katherine Howard', c. 1540, RCT, RCIN 422293.

Hans Holbein, 'Queen Jane Seymour', c. 1536, RCT, RCIN 912267.

Hans Holbein, 'Ring with crest', c. 1532–43, British Museum, SL,5308.78.

Levina Teerlinc, 'Katherine Parr', c. 1544–5, Sudeley Castle.

Lucas Horenbout, 'Henry VIII', c. 1526–7, RCT, RCIN 420010.

Lucas Horenbout, 'Katherine of Aragon', c. 1525, NPG, NPG 4682.

Lucas Horenbout, 'Katherine of Aragon', c. 1525–6, NPG, NPG L244.

Lucas Horenbout, 'Queen Mary I', c. 1525, NPG, NPG 6453.

Martial d'Auvergne, 'Marriage of Henry VI & Margaret of Anjou', *Vigiles de Charles VII*, c. 1475–1500, Bibliothèque Nationale de France, MS Français 5054, f. 126v.

Master John, 'Katherine Parr', c. 1544–5, NPG, NPG 4451.

Michel Sittow, 'Mary Rose Tudor', c. 1514, Kunsthistorisches Museum, Vienna, Inv. No. 5612.

Possibly Lucas Horenbout, 'Jane Seymour', sixteenth century, Sudeley Castle.

Unknown Artist, 'Anne Boleyn', late sixteenth century, based on a work of c. 1533–6, NPG, NPG 668.

Unknown Artist, 'Anne Boleyn', sixteenth century, Hever Castle.

Unknown Artist, 'Anne Boleyn', sixteenth century, Nidd Hall.

Unknown Artist, 'Anne Boleyn', sixteenth century, NPG, NPG 4980(15).

Unknown Artist, 'Catherine of Aragon', c. 1520, NPG, NPG L246.

Unknown Artist, 'Edward IV, with Elizabeth Woodville, Edward V and Richard, Duke of Gloucester', c. 1477, Lambeth Palace Library, MS 265, f. 6v.

Unknown Artist, 'Elizabeth of York', late sixteenth century, based on a work of c. 1500, NPG, NPG 311.

Unknown Artist, 'Elizabeth of York', sixteenth century, RCT, RCIN 403447.

Unknown Artist, 'Elizabeth Woodville', c. 1513–30, RCT, RCIN 406785.

Unknown Artist, 'Elizabeth Woodville', late sixteenth century, RCT, RCIN 404744.

Unknown Artist, 'Elizabeth Woodville', sixteenth century, Queen's College, Cambridge, portrait 88.

Unknown Artist, 'Elizabeth Wydeville', c. 1470, Worshipful Company of Skinners' Fraternity, Guildhall Library, MS 31692, f. 32v.

Unknown Artist, 'Henry VII', c. 1520–40, SoA, LDSAL 332.

Unknown Artist, 'Jane Seymour', c. 1536–40s, Weiss Gallery, London.

Unknown Artist, John Rous, 'The Rous Roll', c. 1483–84 BL, Add MS 48976, f. 7cr.

Unknown Artist, 'Katherine of Aragon', c. 1520, NPG, NPG L246.

Unknown Artist, 'Margaret of Anjou', c. 1475, Worshipful Company of Skinners' Fraternity, Guildhall Library, MS 31692, f. 34v.

Unknown Artist, 'Richard II', c. 1390, Westminster Abbey.

Unknown Artist, 'Talbot Shrewsbury Book', 1445, BL, Royal MS 15 E. vi, f. 2v.

Unknown Artist, 'The Battle of Neville's Cross' in Jean Froissart, *Chroniques*, fourteenth century, Bibliothèque municipale de Besançon, Besançon, MS 864, f. 145v.

Unknown Artist, 'The Family of Henry VIII', c. 1545, RCT. RCIN 405796.

Unknown Artist, 'The Prayer Roll of Margaret of Anjou', c. 1445–55, Bodleian Library, Jesus College, MS 124.

Unknown Artist, 'The Salisbury Roll', 1483–5, BL, Loan MS 90, f. 154r.

William Scrots, 'Katherine Parr', late sixteenth century, NPG, NPG 4618.

Physical Objects

Pietro Da Milano, 'Marguerite d'Anjou', fifteenth century, Milan, gilt bronze, Victoria & Albert Museum (A. 182–1910).

Unknown Artist, 'Chequers Ring', sixteenth century, mother of pearl, gold, rubies, Chequers, Buckinghamshire.

Unknown Maker, 'Lead medal', 1534, lead, British Museum, M.9010.

Printed Primary Sources

Bergenroth, G.A., et al., (ed.), *Calendar of State Papers, Spain*, 13 vols (London, 1862–1954).

Brewer, J.S., (ed.), *Letters and Papers, Foreign and Domestic, of the Reign of Henry VIII, 1509–47*, 21 vols and addenda (London, 1862–1932).

Campbell, W., (ed.), *Materials for a History of the Reign of Henry VII from Original Documents Preserved in the Public Record Office*, 2 vols (London, 1873).
Collins, A.J., (ed.), *Jewels and Plate of Queen Elizabeth I: The Inventory of 1574* (London, 1955).
De Cessolis, J., *The Game and Playe of the Chesse*, ed. Adams, J., (Kalamazoo, 2009).
Hinds, A.B., (ed.), *Calendar of State Papers and Manuscripts in the Archives and Collections of Milan 1385–1618*, 1 vol (London, 1912).
Lemon, R., (ed.), *Calendar of State Papers, Domestic: Edward VI, Mary and Elizabeth* (London, 1856).
Madden, F., (ed.), *Privy Purse Expenses of the Princess Mary* (London, 1831).
Nichols, J.G., (ed.), *Inventories of the Wardrobe, Plate, Chapel Stuff, etc. of Henry Fitzroy, Duke of Richmond, and of the Wardrobe Stuff at Baynard's Castle of Katherine, Princess Dowager* (London, 1855).
Pronay, N., and Cox, J., (eds), *The Crowland Chronicle Continuations: 1459–1486* (London, 1986).
Starkey, D., (ed.), *The Inventory of King Henry VIII: The Transcript*, trans. Ward, P. (London, 1998).
Ullmann, W., (ed.), *Liber Regie Capelle* (London, 1961).

Secondary Sources

Anderson Black, J., *A History of Jewels* (London, 1974).
Anglo, S., *Images of Tudor Kingship* (London, 1992).
Auerbach, E., *Tudor Artists* (London, 1954).
Baldwin, D., *Elizabeth Woodville: Mother of the Princes in the Tower* (Stroud, 2002).
Barrett, E.G., 'Art and the Construction of Early Medieval Queenship: The Iconography of the Join Royal/Imperial Portrait and the Visual Representation of the Ruler's Consort', unpublished PhD thesis, Courtauld Institute of Art, University of London, 1997.
Benz, L., 'Queen Consort, Queen Mother: The Power and Authority of Fourteenth Century Plantagenet Queens', unpublished PhD thesis, University of York, 2009.
Bernard, G.W., 'Anne Boleyn's Religion', *Historical Journal*, 36 (1993), pp. 1–20.
Bolland, C., and Cooper, T., *The Real Tudors: Kings and Queens Rediscovered* (London, 2014).

Campbell, L., *Renaissance Portraits: European Portrait-Painting in the 14th, 15th and 16th Centuries* (New Haven and London, 1990).
Campbell, M., *Medieval Jewellery* (London, 2009).
Cherry, J., *The Middleham Jewel and Ring* (York, 1994).
Coombs, K., *The Portrait Miniature in England* (London, 1995).
Cooper, T., 'Making art in Tudor Britain: New Research on Paintings in the National Portrait Gallery', *British Art Journal*, 9 (2009), pp. 3–11.
Cooper, T., *A Guide to Tudor and Jacobean Portraits* (London, 2008).
Cust, L., 'A Portrait of Queen Catherine Howard, by Hans Holbein the Younger', *BM*, 17 (1910), pp. 192–5, 199.
Denny, J., *Katherine Howard: A Tudor Conspiracy* (London, 2005).
Dolman, B., 'Reading the Portraits of Henry VIII's Queens', in Lipscomb, S., and Betteridge, T. (eds), *Henry VIII and the Court: Art, Politics and Performance* (Farnham, 2013), pp. 115–30.
Drimmer, S., 'Beyond Private Matter: A Prayer Roll for Queen Margaret of Anjou', *Gesta*, 53 (2014), pp. 95–120.
Earenfight, T., *Catherine of Aragon: Infanta of Spain, Queen of England* (Pennsylvania, 2021).
Earenfight, T., *Queenship in Medieval Europe* (Basingstoke, 2013).
Fletcher, J., 'Tree Ring Dates for Some Panel Paintings in England', *BM*, 116 (1974), pp. 250–8.
Fraser, A., *The Six Wives of Henry VIII* (London, 1992).
Frinta, M., 'Observation on Michel Sittow', *Artibus et Historiae*, 30 (2009), pp. 147–51.
Ganz, P., 'Henry VIII and His Court Painter, Hans Holbein', *BM*, 63 (1933), pp. 144, 146, 148–51, 154–5.
Ganz, P., 'Holbein and Henry VIII', *BM*, 83 (1943), pp. 269–73.
Ganz, P., 'Two Unpublished Portraits by Hans Holbein', *BM*, 20 (1911), pp. 31–3.
Gentilini, G., and Mozzatti, T., ' "142 Life-size Figures . . . with the King on Horseback": Baccio Bandinelli's Mausoleum for Henry VIII', in Sicca, C.M., and Waldman, L.A. (eds), *The Anglo-Florentine Renaissance: Art for the Early Tudors* (New Haven, 2012), pp. 203–34.
Greenblatt, S., *Renaissance Self-Fashioning: From More to Shakespeare* (Chicago, 1980).
Hacker, P., and Kuhl, C., 'A Portrait of Anne of Cleves', *BM*, 134 (1992), pp. 172–5.
Harvey, A., and Mortimer, R., (eds), *The Funeral Effigies of Westminster Abbey* (Woodbridge, 1994).
Hayward, M., *Dress at the Court of King Henry VIII* (Leeds, 2007).

Heal, F., *The Power of Gifts: Gift-Exchange in Early Modern England* (Oxford, 2014).

Hepburn, F., *Portraits of the Later Plantagenets* (Woodbridge, 1986).

Hicks, M., *Anne Neville: Queen to Richard III* (Stroud, 2007).

Howard, M., *The Tudor Image* (London, 1995).

Howarth, D., *Images of Rule* (Basingstoke, 1997).

Howey, C.L., 'Dressing a Virgin Queen: Court Women, Dress, and Fashioning the Image of England's Queen Elizabeth I', *Early Modern Women*, 4 (2009), pp. 201–8.

Institute of Historical Research, 'Philippa of Hainault (1310/15–1369) and Richard II', https://archives.history.ac.uk/richardII/philippa.html

Ives, E.W., *The Life and Death of Anne Boleyn* (Oxford, 2004).

Ives, E.W., 'The Queen and the painters: Anne Boleyn, Holbein and Tudor Royal Portraits', *Apollo*, 140 (1984), pp. 49–56.

James, S.E., *Catherine Parr: Henry VIII's Last Love* (Stroud, 2008).

James, S.E., 'Lady Jane Grey or Queen Kateryn Parr?' *BM*, 138 (1996), pp. 20–4.

James, S.E., *The Feminine Dynamic in English Art, 1485–1603: Women as Consumers, Patrons and Painters* (Abingdon, 2009).

Johnson, J., 'Elizabeth of York: Mother of the Tudor Dynasty', in Oakley-Brown, L., and Wilkinson, L.J. (eds), *The Rituals and Rhetoric of Queenship* (Dublin, 2009), pp. 47–58.

Jones, A.R., and Stallybrass, P., *Renaissance Clothing and the Materials of Memory* (Cambridge, 2000).

Laynesmith, J., *The Last Medieval Queens* (Oxford, 2004).

Litten, J., 'The Funeral Effigy: Its Function and Purpose', in Harvey, A., and Mortimer, R. (eds), *The Funeral Effigies of Westminster Abbey* (Woodbridge, 1994), pp. 3–19.

Lloyd, C., *The Royal Collection* (London, 1992).

Mansfield, L., 'Portraits of Eleanor of Austria: From Invisible to Inimitable French Queen Consort', in Broomhall, S. (ed.), *Women and Power at the French Court, 1483–1563* (Amsterdam, 2018).

Mellen, P., *Jean Clouet: Complete Edition of the Drawings, Miniatures and Paintings* (London, 1971).

Phillips, C., *Jewels and Jewellery* (London, 2000).

Phipps Darr, A., 'Pietro Torrigiani and His Sculpture in Henrician England: Sources and Influences', in Sicca, C.M., and Waldman, L.A. (eds), *The Anglo-Florentine Renaissance: Art for the Early Tudors* (New Haven, 2012), pp. 49–80.

Pope-Hennessy, J., *The Portrait in the Renaissance* (London, 1966).

Popham, A.E., 'Hans Holbein's Italian Contemporaries in England', *BM*, 84 (1944), pp. 12–7.

Porter, L., *Katherine the Queen : The Remarkable Life of Katherine Parr* (London, 2011).

Reynolds, A., *In Fine Style: The Art of Tudor and Stuart Fashion* (London, 2013).

Reynolds, G., *The Sixteenth and Seventeenth Century Miniatures in the Collection of Her Majesty the Queen* (London, 1999).

Richards, J.M., 'Mary Tudor as 'Sole Quene?': Gendering Tudor Monarchy', *Historical Journal*, 40 (1997), pp. 895–924.

Roberts, J., (ed.), *Treasures: The Royal Collection* (London, 2008).

Rowlands, J., and Starkey, D., 'An Old Tradition Reasserted: Holbein's Portrait of Queen Anne Boleyn', *BM*, 125 (1983), pp. 88–92.

Russell, G., *Young and Damned and Fair: The Life and Tragedy of Catherine Howard at the Court of Henry VIII* (London, 2017).

Sandford, F., *A Genealogical History of the Kings and Queens of England, and Monarchs of Great Britain, &c. from the Conquest, Anno 1066, to the Year 1677* (London, 1677).

Scarisbrick, D., *Historic Rings: Four Thousand Years of Craftsmanship* (Tokyo, 2004).

Scarisbrick, D., *Portrait Jewels: Opulence and Intimacy from the Medici to the Romanovs* (London, 2011).

Scarisbrick, D., *Rings: Jewelry of Power, Love and Loyalty* (London, 2007).

Scarisbrick, D., *Tudor and Jacobean Jewellery* (London, 1995).

Scott, J., 'Painting from Life? Comments on the Date and Function of the Early Portraits of *Elizabeth Woodville* and *Elizabeth of York* in the Royal Collection', in Kleineke, H., and Steer, C. (eds), *The Yorkist Age* (Donington, 2013), pp. 18–26.

Scott, J., *The Royal Portrait: Image and Impact* (London, 2010).

Sharpe, K., *Selling the Tudor Monarchy: Authority and Image in Sixteenth-Century England* (London, 2009).

Shaw, W.A., 'The Early English School of Portraiture', *BM*, 65 (1934), pp. 171–84.

Sicca, C.M., 'Pawns of International Finance and Politics: Florentine Sculptors at the Court of Henry VIII', *Renaissance Studies*, 20 (2006).

Sinclair, A., (ed.), *The Beauchamp Pageant* (Donington, 2003).

Starkey, D., *Elizabeth* (London, 2000).

Strong, R., *And When Did You Last See Your Father? The Victorian Painter and British History* (London, 1978).

Strong, R., *Artists of the Tudor Court: The Portrait Miniature Rediscovered 1520–1620* (London, 1983).

Strong, R., 'Holbein in England-I and II', *BM*, 83 (1967), pp. 276–81.

Strong, R., 'Holbein in England-III to IV', *BM*, 109 (1967), pp. 698–703.

Strong, R., *Lost Treasures of Britain* (London, 1990).

Strong, R., *Tudor and Jacobean Portraits*, 2 vols (London, 1969).

Tait, H., (ed.), *7000 Years of Jewellery* (London, 1986).

Tillander, H., *Diamond Cuts in Historic Jewellery 1381–1910* (London, 1995).

Tinagli, P., *Women in Italian Renaissance Art* (Manchester, 1997).

Tittler, R., *Portraits, Painters, and Publics in Provincial England, 1540–1640* (Oxford, 2012).

Wardropper, I., 'Between Art and Nature: Jewelry in the Renaissance', *Art Institute of Chicago Museum Studies*, xxv (2000), pp. 6–15, 104.

Warnicke, R.M., *Elizabeth of York and Her Six Daughters-in-Law* (Basingstoke, 2017).

Warnicke, R.M., *The Marrying of Anne of Cleves: Royal Protocol in Tudor England* (Cambridge, 2004).

Weiss, M., *Tudor and Stuart Portraits* (London, 2012).

Whinney, M., *Early Flemish Painting* (London, 1968).

Winter, C., 'Holbein's Miniatures', *BM*, 83 (1943), pp. 266–9.

Woodacre, E., 'Introduction', in Woodacre, E., and Fleiner, C. (eds), *Royal Mothers and Their Ruling Children: Wielding Political Authority from Antiquity to the Early Modern Era* (Basingstoke, 2015), pp. 1–7.

Woodacre, E., *Queens and Queenship* (Leeds, 2021).

Zollner, F., *Michelangelo: The Complete Paintings, Sculptures and Arch* (Berlin, 2017).

5 Goldsmiths and Commissioning Jewels

In 1534 the Imperial ambassador wrote to his master of Henry VIII, 'This king is getting plate of all sorts manufactured, and all the goldsmiths are fully occupied'.[1] For many centuries, there has been a natural connection between the royal court and goldsmiths, and given the penchant for jewels among monarchs and their consorts, royal patronage was crucial.[2] As Maria Hayward has highlighted though, the words 'goldsmith' and 'jeweller' were often interchangeable during this period, and there are examples of both titles being applied to the same person.[3] Monarchs were credited with starting new trends, and the court was at the very centre of fashion, thus providing the ideal outlet for goldsmiths to showcase their work in the hope of securing preferment.[4] As this chapter will demonstrate, kings and queens often had favoured goldsmiths who fulfilled a variety of tasks on behalf of their royal patrons besides creating jewellery.[5] In 1510 for example, Robert Amadas, later Henry VIII's Master of the Jewels, was paid £100 for 'goldsmith's work upon 100 guard jackets', while in 1543 Henry Coldewell was commissioned 'for the impression and making of the great seal and the privy seal of the Court'.[6] The role of the goldsmith could be diverse, and they were often on hand to create special commissions. In order to provide their services to a wider range of people though, goldsmiths also sold smaller, less bespoke items in their shops.[7] This chapter will contextualise the prominence and the role of the goldsmith in the fifteenth and sixteenth centuries, underlining their importance as key figures in the lives of queens. It then

DOI: 10.4324/9781003202592-6

examines the jewels that queens commissioned, seeking to show that it was a regular occurrence for them to employ the services of goldsmiths to create items, for either themselves or others. This in turn accentuated the power that queens wielded over the creation of their own image and the jewels that they chose in order to project their sovereignty.

Goldsmiths

In 1327 the Goldsmiths' Company was founded in London as a guild for the goldsmith trade, but that same century the sumptuary laws had stipulated that the wearing of gold jewellery was limited to the noblest sections of society, thereby maintaining a social hierarchy in terms of display.[8] The result was that the majority of commissions a goldsmith received came from either royalty or the nobility, placing a high level of dependence on these clients. The work of Jessica Lutkin has shown that Henry IV had a great interest in luxury items and spent large sums on goods from goldsmiths.[9] This was continued by his successors, but by the end of the fifteenth century attitudes towards the sumptuary laws had begun to change: other levels of society adorned themselves with jewellery, thereby broadening a goldsmith's potential clientele. Even so, personal commissions were still much in evidence at the royal court, bringing queens into regular contact with the craftsmen. Thus, as Samantha Harper has rightly argued, members of the Goldsmiths' Company enjoyed better access to court than many merchants of other trades, as a result of the valuable nature of the goods that they sold.[10] Harper also highlighted that goldsmiths – unlike other tradesmen – were likely to have personal interaction with the monarch in order to discuss the specifications of commissions.[11]

There is evidence that Jane Seymour and Kateryn Parr chose to employ one goldsmith, Peter Richardson, while the accounts of Elizabeth of York show that in the final year of her life she employed several, including gentlemen named Lybart, Henry Wurley, John Vandelf and Alexander Hove.[12] Similarly, the accounts of Anna of Cleves reveal that she employed the services of a number of goldsmiths, including Peter Richardson, Cornelius Hayes, Robert Cooper and John Hawes.[13] The employment of numerous goldsmiths by these two queens indicates that they played an integral role in their lives, thereby confirming that queens employed the services of goldsmiths on a regular basis. In a further sign of great favour, on one occasion Elizabeth of York made a gift of a buck to two of her goldsmiths, John Vandelf and Lybart.[14]

London was the chief centre for jewellery production in England, followed by York, Chester, Norwich and Exeter.[15] This meant that quality pieces were available across the country, but there was a high concentration of goldsmiths in London, where the goldsmiths' quarter was on Foster Lane, off Cheapside.[16] Some of the most prominent goldsmiths of the period, including Bartholomew Rede, John Shaa and Robert Amadas – all of whom worked for either Edward IV, Richard III, Henry VII or Henry VIII – had shops in Cheapside.[17] The reign of Edward IV had a profound impact on jewellery production and the goldsmiths' trade as a result of the Common Seal that was granted to the Goldsmiths' Company by the King in 1462.[18] This ensured that the eminence of goldsmiths and their industry continued to rise, for the Company had the power to inspect and regulate all gold and silver in the City of London and appointed wardens to oversee this.[19] As such, in 1469 there were as many as 112 foreign master goldsmiths recognised as such, all of whose names appear in the Goldsmiths' Company records.[20] This number confirms the importance of the goldsmith trade to the royal court.

The leading goldsmith of the sixteenth century was acknowledged to be the Italian Benvenuto Cellini, who enjoyed the patronage of the French King François I.[21] At the English court it was also far from unusual for foreign-born goldsmiths to be employed alongside English ones, several of whom worked for consecutive monarchs. Matthew Philip, goldsmith to Henry VI and Margaret of Anjou, provided plate for the coronation of Elizabeth Wydeville, while Hugh Brice had worked for Edward IV and later served Henry VII.[22] Similarly, it was not uncommon for patronage to pass between members of the same family.

Elizabeth Wydeville's surviving accounts name John Amadas as her goldsmith, while his nephew Robert Amadas later became goldsmith to both Henry VII and Henry VIII, and Master of the Jewels.[23] Numerous examples of family members apprenticed to goldsmiths appear in the Goldsmiths' Company books, evidence that this was not unusual.[24]

More than 12 goldsmiths are listed in Henry VII's Chamber Books, including Robert Amadas, John Vandelf, John Shaa and Bartholomew Rede.[25] Several of these were particularly prominent members of the King's court, who all served as royal servants, and some became Mayor of London.[26] Rede also served as a warden of the Goldsmiths' Company, ensuring that high standards were being met within the trade.[27] Such positions show both the diversity of a goldsmith's role and the status with which they were afforded.

Henry VIII also employed a number of goldsmiths, including Peter Van Utricke who hailed from Antwerp.[28] Cornelius Hayes, whose work will be discussed shortly, was highly favoured, while from 1539 Morgan Wolf was given the title of 'the King's Goldsmith'.[29] Neither was it purely goldsmiths who received royal patronage: from at least 1539 to 1545, Henry VIII appointed Richard Atsyll as his official 'graver of precious stones' – Atsyll was also referred to as 'polisher of stones'.[30] Likewise, Alard Plomer or Plomyer, a French jeweller referenced in Chapter 1 in relation to the recasting of part of Jane Seymour's collection, was called 'the King's jeweller' in 1542.[31] He also undertook work for Anna of Cleves.

As well as employing goldsmiths at court, Henry VII and Henry VIII both purchased jewels from goldsmiths abroad.[32] Paris was the largest centre for goldsmiths north of the Alps, with many goldsmiths' shops located near Notre Dame, while Bruges was another important European magnet.[33] Florence, Venice and Prague were also prominent, showing a broad European demographic.[34] Frustratingly, the names of the goldsmiths from whom the kings purchased their jewels are often absent, and Henry VII's Chamber Books contain frequent references to 'a Jueller of Fraunce', or on one occasion to 'Piers Danyell

Jueller off Fraunce', for 'Juelles and other stuff'.[35] Other payments show that he paid for 'certain Juelx bought beyonde the See', while in December 1505 he 'sent over the see in Fraunce and Flaundres for to be emploied vpon certen Juelles and plate'.[36] These examples demonstrate the developments in trade and the European centres for jewellery production to which the court had access. There is no evidence that queens followed the examples set by their husbands in this regard, though they were certainly exposed to and patronised foreign goldsmiths in England.[37]

Commissioning Jewels

The accounts of Edward IV, Henry VII and Henry VIII all reflect their passion for the jewels that were worn to accentuate their wealth and majesty.[38] Those of Henry VII and Henry VIII show that they often bought large quantities of jewels at a time, some of which are likely to have been intended for their wives. Margaret Howell suggested that buying jewels in quantity related to a deep-rooted social convention in the life of the royal court.[39] There is certainly evidence to support this in the accounts of Henry VII; Timothy Schroder has emphasised that the king spent £200,000 on plate and jewels in the period from 1492 to 1509.[40] This was done at regular intervals and often to mark specific occasions when the splendour of the monarchy needed to be underlined. In 1500 for example, the King paid £14,000 'for diverse & many Juells brought oute of Fraunce agenst the marage of my lorde prince [Arthur]', conveying the importance of the marriage and the need to impress.[41] This was a trend continued by Henry VIII, who spent £175,000 in the first 12 years of his reign alone.[42] As Schroder pointed out, this was probably not the full extent of the King's spending.[43]

There is ample evidence that queens followed the examples set by their husbands and were active in commissioning jewellery from goldsmiths, some with greater frequency than others. Chapter 4 referred to patronage as a key aspect of queenship in relation to portraiture, and the surviving evidence shows that many queens in this period also fulfilled this in terms of commissioning jewels. There are exceptions: although Anne Neville certainly wore jewels and is likely to have commissioned pieces, the lack of surviving evidence makes it impossible to confirm her activities.[44] It has been suggested that the Middleham Jewel, a high-status Agnus Dei featuring a sapphire and religious inscriptions, once belonged to her, or else to Cecily Neville.[45] Joanna Laynesmith even proposed Joan Beaufort as a possible owner, while Anthony Pollard provided compelling evidence that Anne Beauchamp, mother to Anne Neville, was responsible for commissioning the jewel.[46] Such an important piece was undoubtedly made by special commission, and probably for reasons that were personal to the owner. The religious engraving and inscription it evinces, all thought to aid women in childbirth, support this view.[47] Yet it is impossible to pinpoint an owner with any certainty.

That queens followed their husbands' lead in commissioning jewellery is evidenced in the accounts of Margaret of Anjou, Elizabeth Wydeville, Elizabeth of York, Anna of Cleves and Kateryn Parr. From the period 1452 to 1453, Matthew Philip was owed £125 10s. for jewellery and goldsmith work for Margaret.[48] This was a sizeable sum, although the details of her purchases are frustratingly unrecorded. Ronald Lightbown pointed out that Margaret's father, René of Anjou, had a great enthusiasm for goldsmiths work, which could in turn have influenced his daughter.[49] Philip was well favoured by both Margaret and her husband, and besides various commissions for Henry VI, had been paid £200 for breaking down the ruby ring Henry had worn at his coronation in Paris 'to make an other Ryng for the Quenes Wedding Ring'.[50] This ring later passed into the ownership of Henry VIII, where it was recorded in his 1530 inventory; 'A silver-gilt box, containing the ring wherewith Henry VI espoused his Queen'.[51] After this it disappears, and its fate is unknown. It was not unusual for queens to employ the same goldsmiths as their husbands, which Elizabeth of York and Anna of Cleves sometimes did, thereby underlining the high regard in which these craftsmen were held.

Margaret of Anjou's jewel bill is even more extraordinary when compared with the payments of her successor, Elizabeth Wydeville. Elizabeth's household was less extravagant than Margaret's, partially accounted for by her smaller income.[52] Her only surviving accounts show that in 1466–1467, £54 was paid to her goldsmith, John Amadas – less than half the amount previously outlaid by Margaret.[53] This is only representative of one year, and may not therefore be typical of Elizabeth's spending habits. Like Margaret, there is no itemised bill that clarifies what this sum covered, but the comparatively low amount could be explained by the differing approaches from the two queens. As a foreign princess Margaret evidently relied on jewellery as a way of broadening her network and accentuating her splendour, and this will be analysed further in Chapter 6. As an English widow, however, Elizabeth Wydeville did not have the same concerns. This was certainly the view of Anne Crawford, who believed that Elizabeth never attempted to spend money on expanding her network as Margaret had done.[54] £54 was nevertheless a significant sum but may be a reflection of Elizabeth's own thriftiness by contrast to her predecessor. Another possibility is that some of Elizabeth's jewels were paid for by Edward IV. Elizabeth's jewel expenditure does, though, seem to have been the exception rather than the rule, a view that is supported by the surviving accounts of her daughter, Elizabeth of York.

Elizabeth of York's accounts provide an interesting point of comparison not only with those of her two predecessors but also with those of her husband. The sums spent by Henry reflect his enthusiasm for jewels and display, and accounts survive covering most of his reign.[55] By contrast, Elizabeth of York's surviving expenses cover just the last year of her life.[56] They are nevertheless interesting because like her predecessor Margaret of Anjou, they reveal that she was capable of spending significant sums on jewels, albeit at key moments. Unlike the accounts of both Margaret and Elizabeth Wydeville, Elizabeth of York's are itemised in several places, allowing us to develop a clearer picture of the way in which she spent her money. They therefore provide more complete evidence of a queen's relationship and interaction with goldsmiths (Table 5.1).

Elizabeth's accounts show that she had regular personal contact with goldsmiths, confirmed by the numerous bills signed by her own hand. Interestingly and predominantly, this contact occurred in November 1502. This does not, however, suggest that this was when she made the greatest number of jewel purchases, as three out of the four entries are bills for items previously ordered – indeed the final entry, dated 24 November in relation to the marriage of her son, Prince Arthur, was a year old, as the wedding had taken place in November 1501. This indicates either that Elizabeth had been slow in settling her goldsmiths' bills, or that it was not unusual for her to receive such bills months after her purchases had been made. Unfortunately, these bills are vague, preventing any further analysis of the nature of Elizabeth's acquisitions.

Elizabeth's accounts do not reflect any preference for specific goldsmiths. In the same manner as those of Henry VII, they show that she used a variety of goldsmiths to complete commissions. Like Margaret of Anjou and Henry VI who favoured Matthew Philip, both Elizabeth and Henry VII employed John Vandelf, with whom Henry settled regular accounts.[57] That some of the goldsmiths employed by Elizabeth differed from those used by her husband – Alexander Hove, for example – suggests that he did not influence her when it came to choosing who would create her jewels, and thus her choices were made independently. As Elizabeth's accounts only survive for one year, and her goldsmiths' payments are largely clustered around the marriage of Prince Arthur, it is difficult to ascertain how regularly she used goldsmiths under normal circumstances. Gifts of jewellery given to her son Henry, however, considered in Chapter 6, indicate that she could be generous. Her payments and those of her husband also show that it was not unusual for monarchs and consorts to purchase pieces from members of the nobility, as Elizabeth did from Sir Richard FitzLewes.[58] Henry VII's Chamber Books reveal that he in turn paid the Marquess of Dorset £100 for 'a ring of gold'.[59] When compared with those of her husband, Elizabeth's

Table 5.1 Payments in Elizabeth of York's accounts relating to jewels: E 36/210

Year	*Description*	*Amount*	*Folio*
11 June 1502	'to William Antyne Coper smyth for spangell[es] sett[es] Square pec[es] sterrys Dropes and point[es] after siluer and gold for garnisshing of Jakett[es] against the disguysing'	20s	40
13 November 1502	's[ir] Richard Lewes knight for a Cheyne of golde w[i]t[h] vij knott[es] wayeng vij onz'	26s 8d	64
17 November 1502	'Lybart goldsmyth for contentac[i]on of a bill signed w[i]t[h] thande of the Quene for certain p[ar]cell[es] of stuf of his occupac[i]on by him deliuered to the quenes gr[ac]e as appereth by the same bill'	£19 7s 1d	66
23 November 1502	'to Henry Wurley of London goldsmyth in p[ar]tie of payement of a Warrant and bill[es] signed w[i] t[h] thandes of the quenes grace' for 'certain stuf of his occupac[i]on'	£60	66
24 November 1502	'John Vandelf and Alexaundr[e] Hove goldsmythes in full contentac[i]on and payement of a bill signed w[i]t[h] thande of the quenes g[ra]ce', for certain pieces 'against the mariage of my lord prince decessed'	£67	67
7 February 1503	'Henry Coote of London goldsmyth in p[ar]tie of payement of C m[a]rk[es] to him due for certain plate deliuered to the quenes g[ra] ce'	£20	86

accounts confirm that the sums she was spending on jewels were considerably lower, most likely in a reflection of their differing financial circumstances. They were though, slightly higher than those of Margaret of Anjou. Prince Arthur's marriage clearly accounts for this, meriting the largest of Elizabeth's costs.

There is less evidence for the spending habits of some of Henry VIII's queens. The wardrobe accounts of Catherine of Aragon from 1515 to 1517 make no mention of jewels, thereby confirming that clothes and jewels were entirely separate entities.[60] Her badly damaged household accounts, referenced by Maria Hayward, show only that in 1520 she employed a goldsmith named Fernando Gawo, who was almost certainly Spanish.[61] A list of New Year's gifts given by Catherine in 1522, analysed in Chapter 6, confirms that she used the services of seven goldsmiths, including Morgan Wolf and Robert Amadas, to produce her gifts.[62] Catherine may have used Gawo for creating her own jewellery, but she certainly patronised a number of others when it came to larger commissions.

The lack of documentary evidence prevents confirmation of specific commissions, but there is ample evidence that Catherine had a preference for objects that displayed her pomegranate badge. It appeared on books, clothes, in stained glass and on architecture, serving as 'visual shorthand' for Catherine's status as Queen of England.[63] This badge also appeared on jewels, and such pieces were made either especially for Catherine or with Catherine in mind, in a reflection of her heritage. There are many examples in the jewel inventory of Henry VIII, but whether Catherine or her husband commissioned these is uncertain. Examples include, 'A golden girdle, well wrought, with roses and pomegranates', and 'A garter with letters of gold; castles and pomegranates', both of which were an acknowledgement of Catherine's origins.[64] Likewise, a surviving silver-gilt vase that may once have belonged to the King was also decorated with the pomegranate.[65] Other pieces appear in an inventory of the goods of Henry's illegitimate son the Duke of Richmond and may have been given as gifts by Henry following his separation from Catherine.[66] Hope Johnston has argued that Catherine's use of the pomegranate provided a distinct way in which she could identify herself with her Spanish roots, despite her role as Queen of England.[67] This also explains why she probably employed a Spanish goldsmith. Henry VIII's jewel inventory shows the influence that Catherine's heritage had on his choices, for several pieces were noted as being 'of Spanish work' or contained some reference to Spain.[68] The collar of gold that Catherine bequeathed to her daughter, Mary, was also noted as having been brought from Spain.[69] Catherine's Spanish origins clearly mattered to her, and there seems little doubt that she had a preference for Spanish craftsmanship when it came to commissioning her jewellery. Similarly, her subjects were able to use her badge as a way of demonstrating their loyalty to the queen, and a sixteenth-century silver-gilt chape found in the Thames in 1989, featuring engravings of the pomegranate, provides evidence of this.[70]

Henry VIII's inventory contains numerous items that featured the initials H and K, such as the pair of gilt flagons 'with Rooses H and k knytt together', but it is impossible to tell which of Henry's three wives who shared this name these were made for.[71] It is likely that an item given to the Lady Mary by the King on 12 December 1542 once belonged to Catherine of Aragon. This was the 'Boke of golde with the Kings face and hir graces mothers'.[72] Mary's jewel inventory also listed 'an Emaurawde wt a Rubie ou it and a great ple (pearl) pendant at the same wt the Halfe Rose and pomegranat on the backeside'.[73] Even after Catherine's death, these items and those in the King's inventory show that traces of her were still extant.

Like Catherine of Aragon, jewellery was made especially for Anne Boleyn, the most recognisable of which were her famous initial jewels. Initialled pieces or items featuring a monogram or emblem show that they must have been commissioned especially for Anne, and thus her jewels would have been crafted either at her own instigation or as gifts. As referenced in Chapter 3, similar initial pieces appear in Kateryn Parr's inventory, such as the 'one H and K with a large Emerode and one large perle pendaunt'.[74] Henry VIII's inventory lists several items of plate and jewellery that featured Anne Boleyn's arms, such as 'one glasse of birrall garnished with gold with the late Queene Annes armes vppon the cover', and 'one Tablet of golde set with small Emerauldes perles and one Dyamounte with H and A'.[75] On one occasion the King even made his son the Duke of Richmond a gift of 'a grete Jugg with a cover gilt, with letters H and A crowned'.[76] Other items appear in the King's inventories featuring his and Jane Seymour's combined initials, thus confirming that this was a favoured design feature that Henry put into practice with many – if not all – of his wives.[77]

An inventory of some of the King's jewels compiled after Anne's death reveals the nature of some of the pieces that are likely to have been commissioned for her. These included a gold enamelled ring with a table diamond featuring the word 'MOSTE' that formed part of Anne's motto, as well as a gold brooch with the letters R.A [Regina Anna] in diamonds.[78] Whether Anne or her husband ordered these specific pieces is uncertain, but we do know that Henry ordered and paid for jewels on her behalf. One such payment was made on 7 April 1532, during the couple's courtship: 'Item the same day paid to the said Rasmus for garnishing of a desk with laten and gold for my lady Anne Rochford xliiij li. xviij s'.[79] Likewise, an inventory of the King's jewels that were to be broken down contains several marginal notes referencing diamonds and rubies that were to be reserved 'for my ladye marques'.[80] Such payments evidently continued after their marriage, as another in the King's accounts recorded: 'delyuerde to his saide highnes a bolle of fyne golde bought of Thomas Trappes goldesmithe, havinge Quene Annes sipher upon the toppe of the cover'.[81] Trappes was a popular contemporary goldsmith who was favoured by Henry VIII and employed to fulfil various commissions.[82]

Several further examples of payments made by Henry for items adorned with jewels for Anne Boleyn can be found in his accounts. These include a receipt dating from around 1536 from his embroiderer, William Ibgrave, 'for the Quenes hindre part of a kirtell the nombre of perles' that were sewn on to this particular garment.[83] Another receipt acknowledged jewels received by Ibgrave from Anthony Denny on the King's behalf, which were to be embroidered on other items of clothing.[84] Finally, a receipt dated 10 May 1536 referenced work done by Ibgrave for embroidering pearls on to the King's doublet and 'the quenys graces slevys'.[85] Ibgrave was clearly a favourite of the royal couple, and he had also worked for Catherine of Aragon.[86] It was evidently not unusual for him to receive joint commissions from the King and Queen, payment for which came from the King's coffers.[87]

Henry VIII patronised many goldsmiths and jewellers, but during Anne Boleyn's ascendancy and reign Cornelius Hayes received both her patronage and that of the King. There is numerous evidence of the work Hayes completed for the couple, including the gems that Henry ordered him to deliver to Anne as gifts at various points in their relationship.[88] In a further testament to the high regard in which the King held Hayes, in 1534 he was entrusted with the task of repairing one of the Crown Jewels; 'a sceptre with the dove broken off', though whether this was the king's or queen's is unknown.[89] Although much of the work Hayes completed was for Anne, the examples of which are discussed in Chapter 6 in relation to gifts, the commissions and payments came directly from the King. In 1534 for example, Thomas Cromwell settled Hayes' bill 'for plate delivered to queen Anne' on the King's behalf.[90] Due to Anne's lack of surviving household accounts, it is impossible to say whether this was an exclusive arrangement, or whether she ordered and paid for separate commissions from Hayes and other goldsmiths – it is probable that she did. Neither is it possible to say whether the generosity Henry displayed to Anne was extended to his other wives, though given the numerous gifts he gave to Katherine Howard it is a strong possibility. Hayes was particularly prominent in his role of resetting gems for Anne Boleyn, of which there is numerous evidence in the gifts she received from the King. Pressures of court finances are likely to have been responsible for jewellery being recast rather than being newly commissioned, and this explains why there are surviving lists of jewels that were delivered to Hayes on the King's behalf.[91] Similar lists from both Hayes and the goldsmith Thomas Alvard survive, revealing the return of completed items of jewellery to Henry.[92] What is unclear though is whether these jewels came from Catherine of Aragon and were recast for Anne, or whether they came from the King's own supplies. It is certainly possible that they had once been Catherine's, for a list of Catherine's belongings refers to two items that were 'Delyvered to the Quenes grace', one of which was a cup made of horn.[93]

Hayes's favour with Henry VIII and Anne Boleyn was highlighted further in 1534 when he was tasked with a particularly important commission, to create a silver cradle in readiness for the royal baby that Anne was expecting (and tragically lost), complete with 'stones that were set in gold in the cradle'.[94] That it was a dual commission emphasised its importance, for Hayes was to work alongside 'Hance, painter' – Holbein, who was employed 'for painting the same Adam and Eve' on the cradle.[95] The high regard in which both men were held was clear, for this was a momentous piece: its commission signifies the importance that was placed on Anne producing a legitimate heir, who was to be showcased in a piece of such magnificence. It was not unusual for artists and jewellers to collaborate on projects, and Holbein certainly designed jewels for Anne Boleyn, although there is no evidence that any of the pieces were actually made.[96] Many of Holbein's jewellery designs from this period still survive, providing 'a record and an advertisement for the latest style in jewelry'.[97] Interestingly, however, Susan Foister suggested that these sketches may not actually have been designs, but rather 'individually owned jewels' that Holbein planned to incorporate into portraits of the owner.[98]

Holbein not only designed a cup in the popular antique style for Jane Seymour, but it was also created.[99] The surviving sketch coupled with the description in Henry VIII's inventory conveys its grandeur (Figure 5.1). Related as being

> one faier standing cupp of golde garnished with Diamountes and perles and this worde bounde to obeye and serve and H and J knytt togethers and in the topp of the cover the kinges armes and Quene Janes armes holden by twoo boyes vnder a crowne Imperiall

though the cup was a celebration of the King's union with Jane, it is unclear whether it was commissioned on her orders or her husband's.[100] Whatever the circumstances it may reflect Holbein's

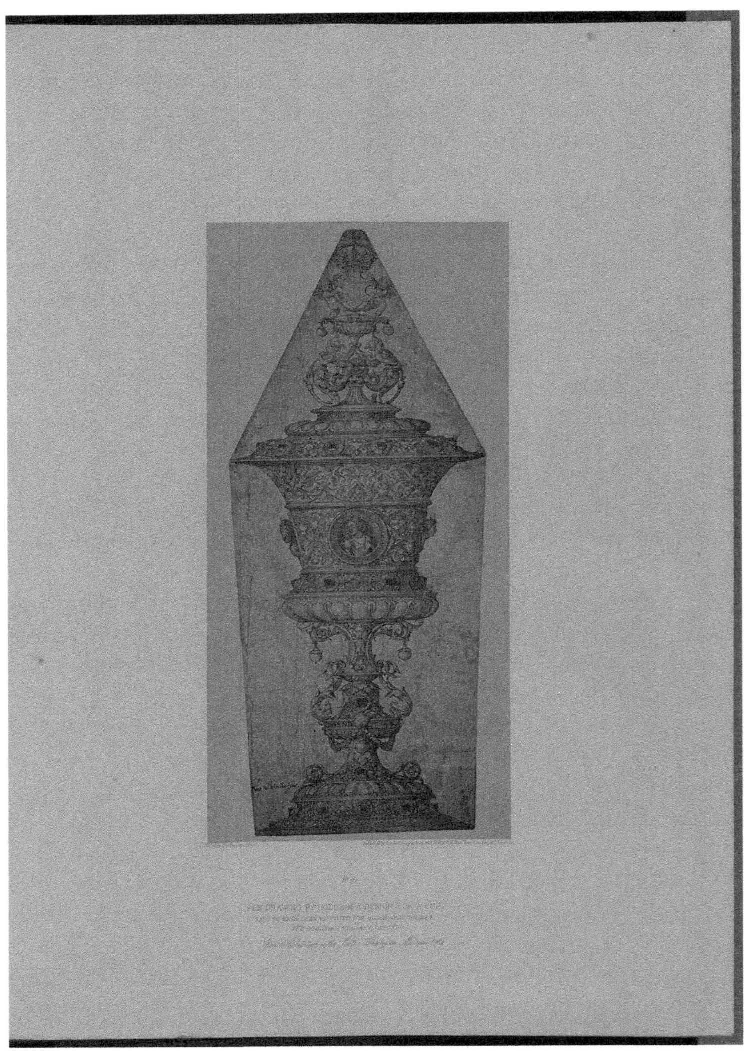

Figure 5.1 Hans Holbein's design for Jane Seymour's cup

Source: Getty Museum Collection. Public Domain. www.getty.edu/art/collection/object/108RTP

desire to earn the patronage of the queen whose masterly portrait he had painted. The cup was unfortunately sold abroad by Charles I in 1625.[101]

Jane Seymour may have been more conscious of projecting an image of majesty than she has hitherto been credited with. The evidence for this comes in the form of another splendid piece of plate listed in Henry VIII's inventory, which was, according to the entry, 'made by Commaundement of late quene jane'.[102] This was described as

> A Bason of golde having in the bussell a Sheelde enameled wherein is the kinges armes crowned borne vpp by a lion crowned and a dragon having a Scripture aboutes the bussell Dieu et mon droit and foure small rooses of gold the border having allso iiij rooses of golde enameled white and redd and the same poysey Dieu et mon droit and an Ewer of golde with an handle to the same standing vppon three dragons heddes the foote chased with braunches haches and Erres enameled redd and in a bordre above that enameled blewe Dieu et mon droite the cover having an aungell standing vppon the knopp holding a sheeld wherein are the kinges armes the bordre thereof chased and garnished with vj rooses white and redd a worme and a fowle with a ring in his mowthe.[103]

Although this piece was made on Jane's orders, the emphasis in the design was her husband's glory, rather than her own. A queen's status made her inseparable from the crown, and thus this object accentuating Henry VIII's power could have been commissioned by Jane in an attempt to signify her own subservience to him, in keeping with her motto, 'Bound to Obey and Serve'.[104]

Jane's employment of the Dutch jeweller Peter Richardson was mentioned earlier in this chapter, and he is known to have made 'juells, woorks, and dyvyses' for her.[105] Richardson first appears in the State Papers in 1536, but it is interesting to consider his employment by two of Jane's successors, Anna of Cleves and Kateryn Parr.[106] This link with the past may indicate nothing more than a preference for Richardson's work, which was certainly true of Kateryn Parr. It is equally possible that, as someone who had experience of serving the royal household, both Anna and Kateryn simply continued to employ him. Given the link, it seems plausible that Katherine Howard had also employed Richardson, but this can only be speculative. Evidently, though, Richardson did not work exclusively for the queen, as the Privy Purse expenses of the Lady Mary show that she paid him £30 in December 1544 for the King's New Year's gift.[107]

Anna of Cleves is the first of Henry VIII's wives for whom some substantial household accounts survive. Although her term as queen was short, she was in frequent contact with a number of goldsmiths. A list of wages shows that Anna was paying 'the goldsmyth', who is unnamed, a regular wage each quarter, totalling 33s. 4d.[108] A similar regular wage also appears in Kateryn Parr's accounts, confirming that the two queens employed a goldsmith to fulfil recurrent commissions for them.[109] In both cases, this is likely to have been Richardson, who is referenced in the accounts of both queens as the queen's goldsmith.[110]

Between February and June 1540, Anna's accounts list seven individual goldsmiths who completed a variety of commissions. Among them were Richardson, Cornelius Hayes and Alard Plomyer. This is an exceptionally high number for so short a period, and she was also spending enormous sums. This strongly suggests that, as a foreign-born queen, Anna was determined to make a positive impression on her new subjects and saw jewellery as a way of creating a majestic image. The nature of her purchases, listed in Table 5.2, confirms this.

As Table 5.2 shows, the sums of money that Anna was spending in a short time are extraordinary. There was also a payment to John Hawes who was described as 'the quenes goldcutter' in settlement of a bill – possibly Hawes had created a cameo for Anna.[111] The items she was purchasing confirm that she was attempting to build an impressive image: the large sums outlaid to Robert Cooper for Anna's saddles suggest that she was eager to be seen by her subjects, and to project this persona to as many people as possible. This is reinforced by the amount that she was spending on single diamonds, as well as other pieces such as the

Table 5.2 Payments in the accounts of Anna of Cleves relating to jewels: E 101/42215 and E 101/422/16

Date	*Goldsmith*	*Object*	*Price*	*Reference*
Unknown	Robert Cooper	'certeyne thing[es] by hym don toward[es] the p[re]formance of the quenes Sadles	£100	E 101/422/15, unfoliated
Unknown	Robert Cooper	'for lyke thyng[es] by hym employed about the quenes Sadles'	£66 13s 4d	E 101/422/15, unfoliated
Unknown	Unknown	'for a Ring floweryd like Roses with Rubies'	£10	E 101/422/16, f. 68v
Unknown	Unknown	Payment for a ring	£30	E 101/422/16, f. 68r.
Unknown	Richard Stakey	'for graving and makyng of the Quenes grac[es] great Seale'	£9	E 101/422/15, unfoliated
Unknown	Garat Harman	'one other table dyamonde'	£25 13s 4d	E 101/422/15, unfoliated
Unknown	Unknown	'for a cuppe w[i]th a cover all gylt weyng xxv ownc[es] & d[em]I quarter	£6 5s 7.5d	E 101/422/15, unfoliated
February–May 1540?	Cornelius Hayes	'for makyng of spangles'	£20	E 101/422/15, unfoliated
17 February 1540	Alard Plomyer	'on[e] broche of the hystorie of Sampson garnysshed w[i]th Dyamons'	£28	E 101/422/15, unfoliated
17 February 1540	Alard Plomyer	'on[e] table dyamond'	£28	E 101/422/15, unfoliated

(*Continued*)

Table 5.2 (Continued)

Date	*Goldsmith*	*Object*	*Price*	*Reference*
2 April 1540	Cornelius Hayes	'for the makyng and goold of the Quenes Chayn'	£24 4s 4d	E 101/422/15, unfoliated
17 April 1540	Unknown	'for ij diamond[es] oon beyng A Rose the o a flour de booe of diamond[es]	£11 13s	E 101/422/15, unfoliated
27 May 1540	Peter Richardson	'for certeyne Juelles & other thyngs '	£46 18s	E 101/422/15, unfoliated
5 June? 1540	Peter Richardson	'for certeyne Juelles by hym made'	£10	E 101/422/16, f. 733r
25 June 1540	Roger Horton	'the makyng w[i]th the sylv[er] of Her grac[es] Trencher knyves'	£4 4d	E 101/422/16, f. 733v

chain, the ring, and the brooch, mentioned in the table. Intriguingly, a brooch described in similar terms later appeared in Henry VIII's inventory: 'a brouche of the force of Sampson sett ouer with dyamountes'.[112] If this was the same piece then Henry had obviously acquired it from his former wife, perhaps as a gift. The purchase of a seal from Richard Stakey shows Anna's awareness of the way in which jewels could aid the administrative aspects of her role. The image of the impressive consort that Anna was eager to create can be seen in other areas of her accounts. For example, she purchased spangles and 'a Crymsen velvet bonet sett wythe buttons of gold and with a fether tasselled with golde and frynged with gold'.[113] In a similar manner to Margaret of Anjou, as a foreign princess Anna is likely to have been more aware of the need to surround herself with splendour. This is certainly borne out by a further payment she made to Robert Cooper on 10 May 1540: Cooper was paid £63 10s 8d 'in full payment of hys byll'.[114] The bill is not itemised, but it confirms that Anna was not averse to investing heavily in material items.

During Kateryn Parr's regency in the summer of 1544, her accounts show that she was in regular contact with Richardson. A payment notes that between May 1543 and May 1544, an unspecified amount was paid to 'P [missing] Goldes [missing]' – presumably Peter Richardson, for the 'p[ro]vysion & making of dyv[er]s & sundrye p[ar]cells of work of golde sylver & p[re]cyous stone made & delyv[er]ed to her hignes use'.[115] Interestingly, however, a further note stated that 'besyd[es] certaine p[ar]cells of broken sylv[er] golde to him delyv[er]ed & deducted in the pryce of his sayd p[ar]celles'.[116] This shows that Richardson was expected to take second-hand jewels in part payment for his services, which seems surprising, given the funds to which Kateryn would have had access. On 20 June 1544, Richardson was paid £20 for spangles to adorn the coats of her footmen, while on another occasion 12d was paid for 'trussing the Queen's jewels, and for going for her goldsmith and silkwoman'.[117] This was not the only occasion on which Kateryn had contact with Richardson that summer, for in September a messenger was rewarded for 'riding for Peter Richardson, the Queen's goldsmith'.[118] Later that same month, Richardson's name appeared again when he was paid 'for certain her affairs, and to speak with Nicholas Cratesere and others about the same affairs'.[119] Although the details of Kateryn's contact with Richardson are unknown, the mention of Nicholas Kratzer holds a clue. As the King's Clockmaker who had been responsible for the design of the astronomical clock at Hampton Court Palace in 1540, Kratzer held an important position at Henry VIII's court.[120] Kateryn Parr evidently had an interest in clocks, as an entry in her accounts notes a payment for the repairs of two.[121] Likewise, not only was she depicted wearing a clock jewel in her Master John portrait, but two items containing clocks appear in her jewel inventory: first, 'a Tablet of golde being a Clock fasshioned like an Harte garnysshed with iij Rubies and one fair dyamounte lozenged', as well as 'a Tablet being therein a Clocke on thoneside the kinges worde wrought of Dyamountes furnysshed and on thother side a Crosse of Dyamountes furnysshed with xxiiiij dyamountes with a button hanging thereat hauing twoo dyamountes and twoo Rubies'.[122] As neither of these items appear in Katherine Howard's inventory, it is reasonable to assume that they were either given to Kateryn or that one or both of these pieces were the topic of conversation between the Queen, Richardson and Kratzer in September 1544, which led to their commission.

Another payment in Kateryn's accounts notes that in 1546 one of her yeoman was sent to convey her goldsmith – presumably Richardson – to her, further evidence that they were in frequent contact.[123] Susan James suggested that it may have been Richardson who was responsible for the creation of the ouche 'with a Crowne conteyning ij Dyamountes one Rubie an Emerode the Crowne being garnysshed with dyamountes and iij perles pendaunte', that Kateryn wears in her Master John portrait.[124] The design of the ouche clearly conveys Katherine's interest in the royal image and the importance of majesty. What is certain is that the ouche came into the possession of Elizabeth I and appears in her 1587 inventory.[125] Anna of Denmark later owned it but ordered it to be broken down, presumably due to the advances in fashion.[126]

Kateryn's accounts bear witness to another important item that was commissioned on her orders. This was a joint commission for cameos created by John Bettes and Giles Gering.[127] While Bettes painted miniatures of both the King and 'the Quenes grace', Gering was paid for having 'engraved in stone' both images.[128] The value of cameos was considered in Chapter 3, but the importance of this commission can be seen by the affixation of Kateryn's seal, and her signature which rarely appears against other payments in her accounts. This suggests that Kateryn dealt directly with both Bettes and Gering, who created the jewels to her specifications. Neither of these items appear in Kateryn's inventories, potentially indicating that she commissioned them in order to bestow elsewhere – possibly to the King, as James suggested, as they were evidently high-status jewels.[129]

Kateryn Parr's accounts cover a wider period than those of Anna of Cleves, yet they provide no further evidence of jewellery that was commissioned on her orders. A number of pieces appear in her inventory that do not match those belonging to Katherine Howard, suggesting that Kateryn either ordered new items or had different tastes to her predecessor and refashioned jewels. Her accounts do, however, show that on one occasion she paid for pearls to be embroidered on to her clothes, further accentuating her love of finery.[130]

Conclusion

This chapter has contextualised the role of the goldsmith in fifteenth- and sixteenth-century England, in order to show that goldsmiths were prominent members of society with regular access to the royal court. This naturally brought them into contact with kings and queens, whose patronage they sought and earned in order to fulfil special commissions on their behalf. The patronage of goldsmiths by the royal family and the court was integral to a goldsmith's survival and reputation, and both Henry VII and Henry VIII favoured several goldsmiths. Samantha Harper was therefore accurate in her assertion that 'goldsmiths were indispensable to the king and his household in a way that no other group of craftsmen or merchants were', yet the same was also true of queens.[131] Evidence of this can be seen with Jane

Seymour, Anna of Cleves and Kateryn Parr, all of whom patronised Peter Richardson, while Anna employed many others during her short term as queen. Such goldsmiths were able to complete commissions on behalf of the queens, such as the elaborate basin that was created on the orders of Jane Seymour.

The surviving accounts of Elizabeth of York, Anna of Cleves and Kateryn Parr confirm both the frequency with which queens were in contact with goldsmiths and that it was not unusual for them to order jewels on a regular basis. These were often commissioned for a number of reasons, and Elizabeth of York's accounts bear testimony to the great expense she outlaid on jewels for the wedding of her son, Prince Arthur. Anna of Cleves was extraordinary, in that the sums of money she spent in a short period of time are likely to have reflected a desire from her to establish herself firmly as England's consort. This, as well as other examples cited throughout this chapter, serves to highlight the way in which queens were able to use their own resources in order to take control of their image, using jewels as a way of doing this. Although commissioning jewels was not the only way in which a queen might acquire pieces, it did provide them with a tangible way of image fashioning. Jewels offered queens an opportunity to showcase their personality and tastes, thereby projecting their majesty in the manner in which they desired.

Notes

1 *L & P*, vii, no. 957.
2 J. Cherry, *Medieval Goldsmiths* (London, 1992), p. 61.
3 Hayward, *Dress*, p. 336.
4 Reynolds, *Fine Style*, p. 15.
5 Anderson Black, *History of Jewels*, p. 133.
6 *L & P*, ii, p. 1446; *L & P*, xviii, part 2, no. 231.
7 Campbell, *Medieval Jewellery*, p. 22.
8 Tait (ed.), *7000 Years*, p. 140.
9 J. Lutkin, 'Luxury and Display in Silver and Gold at the Court of Henry IV', in L. Clark (ed.), *The Fifteenth Century IX* (2010), pp. 157–8.
10 S.P. Harper, 'Royal Servants and City Fathers: The Double Lives of London Goldsmiths at the Court of Henry VII', in M. Allen

and M. Davies (eds), *Medieval Merchants and Money: Essays in Honour of James L Bolton* (London, 2016), p. 177.
11 Ibid, p. 178.
12 E 36/210 f.66–7; *L & P*, xi, no. 519:17; *L & P*, xix, part 2, no. 688.
13 E 101/422/15, unfoliated.
14 E 36/210, f. 83.
15 Scarisbrick, *Tudor and Jacobean Jewellery*, p. 34.
16 Campbell, *Medieval Jewellery*, p. 22; Forsyth, *Cheapside Hoard*, p. 22.
17 GC, MS 1521, f. 28r.
18 Evans, *English Jewellery*, p. 51.
19 W.A. Steward, 'Goldsmiths' and Silversmiths' Work – Past and Present', *Journal of the Royal Society of Arts*, 81 (1933), p. 870.
20 Evans, *English Jewellery*, p. 51; GC, MS 1520.
21 Scarisbrick, *Diamonds*, p. 43.
22 C.L. Scofield, *The Life and Reign of Edward the Fourth*, I (London, 1923), p. 375; *CPR*, 1461–7, p. 268; *CPR*, 1485–1509, p. 38.
23 E 36/207, p. 36; E 36/214, f. 27r; P. Glanville, 'Cardinal Wolsey and the Goldsmiths', in S.J. Gunn and P.G. Lindley (eds), *Cardinal Wolsey: Church, State and Art* (Cambridge, 1991), p. 141.
24 GC, MS 1520; GC, MS 1521.
25 E 36/214, f. 63r; E 101/414/6, f. 36r; BL, Add MS 59899, f. 26v; Ibid, f. 93v. Schroder, 'A Marvel to Behold', p. 37.
26 Harper, 'Royal Servants', p. 177.
27 GC, MS 1520, f. 177r, 253r.
28 *L & P*, ii, p. 1444.
29 *L & P*, xviii, part 1, no. 436.
30 Tait (ed.), *7000 Years*, p. 220; *L & P*, xvi, no. 380.
31 *L & P*, xvii, no. 220.
32 See *L & P*, ii, p. 1465.
33 Campbell, *Medieval Jewellery*, p. 22; C. Weightman, *Margaret of York: The Diabolical Duchess* (Stroud, 2009), p. 29.
34 Campbell, *Medieval Jewellery*, p. 22.
35 E 101/415/3, f. 2r; BL, Add MS 59899, f. 62r.
36 E 101/415/3, f. 19r; E 36/214, f. 10v.
37 Hollis (ed.), *Princely Magnificence*, p. 5.
38 See E 404/74/2; E 36/214, N.H. Nicolas (ed.), *Privy Purse Expenses of King Henry the Eighth from 1529–1532* (London, 1827).
39 Howell, *Eleanor of Provence*, p. 79.
40 Schroder, 'A Marvel to Behold', p. 49.
41 BL, Add MS 7099, f. 68.
42 Schroder, 'A Marvel to Behold', p. 49.
43 Ibid.

44 Hicks, *Anne Neville*, p. 217.
45 Cherry, *Middleham Jewel*, p. 12; J. Cherry, 'Healing Through Faith: The Continuation of Medieval Attitudes to Jewellery into the Renaissance', *Renaissance Studies*, 15 (2001), p. 157.
46 Laynesmith, *Cecily*, p. 14; A. Pollard, 'The Smethon Letter, St Penket and the Tablet of Gold', in M. Aston and R. Horrox (eds), *Much Heaving and Shoving: Late-Medieval Gentry and Their Concerns, Essays for Colin Richmond* (London, 2005), p. 40.
47 Unknown Maker, 'Middleham Jewel', Yorkshire Museum; Cherry, *Middleham Jewel*, p. 34.
48 E 101/410/15; Myers, 'Household of Queen Margaret', p. 10.
49 Lightbown, *European Jewellery*, p. 39.
50 Rymer (ed.), *Foedera*, XI, p. 76.
51 *L & P*, iv, no. 6789.
52 Myers, 'Household of Queen Elizabeth', p. 207.
53 Earenfight, *Queenship*, p. 217; E 36/207, p. 36.
54 A. Crawford, 'The King's Burden?: The Consequences of Royal Marriage in Fifteenth-Century England', in R.A. Griffiths (ed.), *Patronage, the Crown and the Provinces: In Later Medieval England* (Gloucester, 1981), p. 50.
55 See E 101/414/6; E 101/414/16; E 101/415/3; E 36/214; BL, Add MS 59899.
56 E 36/210.
57 See BL, Add MS 59899, f. 3v, 7v, 44v.
58 E 36/210, f. 64.
59 BL, Add MS 7099, f. 6.
60 E 101/418/6; See Beer, 'Practices and Performances', p. 91.
61 See Hayward, *Dress*, p. 336; BL, Cotton MS Appendix LXV.
62 *L & P*, Addenda I, no. 367.
63 H. Johnston, 'Catherine of Aragon's Pomegranate, Revisited', *Transactions of the Cambridge Bibliographical Society*, 13 (2005), p. 155.
64 *L & P*, iii, no. 463.
65 T. Schroder, 'A Royal Tudor Rock-Crystal and Silver-Gilt Vase', *BM*, 137 (1995), p. 256.
66 Nichols (ed.), *Inventories*, p. 5.
67 Johnston, 'Catherine of Aragon's Pomegranate', p. 154.
68 *L & P*, iii, no. 463.
69 BL, Cotton MS Otho C X, f. 216r.
70 H. Forsyth, 'An Inscribed Sixteenth-Century English Silver-Gilt Chape', *BM*, 138 (1996), p. 392.
71 SoA, MS 129, f. 86v.
72 Madden (ed.), *Privy Purse Expenses*, p. 178.
73 Ibid, p. 192.
74 SoA, MS 129, f. 178v.
75 Ibid, f. 28v, 188v.

76 Nichols (ed.), *Inventories*, p. 13.
77 BL, Royal Appendix MS 89, f. 21r-v.
78 Ibid, f. 32v, 33v.
79 Nicolas (ed.), *Privy Purse Expenses*, p. 123.
80 BL, Royal MS 7 C XVI, f. 41r-v.
81 W.B.D.D. Turnbull (ed.), *Account of the Monastic Treasures Confiscated at the Dissolution of the Various Houses in England* (Edinburgh, 1836), p. 97.
82 *L & P*, vii, no. 10.
83 BL, Royal MS 7 C XVI, p. 33.
84 Ibid, p. 36.
85 Ibid, p. 37.
86 See Hayward, *Dress*, p. 327; Beer, 'Practices and Performances', p. 110.
87 E 315/242/3, f. 22v.
88 *L & P*, v, no. 276.
89 *L & P*, vii, no. 10.
90 *L & P*, vii, no. 137.
91 BL, Royal MS 7 C XVI, f. 48r.
92 Ibid, f. 53; Ibid, f. 35.
93 Nichols (ed.), *Inventories*, p. 39.
94 *L & P*, vii, no. 1668.
95 Ibid.
96 J. Rowlands, *Holbein: The Paintings of Hans Holbein the Younger* (Oxford, 1985), p. 88; Hayward, *Dress*, p. 188.
97 Hans Holbein, 'Drawing', c. 1532–43, British Museum, SL, 5308.37 for example; A.R. Jones and P. Stallybrass, *Renaissance Clothing and the Materials of Memory* (Cambridge, 2000), p. 41.
98 S. Foister, *Holbein and England* (New Haven and London, 2004), p. 40.
99 Hans Holbein, 'Jane Seymour's Cup', c. 1536, Ashmolean Museum, Oxford, WA1863.424. See also Schroder, 'A Marvel to Behold', p. 195.
100 SoA, MS 129, f. 15v.
101 See J.F. Hayward, *Virtuoso Goldsmiths and the Triumph of Mannerism, 1540–1620* (London, 1976), pp. 299–300 for another piece potentially designed by Holbein.
102 SoA, MS 129, f. 26r.
103 Ibid.
104 Benz, *Three Medieval Queens*, p. 167.
105 *L & P*, xi, no. 519.
106 Schroder, 'A Marvel to Behold', p. 181.
107 Madden (ed.), *Privy Purse Expenses*, p. 170.
108 E 101/422/15, unfoliated.
109 E 315/340, f. 49v-50r.

110 E 101/422/15, unfoliated.
111 Ibid.
112 SoA, MS 129, f. 161r.
113 E 101/422/15, unfoliated.
114 Ibid.
115 E 315/161, f. 214r.
116 Ibid.
117 Ibid, p. 18; *L & P*, xix, part 2, no. 688.
118 *L & P*, xix, part 2, no. 688.
119 Ibid.
120 L. Worsley and D. Souden, *Hampton Court Palace: The Official Illustrated History* (London, 2005), p. 38.
121 E 315/161, p. 83
122 SoA, MS 129, f. 179v-180r.
123 E 314/22, p. 7.
124 SoA, MS 129, f. 178r; Master John, 'Katherine Parr', NPG; James, 'Lady Jane Grey or Queen Kateryn Parr?', pp. 20–4.
125 BL, Royal MS Appendix 68, f. 26r.
126 National Library of Scotland, MS 31.1.10. f. 19v.
127 E 314/22, p. 18.
128 Ibid.
129 James, *Feminine Dynamic*, p. 103.
130 E 101/423/12, unfoliated.
131 Harper, 'Royal Servants', p. 179.

References

Manuscript Sources

Kew, The National Archives

EXCHEQUER

E 36 Treasury of Receipt, Miscellaneous Books.
E 101 King's Remembrancer, Various Accounts.
E 314 Court of Augmentations, Miscellaneous Books.
E 315 Court of Augmentations and Predecessors, Miscellaneous Books.
E 404 Warrants for Issue.

LONDON, BRITISH LIBRARY

Additional Manuscripts 7099, 59899.
Cotton Manuscripts Appendix LXV, Otho C X.
Royal Manuscripts Appendix MS 68, Appendix MS 89, 7 C XVI.

LONDON, GOLDSMITHS' COMPANY

MS 1520 Minute Book A, 1444–1516.
MS 1521 Minute Book B, 1492–7.

LONDON, SOCIETY OF ANTIQUARIES

MS 129 Inventory of King Henry VIII.

EDINBURGH, NATIONAL LIBRARY OF SCOTLAND

MS 31.1.10 Anna of Denmark's Jewel Inventory.

Portraits

Hans Holbein, 'Drawing', c. 1532–43, British Museum, SL, 5308.37.
Hans Holbein, 'Jane Seymour's Cup', c. 1536, Ashmolean Museum, Oxford, WA1863.424.
Master John, 'Katherine Parr', c. 1544–5, NPG, NPG 4451.

Physical Objects

Unknown Maker, 'Middleham Jewel', fifteenth century, gold and sapphire, Yorkshire Museum, YORYM: 1991.43.

Printed Primary Sources

Brewer, J.S., (ed.), *Letters and Papers, Foreign and Domestic, of the Reign of Henry VIII, 1509–47*, 21 vols and addenda (London, 1862–1932).
Brodie, R.H., Black, J.G., and Maxwell Lyte, H.C., (eds), *Calendar of the Patent Rolls Preserved in the Public Record Office, 1476–1509*, 3 vols (London, 1901–16).
Madden, F., (ed.), *Privy Purse Expenses of the Princess Mary* (London, 1831).
Nichols, J.G., (ed.), *Inventories of the Wardrobe, Plate, Chapel Stuff, etc. of Henry Fitzroy, Duke of Richmond, and of the Wardrobe Stuff at Baynard's Castle of Katherine, Princess Dowager* (London, 1855).
Nicolas, N.H., (ed.), *Privy Purse Expenses of King Henry the Eighth from 1529–1532* (London, 1827).
Rymer, T., (ed.), *Rymer's Foedera*, 16 vols (London, 1739–45).

Turnbull, W.B.D.D., (ed.), *Account of the Monastic Treasures Confiscated at the Dissolution of the Various Houses in England* (Edinburgh, 1836).

Secondary Sources

Anderson Black, J., *A History of Jewels* (London, 1974).

Beer, M.L., 'Practices and Performances of Queenship: Catherine of Aragon and Margaret Tudor, 1503–1533', unpublished PhD thesis, University of Illinois, 2014.

Benz St John, L., *Three Medieval Queens: Queenship and the Crown in Fourteenth-Century England* (Basingstoke, 2012).

Campbell, M., *Medieval Jewellery* (London, 2009).

Cherry, J., 'Healing Through Faith: The Continuation of Medieval Attitudes to Jewellery into the Renaissance', *Renaissance Studies*, 15 (2001), pp. 154–71.

Cherry, J., *Medieval Goldsmiths* (London, 1992).

Cherry, J., *The Middleham Jewel and Ring* (York, 1994).

Crawford, A., 'The King's Burden?: The Consequences of Royal Marriage in Fifteenth-century England', in Griffiths, R.A. (ed.), *Patronage, the Crown and the Provinces: In Later Medieval England* (Gloucester, 1981), pp. 33–56.

Earenfight, T., *Queenship in Medieval Europe* (Basingstoke, 2013).

Evans, J., *English Jewellery: From the Fifth Century A.D. to 1800* (London, 1921).

Foister, S., *Holbein and England* (New Haven and London, 2004).

Forsyth, H., 'An Inscribed Sixteenth-Century English Silver-Gilt Chape', *BM*, 138 (1996), pp. 392–3.

Forsyth, H., *The Cheapside Hoard: London's Lost Jewels* (London, 2013).

Glanville, P., 'Cardinal Wolsey and the Goldsmiths', in Gunn, S.J., and Lindley, P.G. (eds), *Cardinal Wolsey: Church, State and Art* (Cambridge, 1991), pp. 131–48.

Harper, S.P., 'Royal Servants and City Fathers: The Double Lives of London Goldsmiths at the Court of Henry VII', in Allen, M., and Davies, M. (eds), *Medieval Merchants and Money: Essays in Honour of James L Bolton* (London, 2016), pp. 177–93.

Hayward, J.F., *Virtuoso Goldsmiths and the Triumph of Mannerism, 1540–1620* (London, 1976).

Hayward, M., *Dress at the Court of King Henry VIII* (Leeds, 2007).

Hicks, M., *Anne Neville: Queen to Richard III* (Stroud, 2007).
Hollis, J., (ed.), *Princely Magnificence: Court Jewels of the Renaissance, 1500–1630* (London, 1980).
Howell, M., *Eleanor of Provence: Queenship in Thirteenth Century England* (Oxford, 1998).
James, S.E., 'Lady Jane Grey or Queen Kateryn Parr?' *BM*, 138 (1996), pp. 20–4.
James, S.E., *The Feminine Dynamic in English Art, 1485–1603: Women as Consumers, Patrons and Painters* (Abingdon, 2009).
Johnston, H., 'Catherine of Aragon's Pomegranate, Revisited', *Transactions of the Cambridge Bibliographical Society*, 13 (2005), pp. 153–73.
Jones, A.R., and Stallybrass, P., *Renaissance Clothing and the Materials of Memory* (Cambridge, 2000).
Laynesmith, J.L., *Cecily Duchess of York* (London, 2017).
Lightbown, R.W., *Mediaeval European Jewellery* (London, 1992).
Lutkin, J., 'Luxury and Display in Silver and Gold at the Court of Henry IV', in Clark, L. (ed.), *The Fifteenth Century IX* (2010), pp. 155–78.
Myers, A.R., 'The Household of Queen Margaret of Anjou, 1452–3', *BJRL*, 50 (1957–8), pp. 79–113.
Myers, A.R., 'The Household of Queen Elizabeth Woodville, 1466–7', *BJRL*, 50 (1967–8), pp. 207–15.
Pollard, A., 'The Smethon Letter, St Penket and the Tablet of Gold', in Aston, M., and Horrox, R. (eds), *Much Heaving and Shoving: Late-Medieval Gentry and Their Concerns, Essays for Colin Richmond* (London, 2005), pp. 138–44.
Reddaway, T.F., 'The London Goldsmiths Circa 1500', *Transactions of the Royal Historical Society*, 12 (1962), pp. 49–62.
Reynolds, A., *In Fine Style: The Art of Tudor and Stuart Fashion* (London, 2013).
Rowlands, J., *Holbein: The Paintings of Hans Holbein the Younger* (Oxford, 1985).
Scarisbrick, D., *Diamond Jewelry: 700 Years of Glory and Glamour* (London, 2019).
Scarisbrick, D., *Tudor and Jacobean Jewellery* (London, 1995).
Schroder, T., *'A Marvel to Behold': Gold and Silver at the Court of Henry VIII* (Woodbridge, 2020).
Schroder, T., 'A Royal Tudor Rock-Crystal and Silver-Gilt Vase', *BM*, 137 (1995), pp. 356–66.
Scofield, C.L., *The Life and Reign of Edward the Fourth*, 2 vols (London, 1923).

Steward, W.A., 'Goldsmiths' and Silversmiths' Work – Past and Present', *Journal of the Royal Society of Arts*, 81 (1933), pp. 865–76.

Tait, H. (ed.), *7000 Years of Jewellery* (London, 1986).

Weightman, C., *Margaret of York: The Diabolical Duchess* (Stroud, 2009).

Worsley, L., and Souden, D., *Hampton Court Palace: The Official Illustrated History* (London, 2005).

6 Gifts of Jewels

'The gift was a process, rather than exclusively a material entity', and thus, Felicity Heal stated, 'there was a present or reward for every circumstance'.[1] The gift-giving process formed an integral part of life at fifteenth- and sixteenth-century courts. As a vital part of queenship, it was one in which queens were fully immersed. Gifts were given in order to mark a number of occasions, yet as will be seen, the giving of jewellery by queens was not a common occurrence – plate or money by means of reward was more usual. When such gifts were given by queens, it not only was a sign of great favour but was also likely an attempt to network and secure loyalty. This kind of patronage was a crucial part of building and expanding a queen's circle, and gifts of jewels provided them with tangible tools to enable them to do this. However, as examples of gifts of jewels given by Katherine Howard underline, they could also be used as bribes. Jewels given to queens marked every great event in her life and would be expected by consorts and the royal family on occasions such as births, christenings, marriages and deaths.[2] Ample examples of such gifts will be examined in this chapter, which will analyse the way in which queens gave, received and used jewels in the context of gift giving to mark a number of occasions: New Year, gifts between family members, piety, diplomacy and bribes, and prizes.[3] The examples in this chapter will show how gifts of jewels aided and enhanced relations with a queen's husband and family, her construction of networks at and beyond the court, and her diplomatic standing. It will further convey the way that

DOI: 10.4324/9781003202592-7

such gifts accentuated a queen's status both as an individual and within her court, adding another dimension to the projection of majesty.

The Context of Gift Giving

In theory giving a gift was a voluntary process – as was the case with bequests made in wills – and as Heal asserted, the spirit of the gift had to appear to be freely given.[4] In reality though, it was part of a reciprocal process in which 'the recipient feels obligated to reciprocate with a counter-gift, although not explicitly compelled to do so by any existing authority'.[5] Not all items received had been freely given and could therefore cause problems when taken out of context. According to the account of Cardinal Wolsey's servant George Cavendish, during Henry VIII's courtship of Anne Boleyn, Sir Thomas Wyatt, a rival suitor, 'caught from her a certain small jew'el hanging by a lace out of her pocket'.[6] He refused to return it, and when the King boasted of having won Anne's love and produced a ring she had given him as proof of it, Wyatt supposedly countered it by flaunting the jewel he had previously taken from Anne, much to the King's dismay.[7] Gifts of jewels therefore served as signs of affection in a relationship, and in arousing jealousy in a third party.

The practice of royal gift giving had been established in England for many centuries, with examples dating back to the Roman period.[8] Gifts were often chosen with a great deal of care, for as Helen Maurer related, 'Gift giving made an important statement about the giver's status, wealth and generosity. Likewise, it involved recognition of the recipient's status'.[9] For those who received gifts from a queen, it was a sure sign of the favour in which they were held. This is in keeping with the argument of Natalie Zemon Davis, who asserted that 'In a sense, the whole patronage system was carried on under the rhetoric of gifts'.[10] It was not just the object itself but also the mode of presentation that mattered.[11] The size and quality of the present were dependent on the social status and the relationship of the parties involved, but if chosen correctly both individuals and families.[12]

Surviving receipts and gift rolls from the period reveal the nature of gifts given and received by monarchs and their consorts, from the humble to the elaborate. The Queen's Book of Elizabeth of York, for example, shows that she frequently gave rewards to subjects who brought humble gifts of fruit and cheese, among other things.[13] Her accounts are littered with such references and show that gifts such as these were more frequent than personal gifts from friends and family members. Similar surviving examples in the Chamber Books of Henry VII and the accounts of Anna of Cleves and Kateryn Parr show that such rewards were standard practice.[14] In 1540 for example, Anna provided a reward to a subject 'for bryngіng of twoo larks to your grace', while in 1547 Kateryn rewarded a woman who brought her strawberries.[15] Much can be gleaned about the gift-giving practices of queens from surviving documentary sources, and the way in which they deployed their finances.

Although there are many records of gifts given to and by queens during this period, there are likely to have been occasions on which gifts of jewels went unrecorded. Olga Dmitrieva and Tessa Murdoch believe that this lack of record can be explained because by the fifteenth century, gift giving had become such a long-standing tradition that it had become trivial.[16] The result was that many gifts were barely mentioned in contemporary sources. Similarly, there are often occasions when jewellery gifts are described as a 'token'. Heal explained that tokens 'were often small gifts, accompanying letters or messages, expressing the goodwill of the sender', a description that accurately matches the numerous surviving examples.[17] In 1519, Thomas Boleyn referred to the French Queen Claude's intention to send Catherine of Aragon a token, while in 1522 Henry VIII received a token of a ring from his sister Margaret, Queen of Scotland.[18] Likewise, when the Lady Mary hoped to be reconciled with her father in 1536 she sent a token, hoping that 'the King may send her a token' in return as a sign of goodwill.[19] Rings were a popular choice of token, and examples of their use are frequent throughout this period. Katherine Howard gave a rather larger token to Lady Rutland: 'a peir of beades of mother of peerll garnesshed with golde'.[20] Katherine used beads as gifts on other occasions and perhaps chose them for their versatility.

New Year's Gifts

The main season for gift exchange was New Year. Although it was not the only time of year when gifts were traditionally exchanged, the gifts given at Lent and Easter were more often associated with the themes of Christianity. Unfortunately, there are no extant examples of gifts of jewels that were given or received by the queens in this period on these occasions. New Year was the most public occasion for giving gifts, and Heal suggested that it was the responsibility of the subject to present their monarch with a gift, which would be rewarded with a gift in return.[21] In both instances, gifts were rarely given either to or from the monarch and his consort personally. Instead, a servant or associate was often appointed to deliver them, and they would also be rewarded. Margaret of Anjou's accounts, for example, record payments to the servants of the Duchess of Bedford alongside others.[22] Comparably, the Queen's Book of Elizabeth of York lists rewards given to servants of the Bishop of Exeter, the Archbishop of Canterbury and Margaret Beaufort, among others, all of whom brought the Queen gifts at New Year 1503.[23] The list of Catherine of Aragon's New Year's gifts shows that one of her ladies or a member of her household delivered them – often the same one.[24] Gifts were frequently given to queens via an agent, and at New Year 1537 Lady Lisle's representative delivered 'a pair of beads of "granatts" [garnets] with gold' to Jane Seymour.[25] The same year, the Lady Mary's accounts show that she rewarded 'one of the Page of the quenes Chambr for bringing hir grace new yeres gyfte to my lade grace', and a similar reward was made to Kateryn Parr's servant in 1544.[26] Though the nature of sending a gift was a personal one, which often incurred great expense – particularly on behalf of the courtier – these examples emphasise how it could become an impersonal experience simply by the manner in which it was delivered. The use of an intermediary disassociated the giver and the recipient but can be partially explained by the frequent absence of members of the nobility from court at New Year. Thus, it was not only a custom but sometimes a practical issue. Occasionally though, courtiers would gather in person to present their offerings to the monarch.[27] At New Year 1538 for example, John Husee recalled, 'The King stood leaning against the cupboard, receiving all things, and Mr Tywke [Tuke] at the end of the same cupboard penning all things that were presented'.[28] Though this example shows that Henry could receive his gifts in person, it was more commonplace for gifts to be presented via a member of the monarch or consort's household.

Zemon Davis pointed out that since the Roman period there have been two different types of New Year gift: gifts of good omen that could be given to recipients of any rank and reciprocal gifts that required something in return.[29] It was the latter that was primarily in practice during this period, and numerous gift rolls survive bearing testimony to the gifts that were given to and by the monarch.[30] In England this practice had begun in the thirteenth century and thus was well established by the fifteenth century.[31] Making a gift of jewellery to a queen was a popular choice but to receive one in return was a rarity. When a monarch and their consort gave jewels on this occasion, the value of the jewel was marked against the rank of the recipient, reflected in the accounts of Margaret of Anjou.[32] It was though, more common for courtiers to receive plate.[33] By using the surviving evidence from 1532, 1534 and 1539, Maria Hayward demonstrated that the amount of plate purchased from goldsmiths by Henry VIII for his courtiers was substantial, with the most pieces bought in 1534.[34] This was a practice that was later emulated by Elizabeth I, whose New Year's gifts to her courtiers likewise consisted of plate each year.[35]

All the queens in this period would have participated in New Year's gift giving, as it provided an ideal opportunity for them to forge bonds of loyalty within their courts.[36] Unfortunately, the evidence for their activities is slender in some instances. There is, for example, no record of Elizabeth Wydeville's gift-giving habits at New Year or elsewhere, while the only comment made in relation to Anne Neville comes from the Crowland Chronicler. He remarked upon the 'vain exchanges of clothing between Queen Anne and Lady Elizabeth, eldest daughter of the dead king [Edward IV]', that took place at Christmas 1484.[37] This fragment of information provides further evidence of the rarity with which queens bestowed jewels as gifts, even among members of their own family.

Margaret of Anjou's Jewel Accounts

There is more surviving evidence for the New Year's gift giving of Margaret of Anjou than any other queen in this period. Five of Margaret's jewel accounts survive, recording the recipients of the Queen's New Year's gifts from the period 1446 to 1453.[38] Margaret's two Keepers of the Jewels, John Norris and Edward Ellesmere, created these accounts, noting the nature of the gift each recipient received. The recipients are listed in order of rank, and the presents that they were given reflected this. Some of the accounts are damaged in places and this is particularly true of E 101/410/2, covering 1448–1449, which is also faded. It is therefore difficult to extract precise information from all of these documents.

Alec Myers's study of Margaret's household demonstrated that she was a particularly generous giver of jewels at New Year.[39] This may have been because, as emphasised by Beer, gifts were of special importance to foreign-born queens who needed to forge new relationships within their realms.[40] Myers made a close examination of E 101/410/8, Margaret's jewel account covering 1452–1453.[41] As both this and the other surviving accounts show, Margaret was bountiful to her servants. Given the lack of comparative source material for other contemporary queens, it is impossible to ascertain whether Margaret's generosity was unique, or if she conformed to the expected gift-giving patterns of queens. The surviving evidence does suggest that the nature of gifts given by other queens at New Year did not consist of jewels on anywhere near the same kind of scale. Kateryn Parr, for example, chose to make her household gifts of clothes on one occasion.[42] This makes Margaret's accounts even more significant and allows us to draw some interesting conclusions.

The first three accounts covering 1445–1446, 1446–1447 and 1448–1449 show that the number of recipients was relatively stable with no great changes – more than one hundred recipients were listed on the first two accounts and probably a similar number on the latter.[43] Myers nevertheless established that Margaret's finances were in a terrible state.[44] Yet, 'so strong was the social compulsion' to make such gifts at New Year, that coupled with Margaret's generosity the list of recipients was long.[45] With the onset of the 1450s, there is a marked change, and it is interesting to consider what impact the political climate had on Margaret's gift giving. In 1451 for example, England lost the Duchy of Aquitaine, and Margaret's accounts for 1451–1452 show that she gave gifts to approximately just under two hundred people – the highest number listed in any of her accounts.[46] This could have been Margaret's attempt to rally support in the aftermath of the loss of Aquitaine. Similarly, Maurer recognised that the same year Margaret's failure to bear an heir was causing political tensions in the country to run high, a further reason for her to try to make allies.[47] The number of recipients listed in her 1452–1453 accounts dipped to roughly half of what they had been the previous year, and this is likely to be accounted for by the fact that Margaret suspected she may have been pregnant, although, as Maurer highlighted, she could by no means have been certain of this.[48]

Margaret's finances undoubtedly impacted upon those who received a New Year's gift, and her accounts demonstrate how changeable this could be. Many of the recipients listed were members of Margaret's household and appear in more than one account: for example, Elizabeth Grey, who is likely to have been Margaret's successor, Queen Elizabeth Wydeville, and Rose Merston, both the Queen's ladies.[49] Women are prominent in all of Margaret's gift lists, which is indicative of the female networking that was happening around the queen.[50] The surviving evidence for the gift-giving patterns of other queens supports this, and though not always taking place at New Year suggests that they were attempting to do the same. Furthermore, members of Margaret's household often received the same gift in a clear reflection of rank. In 1453 for example, they were all given ornamented chopins.[51] Maurer proposed an alternative theory, asserting that Margaret may simply have liked the women she gave gifts to and wished to reward them; this too is a plausible explanation, particularly in the cases of some of her unmarried ladies to whom the Queen was especially generous.[52]

The recipients of Margaret's gifts are typically listed in order of rank, with the King, leading clergy and nobility at the top. The same names appear on numerous occasions throughout the gift lists, including the Duke and Duchess of Suffolk, and the Duchess of Bedford, among others.[53] This suggests not only continuity in the relationships the Queen was building with her nobility but also, as a foreign-born queen, a desire to foster good relations with her subjects. This confirms the arguments of both Beer and Earenfight, who asserted that an effective way 'to build strong ties among the nobility was to bestow largesse in the form of hospitality and the exchange of gifts'.[54]

There are instances on which Margaret's gifts were not as lavish as they had been on previous occasions, and it seems likely that this reflected the depletion in her funds at the time. In 1453 the Duchess of Somerset was the only person of rank to receive an individual gift – a jewelled saltcellar worth £28.[55] Myers argued that Margaret gave fewer and less-expensive gifts in 1453 than she had in the years immediately following her arrival in England, a circumstance that he attributed to her increasingly stretched financial circumstances.[56] As noted previously, however, Margaret may have suspected her pregnancy at this time but also had a strong ally in the form of the Duke of Somerset. This meant that she had little need to buy male political support through gifts, which may partially account for there being fewer distributed.

Tudor Queens

Jewels provided monarchs with a potential supply of readymade gifts that did not incur additional costs. Evidence of this appears in the early years of the reign of Henry VI, who was fond of presenting gifts of jewels to those closest to him at New Year. In 1437 it was recorded that he gave his mother, Katherine of Valois, a 'tabulett of golde with a crucifixe', while his step-grandmother Joan of Navarre also received a tablet.[57] Remarkably, while Katherine's gift was purchased from a goldsmith, Joan's had once been given to 'the Kynge by my lady of Gloucestre'.[58] Several other recipients were also given items that had once been the King's personal property, signifying the way in which Henry was able to recycle jewels in order to create new gifts and save money. That Henry chose to purchase his mother's gift does, though, suggest a warm relationship between the pair. Henry VI was not alone in this respect, and Henry VIII followed the same pattern. As Hayward has highlighted, the King's jewel house provided a source of readymade gifts that did not present the King with additional costs yet still made an impressive statement.[59]

The most costly and elaborate gifts exchanged at New Year were naturally between the king and queen, which, as Beer suggested, provided a tangible way of demonstrating the strength of the royal relationship.[60] James IV of Scotland frequently gave jewels to his wife Margaret Tudor at New Year, including two sapphire rings that were gifted in 1504.[61] This trend was also employed by Henry VIII, who sent word to the recently arrived Anna of Cleves in January 1540 that he had brought her an expensive gift, which consisted of 'a partlet furred with sables and sable skins for her neck, with a muffler furred and a cap'.[62] He was considerably more generous to Katherine Howard, and eight pieces of jewellery in her inventory can be identified as New Year's gifts given in 1541.[63] This was influenced by Henry's passion for his fifth wife, and he continued to lavish other items of jewellery upon her throughout the course of their short marriage.[64] Unfortunately, there are no surviving examples of gifts that she made to him in return. It is certain that she made such gifts, as evidence in her jewel inventory and a report of New Year 1541, analysed later in this chapter, confirm that she too could be generous when it came to giving gifts.[65] By contrast, on one occasion Kateryn Parr had presented her husband with an elaborate New Year's gift of 'a faire Standdishe with a deske of gold'.[66]

Henry VIII's queens exchanged New Year's gifts with their contemporaries 'as a means of making and maintaining a network of patronage'.[67] Like Margaret of Anjou, they distributed gifts to members of their households and evidently gave this a great deal of prior thought. In autumn 1533, Thomas Cromwell had heard that Anne Boleyn planned to give 'palfreys and saddles for her ladies'.[68] The will of Lady Maud Parr refers to 'beades of lignum alweys dressed with goulde' that had been given to her by Catherine of Aragon, but it is unclear on what occasion.[69] It may have been a special sign of favour for a list of New Year's gifts distributed by Catherine in 1522 shows that she only gave jewels to those of the highest rank, while the majority of her household received plate.[70] Beer, however, suggested that this list was one of intimacy rather than status, and of the ten recipients who did receive jewels – all of which were women – the gifts were listed as having come from 'the Queen's store', rather than being newly purchased.[71] As the earlier example of Henry VI has shown, this was not unusual, and Catherine's list also reveals that she had herself received most of these pieces as gifts. The 'gold ring with a heartshaped diamond and 9 little granades or rybewes' that Catherine gave to her sister-in-law, Mary, for example, had previously been given to her by the Bishop of Carlisle.[72] Similarly, a gold pomander that Mary had given to Catherine was bestowed upon Lady Boleyn.[73] Nevertheless, Beer has shown that Catherine was at the centre of a significant gift exchange at court, spending between £350 and £424 per year on gifts between 1524 and 1530 – not solely at New Year – thereby allowing the Queen to create networks of allegiance with her English courtiers through the distribution of valuable gifts.[74] Jewels were greatly prized both 'for their social prestige and their appearance', and thus to receive such a gift from the queen was a singular honour – one that in reality few people ever experienced.[75] Yet at New Year 1541 Katherine Howard made gifts of jewels to two of her ladies. A pair of beads were given to the King's niece, Lady Margaret Douglas, while Katherine's maternal half-sister, Lady Baynton, was the recipient of a 'Gurdell of Goldesmytheswerke conteignyng viij peces of one sorte and xv of another'.[76] That these two ladies were the only members of Katherine's household to receive jewellery from the Queen underlines their familial relationship with her.

It is improbable that queens provided gifts for everyone at court, for the surviving gift rolls confirm that the King exchanged gifts with groups of people who were clearly identified by their social standing.[77] The same is likely to be true of the queen. In 1535 for example, Lady Lisle's agent informed her that 'I send you the Queen's [Anne Boleyn] New Year's gift, a pair of gold beads, weighing, with their tassels, 5 oz'.[78] In a further complimentary gesture that suggested intimacy, the beads were 'of her grace's own wearing'.[79] As Lady Lisle was married to the King's illegitimate maternal uncle, such a gift may have been an acknowledgement of their familial proximity to one another.[80] This was not the only occasion on which Lady Lisle received a gift from one of Henry VIII's queens, for in 1537 she was the recipient of an unknown New Year's gift from Jane Seymour.[81] Some of the gifts distributed by the King were on behalf of himself and his consort, for at New Year 1541 the Imperial ambassador related that following the receipt of gifts from the King's daughter, Lady Mary; in return she was sent 'two magnificent New Year's gifts from himself and the Queen [Katherine Howard]'.[82] Unfortunately there is no indication as to what these were.

Henry VIII's gift rolls provide examples of the gifts given to the King, and those he gave in return.[83] In 1534, for example, the Bishop of Carlisle gave him 'a ring of golde with a diamant'.[84] That such detailed lists were kept indicates the importance that was placed on the process of giving gifts to kings, although it is unclear when this began.[85] Also in 1534, Anne Boleyn made her husband a particularly elaborate gift:

> a goodly gilte bason hauyng a raille or boarde of golde in the middest of the bryme garnished with rubies and pearls wherin standeth a fountein also hauyng a raille of golde about it garnished with diamants. Out wherof issueth water at the teets of three nayked women standing aboute the foote of the same founteyn.[86]

On Anne's first New Year as Queen of England, her choice of gift was an attempt to make an awe-inspiring statement of her exalted status and majesty.[87] It was undoubtedly intended to impress her court as much as her husband, thereby underlining the ways in which gifts of jewels could serve several purposes.

Although highly unusual and thus serving to reinforce the unprecedented nature of queenship during this period, there are examples of Henry VIII's queens giving New Year's gifts to one another. Kateryn Parr did this on at least one occasion but so too did Katherine Howard. Anna of Cleves joined the court at Hampton Court Palace at New Year 1541. She was warmly received by her former husband and the new queen – her own former lady-in-waiting, and 'At this time the King sent his Queen a present of a ring and two small dogs, which she passed over to lady Anne'.[88] This was presumably done with the King's approval and not only reveals Katherine Howard's kindly nature but shows that she felt secure enough in her position to make such a personal gift, given to her by her husband, to her predecessor and former mistress. The recycling of gifts – thereby offering a piece of personal property – was seen as a sign of favour, as Katherine doubtless intended.[89]

If a New Year's gift was not received, it was a sure sign of disfavour. In 1537 Sir George Lawson – who usually received a gift from the King – was so concerned when he received nothing that he was forced to check with Thomas Cromwell that he had not caused offence.[90] Such was the impact that a lack of gift could cause. Further evidence of this appeared in 1532 when Catherine of Aragon was in disgrace, underlined by the fact that 'The King has sent her no present, and has forbidden the Council and others to do so, as is usual'.[91] Though Catherine was also banned from sending Henry a gift, she ignored his instructions. She sent a gold cup, but as the Imperial ambassador Chapuys reported, 'the King refused it'.[92] There could be no clearer indication that Catherine was out of favour, and the cup 'was sent back to the Queen'.[93] The refusal to both give and receive a gift served as tangible evidence of Catherine's disgrace and is in stark contrast to the treatment meted out to Anne Boleyn that year. Though she was not queen, in a visible display of her heightened importance, for the first time Anne was listed as an official recipient of a New Year's gift from the King.[94] She had received such gifts from him on previous occasions, yet her appearance on the gift rolls for this year is noteworthy. It denotes a change in the nature of her relationship with Henry and suggests that both parties now recognised that it had become more official. This in turn underlines that they both believed that their marriage would be concluded shortly.

Family

Jewels were a popular choice of gift not only between queens and their husbands but also with their children. At New Year 1540, for example, the Lady Mary made her half-brother Prince Edward a gift of a gold brooch with the image of St John the Baptist set with a ruby, while she received jewels from both Edward and her half-sister Elizabeth in 1543.[95] Such gifts were not unusual for Mary, whose accounts and jewel inventory show that she frequently gave jewels to friends and members of her family.[96] Moreover, having spent a great deal of time with both Elizabeth and Edward in their youths, her relationships with her two younger half-siblings were warm at this time. Anna of Cleves was on such good terms with Mary that she continued to exchange gifts with her after her marriage to Henry VIII had been dissolved. These gifts included 'Spayneshe Silke' sent by Anna, and Mary's accounts note several payments to Anna's servants by way of reward for delivering gifts.[97] Kateryn Parr also shared a good relationship with her stepchildren and Anna of Cleves, and her accounts show that at New Year 1544 she gave cloth of silver for kirtles to Mary, Elizabeth and Anna, and clothes to Prince Edward.[98] That Kateryn chose to include Anna is perhaps not only a sign that, like Henry, she considered her to be part of the family but also an acknowledgement of Anna's status. Kateryn's fondness for jewellery has been noted throughout the course of this book, and at New Year 1547 she gave her stepson Prince Edward a gift of a jewel containing miniatures of herself and the King.[99] A gift of this nature was characteristic of Kateryn, who distributed miniatures of herself to her friends and family as related in Chapters 3 and 4. This was not the only occasion on which Kateryn had given jewels to her stepchildren for New Year, as another year she gave her stepdaughter Mary 'a Boke of golde set with Rubies' and 'a payr of Braceletts set with small ples [pearls]'.[100] Kateryn's surviving accounts confirm that such gifts were by no means a regularity and serve once more to reinforce the significance and value that was placed on jewels. It was nevertheless the second known instance on which she had given Mary such a gift, for shortly after Kateryn's marriage she had presented Mary with a pair of diamond and ruby bracelets, one of which contained an emerald.[101] This gift was of particular importance, as it signified an attempt on Kateryn's part to engineer good relations during the transition of their relationship to stepmother and stepdaughter. Bracelets were given as tokens of love and remembrance, which may explain their choice.

Aside from New Year, gifts were frequently exchanged between family members in order to mark a variety of other occasions. For kings and queens, this process could begin with courtship. Heal suggested that courtship gifts could be viewed as 'a deferred promise of future performance', and this is most clearly in evidence in the relationship of Henry VIII and Anne Boleyn.[102] Jewels were one of the most tangible ways of conveying love and affection, and most stages of the couple's courtship were marked by gifts of jewels. The King's surviving letters to Anne reference several: 'seeing I cannot be present in person with you I send you the nearest thing to that possible, that is, my picture set in bracelets, with the whole device'.[103] The inclusion of a portrait within the jewels is reflective of the highly personal nature of this gift. It was clearly an attempt to win Anne's favour, but her apprehension as to the nature of their relationship was underlined in the choice of jewel she sent in return. Crafted like a ship in stormy waters with a single damsel aboard, the jewel was symbolic of how Anne perceived her situation. It demonstrates how jewels could be used to convey messages, something that was adopted with increasing frequency during the Elizabethan period.[104] The meaning of the gift was fully understood by the King, who responded by thanking Anne not only for the jewel but 'for the pretty interpretation and too humble submission made by your benignity'.[105]

As the relationship between Anne and Henry became increasingly serious, so too did the regularity with which the King bestowed jewels upon her. His 1531 accounts record numerous gifts for Anne from goldsmith Cornelius Hayes. These gifts do not, however, appear to have stemmed solely from 1531, and seem to have been gifted over the course of several years (Table 6.1).[106]

The first gift of an emerald ring was delivered alongside 'numerous other presents of jewelry', although the details of these are not recorded.[107] Likewise, several other items listed in

Table 6.1 Gifts of jewels given to Anne Boleyn by Henry VIII: *L & P*, v, no. 276

Possible Date	*Gift*
1527	Bracelets featuring a portrait of the King
1527	'a ring set with emeralds'
1531	'a little book with crown gold'
1531	'A ring with a table diamond'
1531	'a diamond in a brooch of Our Lady of Boulogne'
1531	'19 diamonds for her head'
1531	'Two bracelets for her, set with 10 diamonds and 8 pearls'
1531	'19 diamonds set in trueloves of crown gold'
1531	'21 rubies set in roses of crown gold'
1531	'A borasse flower of diamonds for her'
1531	'Two borders of gold for her sleeves, set with 10 diamonds and 8 pearls'
1531	'Two buttons of crown gold, set with 10 diamonds and 40 pearls'
1531	'2 diamonds on two hearts, for her head'
1531	'21 diamonds and 21 rubies set upon roses and hearts'
1531	'a dial and a tablet'
1531	'Five diamonds and 4 pieces of Paris work'
1531	'10 buttons of gold, set with diamonds'

the table were delivered with other pieces that are not specifically described. This suggests that they were either of lesser value or that the quantities were too great, and therefore too laborious to record. As the contents of the table show, the jewellery that Anne received was varied and highly ornamented but also contained practical items, such as buttons. If these jewels took her personal preferences into account, then she seems to have been particularly fond of diamonds, which appear frequently. Several of the jewels are indicative of the nature of Anne's relationship with the King and have a romantic theme to them, such as the diamonds and rubies 'set upon roses and hearts'.[108] This is a testimony to the strength of Henry's feelings for Anne, despite the longevity of their courtship.

St Valentine's Day was a popular choice for making a gift to a loved one, yet there are few examples of gifts that can be connected to queens.[109] However, a payment in the 1540 accounts of Anna of Cleves shows that she paid £6 5s 7.5d. for a gilt cup 'whyche your grace gave unto M[aste]r Cecell [Cecil] beyng yo[u]r g[ra]ces valentyne'.[110] This is the only direct evidence we have of a queen bestowing such a gift to mark this occasion and indicates that Valentine's Day must therefore have been celebrated in some form at the Tudor court. An inventory of Henry VIII's jewels dating from 1530 lists 'five valentines of goldsmith's work', but it is unclear if this was a specific type of jewel or if it was linked to the occasion.[111] One piece that certainly had a romantic theme came from Catherine of Aragon: 'A blue heart and H and K. With white letters and a lock to it. With two hands holding a heart, with a hanging pearl, given by the Queen'.[112] The occasion on which this jewel was given though is unknown. Other items that appear in the inventories of Henry's wives reveal the popularity of romantically themed jewellery and could have been intended as Valentine's gifts. Anne Boleyn was given various pieces shaped like hearts, including two pieces listed in the earlier table: '2 diamonds on two hearts, for her head', on 5 February 1531.[113] The date on which this piece was given makes it plausible that it was a Valentine's gift. A more certain example of a Valentine's gift appears in the jewel inventory of the Lady Mary. This shows that she was given 'a Broche of golde enamyled blacke with an Agate of the Story of Abrahm with iiij small Rockt Rubies' by Sir Anthony Browne, 'drawing hir grace to his Valentyne'.[114] As Sir Anthony was both a married man and highly trusted by the King, this gift was intended as no more than a friendly gesture.

A queen's marriage was a key lifecycle event, and gifts of jewels might therefore be expected on this occasion as they 'added festivity and courtesy to the formalities of contract'.[115] There is a lack of evidence in connection with most of the English queens of this period; however, notes in Katherine Howard's inventory show that King gave the bulk of the jewels listed to her 'at the time of the solemnization of their marriage'.[116] The examples of jewels given to Margaret of Anjou by Henry VI discussed in Chapter 7 in relation to the Crown Jewels are also likely to have been wedding gifts. In the seventeenth century, Sir Francis Bacon claimed that following the marriage of Henry VII and Elizabeth of York in 1486, 'Gifts flowed freely on all sides and were showered on everyone, while feasts, dances and tournaments were celebrated with liberal generosity to make known and to magnify the joyful occasion and the bounty of gold, silver, rings and jewels'.[117] Unfortunately, there is no contemporary evidence with which to corroborate this claim. Evidence does survive in connection with the marriage of Mary Tudor to the French King, Louis XII, in 1514. The Earl of Worcester reported to Cardinal Wolsey that Louis had presented his bride with 'the goodliest and the rychest sight of Jouelles [missing words] I saw. I wold never have believed it if I had not seen [missing word]'.[118] Not only did Louis provide Mary with 'lvi great peces that I sawe of dyamonds and Rubies vii of the grettest perles that I have seen', but among other splendid jewels he also gave her 'a marvellous greate pointed diamond, with a Rubye almost two inches longe, withoute foil, which was esteemed by some men at ten thousand marks'.[119] Such lavish gifts show not only Louis's enthusiasm for Mary and his determination to be generous, but the jewels also provided a way to emphasise his wealth and magnificence to his foreign bride and her family. By the same token, both Ferdinand of Aragon and Isabel of Castile presented their daughter-in-law, Margaret of Austria, with jewels upon her marriage to their son

Prince Juan. Among the pieces given to Margaret was a string of 48 pearls which came from Isabel.[120] Gifts were an integral part of these joyous occasions, further emphasising the regality of the monarch.

The marriages of a queen's children marked another key life-cycle event, and it was not unusual for money to be outlaid on jewels in preparation. This was an important part of conveying the wealth of the dynasty and was of particular consequence to Henry VII and Elizabeth of York, with their newly established Tudor dynasty. Henry VII's Chamber Books record that in 1501 he spent the extravagant sum of £14,000 'for diverse and many juells brought oute of Fraunce agenst the marage of my Lorde Prince', Arthur to Catherine of Aragon.[121] Some of these may have been used at the time of Catherine's reception into London, when the *Great Chronicle of London* recorded that 'the said pryncesse accompanyed with many lordis and ladyes In moost sumptuous wyse apparaylid' prepared to enter the city.[122] Equally likely is that the jewels displayed on this occasion had been a part of Catherine's wedding trousseau, as throughout the course of the marriage negotiations Henry VII had made it clear to her parents that they 'are to dress their daughter suitably to her rank (honorifice), and to give her as many jewels, etc., for her personal use, as becomes her position'.[123] Catherine's dowry partially consisted of jewels, which led to a dispute between Henry VII and the Spanish sovereigns following Arthur's death in 1502 over their return.[124] Timothy Schroder noted that many of the pieces of gold and silver plate that Catherine brought with her from Spain were listed as gifts to Henry VIII in the 1521 Jewel Book, but no details of specific jewels are known.[125] That jewels could be used to form part of a foreign bride's dowry once more emphasises the value that was placed on precious objects.

Some of Henry VII's expenditure for his eldest son's wedding may be accounted for by the gifts he made to Catherine in 1502. In order to help quell his daughter-in-law's homesickness when her Spanish servants were destined for home, Henry VII summoned his jeweller who had 'many rings, and huge diamonds, and jewels of most goodly fashion'.[126] Catherine was permitted to choose a piece, while her ladies then followed suit. Such a gift displayed both Henry's generosity and majesty and is seemingly in keeping with his character – contrary to his traditional reputation as a miser.[127] Indeed, further evidence of both of these elements of Henry's personality can be seen in the preparations for the marriage of his daughter, Margaret, to the King of Scotland in 1503. On this occasion 'sertain juells, plate, and other stuff' were bought for both Margaret and the King at a cost of £16,000.[128]

Queens could receive jewellery from their husbands as signs of affection. Henry VII's Chamber Books show that he regularly gave Elizabeth of York jewels or money with which to buy them. In 1492 for example, he gave 'the Quenes grace for golde wyer' £2 6s. 8d, presumably to adorn items of clothing.[129] In May 1497 he gave Elizabeth a further £31 10s. 'for juels'.[130] It is interesting to consider that Henry did not choose his wife's jewels himself, which suggests that this particular gift was not a personal one. Alternatively, it could be that he simply preferred to allow Elizabeth to buy something of her own choice, or that he was reimbursing her for items she had already purchased. Although the Queen's Book containing Elizabeth's expenses covers only 1502 and 1503, it reveals no such similar gifts to her husband.[131] This could be as a result of her straightened finances, rather than her feelings towards him, for Henry's accounts show that on other occasions he had given Elizabeth money for the purpose of clearing her debts, and this continued for some time after her death.[132]

An entry in the accounts of Anna of Cleves shows a payment in 1540, possibly in July, to 'my Lady of Rutland for a Reward whyche she gave for your grace for a fayer flower curiously wrought & sent to the kyngs highnes'.[133] That Anna was making gifts of jewels to her husband at a time when her marriage was coming to an end may be indicative of her desire to earn the King's favour. However, Anna's example shows that even following the breakdown of a royal marriage, it was still possible for a couple to exchange gifts. Following her separation from Henry VIII in July 1540, it was observed that Anna 'sent his Highness a ring for a token' as a sign of the goodwill she bore towards him.[134] More poignantly, she also sent him 'the ring delivered unto her at their pretensed marriage, desiring that it might be broken in pieces as a thing which she knew of no force or value'.[135] Henry's generosity to Anna in thanks for her co-operation in the annulment of her marriage has been noted in Chapter 2 in relation to the jewels he bestowed upon her, thus in material terms it was to Anna's advantage to do so. This act of kindness on behalf of the King conveys his determination that Anna 'will be considered as the King's sister, and have precedence over all ladies in England, after the Queen and the King's children'.[136] Similarly, that the former married couple exchanged New Year's gifts in both 1541 and 1542 is proof that they remained on good terms.[137]

Bearing her husband a child was a crucial moment in a queen's life, and it was not unusual for her to receive gifts of jewels upon this occasion. For kings this provided a tangible way of rewarding their wives, and there is evidence that Edward IV chose to do this at least once. His accounts record that in 1466 he spent £125 on 'an ouch agenst the tyme of the birth of our moost dere daughter Elizabeth', which was presumably given to Elizabeth Wydeville.[138] The cost of the jewel was substantial and serves as confirmation of the King's joy. There is no evidence to suggest that Edward gave Elizabeth similar gifts following the births of their subsequent children, and it could be that this was a unique gift ordered to mark the birth of the couple's first child. It is also possible that this jewel was purchased prior to the baby's birth in hopeful anticipation that Elizabeth would provide Edward with a son. This would certainly explain why such a large sum was paid.

Gifts were also given to the midwives who delivered royal children by way of reward. When Marjory Cobb delivered the future Edward V in 1470, she was rewarded with a grant of £10 for life, and this was probably a standard sum, for when Henry VIII's first son was born in 1511, his godfather the French King rewarded the midwife with the same amount.[139] The christening of royal children presented another important opportunity for the giving of gifts, and the account of the christening of Princess Bridget in 1480 reveals that following the ceremony 'the godfather and the godmoders gave great gyftes to the said princess'.[140] The details of these gifts are not recorded, but it is possible that they consisted of jewelled items or plate. Queens also provided christening gifts to other children, particularly if they had been asked to stand as godparents. We see evidence of this in Kateryn Parr's accounts, which show that in July 1547 she made a gift of a bowl for the christening of Lady Margaret Douglas's child.[141] It was usual for godparents to send gifts, but for queens they provided another way of fostering good relations and ensured secured loyalty.

Jewels could be an indication or reflection as to the intimate nature of the relationship between a queen and her husband, but queens also used them as a sign of affection to their children. An inventory of jewels belonging to Prince Henry (later Henry VIII) shows that his mother, Elizabeth of York, gave him two items. The first of these was a cross 'sett with v table diamounds t iii. good ples [pearls]', as well as 'a ryng enameld with a ruby'.[142] Elizabeth was renowned for her deep religious faith, and this explains why she chose the gift of a cross. The other item was 'a ryng enameld with a ruby'; the inventory shows that Henry received other gifts of rings, including from his father and Catherine of Aragon, but the date and occasions of these gifts are not recorded.[143]

Katherine Howard's inventory confirms that she made gifts to her stepdaughters. Two pieces of jewellery were given to the Lady Elizabeth on unknown dates: a pair of beads, and 'oone other Brooche of Golde wherin is set an antique hed of agate vj very small Rubyes and vj verey small Emeraldes litle thing worthe'.[144] The brooch was listed as being of little value, which suggests that it was a token gift, given to a girl who would have been no more than eight years old. That two gifts were made though is expressive of a close relationship between Katherine and her stepdaughter. This is borne out by contemporary reports, and while contemporaries hinted at a cool relationship between Katherine and her eldest stepdaughter, Mary, this did not prevent Katherine from making Mary a gift of a pomander.[145]

Piety

Gifts that showcased a monarch's piety were common, and both Henry VII's Chamber Books and Henry VIII's accounts pre-Reformation record regular payments to various religious houses.[146] As an essential part of Christian duty, charity formed an integral part of a queen's role.[147] Indeed, as Anne Crawford stated, 'queens were leaders of domestic society', and thus their appearances of piety could wield great influence over others.[148] Prior to the Reformation, queens were expected to demonstrate piety, and though the Reformation ensured that gifts to religious houses were no longer forthcoming, queens were nevertheless expected to continue their charitable works. Frequent examples of this appear in the accounts of Kateryn Parr, who on one occasion gave money 'to a pore woman at Westminster', and on another 'to a blynde woman'.[149]

Queens often gave gifts to religious institutions on Saints days, and Henry VIII's accounts reference numerous payments made on behalf of Catherine of Aragon on these occasions.[150] Similarly, Elizabeth of York often made offerings at various religious houses, but both queens made these gifts in cash.[151] Between March 1502 and March 1503, Elizabeth made 38 offerings to various religious institutions and can therefore be accurately classified as 'a consort whose piety and charity were truly queenly'.[152] Catherine of Aragon made comparable offerings, although the evidence for her gifts is more sporadic due to their appearance in Henry VIII's accounts.[153] Crawford asserted that there is no evidence that Margaret of Anjou was anything other than conventionally pious, but Margaret did use jewels as a way of emphasising her religious devotion. At New Year 1453 Margaret gave the shrine at Walsingham a gold plaque garnished with pearls, sapphires and rubies, which showed an angel holding a cross.[154] This is the only specific example of a queen giving jewels to a religious house in this period, and although other queens are known to have visited Walsingham – chiefly Elizabeth Wydeville with Edward IV in 1469, presumably to ask for help in conceiving a son, and Catherine of Aragon – no such gifts are recorded.[155] Margaret's gift is likely to have had a double meaning, for though she had been married since 1445 she had yet to produce a child. As mentioned earlier in this chapter, by early 1453 Margaret 'may have been hopeful' that she was pregnant, and thus the gift to Walsingham – a shrine particularly linked with fertility – was the Queen's way of rendering thanks: she gave birth to her son in October that same year.[156]

It was not just queens who chose to use gifts of jewels in this way. In 1541 it was reported that Margaret Beaufort had once given a church 'a gold crown with stones and jewels', and indeed, her will provides numerous examples of gifts that she made to religious institutions.[157] Such gifts were not therefore exclusive to monarchs and their consorts and were one of the most popular ways of conveying religious devotion. As the King's mother, Margaret behaved in a semi-regal manner, and her gifts are likely to have been reflective of others made by contemporary queens.[158] Gifts made to religious institutions were one of the most effective ways of a queen expressing piety, which was in turn integral for a consort.[159] Following the Reformation and the Dissolution of the Monasteries, however, such displays no longer occurred and queens found other ways of expressing their piety – including through their jewels.

Diplomacy and Bribes

Public displays of generosity were a vital part of monarchy and so too was diplomacy. Gifts formed an important tool with which to aid monarchs and consorts, particularly in relations between different European rulers.[160] Political gifts were always expected to yield some kind of return – often in terms of benefits – and they could be useful in securing peace and enhancing foreign relations.[161] Given the physical distance between European rulers, ambassadors played a vital role in gift distribution, and without suitably rich gifts ambassadors 'had little hope of being successful'.[162] It was often they who presented gifts to monarchs and their consorts on behalf of their foreign masters, and they were also frequently responsible for distributing bribes to those in influential positions at court. Glenn Richardson has shown that in the early years of Henry VIII's reign, the King was making rich gifts to members of François I's embassy in order to ensure smooth relations between the two countries.[163] Comparably, in his excellent work about sixteenth-century diplomacy, Garrett Mattingly noted that the Imperial ambassador, Chapuys, 'spent a good deal on outright espionage', in order to glean information.[164] Mattingly went as far as to state that 'Chapuys's intelligence apparatus represents about the most diversified development of the sixteenth century'.[165] However, there are other examples of gifts that were made in order to ensure that the recipient spoke favourably on behalf of the giver's party. Thomas Cromwell received a steady stream of gifts throughout his period in office from a number of recipients, all of which were carefully recorded.[166] Not all of these came from abroad, and many were from those who were either members of or associated with the court, who sought his help and believed that a gift would help to secure his personal loyalty and intervention.

There were occasions, albeit rarely, when opportunities for monarchs to offer gifts personally presented themselves. For example, when Lord Louis of Gruuthuyse visited Edward IV's court in 1472, Louis was given 'a cuppe of golde garnished with pearl and in the middest of the cuppe is a greate pece of an unicornes horne', the cover of which contained 'a greate zafer [sapphire]'.[167] This was the first of several gifts Edward made to his guest, and the surviving narrative of the visit confirms that its purpose was to impress the King's resplendence upon Louis. Although Elizabeth Wydeville is not specifically mentioned in regard to the gift giving, she certainly witnessed it and took part in the entertainments that were staged.[168] It is plausible that on this occasion and others, she may have played a more significant role in diplomatic negotiations: in an attempt to persuade Elizabeth to use her influence with her husband to the giver's advantage, it is possible that Elizabeth – and perhaps other contemporary queens – were given gifts that went unrecorded.

More direct evidence of the queen's involvement in the diplomatic gift giving process appears when Catherine of Aragon accompanied her husband to France for the Field of the Cloth of Gold in 1520. Theresa Earenfight convincingly argued that Catherine was one of Henry VIII's 'closest advisers on international diplomacy', and there is certainly evidence of it here.[169] At the famous meeting between the French and English kings, it was observed that not only did Henry VIII and François I make one another gifts of rich jewels but that 'The Queen of England gave a very beautiful diamond and a ruby in a ring to the most Christian King; and the Queen of France gave two other rings of equal value to the King of England'.[170] Queens were therefore able to participate in diplomatic proceedings, providing gifts that were of parity to one another in order to support their husband's negotiations. Given Catherine's origins and loyalty to her home country, however, François must have been aware that she viewed an English alliance with Spain more favourably.

In another context, we know that Catherine exchanged gifts with her former sister-in-law, Margaret of Austria. Although the nature of Catherine's gifts to Margaret are unknown, Margaret sent a gift of paternoster beads that were probably intended for both Catherine and Henry.[171] Gifts such as these were important, for as Earenfight asserted, as women in power who played important – albeit different – roles in the affairs of their respective countries, Catherine and Margaret were 'obliged to offer gifts to cement the diplomatic and familial ties' between them.[172]

Though she was not yet a queen, in 1532 Anne Boleyn was given the opportunity to participate directly in diplomatic gift giving. Having accompanied Henry VIII to Calais, François I made Anne an extravagant gift of 'a diamond worth 15,000 or 16,000 cr'.[173] The significance of this was substantial, for it served as an acknowledgement of Anne's heightened status and the French King's belief that she would soon be queen, as well as his acceptance of her in that role. A gift in such circumstances was highly unusual and was tangible evidence of François's support for Anne's marriage. The value of the gift is notable, as in turn it reflected the wealth both of François and of France and served as evidence of his power – something that François wanted to reinforce to both Anne and Henry. It also demonstrated François's determination to form a friendly alliance with England, for as Heal argued, when an alliance was sought gifts had to flow generously.[174] Making Anne an expensive gift provided François with the ideal outlet to pursue negotiations, and he evidently believed – rightly – that he would have greater success with Anne than he could have hoped for with her predecessor.

Gifts were an important part of upholding the regal image of majesty and the vision of wealth that monarchs were keen to portray, and queens often played a leading part in this. In preparation for the visit of Claude d'Annebaut in 1546, Henry VIII ordered five licenses for French, Flemish and Italian jewellers to bring to England

> almaner juelles, perlles, precious stones, as well set in gold and embrawdred in garmentes as unsett, almaner goldsmythes worke of golde and sylver, almaner sortes of skynnes and ffurres of sables and lusardes, clothes, newe gentlelesses of what facion or value the same be, wrought and set or unwrought and not set, in gold or otherwise as he or they shall thinke best.[175]

These were not all intended for Henry's use but also to enhance the splendour of 'our derest wief the Quene' and his daughter Mary.[176] These jewels were not itemised, but the importance that Kateryn placed on the visit is underlined by the further orders she gave in spring 1546 for the jeweller Mark Mylloner of London to provide 635 aiglettes of gold, set in purple ribbon, and gloves trimmed with buttons of diamonds and rubies.[177] The ordering of these additional items suggests a particular awareness from Kateryn of the need to impress – possibly because the visit of d'Annebaut marked one of the only instances in which she had been directly involved in a diplomatic visit. It is possible that some of the aiglettes are the same as those that appear in her queenly inventory, referenced in Chapter 3.[178] As has been previously emphasised, Kateryn was particularly conscious of the usefulness of the royal image as a propaganda tool, partially because of her own relatively humble origins. 1546 was not the first time she had projected this image, and when the Duke of Najera visited England in 1544 her jewels drew comment. It was then observed that 'Suspended from her neck were two crosses, and a jewel of very rich diamonds, and in her head-dress were many and beautiful ones. Her girdle was of gold, with very large pendants'.[179]

Prizes and Rewards

Throughout the fifteenth century and the early decades of the sixteenth century, tournaments were a regular occurrence at the royal court. These were often elaborate and were commonly staged in order to celebrate momentous occasions, such as marriages or coronations. The prizes for the victors of such tournaments were often jewels, and the Chamber Books of Henry VII show that in July 1505 he paid Bartholomew Rede £8 for 4oz of gold 'made in Ryng[es] for the Just[es] at Riche[mount]'.[180] The task of distributing such prizes was typically a female prerogative that conformed with the rules of chivalry.[181] In 1466 Edward IV's ordinances for jousting stated that either the queen or the ladies present were to be given the honour of 'the attributone and gyfte of the prize'.[182] The queen was therefore often directly involved in this process.

In another example of a key lifecycle event in which the giving of jewels was involved, at a tournament held in celebration of Elizabeth Wydeville's coronation in 1465, it was probably the Queen who presented Lord Stanley with a ruby ring.[183] Similarly, Catherine of Aragon is likely to have distributed the letters 'H' and 'K' in gold, which were created for the victors of the jousts held in February 1511 in celebration of the birth of her short-lived son, Henry, Duke of Cornwall.[184] Catherine's wardrobe accounts for 1515–1517 also show that on one occasion she lent a member of her household, Alexander Frognall, money for 'an H of gold'.[185] It is unclear, though, whether this was intended as a prize for a joust, or perhaps as some other kind of gift. Catherine was certainly involved in the giving of prizes at the Field of the Cloth of Gold, for the Venetian ambassador reported that during the visit 'the Queen gave orders to make presents to some of the jousters', which 'consisted of jewels, or rings, or collars, and the like'.[186] In the same manner as Catherine had given gifts to the French King, she and the French Queen, Claude, distributed prizes to the other's husband following the jousts: 'the Queen of France gave the prize and honour of the joust to the King of England, namely, a diamond and a ruby in two rings; the Queen of England doing the like by the most Christian King'.[187] These jewels allowed both queens to reinforce the messages they had given with their earlier gifts.

Queens did not exclusively adopt the role of prize givers, and at a tournament held to celebrate the wedding of Prince Richard to Anne Mowbray in 1478 it was the Prince's elder sister, Elizabeth of York, who participated in the prize giving. The prizes were gems set with golden letters, and among the fortunate recipients was Sir Richard Haute who received a gold 'E' set with a ruby.[188] Jewels given at tournaments provided an ideal reward for the feats of those who excelled in bravery. The giving of jewels as tournament prizes links with the notion that such gifts were an indication of favour. This favour was also highlighted in the examples of gifts of jewels that were given by queens, and links with Beer's observation that courtiers were interested in who the queen favoured and rewarded.[189]

Knowing that the relationship between Cardinal Wolsey and Anne Boleyn was far from harmonious, when Wolsey lay ill in the 1520s Henry VIII urged Anne to send him a gift as a sign of her goodwill towards him. Dutifully, Anne 'took incontinent a tabulet of gold hanging at her girdle, and delivered it to Master Buttes with very gentle and comfortable words and commendations to the Cardinal'.[190] In this instance, the intimacy of the gift – taken from Anne's own person – was significant and was intended to smooth relations and as a show of friendship to reassure Wolsey that his relationship with Anne was amicable. Though Anne was not queen at that time, she was wielding power on an almost royal scale. Hers demonstrated perfectly that the 'gift that was a seal of royal favour might provide a security that might mean the difference between life and death'.[191] Anne also made other intimate gifts, such as in 1535 when she gave Lord Leonard Grey a gift of a chain of gold from her waist, worth 100 marks, and a purse of 20 sovereigns.[192] In this instance, the monetary value was of less importance than the symbolic gesture of receiving a gift that had been the queen's property. There could be no greater demonstration of favour, and Anne's was a pattern of behaviour that was followed by all queens in order to widen their networks and secure loyalties.

Evidence in support of this can be found in Katherine Howard's inventory, which shows that she gave jewels to her ladies and family. Five of these have already been discussed within the relevant context earlier in this chapter, but all of the gifts given by Katherine are revealing in terms of her relationships with the women around her. All of the recipients were linked to her in some way, including the Countess of Surrey, the wife of Katherine's cousin, to whom the Queen gave the gift of a brooch for an unspecified reason.[193] Another gift was made to mark a special occasion:

> one peir of beades of Cristall garnesshed with golde being of them xl/betwixt euery of them a pece of goldesmytheswerke/and viij beades of golde ennamuled blewe and set with stones/hauyng also a pillor of Cristall with aman of golde in the same/and with a tassell of venice golde.

These were given 'by the Quene to the Lady Carew late Mrs Borrys [Norris] ageynst her Marriage'.[194] Lady Carew was one of Katherine's ladies, but there is no evidence of Katherine providing similar gifts against the marriage of any of her other ladies. Nevertheless, this is likely to have been expected practice as the jewel inventory of Katherine's eldest stepdaughter, Mary, reveals that she too made gifts of jewels to her friends and ladies upon their marriages.[195] However, the accounts of both Anna of Cleves and Kateryn Parr provide testimony that such gifts were unusual, for both show that rewards for good service usually appeared in the form of cash.[196]

Not all rewards of jewels for good service to the queen came directly from her. Following the death of Jane Seymour in October 1537, her jewel inventory reveals that of the 508 items individually listed, the King gave away as gifts.[197] In a similar manner to the gifts made by Katherine Howard, most of these were given to members of Jane's household, but here too there is evidence to suggest that rank and favour came into play. While Lady Rochford, former sister-in-law of Anne Boleyn, Lady Russell, wife of one of the King's privy councillors, and a Mr Long were each given 'a Tabelet of golde', other ladies were given several pieces.[198] Lady Zouche was a particularly fortunate recipient, receiving two borders of gold, while her husband was given a brooch of gold.[199] In what may have been an indication of rank, given that it is one of the most detailed items described, the King's daughter Lady Elizabeth received 'a litle booke of golde with the Salvation of oure Lady'.[200] Elizabeth was the only giftee to receive a book, and this could have been a reflection of her scholarly abilities or to encourage her in them. What is not known, however, is whether these gifts were made at Jane's request before her death – in which case she may have given some indication as to who she wanted to reward and with which items – or whether it was a decision made by the King. In either scenario, that some of the recipients were given more than one piece of jewellery could be a sign of the esteem in which the late queen and possibly the King had held them. Kings using jewels to reward members of their consort's household was not exclusive to the English court, for James IV of Scotland also made gifts of jewels to the ladies of his wife, Margaret Tudor, albeit at New Year.[201]

Jane Seymour's jewel collection provided her husband with an effective way of rewarding the good service shown to his former queen, while not incurring any costs. It is possible though that it indicated something more. Although Henry was giving away jewels that had primarily been Jane's personal property, that he was so quick to dispose of them suggests that – on a personal level at least – he was in no hurry to replace her with a new queen. This supports Henry's own assertion to François I, made shortly after Jane's death, that 'Divine Providence has mingled my joy with the bitterness of the death of her who brought me this happiness'.[202] Some of the more practical items in Jane's collection, such as buttons, were acquired by the King and used to adorn his own clothes, while as discussed in Chapter 1, several other pieces were broken down.[203]

Other jewels given by queens in reward were highly inappropriate and were taken as bribes. There are two instances of this during this period, the first of which became apparent during the trial of Anne Boleyn in May 1536. Here it was claimed that the Queen had enticed her brother, Lord Rochford, to commit incest with her not only by alluring him with her body but 'also with kisses, presents, and jewels'.[204] Though it is certainly possible, if not likely, that Anne gave jewels to her brother throughout her period as queen, this example shows how gifts could look suspicious when taken out of context. It also emphasises the negative connotations that could be attached to the way in which jewels were used. The accusation in the trial proceedings illustrates how Anne's accusers believed they could manipulate the gift giving process in order to provide evidence of Anne and Rochford's guilt.[205]

By contrast, the accusation that Katherine Howard used jewels as a form of bribery was fully justified. When the Queen's infidelity was discovered in November 1541, so too was the fact that she had been giving gifts to her lover, Thomas Culpeper. According to Culpeper's deposition, when he met Katherine in her apartments she 'gave him by her own hands a fair cap of velvet garnished with a brooch and three dozen pairs of aglets and a chain'.[206] During Culpeper's trial, it was also revealed that Katherine had given 'divers gifts and sums of money' to her secretary and former lover, Francis Dereham.[207] Katherine's gifts were doubtless intended to reflect her devotion to Culpeper, and in Dereham's case as a bribe in order to silence him in regard to her previous indiscretions. This is supported by the gift Katherine made to Alice Wilkes, a member of her household who had known the Queen prior to her marriage. Wilkes was given rich gifts of 'upper and nether habiliments of goldsmith's work for the French hood and a tablet of gold'.[208] Such gifts suggest that Katherine expected something in return, chiefly the silence of those who could have provided evidence against her. Katherine's example shows how gifts could aid inappropriate queenly behaviour, though it was nevertheless in keeping with the way in which queens used jewels to secure and reward loyalty.

Conclusion

Throughout the fifteenth and sixteenth centuries, gifts were used in a variety of contexts by both kings and their consorts, and were 'a powerful means of expressing rank and importance'.[209] Symbolic in many ways, gift giving was an expected part of queenship and served as a physical message to the recipient. To receive a gift of a jewel from a queen was an uncommon occurrence and therefore served to show or underline an important point. Gifts of jewels marked the most important events in a queen's life, be it marriage, the birth of an heir, or diplomatic duties. As Zemon Davis effectively argued, and as this chapter emphasises, gifts of jewels could be used to express affection and loyalty but were also a means to garner support, self-interest and advancement.[210] New Year's gifts were those traditionally given and received by queens each year, yet there were many other occasions on which queens gave and received jewels. Not only could jewels serve as tangible signs of affection between a queen and her husband, children, and other family members, but this could in turn be extended to friends and servants. In these latter instances, they served as something more, for they were ways of aiding the queen's construction and consolidation of her network both at court and beyond. Jewels provided a solid way of offering thanks for good service, showcasing the wealth of the monarchy and country, and helping to ensure that smooth relations between nations were exercised. By contrast, examples cited during Anne Boleyn's trial and the fall of Katherine Howard serve as evidence of the way in which gifts of jewels could be used to provide detrimental evidence to highlight a queen's conduct and draw attention to her unacceptable behaviour. Gifts were an integral part of queenship and the politics surrounding royal life, but gifts of jewels helped to accentuate the status of the queen both as an individual and within her broader network. The gift of jewels could be symbolic of both exaltation and disgrace and provided queens with an effective means of demonstrating their power. This in turn offered them a tangible way of fashioning and enhancing their own image, thereby adding another dimension to the projection of majesty.

Notes

1 Heal, *Power of Gifts*, pp. 23 + 114.
2 Ibid, p. 4.
3 Hollis (ed.), *Princely Magnificence*, p. 5.
4 Heal, *Power of Gifts*, p. 6.

5 Earenfight, *Queenship*, p. 39.
6 G. Cavendish, *The Life and Death of Cardinal Wolsey*, ed. R.S. Sylvester (London and New York, 1959), pp. 426–7.
7 Ibid.
8 See I.K. Ben-Amos, *The Culture of Giving: Informal Support and Gift-Exchange in Early Modern England* (Cambridge, 2008).
9 Maurer, *Margaret of Anjou*, p. 86.
10 Zemon Davis, *The Gift in Sixteenth-Century France* (Oxford, 2000), p. 62.
11 Heal, *Power of Gifts*, p. 35.
12 Eichberger, 'A Courtly Phenomenon', in Eichberger (ed.), *Women of Distinction*, p. 287.
13 E 36/210, f. 31, 38.
14 See E 36/214, f. 13r for example.
15 E 101/422/16, f. 68r; E 315/340, f. 26r.
16 O. Dmitrieva and T. Murdoch (eds.), *Treasures of the Royal Courts: Tudors, Stuarts and the Russian Tsars* (London, 2013), p. 25.
17 Heal, *Power of Gifts*, p. 32.
18 *L & P*, iii, no. 446; *L & P*, iii, no. 2725.
19 *L & P*, x, no. 1079.
20 BL, Stowe MS 559, f. 65r.
21 Heal, *Power of Gifts*, p. 93.
22 E 101/410/8.
23 E 36/210, f. 84–5.
24 *L & P*, viii, no. 15; *L & P*, Addenda 1, no. 367; Beer, *Queenship*, p. 110.
25 *L & P*, xii, part 1, no. 450.
26 Madden (ed.), *Privy Purse Expenses*, pp. 9, 143.
27 Hollis (ed.), *Princely Magnificence*, p. 10.
28 *L & P*, xiii, part 1, no. 24.
29 Zemon Davis, *The Gift*, pp. 23–4.
30 See E 101/421/4, E 101/420/15, E 101/421/13 for examples during the reign of Henry VIII; BL, RP 294 for Mary I & Elizabeth I.
31 Lutkin, 'Luxury and Display', p. 157; Stratford (ed.), *Richard II*, p. 66.
32 Campbell, *Medieval Jewellery*, p. 23.
33 M. Hayward, 'Gift Giving at the Court of Henry VIII: The 1539 New Year's Gift Roll in Context', *Antiquaries Journal*, 85 (2005), p. 9.
34 Ibid, pp. 35–7.
35 See J. Lawson (ed.), *The Elizabethan New Year's Gift Exchanges 1559–1603* (Oxford, 2013).
36 Beer, *Queenship*, p. 105.

37 Pronay and Cox (eds), *Crowland Chronicle*, p. 175.
38 E 101/409/14; E 101/409/17; E 101/410/2; E 101/410/8; E 101/410/11.
39 Myers, 'Household of Queen Margaret', pp. 79–113.
40 Beer, *Queenship*, pp. 104–5.
41 Myers, 'Jewels of Queen Margaret', pp. 113–31.
42 E 101/423/12, unfoliated.
43 E 101/409/14; E 101/409/17; E 101/410/2.
44 Myers, 'Household of Queen Margaret', p. 114.
45 Myers, 'Jewels of Queen Margaret', p. 114.
46 E 101/410/8.
47 Maurer, *Margaret of Anjou*, p. 42; E 101/410/11.
48 Maurer, *Margaret of Anjou*, p. 43.
49 E 101/409/14; E 101/410/8.
50 Maurer, *Margaret of Anjou*, p. 86.
51 E 101/410/8. They are described as 'x chopynes goderoned parcellatim deauratos ponderantes xij marcas et j quarteriam troie'.
52 Maurer, *Margaret of Anjou*, pp. 86–7; Laynesmith, *Last Medieval Queens*, p. 228.
53 E 101/409/14; E 101/409/17; E 101/410/2.
54 Earenfight, *Queenship*, p. 37.
55 Myers, 'Jewels of Queen Margaret', p. 114; Maurer, *Margaret of Anjou*, p. 90.
56 Myers, 'Jewels of Queen Margaret', p. 114.
57 Cited in S. Bentley (ed.), *Excerpta Historica: Or, Illustrations of English History* (London, 1831), pp. 148–9.
58 Ibid, p. 149.
59 Hayward, 'Possessions', p. 202.
60 Beer, *Queenship*, p. 105.
61 Ibid, p. 106.
62 *L & P*, xv, no. 850:7.
63 BL, Stowe MS 559, f. 55r-68r.
64 Ibid.
65 BL, Stowe MS 559, f. 55r-68r; *L & P*, xvi, no. 436.
66 SoA, MS 129, f. 199r.
67 Hayward, *Dress*, p. 157.
68 *L & P*, vi, no. 1194.
69 Nichols and Bruce (eds), *Doctors' Commons*, p. 14.
70 *L & P*, Addenda 1, no. 367.
71 Ibid. Beer, *Queenship*, p. 111.
72 *L & P*, Addenda 1, no. 367.
73 Ibid.
74 Beer, *Queenship*, pp. 108, 110.
75 Myers, 'Jewels of Queen Margaret', p. 113.
76 BL, Stowe MS 559, f. 65r, 61v.

77 Hayward, 'Gift Giving', p. 129.
78 *L & P*, viii, no. 46.
79 M.C. Byrne (ed.), *The Lisle Letters,* ii (Chicago, 1981), p. 213.
80 D. Grummitt, 'Plantagenet, Arthur, Viscount Lisle', *ODNB*.
81 *L & P*, xii, part 1, no. 494.
82 *L & P*, xvi, no. 436.
83 E101/420/4; E101/420/15; E101/421/13.
84 E101/421/13, p. 1.
85 Beer, *Queenship*, p. 106.
86 Ibid.
87 Hans Holbein, 'Table fountain design for Anne Boleyn', 1533–4, Öffentliche Kunstsammlung, Basel, 1662.165.89.
88 *L & P,* xvi, no. 436.
89 Hayward, 'Gift Giving', p. 137.
90 *L & P,* xii, part 1, no. 968.
91 *L & P,* v, no. 696.
92 Ibid.
93 Ibid.
94 E 101/420/15, p. 1.
95 BL, Add MS 11301, f. 12r; Madden (ed.), *Privy Purse Expenses*, p. 96.
96 Madden (ed.), *Privy Purse Expenses*, pp. 175–201.
97 Ibid, pp. 159, 118, 121.
98 E 315/161, f. 210r.
99 *L & P*, xxi, part 2, no. 686.
100 Madden (ed.), *Privy Purse Expenses*, p. 185.
101 Ibid.
102 Heal, *Power of Gifts*, p. 65.
103 *L & P,* iv, no. 3321.
104 Scarisbrick, *Tudor and Jacobean Jewellery*, pp. 42–69.
105 *L & P,* iv, no. 3325.
106 *L & P*, v, no. 276.
107 Ibid.
108 Ibid.
109 Hayward, *Dress*, p. 236.
110 E 101/422/15, unfoliated.
111 *L & P*, iv, no. 6789.
112 Ibid.
113 *L & P*, v, no. 276.
114 Madden (ed.), *Privy Purse Expenses*, p. 177.
115 Zemon Davis, *The Gift*, p. 29.
116 BL, Stowe MS 559, f. 55r.
117 F. Bacon, *The History of the Reign of King Henry VII,* ed. B. Vickers (Cambridge, 1998), p. 32.

118 BL, Cotton Caligula D VI, f. 201v.
119 Ibid; Ibid, f. 203r.
120 Cremades (ed.), *Inventarios*, iii, p. 2372.
121 BL, Add MS 7099, f. 68.
122 A.H. Thomas and I.D. Thornley (eds), *The Great Chronicle of London* (London, 1983), p. 297.
123 *CSPS*, i, p. 5.
124 See *CSPS*, i, no. 287; *CSPS*, i, no. 364; *CSPS*, i, no. 448.
125 Schroder, 'A Marvel to Behold', p. 95.
126 G. Kipling (ed.), *The Receyt of the Ladie Kateryne* (London, 1990), pp. 77–8.
127 See S. Anglo, 'Ill of the Dead: The Posthumous Reputation of Henry VII', *Renaissance Studies*, 1 (1987), pp. 27–47.
128 BL, Add MS 7099, f. 82.
129 Ibid, f. 4.
130 Ibid, f. 40.
131 E 36/210.
132 BL, Add MS 59899, f. 56–7, 62r; E 101/414/6, f. 119r.
133 E 101/422/16, f. 735r.
134 *L & P*, xv, no. 925.
135 Ibid.
136 *L & P*, xv, no. 899.
137 *L & P*, xvi, no. 436; *L & P*, xvii, no. 63. In 1541 Anna sent the King two horses with violet velvet trappings, and in 1542 she gave some pieces of cloth. In return, in 1542 she received some glass pots and flagons.
138 E 404/74/2, p. 20.
139 *CPR*, 1467–77, p. 547; *L & P*, i, no. 670.
140 BL, Stowe MS 1047, f. 204v.
141 E 315/340, f. 25v.
142 F. Palgrave (ed.), *The Antient Calendars and Inventories of the Treasury of His Majesty's Exchequer*, I (London, 1836), p. 393.
143 Ibid, p. 394.
144 BL, Stowe MS 559, f. 57v.
145 In December 1540, Chapuys reported that Katherine 'was offended because the Princess did not treat her with the same respect as her two predecessors', *L & P*, xvi, no. 314. There is no evidence suggestive of a close relationship between the two women; BL, Stowe MS 559, f. 67r.
146 See E 101/414/6, f. 41; E 36/215, f. 484; BL, Add MS 21481, f. 241v for examples.
147 Heal, *Power of Gifts*, p. 26.
148 A. Crawford, 'The Piety of Late Medieval English Queens', in C.M. Barron and C. Harper-Bill (eds), *The Church in Pre-Reformation*

Society: Essays in Honour of F.R.H Du Boulay (Woodbridge, 1985), p. 48.

149 E 315/340, f. 21r, 23v.

150 E 36/215, f. 11, 92.

151 E 36/210, f. 41, 52; E 36/215, f. 11/92.

152 E 36/210, f. 30, 81; Crawford, 'Piety', p. 51.

153 E 36/215, f. 252; E 36/216, f. 75v.

154 E 101/410/8. Myers translation of the original text is as follows: 'vnum tabulettum auri garnisatum in borduris eiusdem cum x trochis peru- larum, v saphires, et v baleys cum vno angelo in medio, habenti caput vinus camewe et in medio eiusdem sursum vnum bonum saphirum et tenenti inter manus suas vnam crucem garnisatam cum vno rubie et ix perulis orientis'. Myers, 'Jewels of Queen Margaret', p. 124.

155 J.C. Dickinson, *The Shrine of Our Lady of Walsingham* (Cambridge, 1956), p. 35; In her will Catherine of Aragon asked that someone should 'go our Lady of Wallsingham' on her behalf. BL, Cotton MS Otho C X, f. 216r.

156 Maurer, *Margaret of Anjou*, p. 43.

157 *L & P*, xvi, no. 234; PROB 11/16/419.

158 S. Fisher, '"Margaret R": Lady Margaret Beaufort's Self-fashioning and Female Ambition', in Fleiner and Woodacre (eds), *Virtuous or Villainess?*, pp. 151–72; See also Jones and Underwood, *King's Mother*, pp. 69–70.

159 Earenfight, *Queenship*, p. 23.

160 See M. Auwers, 'The Gift of Rubens: Rethinking the Concept of Gift-Giving in Early Modern Diplomacy', *European History Quarterly*, 43 (2013), pp. 421–41.

161 Dmitrieva and Murdoch (eds), *Treasures*, p. 24.

162 Z. Biedermann, A. Gerritsen, and G. Riello (eds), *Global Gifts: The Material Culture of Diplomacy in Early Modern Eurasia* (New York, 2017), p. 2.

163 G. Richardson, '"As Presence Did Present Them": Personal Gift-Giving at the Field of Cloth of Gold', in Lipscomb and Betteridge (eds), *Henry VIII and the Court*, p. 50.

164 G. Mattingly, *Renaissance Diplomacy* (London, 1955), p. 244.

165 Ibid, p. 246.

166 See *L & P*, vii, no. 763; *L & P*, xii, part 1, no. 640.

167 BL, Stowe MS 1047, f. 224r. See also C.L. Kingsford, *English Historical Literature in the Fifteenth Century* (Oxford, 1913), p. 387.

168 BL, Stowe MS 1047, f. 223r-224v.

169 Earenfight, *Catherine of Aragon*, p. 2.

170 *CSPV*, iii, no. 79.

171 Earenfight, *Catherine of Aragon*, p. 134.
172 Ibid.
173 *L & P*, v, no. 1485.
174 Heal, *Power of Gifts*, p. 150.
175 *L & P*, xxi, part 1, no. 1383:96.
176 Ibid.
177 *L & P*, xxi, part 2, no, 769:19.
178 SoA, MS 129, f. 183v.
179 F. Madden (ed.), 'Narrative of the Visit of the Duke of Najera', *Archaeologica XXIII* (1831), pp. 344–57.
180 BL, Add MS 59899, f. 93v.
181 Laynesmith, *Last Medieval Queens*, p. 245.
182 BL, Stowe MS 1047, f. 209r.
183 Laynesmith, *Last Medieval Queens*, pp. 109–110.
184 See S. Anglo, *The Great Tournament Roll of Westminster: Historical Introduction* (Oxford, 1968).
185 E 101/418/6, f. 14r.
186 *CSPV*, iii, no. 50.
187 *CSPV*, iii, no. 95.
188 W.G. Searle (ed.), *The Narrative of the Marriage of Richard, Duke of York with Anne of Norfolk, 1477* (Cambridge, 1867), pp. 39–40; See also BL, Stowe MS 1047, f. 211r-v.
189 Beer, *Queenship*, p. 101.
190 Cavendish, *Life and Death*, p. 82.
191 Heal, *Power of Gifts*, p. 116.
192 *L & P*, ix, no. 700.
193 BL, Stowe MS 559, f. 57v.
194 Ibid, f. 64v.
195 Lady Neville was given a 'Broche of gold of Historie of moyses set with ij litle Diamonds'. See Madden (ed.), *Privy Purse Expenses*, p. 192.
196 E 101/422/16, f. 68v; E 315/340, f. 21r-32v.
197 BL Royal MS 7 C XVI, f. 18r-31r.
198 Ibid, f. 22r.
199 Ibid, f. 26r, 27v.
200 Ibid, f. 21v.
201 Beer, *Queenship*, p. 107.
202 *L & P*, xii, part 2, no. 972.
203 BL, Royal MS 7 C XVI, f. 29r.
204 *L & P*, x, no. 876.
205 Ives, 'Fall of Anne Boleyn Reconsidered', p. 657.
206 SP 1/167/157–9.
207 *L & P*, xvi, no. 1395.
208 *L & P*, xvi, no. 1339.
209 Earenfight, *Catherine of Aragon*, p. 31.
210 Zemon Davis, *The Gift*, p. 22.

References

Manuscript Sources

Kew, The National Archives

EXCHEQUER

E 36	Treasury of Receipt, Miscellaneous Books.
E 101	King's Remembrancer, Various Accounts.
E 315	Court of Augmentations and Predecessors, Miscellaneous Books.
E 404	Warrants for Issue.

PREROGATIVE COURT OF CANTERBURY

PROB 11 Registered Copy Wills.

SPECIAL COLLECTIONS

SP State Papers

LONDON, BRITISH LIBRARY

Additional Manuscripts	7099, 11301, 21481, 59899.
Cotton Manuscripts	Caligula D VI, Otho C X.
Royal Manuscripts	7 C XVI.
RP	294.
Stowe Manuscripts	559, 1047.

LONDON, SOCIETY OF ANTIQUARIES

MS 129 Inventory of King Henry VIII.

Portraits

Hans Holbein, 'Table fountain design for Anne Boleyn', 1533–4, Öffentliche Kunstsammlung, Basel, 1662.165.89.

Printed Primary Sources

Bacon, F., *The History of the Reign of King Henry VII*, ed. Vickers, B. (Cambridge, 1998).

Bentley, S., (ed.), *Excerpta Historica: Or, Illustrations of English History* (London, 1831).

Bergenroth, G.A., et al. (ed.), *Calendar of State Papers, Spain*, 13 vols (London, 1862–1954).

Brewer, J., et al., (ed.), *Letters and Papers, Foreign and Domestic, of the Reign of Henry VIII, 1509–1547*, 21 vols (London, 1862–1932).

Brodie, R.H., Black, J.G., and Maxwell Lyte, H.C. (eds), *Calendar of the Patent Rolls Preserved in the Public Record Office, 1476–1509*, 3 vols (London, 1901–16).

Brown, R., et al., (ed.), *Calendar of State Papers, Venice*, 38 vols (London, 1864–1947).

Byrne, M.C., (ed.), *The Lisle Letters*, 6 vols (Chicago, 1981).

Cavendish, G., *The Life and Death of Cardinal Wolsey*, ed. Sylvester, R.S. (London and New York, 1959).

Cremades, F.C., (ed.), *Los inventarios de Carlos V y la familia imperial*, 3 vols (Madrid, 2010).

Kipling, G., (ed.), *The Receyt of the Ladie Kateryne* (London, 1990).

Knighton, C.S., (ed.), *Calendar of State Papers Domestic Series of the Reign of Edward VI 1547–1553* (London, 1992).

Lawson, J., (ed.), *The Elizabethan New Year's Gift Exchanges 1559–1603* (Oxford, 2013).

Madden, F., (ed.), 'Narrative of the Visit of the Duke of Najera', *Archaeologica*, XXIII (1831), pp. 344–57.

Madden, F., (ed.), *Privy Purse Expenses of the Princess Mary* (London, 1831).

Nichols, J., and Bruce, J., (eds), *Wills from Doctors' Commons: A Selection from the Wills of Eminent Persons Proved in the Prerogative Court of Canterbury, 1495–1695* (London, 1863).

Palgrave, F., (ed.), *The Antient Calendars and Inventories of the Treasury of His Majesty's Exchequer*, I (London, 1836).

Pronay, N., and Cox, J. (eds), *The Crowland Chronicle Continuations: 1459–1486* (London, 1986).

Searle, W.G., (ed.), *The Narrative of the Marriage of Richard, Duke of York with Anne of Norfolk, 1477* (Cambridge, 1867).

Stratford, J., (ed.), *Richard II and the English Royal Treasure* (Woodbridge, 2012).

Thomas, A.H., and Thornley, I.D., (eds), *The Great Chronicle of London* (London, 1983).

Secondary Sources

Anglo, S., 'Ill of the Dead: The Posthumous Reputation of Henry VII, *Renaissance Studies*, 1 (1987), pp. 27–47.

Anglo, S., *The Great Tournament Roll of Westminster: Historical Introduction* (Oxford, 1968).

Auwers, M., 'The Gift of Rubens: Rethinking the Concept of Gift-Giving in Early Modern Diplomacy', *European History Quarterly*, 43 (2013), pp. 421–41.

Beer, M.L., *Queenship at the Renaissance Courts of Britain: Catherine of Aragon and Margaret Tudor, 1503–1533* (Fakenham, 2018).

Ben-Amos, I.K., *The Culture of Giving: Informal Support and Gift-Exchange in Early Modern England* (Cambridge, 2008).

Biedermann, Z., Gerritsen, A., and Riello, G., (eds), *Global Gifts: The Material Culture of Diplomacy in Early Modern Eurasia* (New York, 2017).

Campbell, M., *Medieval Jewellery* (London, 2009).

Crawford, A., 'The Piety of Late Medieval English Queens', in Barron, C.M., and Harper-Bill, C., (eds), *The Church in Pre-Reformation Society: Essays in Honour of F.R.H Du Boulay* (Woodbridge, 1985), pp. 48–57.

Dickinson, J.C., *The Shrine of Our Lady of Walsingham* (Cambridge, 1956).

Dmitrieva, O., and Murdoch, T., (eds.), *Treasures of the Royal Courts: Tudors, Stuarts and the Russian Tsars* (London, 2013).

Earenfight, T., *Queenship in Medieval Europe* (Basingstoke, 2013).

Earenfight, T.M., *Catherine of Aragon: Infanta of Spain, Queen of England* (Pennsylvania, 2021).

Eichberger, D., 'A Courtly Phenomenon from a Female Perspective', in Eichberger, D. (ed.), *Women of Distinction.* (Leuven, 2008), pp. 286–95.

Fisher, S., ' "Margaret R": Lady Margaret Beaufort's Self-fashioning and Female Ambition', in Fleiner, C., and Woodacre, E. (eds), *Virtuous or Villainess? The Image of the Royal Mother from the Early Medieval to the Early Modern Era* (Basingstoke, 2016), pp. 151–72.

Grummitt, D., 'Plantagenet, Arthur, Viscount Lisle', *ODNB*, https://doi.org/10.1093/ref:odnb/22355

Hayward, M., *Dress at the Court of King Henry VIII* (Leeds, 2007).

Hayward, M., 'Gift Giving at the Court of Henry VIII: The 1539 New Year's Gift Roll in Context', *Antiquaries Journal*, 85 (2005), pp. 125–75.

Hayward, M., 'The Possessions of Henry VIII: A Study of Inventories', unpublished PhD thesis, London School of Economics and Political Science, University of London, 1998.

Heal, F., *The Power of Gifts: Gift-Exchange in Early Modern England* (Oxford, 2014).

Hollis, J., (ed.), *Princely Magnificence: Court Jewels of the Renaissance, 1500–1630* (London, 1980).

Ives, E., 'The Fall of Anne Boleyn Reconsidered', *EHR*, 107 (1992), pp. 651–64.

Jones, M., and Underwood, M.G., *The King's Mother: Lady Margaret Beaufort Countess of Richmond and Derby* (Cambridge, 1992).

Kingsford, C.L., *English Historical Literature in the Fifteenth Century* (Oxford, 1913).

Laynesmith, J., *The Last Medieval Queens* (Oxford, 2004).

Lutkin, J., 'Luxury and Display in Silver and Gold at the Court of Henry IV', in Clark, L. (ed.), *The Fifteenth Century IX* (2010), pp. 155–78.

Mattingly, G., *Renaissance Diplomacy* (London, 1955).

Maurer, H.E., *Margaret of Anjou: Queenship and Power in Late Medieval England* (Woodbridge, 2003).

Myers, A.R., 'The Household of Queen Margaret of Anjou, 1452–3', *BJRL*, 50 (1957–8), pp. 79–113.

Myers, A.R., 'The Jewels of Queen Margaret of Anjou', *BJRL*, 42 (1959), pp. 113–31.

Richardson, G., ''As Presence Did Present Them': Personal Gift-giving at the Field of Cloth of Gold', in Lipscomb, S., and Betteridge, T. (eds), *Henry VIII and the Court* (Farnham, 2013), pp. 47–64.

Scarisbrick, D., *Tudor and Jacobean Jewellery* (London, 1995).

Schroder, T., *'A Marvel to Behold': Gold and Silver at the Court of Henry VIII* (Woodbridge, 2020).

Zemon Davis, N., *The Gift in Sixteenth-Century France* (Oxford, 2000).

7 The Crown Jewels

'Splendour was a royal obligation', as Philippa Glanville observed, something that the very existence of the Crown Jewels emphasises.[1] By right of their rank, all ten queens in this period theoretically had access to and were permitted to use these jewels. However, the evidence discussed in this chapter suggests that it is unlikely that the latter four wives of Henry VIII ever did so. The Crown Jewels were, and remain, the principal jewels in royal ownership, not only for their monetary value but also in terms of their historical importance. This chapter will establish the significance of the Crown Jewels, drawing on examples from other European countries as a point of contrast to highlight their prominence as a distinctive collection that played a unique role among the jewellery collections of queens. In order to do this, the specific pieces and regalia used by queens will be analysed, together with the role that they played in coronations and ceremonial occasions. This will demonstrate the way in which the Crown Jewels were unique in aiding queens with the projection of majesty and asserting their divine right to reign alongside their husbands.

As the only jewels that were intended and reserved solely for the use of a king and his consort, the Crown Jewels were and are a unique entity. Their very creation specifically denoted rank, thereby reinforcing the importance of the wearer.[2] Although they were functional as well as decorative, they served a completely different purpose to other jewels and had a political role to play in the symbolism of monarchy. They were 'symbols of

DOI: 10.4324/9781003202592-8

[monarchs'] worldly authority and the divine power bestowed on them'.[3] As a collection of jewels that were inherited by a monarch upon their accession and passed on to their successors, the Crown Jewels did not form a part of the monarch's or a consort's personal collection. They were instead pieces that were owned by the state and reserved for their use, primarily on ceremonial occasions.

Crown jewels in some form have been an integral part of European and other enlightened societies for many centuries, the evidence for which stems from surviving crowns that date from the Iron Age.[4] These examples show a longstanding association with figures of authority, one that continues to this day. The Romans and Saxons also used crowns as a way of identifying their rulers, and it was the Saxons who developed this idea.[5] Collections of royal regalia came into being, and their inclusion in the coronation ceremony that was firmly established in the seventh and eighth centuries became a crucial part of this process.[6] It was the view of Prince Michael of Greece, however, that 'Charlemagne's coronation can be called the ancestor of all European coronations', and Charlemagne was a ruler with whom successive French kings were eager to be associated.[7] In contrast with the examples set in England and France, in Sweden Erik Knutsson was the first known king to be crowned in the thirteenth century, but the concept of regalia did not appear until three centuries later.[8] His example serves to convey the differing traditions and importance placed on ceremonial by other European countries. By the Norman period, in England, the idea of regalia was defined by Anna Keay as 'precious metal or jewelled objects borne by and identifying a king' and was a recognised concept, but they had yet to gain the symbolic value that would later become attached to them.[9] As she related, the symbolic value of the Crown Jewels came in the century following the Normans, when the monks of Westminster Abbey claimed that Edward the Confessor had left his collection of jewels in their safekeeping to be used at the coronation of every future English monarch.[10] There is no evidence to suggest that this tale was true, but as Edward was greatly revered as a saint the story gathered momentum. As a result, by the time of Henry III's coronation in

1220, his crown was believed to have been used by Edward, and 'The concept of a hereditary collection of regalia had come into being'.[11] An inventory of Henry's regalia, however, reveals that his crown was referred to as 'A golden crown entirely adorned with divers stones', and it was not until 1450 that any of the royal jewels were described in inventories as 'Relics of the Holy Confessor'.[12] From that time on, the crown used at the coronation of kings was called St Edward's Crown, even though it is unlikely to have originated with the Saxon King.

English kings were not alone in their desire to associate themselves with antiquity. When Ivan the Terrible had himself crowned first Tsar of Russia in 1547, his claim that his crown dated from the tenth century was an attempt to reinforce his legitimacy.[13] Such an action accentuates the importance that was attached to the role jewels played in enforcing majesty, and Ivan was not the only monarch to recognise this. In Scotland James V claimed that Robert the Bruce had worn his crown, although it had been commissioned on James's orders.[14] The need to associate themselves with powerful monarchs from the past reveals a desire from rulers to enhance their own greatness, and jewels provided the perfect tangible tool for them to do so.

As a concept, Clare Phillips suggested that Crown Jewels as a separate entity from a monarch's personal collection, derived from the French King François I (Bijoux de la Couronne).[15] Her justification for such a claim is that in 1530 François I had declared eight pieces to be heirlooms of the French kings – other monarchs quickly followed suit.[16] But, although this was only then the case in France, in England the idea of a separate set of regalia for use at coronations had long been established. In the same manner as a monarch's personal jewel collection, the Crown Jewels were not so simply defined. They fell into two subcategories: regalia used solely at the coronation of a monarch, which in England became known as St Edward's regalia during the reign of Henry III, and state regalia that could be worn for other ceremonial occasions.[17] Collectively these two sub-categories formed the Crown Jewels. Most contemporary sources primarily relate to the coronation regalia, and thus it is these pieces that will be predominantly discussed in the regalia section of this chapter. This will signify the role that they played in conveying a queen's resplendence and establishing her as a legitimate consort.

Context and Significance of the Crown Jewels

The physical appearance of the Crown Jewels that were used for coronations generally did not reflect the personal tastes of individual kings and their consorts, although this did not prevent monarchs from attempting to put their own stamp on the collection. Henry III's inventory lists 22 items, not all of which were regalia. 'One pair of new sandals and stockings of red samite with an orphrey' are listed, and comparable items are also found in Edward III's inventory of regalia.[18] The sandals of red samite are worthy of comment, for it is possible that this stemmed from the tradition of imperial Roman regalia, whereby red boots were worn as a symbol of divine majesty.[19] Though only one crown is listed in Henry III's inventory, there were four in Edward III's collection.[20] By the reign of Henry VIII though, few of these earlier medieval pieces remained, having been replaced by various others. This was partially influenced by the lessening emphasis that was placed on the magical and mysterious ways of the monarchy that came with the Renaissance. This resulted in objects 'of a purely precious nature' being introduced to the Crown Jewel collection, such as the 'pece of an Vnicornes horne' that was found in Henry VIII's hoard.[21] Some of the new jewels did, however, serve a greater purpose. For example, either Henry VII or Henry VIII probably commissioned the Tudor State Crown that first appears in a 1521 inventory, and which became the most important object in the Tudor collection.[22] Its importance is emphasised by its detailed description, coupled with its appearance in many contemporary portraits.[23] It was not worn for coronations but instead for state occasions such as the opening of Parliament. It was such an influential piece that it was believed to be the inspiration for the crown that was made for Eric XIV of Sweden in the mid-sixteenth century, thereby demonstrating the impact that jewellery design could have on other European rulers who were eager to emulate the splendour of their contemporaries.[24]

Separate sets of coronation regalia and state regalia were made for the use of the king and queen, but it is unclear precisely when this came into being. It was not until 1450 during the reign of Henry VI that three pieces were specifically listed as being for the queen's use: 'for the coronation of the queen, a crown and two rods'.[25] These items may have been made especially for Margaret of Anjou, as there is evidence that jewels were commissioned for her coronation. All that can be said with certainty is that they were added to the collection at some point between the reigns of Edward III and Henry VI. Certainly, after 1450 additional pieces of regalia were commissioned for the use of the queen's coronation. This development of the queen's regalia indicates the increasing prominence of the role that queens were expected to play and the significance of her power, thereby supporting the argument of Pauline Stafford that queens were an important part of the spectacle of royalty.[26]

Unless alterations or repairs were required, the Crown Jewels rarely fell victim to the rapidly changing fashions of the time. Surviving contemporary descriptions suggest that much of the regalia used at the coronations of kings and queens between 1445 and 1533 was the same, demonstrating a powerful link with monarchical predecessors that kings and queens wished to uphold. This was something that, unlike other jewels, evidently took precedence over contemporary fashions and enforces the power of tradition. Once again, it emphasises the value that was placed on antiquity, and the way in which objects that had been used by a monarch's predecessor served to underline legitimacy. Abroad, the Imperial Crown of the Holy Roman Empire was used in a similar way. Though it was claimed to have associations with Charlemagne, it was almost certainly made for the coronation of Otto the Great in 962 and its use was retained in coronation ceremonies until the nineteenth century.[27] Although not used by Charlemagne, the age of the crown still conveys the value that successive monarchs placed on it.

Aside from their political significance, monarchs did recognise the monetary value of the Crown Jewels, and as such they provided a useful tool for pawning. Evidence for this appears in Edward III's inventory, with 'the great crown of the king which was lately pledged in the parts of Flanders'.[28] This crown was, though, apparently 'worth nothing'.[29] Pawning was a trend that was adopted elsewhere in Europe, as Christian IV of Denmark was also obliged to pawn his crown in the 1640s.[30] As time progressed, in England the Crown Jewels continued to provide a valuable source of income: in the seventeenth century, Henrietta Maria was forced to sell them in order to raise funds to support her husband's forces against the Parliamentarian rebels.[31] Using the jewels in such a way signifies that in times of financial crisis, the historical importance of the Crown Jewels did not outweigh their ability to resolve economic problems.

The Crown Jewels have been acknowledged as the most important items in the royal collection for centuries, yet it is the crown that has been viewed as the ultimate symbol of monarchy and remains so to this day. Though it was not common practice for queens to wear crowns and state regalia regularly, in symbolic terms the crown held great significance for them. In all of her surviving likenesses, Margaret of Anjou is depicted wearing a crown: the Milanese sculptor Pietro da Milano struck her image on a medal that is likely to have been cast in 1462 – the earliest likeness of an English queen wearing an imperial crown – which conveys its importance in the eyes of her contemporaries.[32] The reason for the medal's creation is unclear, but Milano's patron was Margaret's father, René of Anjou, so it is possible that it was made at his request.[33] During the Renaissance, an interest in the Roman period led to a revival of the medallic portrait bust, and although arguably René slightly predates this it is plausible that it was from here that his interest stemmed.[34] Henry V had only recently introduced the trend for imperial, or closed crowns, and this is in keeping with Roy Strong's argument that fifteenth-century English preoccupations with the imperial crown were probably connected with England's claims to France.[35] Nevertheless, this trend was repeated throughout Europe. Frederick Hepburn claimed that Margaret's depiction with an imperial crown would have automatically identified her as queen to her contemporaries.[36] He also stated that 'The imperial crown was, at its most basic level, the supreme symbol of sovereign authority over the inhabitants of the realm of England'.[37] This makes Margaret's image all the more noteworthy, for though she wore her crown by right of her husband, on the medal she is shown facing left in the manner of a male sitter. Hepburn contended that this confirms the view that she was being presented not as Henry's consort, but as a more powerful ruler in her own right.[38] As the medal is likely to have been cast when Margaret was attempting to assert her authority in the light of her husband's illness, it is certainly plausible that this was the case and that the medal provided a means of doing so.[39]

The association of the crown with immortality made it even more significant. Julie Ann Smith, however, suggested that for queens the crown represented virginity rather than authority.[40] Although not all of the queens in this period were virgins at the time of their coronations – notably Anne Boleyn, who was six months pregnant – it is a valid point. That Elizabeth Wydeville was not a virgin at the time of her marriage drew disapproving comment from a foreign chronicler, who remarked, 'Although the coronation in England demands that a king should marry a virgin whoever she may be, legitimately born and not a widow, yet the king took this one against the will of all his lords'.[41] The point was that all queens needed to be seen to emulate virgins and adorned themselves in such a way as to support this view. For example, during Margaret of Anjou's coronation procession, she wore 'white damask poudred with gold', in a symbolic gesture of virginity that was adopted by the other queens in this period.[42] The way in which their jewels aided this representation will be analysed later in this chapter, but it was of the utmost importance that 'The public body of the queen at her coronation was virginal whatever the physical individual truth might be'.[43]

The association with virginity reflected a desire from queens to identify themselves with the Virgin Mary, and they were able to do this through their jewels.[44] This can be seen in surviving likenesses of Margaret of Anjou, Elizabeth Wydeville, Anne Neville and Elizabeth of York, in which all four queens wear crowns. An imperial crown, like that worn by Margaret of Anjou in her medal portrait, also appears in an image of Elizabeth of York in the St George's altarpiece in the Royal Collection discussed in Chapter 4.[45] As Alison Weir has suggested, it bears great similarities to the crown that Anne Neville wears in the Rous Roll (Figure 7.1).[46] If this was indeed the case, then it confirms the importance that this particular crown held in the queen's collection of Crown Jewels, and presumably Elizabeth Wydeville would also have had access to it. That images of Margaret of Anjou, Elizabeth Wydeville, Anne Neville and Elizabeth of York all feature crowns can be partially explained by the association of the Virgin Mary as the Queen of Heaven, an image that medieval queens were keen to emulate as it added to the notion of queenly authority.[47] Marian devotion was a key aspect of late medieval piety, providing a further explanation for the connection. The association of Mary with queenship stemmed from her use of the crown of 12 stars, and the influence that she had on queens and their appearance during this period can be seen across many spheres.[48] For example, although many of the queens were not virgins at the time of their coronations, this did not prevent them from attempting to emulate Mary's example by wearing their hair loose as a token gesture. This is confirmed in two contemporary images of Margaret of Anjou and Elizabeth Wydeville.

That of Margaret of Anjou appears in a prayer roll in the Bodleian Library, dating from between 1445 and 1455.[49] Adorned in regalia, Margaret is portrayed in a blue robe with a red cloak representative of the Virgin Mary, and as Sonja Drimmer related, the text shows that Margaret was either seeking the Virgin's aid or praising her.[50] Drimmer asserted, 'Queenship is figured here as a conventionally Marian enterprise', and the same is true of the image of Margaret's successor.[51]

Elizabeth Wydeville's likeness was produced in the 1470s to mark her membership of the Skinners of London, and like Margaret's image, she is shown dressed as the Virgin Mary wearing blue and red robes.[52] The blue cloak in particular conveys the idea of Mary being the Mother of Mercy, and this is confirmed in the legend on the image which refers to 'oure blissed Lady and Moder of Mercy'.[53] The inclusion of a crown, orb and sceptre is significant, for though by this period it had become usual for queens to be invested with a crown and sceptre, both of which also feature in the image of Margaret, they were not normally

Figure 7.1 Anne Neville depicted in the Rous Roll

Source: © The History Collection/Alamy Stock Photo

given the orb at their coronation – with the exception of Elizabeth of York, and later Karin Månsdotter, Swedish consort of Eric XIV.[54] Karin's humble origins make this depiction even more unusual. It was, nevertheless, not uncommon for queens to be depicted carrying the orb, and it was intended to show that God had set the monarch as vice-regent over his great Christian kingdom.[55] As Joanna Laynesmith suggested, that queens were shown with the same regalia as Mary is indicative that there was 'a blurring of the understanding of their roles in popular perceptions'.[56]

By the time of Catherine of Aragon's reign, representations of queens had begun to change, and neither she nor any other of Henry VIII's wives were depicted wearing crowns.[57] The onset of the Reformation had an impact on traditional ideas, for Mary was no longer seen as an integral part of Tudor ideals of queenship. Luther and other religious reformers doubtlessly influenced this, seeking to 'downgrade Mary', and exploit the 'vessel' theory expressed by Emperor Constantine V in the eighth century, whereby Mary was viewed as 'no more than an empty purse' following Christ's birth.[58] Her degradation did not reduce the power of queens, though it did remove a means of advertising their authority by linking them to Mary. The Reformation also ensured that the mysticisms of the church that had been associated with monarchy were no longer so closely adhered to. Equally, the decreasing frequency with which queens were expected to wear their crowns could also account for the lack of visual representations.[59] Ceremonial crown-wearing days were not a regular feature in the Tudor regime, although they had been an integral part of medieval monarchy and will therefore be addressed later in this chapter. This does not indicate a lessening of importance for the crown as a symbol, for images of Henry VIII with his crown survive.[60] Indeed, the crown was still identified as a crucial aspect of sixteenth-century monarchy, as its appearance in Elizabeth I's coronation portrait confirms.[61] This example was noteworthy because of the crown's symbolism emphasising Elizabeth's status as a queen regnant, in contrast to Henry VIII's wives who were all consorts.

Pieces and Regalia

Two vital sources provide information about the Crown Jewels during the Tudor period. The first is the 1547 inventory of Henry VIII's belongings, where, as the first items listed, the value of the Crown Jewels is undoubted.[62] No reference is made to their monetary worth, but their significance is self-explanatory. Of the 18 items listed, 15 relate to the king, serving to underline his precedence over his female consort. For example, 'the Kinges Crowne of golde', refers to the crown commissioned by either Henry VII or Henry VIII, known as the Tudor State Crown.[63] Unlike St Edward's Crown, the Tudor State Crown was not used for coronations and was instead adopted by the king for ceremonial occasions. As will soon become clear, however, the 1547 inventory did not contain all the regalia that was adorned by monarchs and consorts for coronations, and several items were stored separately.

The symbolic importance of the crown was such that following the coronation ceremony of Catherine of Aragon in 1509, among the decorations at the Palace of Westminster was a fountain topped with 'a greate Croune Emperiall'.[64] Crowns were constructed of the most expensive materials, and they were indeed the most important objects a goldsmith would ever have to make.[65] They also accounted for the biggest items of expenditure on luxury objects within the royal family and could be used as an expression of a monarch's personal tastes on occasion.[66] Ivan the Terrible took advantage of this when he ordered the creation of the Crown of Kazan in 1552. The design of the crown greatly resembles the Cathedral of St Basil, which had been built by Ivan in order to celebrate his military victories.[67] Such a design was Ivan's way of expressing his strength through his regalia, a point that none of his subjects could have missed.

In England, St Edward's Crown was the most important crown in the collection in historical terms. It was an object that Keay described as 'the defining symbol of English kingship', and it held similar importance to queens.[68] Although St Edward's Crown was reserved for crowning male monarchs, during the coronation of Anne Boleyn, a contemporary observed that 'the archbysshop set the crown of St Edward on her head'.[69] Alice Hunt believed that this was a deliberate choice, as the visual link with St Edward articulated Anne's lawful right to rule.[70] Joanna Laynesmith supported this view, asserting that the use of regalia in this way emphasised a positive difference between Anne and most other queens.[71] This was necessary in order to reinforce her exalted status, but there is no evidence that any of the other queens in this period were crowned with St Edward's Crown. This oxymoronic example also shows that queens were permitted to use the same regalia as kings when it was not in use, placing them on a level with their husbands.

The counterpart made to match St Edward's Crown and used by queens for the coronation ceremony was Queen Edith's Crown. Described in an inventory dating from 1649 as 'Silver gilt Enriched with Garnetts, foule pearle, Saphires and some old stones', it is likely to have been this crown that was used for the coronations of all of the queens in this period, with the exception of Anne Boleyn.[72] That it was made from silver gilt rather than gold in the same manner as St Edward's Crown was a reflection of the superiority of the king, underlining that his coronation held greater importance than that of his consort.[73] Despite its name and association with St Edward the Confessor's consort, Queen Edith's crown was almost certainly made in the late fourteenth or early fifteenth century and differed from the queen's crown described in the 1547 inventory.[74]

Only three items in the 1547 inventory were specifically linked to the queen, foremost of which was the state crown:

> Item the quenes Crowne of golde the border sett with vj Saphires nott all of one fynes twoo lesse Saphires vj ballaces nott fyne and viij small perles Item vj crosses of gold euerie crosse sett with a Saphire a ballace and iiij/perles nott greate Item vj flower de luces of gold euerie flower de luce sett with a ballace a Saphire and v small perles the Saphire and ballace nott fyne with a Dyamounte and A crosse of golde nott garnished with a Cappe in it of purple vellat with a roll in it weying togethers liij ounces.[75]

This crown varied from Queen Edith's Crown and did not form a part of the regalia used for the coronation of a queen. In the same manner as the Tudor State Crown used by the king, its use was probably intended for other ceremonial occasions, and it could have been commissioned at the same time as its male counterpart. Alternatively, it could have been made for the coronation of Anne Boleyn – a contemporary account recorded that after her anointing, 'the bysshop toke the crown of St Edward from her head; and put her upon the crown made for her'.[76] This is the only reference to a crown being made specifically for one of Henry VIII's queens, and there is no documentary evidence to suggest that any of the King's other wives ever wore it. If the report of the Milanese ambassador is to be believed, its creation is likely to have been influenced by the King's separation from Catherine of Aragon. Writing on 3 June 1533, just two days after Anne's coronation, the ambassador reported that Henry had previously given orders 'requiring the crown for the coronation of the new queen'.[77] When Master Sadocho, who had been charged with guarding the crown, refused to hand it over because of his previous oath to Catherine of Aragon, the ambassador claimed that the King was left with no choice but to have 'another crown made for the coronation of the new queen'.[78] This explains why a new crown was made, which may have been the same as that recorded in the 1547 inventory. The significance of the Queen's Crown in projecting the royal image can be seen by its inclusion in a seventeenth-century portrait of Henrietta Maria, which provides the only surviving visual representation of this most crucial piece of queens' jewellery.[79] This not only serves as evidence of its appearance but also shows that it had passed from queen to queen since at least the reign of Henry VIII – possibly even before.

Two further pieces reserved for the queen's use are mentioned in the 1547 inventory. First, 'Item a Sceptre of gold with a dove on the knoppe for the Queene weying vj oz quarter'.[80] It is unclear precisely when this item was made, but descriptions of the coronations of Elizabeth Wydeville, Anne Neville and Elizabeth of York all refer to sceptres, and given its inclusion in images of Margaret of Anjou it is probable that both she and Catherine of Aragon also used them.[81] Likewise, a contemporary account made reference to Anne Boleyn being handed 'the Scepter of golde in her right hande, and the rodd of justice with the dove in her left hande'.[82] This second item is likely to be the same as that listed in the 1547 inventory. The sceptre also appears in a shorter inventory created in 1606, in which it is described as 'Item a small Scepter for the Queene with a Dove vpon the Top'.[83] Both the 1547 and the later detailed 1649 inventories listed sceptres that were specifically allocated for the queen's use, and here there was an obvious reflection in the king's superiority. While the king's sceptre was made of gold, the *Liber Regalis*, which set out the protocol for the crowning of a king and his consort, stated that a queen's sceptre should be made of gilt.[84] However, Elizabeth Wydeville is known to have used St Edward's staff, which was the same as that used by kings.[85] It is also likely that St Edward's was the same sceptre as that used by Elizabeth of York, described as 'the scepter of gold in her right hand', and the one referred to in similar terms that was used by Anne Boleyn.[86] That Elizabeth Wydeville and Anne Boleyn were given permission to use this item is momentous and serves to underline the crucial role jewels played in assisting with the reinforcement of a queen's status, necessary in both of these instances.[87]

The second item of queen's jewellery listed in the 1547 inventory was 'a Serclett of gold for the quene sett with a faier Emerade foure faier Saphires foure rooses of Dyamountes foure ballaces all sett in Rooses and xiiij perles like of one sorte weying with the Silke xviij oz di'.[88] This circlet was the same as that worn by Catherine of Aragon in her coronation procession, described as 'a gold circlet, newe made for her, set with an emerald, sapphires, rubies, diamonds and pearls'.[89] This description allows us to date the creation of the circlet precisely, and it was probably the same circlet that a contemporary observer of Catherine's coronation saw when relating that the Queen wore 'on her hedde a Coronall, set with many riche orient stones'.[90] Its inclusion among the Crown Jewels suggests that Anne Boleyn also used it, for in her coronation procession she was seen to have been wearing a 'circlet as she had the Saturday', described simply as 'a Circlet of golde, garnished with precious stones'.[91] Catherine's circlet disappeared into the collection of Lord Protector Somerset, and from there its fate is unknown.[92]

With the abolition of the monarchy in 1649, so too vanished the importance attached to the Crown Jewels. It was because of their association that they were 'totallie Broken and defaced', in a visible attempt to dismantle all objects affiliated with royal authority.[93] As a result, a collection that was hundreds of years old was destroyed, for as Claude Blair recounted, by 1650 'both the venerable Regalia of St Edward and the rich crowns and ensigns of Tudor and Stuart monarchy, symbols of a very different absolutism from that of the eleventh century, were no more'.[94] Their historical value was of little importance to the Parliamentarians, but the government did at least recognise their monetary value. It was for this reason that a further inventory of the Crown Jewels was compiled, in order to establish their worth before they were broken up.[95] The 1649 inventory confirms that few of the Crown Jewels listed in the 1547 inventory had undergone any significant changes.[96] However, the monetary values placed on each item did not reflect their historical or symbolic magnitude. They do nevertheless prove that the king's regalia was considered to be more valuable than the queen's: while the Tudor State Crown was valued at £1,100, at £338 the queen's was believed to be worth about a third as much.[97] This is partially because the king's crown was both heavier and contained more stones, another clear indication of status. The iconic St Edward's Crown was valued at £248, while 'Queene Ediths Crowne formerly thought to be of Massy gould but vpon triall found to be of Siluer gilt' was believed to be worth just £16.[98] Jennifer Loach argued that so few people had seen St Edward's Crown at close range prior to its destruction that its appearance remains a mystery.[99] Certainly, there are few contemporary descriptions of it, and no images. Neither St Edward's nor Queen Edith's crowns appeared in the 1547 inventory, and the reason for this seems to have been because they were held in storage at Westminster Abbey, rather than being a part of the main ceremonial collection in the custody of the monarch.

The destruction of the medieval Crown Jewels means that we no longer have the majority of the physical objects to use as sources for this period – all that survives is the medieval Coronation Spoon.[100] When the present collection was remade in 1660 in preparation for the coronation of Charles II, it was largely modelled on the appearance of the old, confirming that fashions were not a decisive factor in their composition.[101] More important was the association with dynastic continuity at a time when the monarchy had only recently been re-established. For the most part though, we are primarily reliant on the surviving inventories, contemporary descriptions and images, which provide a relatively complete picture of the collection as it once was.

Coronations and Royal Ceremonial

Surviving accounts of the coronations of the queens of this period confirm that 'a coronation had become the greatest festivity of any reign'.[102] The first full account of an English queen's coronation is that of Eleanor of Provence in 1236, and as time progressed so too did the level of ceremony.[103] Theresa Earenfight argued that while a king's coronation legitimated his right to rule, 'a queen consort's coronation legitimised only their union and the offspring of the marriage'.[104] There are numerous examples during this period that contradict this line of thought. When Elizabeth of York gave birth to her first child in September 1486 her coronation had not taken place, yet the legitimacy of her son was beyond question.[105] Similarly, though Jane Seymour had not been crowned when her son was born in October 1537, both his legitimacy and the validity of Jane's marriage were undoubted.[106] Neither Anna of Cleves, Katherine Howard nor Kateryn Parr were crowned, yet nobody questioned their right to rule as consorts. It is clear then, that the coronation of a queen was something more, and unrelated to her marriage.

The coronation was an important confirmation of royal authority, and the Crown Jewels formed an intrinsic part of that process. A coronation confirmed a monarch's right to rule, and as such it was often the case – although not always and by no means compulsory – that a king's spouse should undergo the same ceremonies. Yet for queens the coronation was of particular importance, for as Laynesmith argued, it was 'the one rite of passage which queens did not share with other women and it most explicitly established their unique role. This was also the occasion upon which the widest variety of ideologies of queenship were expressed'.[107] It was a ritual that set a queen apart from her female contemporaries and reinforced her superior rank. Earenfight supported this view, expressing the belief that 'a coronation symbolised the intimate association with the powerful mythical quality of royalty, transmitted enormous power and elevated her status among women'.[108]

As was both customary and expected, the first six queens in this period enjoyed the privilege of a coronation, but – in a break from tradition – the latter four were denied the opportunity. Plans for Jane Seymour's coronation were in train before her marriage had even taken place; in May 1536 John Husee reported, 'A new coronation is expected at Midsummer', and by all accounts it was to be a grand occasion, for another contemporary noted that 'the King intends to do wonders'.[109] Such was the confidence that Henry VIII had in his marriage to Jane before it had even been solemnised, but it was not scheduled until October. It was then observed, 'The Queen's coronation which was to have taken place at the end of this month is put off till next summer, and some doubt it will not take place at all. There is no appearance that she will have children'.[110] Although the true reason behind the postponement was an outbreak of plague, that such rumours were circulating shows how the coronation of a queen was believed to be associated with her ability to produce children.[111] In a European context, Holly Hurlburt has shown that childbearing and the queen's coronation were closely linked, because with the responsibility of bearing an heir came too the possibility of a regency.[112] Thus, coronations carried 'direct political import'.[113] In Jane's case, there does seem to be an element of truth in the link between the coronation and her capability of bearing an heir, because although there were murmurs of plans for Jane's coronation, by the time of her death in October 1537 no firm arrangements had been made. This could have been a strategy Henry intended to employ with his following wives, with the exception of Anna of Cleves. Despite his obvious distaste for Anna, a coronation was both planned and expected. In March 1540 the French ambassador reported that it would take place at Whitsuntide, and the following month referred to the preparations.[114] It was the lack of these plans materialising that drew attention to the fact that all was not well in Anna's marriage, underlining the importance contemporaries placed on this ceremony. As Retha Warnicke asserted, Anna's coronation was not only necessary in order to 'offer the appearance of divine approval for her queenship but also provide an affirmation of Henry's commitment to her as his consort'.[115] However, Warnicke correctly argued that as the King had been unable to consummate his marriage with Anna, 'absolutely no chance existed that this highly sacred and expensive ritual would appear on the royal schedule that spring'.[116] In this instance the King allowed his personal feelings to dictate his policy, thereby emphasising his determination to be rid of his fourth wife.

There is no evidence to suggest that plans were made for Katherine Howard and Kateryn Parr to be crowned, although in 1541 rumours circulated that the former would be anointed in York if she produced a male heir.[117] This is indicative of talk that was spreading at court and could reflect the King's own feelings that Katherine would only receive a coronation if she produced a child. In circumstances such as these, coronations, in the words of John Carmi Parsons, 'consecrated queens as lawful royal consorts and mothers of legitimate royal heirs'.[118] If this was true then given Henry's marital history it is hardly surprising and shows his unwillingness to spend money on a coronation unless he was given something in return. The lack of coronations for the latter four of his wives is, though, even more remarkable, given that the next queen consort, Anna of Denmark, was given a coronation alongside her husband James I in 1603.[119] At this time Anna had already produced two surviving male heirs, as well as a daughter.[120] Although none of Henry's latter four queens were crowned, they were still considered to be queens by their contemporaries and were addressed as such. Even so, their lack of coronation serves to highlight the differences between a reigning monarch, for whom a coronation was obligatory, and a consort, whose coronation was optional. It was the decision of their husband as to whether a coronation was staged.

Their rank automatically gave them access to the Crown Jewels, yet there is no evidence that the latter four of Henry VIII's wives ever used them. Not only is this supported by their lack of coronations but also because the stately occasions on which crowns had been used in the past were in decline by this period. Kateryn Parr in particular found other ways to highlight her status as previous chapters have shown. Majesty could be expressed not solely through the Crown Jewels but also in a queen's personal and queenly collection.

Consorts were frequently crowned in the same ceremony as their husbands, and this was a practice that was employed for Anne Neville in 1483 and Catherine of Aragon in 1509. As both women were married at the time that their husbands were crowned, it was naturally expected that the kings' consorts would share the same coronation ceremony. The precedent for a double coronation had been employed regularly over time, though the coronation of Anne Neville and Richard III was the first double coronation since that of Edward II and Isabella of France in 1308.[121] This probably explains both why its details were so well recorded by contemporaries and why it attracted such interest.[122] For both Anne Neville and Catherine of Aragon though, the emphasis was primarily on their husbands. This becomes evident when studying the surviving wardrobe accounts, which reveal that the majority of preparations that were put in place were for the king.[123] Equally, most contemporary accounts of Richard III's coronation, which was viewed as extraordinary due to his usurpation, focus on the King rather than his consort.[124] The same was true of the jewels used, and for Henry VIII included 'the crowne the septre and the Rodde with all things thereto pertyning to be deliuered unto the king by the Clerke of the Juell howse when Seint Edward's Crowne is taken of his hed after wards'.[125]

Margaret of Anjou, Elizabeth Wydeville, Elizabeth of York and Anne Boleyn were crowned separately from their husbands, and all underwent slightly different conventions and levels of ceremony. Staged the same year as her marriage to Henry

VI, the preparations for Margaret of Anjou's coronation were approached with the utmost seriousness, as is reflected in the cost. The exorbitant sum of £7,000 was taken from a half-fifteenth granted in the Parliament of 1445 to pay off debts incurred for jewels and clothing for the queen's coronation.[126] Her marriage had signalled the cementing of a crucial alliance for peace between England and France, orchestrated by Henry VI and the Duke of Anjou – one that had been unpopular in England due in part to the lack of a dowry on Margaret's part.[127] For this reason it was deemed necessary for Margaret's coronation to showcase an extraordinary level of splendour. Henry VI spent lavishly on jewels for his new queen, and a letter to the King's treasurer shows that he had ordered

> a Pusan of Golde, called Ilkyngton Coler, Garnished with iv Rubees, iv greet Sappurs, xxxii greet Perles, and liii other Perles. And also a Pectoral of Golde garnished with Rubees, Perles and Diamonds, and also with a greet Owche Garnished with Diamondes, Rubees, and Perles.[128]

It seems likely that these jewels were intended to form a part of Margaret's personal collection, rather than becoming absorbed into the Crown Jewels, because Henry gave orders that the first two of these pieces ought to be given 'unto oure saide Wyf of our Guft'.[129] Although the sum spent on jewels for Margaret was extraordinary, it could be that some new jewels were purchased for the coronation of each queen. In 1465 for example, the London goldsmith Matthew Philip provided a gold cup and basin for the coronation of Elizabeth Wydeville.[130] The earlier example of Anne Boleyn also shows that it was possible for new crowns to be made for queens.

In the instances of all six queens who were given coronations, the ceremony did not simply take place on one day but was instead celebrated over the course of several days. This not only gave the king the opportunity to showcase his wealth and magnificence but was a chance for him and his consort to be seen by their subjects, and 'to provide the populace with entertainment'.[131] Elaborate levels of ceremonial served to bind people to their monarch, as each king was doubtless aware.[132] The pageantry that accompanied such occasions necessitated an impressive display of jewels, and contemporary records show that no expense had been spared for Elizabeth of York's coronation.[133]

The coronation became key to legitimising a queen's status in her realm, and this is the crucial point when highlighting how it differed from her marriage to a king.[134] Additionally and vitally, it also 'secured her prominence in the royal family as part of a monarchical couple'.[135] This was particularly important, necessary and apparent in the coronations of Elizabeth Wydeville (26 May 1465) and Anne Boleyn (1 June 1533), both of whom were given sumptuous individual coronations. Weeks before Anne's took place, the Imperial ambassador Chapuys reported rumours that she was to appear 'magnificently arrayed, no difficult matter for her to accomplish since she is in possession of all the Queen's jewels, and wears them on all occasions'.[136] Thanks to contemporary accounts we know that the rumours were correct. Detailed descriptions of both Anne and Elizabeth Wydeville's coronations survive, signifying that there were many parallels in the ways in which they were both conducted.[137] These were the only instances that commoners were ever crowned queens of England, and although a high level of pageantry and display were standard in coronation celebrations, at these times they were deemed especially necessary in order to highlight the rapidly exalted status of the queens'.[138] They also served as a useful tool to distract the populace's attention from Elizabeth and Anne's low-born origins. Arlene Okerlund described Elizabeth Wydeville's coronation as Edward IV's attempt to present 'his beautiful Queen as a jewel ensconced in a setting of regal pomp and circumstance'.[139] Anne Boleyn's coronation provided an opportunity not only to reaffirm Henry VIII's authority and consolidate Anne's status as queen but also to draw support and dispel some of her unpopularity.[140] Moreover, as Hunt emphasised, her visible pregnancy 'contributed to the establishment and legitimation of the new Tudor supremacy'.[141] Unfortunately, the ploy to increase Anne's popularity was unsuccessful.

The protocol and procedure for a queen's coronation had been laid out in the *Liber Regalis* (Royal Book) in the late fourteenth century, which stipulated the rules for both a double coronation and 'the day on which the queen is to be crowned by herself'.[142] The lower status of a queen compared with her husband was reflected in the coronation orders. For example, the *Liber Regalis* clearly stated that if a queen were to be crowned in the same ceremony as her husband, then 'a throne must likewise be prepared for her on the left-hand side of the king's throne, which must be somewhat higher'.[143] Additionally, in theory either a priest or a bishop could perform the coronation ceremony of a queen, whereas only a bishop was permitted to crown a king. Despite this, there is no record of a priest ever performing a queen's coronation ceremony.[144]

In keeping with the terms of the *Liber Regalis*, the coronation of a queen began with her ceremonial procession from the Tower of London to the Palace of Westminster. Traditions that had been in place for years were adhered to during this display, for in an indication of the value that was placed on the *Liber Regalis*, each of the queens complied with the rules that had been laid out. These specified that a queen should wear her hair 'decently let down on to her shoulders' in a symbol of virginity and that she 'shall wear a circlet of gold adorned with jewels to keep her hair the more conveniently in order on her head'.[145] The earlier discussion shows that both Catherine of Aragon and Anne Boleyn wore a circlet – possibly the same one, and prior to her coronation Margaret of Anjou was reported to be wearing 'a coronall of gold, riche perles and precious stones'.[146] This could have been the same coronet worn by both Anne Neville, described as 'a rych serkelet of golde with many preciouse perles and stones sett therin', and Elizabeth of York, who wore 'a Circlett of golde richely garnyshed with perle and precious stones'.[147] The generalisation in the description of these items makes it impossible to clarify if they were the same. It is certainly possible, however, that they were different: from at least the late fourteenth century, it had been customary for the crown worn by a queen in her coronation procession to be given to her by the king, so it may be that the circlets worn by all of the queens were unique and individual.[148] If indeed all, or at least some of the queens were gifted their coronets and circlets, it serves to exemplify the personal as well as dynastic nature that ceremonial jewels could adopt – the coronet was not a part of St Edward's regalia, and thus it was not used in the coronation ceremony. Queens were expected to continue wearing their coronet or circlet as their coronation ceremony began: the stipulations for Anne Neville's coronation related that she should be 'bareheded weringe a rounde circle of gold set with perill and precious stones' from the moment she left the Tower.[149] The *Liber Regalis* asserted that when 'the circlet which she wore on her head has been laid aside', she could be anointed with holy oil.[150] This symbolises that it was only at this most holy of moments that a queen was required to be unadorned with jewels, and at every other important point in the ceremony she would be equipped with some form of regalia.

Following her anointing, the *Liber Regalis* ordered, 'Then shall the ring be given to her by the consecrator', followed by a prayer.[151] In England the ruby became the traditional stone for coronation rings, a trend started by Henry III and reflective of the belief that it inspired love and reverence towards its wearer.[152] 'A golden ring with a ruby' can be found in Henry's inventory, but it does not appear in later inventories.[153] This is highly suggestive that the ring did not hold the same historical significance as other pieces of the coronation regalia and was not passed to successive monarchs. It indicates that it was instead commissioned by individual monarchs with their own personal tastes in mind, to use and dispose of at will, and stored separately from the coronation regalia. Evidence in support of this can be found for Henry VI, whose ruby coronation ring was delivered to goldsmith Matthew Philip, 'to make anew for the Queen's wedding ring'.[154] This serves as a further example of recycling and the dual purpose of jewels. Additionally, in both Henry VIII's 1519 and 1530 inventory of personal jewels can be found 'A ruby ring wherewith the King was sacred', further proof that the ring was kept separately.[155] Very little is known about the ring provided for use by queens, and it is impossible to clarify whether successive queens used the same one. No mention is made of a ring during the ceremony of Elizabeth Wydeville, but given the emphasis on the *Liber Regalis* it is likely that there was one.[156] The only detail given about Anne Neville's coronation ring is that it was provided by Lord Lovell in his capacity as Chamberlain of the King's Household, and this lends credence to the possibility that it was commissioned especially for her use.[157] The *Little Device* was a document that set out the expectations for a coronation and was used by Henry VII, who it was assumed would be crowned with Elizabeth of York.[158] This related that the queen would be presented with 'a riche Ring' that had been blessed.[159] It is likely that this was conformed to, but the only detail that was noted in the contemporary account of Elizabeth's coronation was that it was placed 'upon her fourthe finger'.[160]

Once the queen had been given her ring, 'Then shall the crown be blessed', before 'the Archbishop or Bishop shall place the crown on the queen's head'.[161] As discussed earlier in this chapter, for the most part the crown that was used by queens during this period was Queen Edith's Crown. Initially, a queen would only be invested with the crown and a ring, but the changing and growing prominence of a queen's status can be seen over time, when gradually more regalia was introduced into a queen's coronation ceremony.[162] This was in keeping with the stipulations of the *Liber Regalis*, which stated that once a queen had been invested with the crown, she ought to be delivered 'the sceptre into her right hand, and the rod into her left'.[163] Both of these pieces were topped with a dove with its wings displayed as specified in the *Liber Regalis*, symbolising the quality of gentleness attributed to a queen.[164] The sceptre also denoted the royal power of command and was a reminder to the sovereign of the importance of justice.[165] For queens, this became particularly essential as their roles as intercessors with their husbands grew in prestige.[166] The inclusion of the sceptre in a queen's coronation ceremony was therefore paramount. In contrast to two of her contemporaries, who, as related earlier, were presented with St Edward's staff usually reserved for the king's use, Anne Neville used only the crown and a ring, as well as a sceptre and a rod.[167] Given that Anne shared her husband's coronation, the most important regalia would have been reserved for Richard's use.

The coronation was undoubtedly the most important occasion on which a queen would wear regalia. In a clear affirmation of the majesty of the occasion, she was likely to continue wearing it throughout her coronation banquet in Westminster Hall. During the coronation banquet of Elizabeth Wydeville, for example, it was noted that the queen removed and replaced her crown several times.[168] The use of the Crown Jewels was not, however, restricted solely to a monarch's coronation. During the medieval period, crown-wearing days were a regular occurrence and were at their peak during the reign of Henry VI. Growing progressively elaborate, by the reign of Henry VI the king formally wore his crown on six important religious feasts: Christmas, Epiphany, Easter, Whitsun, All Saints and one or both of the feasts of St Edward – this not only was a display of the king's piety but was another way of projecting sovereignty.[169] Such days were based on the medieval beliefs in the mysteries of a monarch's power, but changing times meant that by the reign of Henry VII the importance of this ceremony had declined.[170] This was reflected when the king wore his crown for just one instance each year – both Henry VII and Henry VIII only wore it at Epiphany.[171] On one of these occasions, a contemporary writing in 1488 observed, 'The King and the Quene wer coronned'.[172] This suggests that queens followed the same traditions as their husbands and were expected to share in this spectacle in order to enhance the king's majestic image. The crowns worn by kings and their consorts at these junctures were a part of the state regalia, rather than that used for coronation ceremonies. It is likely that they were created for moments like this, when image was of the utmost importance. Kings also donned crowns at the State Opening of Parliament, and this too is indicative of the formality of the event.[173] Queens were not generally a part of this ritual and were therefore not expected to participate. In one instance, however, a contemporary observed that when Edward IV came to open Parliament, 'wheder come the quene crowned', emphasising Elizabeth Wydeville's role in supporting her husband at important moments.[174]

Crowns were also worn at other times when a monarch and their consort wanted to make a statement. While in York in 1483 Richard III was seen wearing his crown and sceptre, 'after whom marched in order quene Anne his wife likewyse crouned'.[175] At ceremonial events like this, the use of the crown reflected the importance that was placed on the projection of the royal image. Such a move was a very deliberate attempt to curry support for Richard and Anne's accession: the regalia played an essential part in assisting with this and showcasing the couple's grandeur.

Crowns could also serve a very different purpose and were often given to brides as wedding presents, which may account for the payment of a crown for Margaret Tudor in the Scottish treasurer's accounts in the summer of 1503.[176] This could also have been the case with both Margaret of Anjou and her predecessor, Katherine of Valois, for whom images survive depicting their marriages. A portrayal of the marriage of Henry V and Katherine of Valois, taken from the *Chroniques de France*, shows both the King and his bride wearing crowns, as does that of Henry VI and Margaret of Anjou, discussed in Chapter 4.[177] Notably, though, no mention is made of a crown in the payments made for jewels in preparation for Margaret's arrival.[178] This suggests either that Margaret did not receive a crown as a wedding gift or that the record for payment is no longer extant. Anna of Cleves, although not wearing a crown, adorned 'a rytch cronett of stones and pearle sett with rosemarie' for her wedding to Henry VIII, and she is the only one of Henry's wives for whom such a detail survives.[179] This could reflect a general pattern that such coronets or crowns were also adopted for the other five wives, in an indication of their newfound status.

The trend for using crowns to mark marriages is borne out by two surviving crowns from this period, at least one of which is of English origin. Originally made for Richard II's consort Anne of Bohemia, the crown of Princess Blanche, daughter of Henry IV, was intended to serve as a wedding coronet when she married Ludwig III of Bavaria in 1402.[180] Though it was of vital importance that the crown should express the wealth of Blanche's family, its primary purpose was more personal and regarded as 'essential to the wedding ceremony'.[181] Interestingly, though, there was a distinct lack of wealth within the families of some foreign princesses marrying into England, as previously recognised with Margaret of Anjou.[182] The same was not true of Catherine of Aragon, who, as Chapter 6 noted, brought a dowry partially consisting of jewels. The appearance of Princess Blanche's crown provides visual evidence as to the design and make-up of medieval crowns, and unlike the crowns worn by queens at their coronations, crowns such as this, which were more personal in nature, could be made from gold rather than gilt.[183] This was not exclusive and was not true of the other crown from this period, which was made slightly later for Margaret of York, Duchess of Burgundy.[184] Fashioned from silver gilt, Margaret's crown incorporated not only personal elements, such as the inclusion of her name, but also political allegiances, as evidenced in the addition of the enamelled white roses, which proudly declared Margaret's heritage. Margaret may even have worn this piece at her wedding to Charles, Duke of Burgundy, as she was described as being 'rychely coroned'.[185] Queens could also wear crowns at the weddings of their offspring. Isabel of Castile, for example, wore her crown at the wedding of her son Juan to Margaret of Austria in 1497.[186] This was a display not only of her regal status but of the solemnity of this consequential royal event.

Crowns could be worn for other important moments in a queen's life. *The Beauchamp Pageant* depicts Katherine of Valois wearing her crown following the birth of her son, the future Henry VI.[187] It is improbable that Katherine really wore her crown at this time, but such a portrayal emphasises the magnitude that was placed on royal regalia in projecting her queenly status at this integral moment: she had provided her husband with a male heir, and the image of the crown enhanced her triumph. There is no evidence that any of the other queens wore their crowns or adopted state regalia at such times or were depicted in such a manner. The peak in popularity of crown wearing in the fourteenth century partially explains this, but by the end of the century fashions had begun to change. The result was that headdresses became more popular, as portraits of Elizabeth Wydeville and her successors convey, and the use of coronals declined.[188] They were, though, still worn on state occasions.

The gravity of the crown rested in more than just material terms. This becomes apparent in the transition between Catherine of Aragon and Anne Boleyn. The author of the *Chronicle of King Henry VIII of England* noted that even prior to her marriage, Anne insisted that Catherine ought to surrender her jewels and crown – a right only afforded to the queen. In support of this, the reports of the Imperial ambassador related that

> Tallebout (the earl of Shrewsbury) keeps in his hands, as belongs to his office, the queen of England's crown; and since neither he nor any of his house ever incurred reproach, he would take care not to allow it to be put upon any other head.[189]

The King willingly complied with Anne's demands, leading the author of the *Chronicle* to report that Catherine retorted, ' "Although they take my crown," said the blessed lady, "I shall never cease to be Queen." '[190] The physical crown was viewed as the ultimate materialistic representation of queenship, but Catherine's behaviour reflects her belief – and that of many of her contemporaries – that it was only a symbol and not a physical requirement of being a queen.

The gravity attached to crowns in life was also evidenced in death. The account of Elizabeth of York's funeral describes her effigy as being richly adorned with 'her very rich crowne on her hed'.[191] In an important reinforcement of her position, she had a sceptre, and 'her fyngers well garneshed with rynge of gold and presyous stones'.[192] These symbols served as important reminders of majesty and were not afforded to any other queens in this period, with the possible exception of Anne Neville. They could also have been intended as a subtle acknowledgement of Elizabeth's dynastic legitimacy: she had a claim to be a queen in her own right, although her cousin the Earl of Warwick was heir to the House of York in the male line.[193] Anne Neville could have been afforded a similar degree of ceremony, for though no details of the proceedings for her funeral survive, the Crowland Chronicler reported that she 'was buried at Westminster with no less honours than befitted the interment of a queen'.[194] Anne, then, was clearly buried with some degree of pomp. The concept of funeral regalia was not exclusive to England. In Bohemia pieces remain dating from the fourteenth century, while in

France Queen Jeanne d'Evreux instructed that following her death her crown should be placed on her head.[195] A crown of Isabel of Castile's that was probably a funeral ornament still survives in Granada Cathedral, and these examples all evoke the importance that was attached to a monarch's regalia in ensuring that their royal identity continued to be remembered after their death.[196] It was also possible for a monarch to be buried with their crown, as the excavations of Gustav I Vasa of Sweden and his three wives revealed.[197]

Conclusion

The Crown Jewels were the singular most important set of jewels in a monarch's possession. Although not owned by them personally, they formed a fundamental part of state property that helped to ensure that the monarch and his consort were able to fulfil their ceremonial duties. Unlike other jewels, St Edward's regalia within the Crown Jewel collection were the only pieces that could be worn by queens at their coronation, and as such were only used by the first six queens in this period. This was the only occasion on which a queen had access to St Edward's regalia, as its use for coronations rendered it redundant elsewhere in a queen's life. The same was true of regalia used at the coronations of other European monarchs, and thus England's traditions were by no means unique.

In contrast to coronation regalia, state regalia, which included the Queen's State Crown, could be worn alongside other items of jewels that formed a part of the queen's collection. Examples of these items can be found in the inventories of Katherine Howard and Kateryn Parr.[198] While the later medieval queens wore crowns for events besides their coronations, there is no evidence to suggest that any of Henry VIII's wives ever did. This is accounted for by the decline in ceremonial occasions such as 'crowning wearing days', influenced by the Renaissance and the Reformation, which brought with it a desire for less-ornate ritual. Following Henry's break with Rome, he also felt a greater need to assert his authority in his kingdom as an individual. Though none of his wives seem to have made regular use of the state regalia that included the State Crown, they did at least make full use of the queenly collection of jewels that each one in turn was given upon acquiring their role. That they had easier access to these objects, which were in their custody, than the state regalia that was not, is also likely to account for their prominence.

The Crown Jewels played a vital role in assisting both king and queen with the projection of majesty that was an integral part of fifteenth- and sixteenth-century monarchy. They contributed to the aura of sovereignty, and this was most clearly in evidence on occasions such as coronations, when the jewels were clearly displayed to emphasise the monarch's splendour. In a reflection of the changing times, over time the appearance and use of the collection changed. Nevertheless, Hunt's assertion that 'the objects of the regalia are inextricable from the right of the office that they symbolise' ensured that the Crown Jewels remained the epitome of sovereignty.[199]

Notes

1 Glanville, *Silver*, p. 19.
2 Tait (ed.), *7000 Years*, p. 20.
3 Chadour-Sampson and Bari, *Pearls*, p. 49.
4 A. Keay, *The Crown Jewels: The Official Illustrated History* (London, 2012), p. 9.
5 Ibid, p. 10.
6 Ibid, p. 12.
7 Prince Michael of Greece, *Crown Jewels* (New York, 1983), p. 8.
8 U. Landergren (ed.), *The Treasury: The Regalia and Treasures of the Realm* (Stockholm, 2009), p. 3.
9 Keay, *Crown Jewels*, p. 15.
10 Ibid, p. 17.
11 Ibid.
12 L.G. Wickham Legg (ed.), *English Coronation Records* (Oxford, 1901), p. 191.
13 Prince of Greece, *Crown Jewels*, p. 12.
14 Ibid, p. 80.
15 Phillips, *Jewelry*, p. 78; Scarisbrick, *Diamonds*, p. 43.
16 Phillips, *Jewelry*, p. 78.
17 See R. Strong, *Coronation: A History of Kingship and the British Monarchy* (London, 2005), pp. 77–8.
18 Wickham Legg (ed.), *Coronation Records*, pp. 55–6, 80.

19 P. Longworth, 'Legitimacy and Myth in Central and Eastern Europe', in S.J. Kirschbaum (ed.), *Historical Reflections on Central Europe: Selected Papers from the Fifth World Congress of Central and East European Studies* (Basingstoke, 1999), p. 6.
20 Wickham Legg (ed.), *Coronation Records*, pp. 55–6, 80.
21 Prince of Greece, *Crown Jewels*, p. 16; SoA, MS 129, f. 7v.
22 The original manuscript inventory is unavailable, but a transcript of it is printed in E. Trollope (ed.), 'King Henry VIII's Jewel Book', *Associated Architectural Societies*, 17 (1883–4), p. 160.
23 SoA, MS 129, f. 7r; D. Mytens, 'King Charles I', 1631, NPG, NPG 1246.
24 Landergren (ed.), *Treasury*, p. 13.
25 Wickham Legg (ed.), *Coronation Records*, p. 192.
26 P. Stafford, *Queens, Concubines and Dowagers, Dowagers: The King's Wife in the Early Middle Ages* (London, 1983), p. 108.
27 Prince of Greece, *Crown Jewels*, p. 26; E. Morgan, '"Lapis Orphanus" in the Imperial Crown', *Modern Language Review*, 58 (1963), pp. 210–14.
28 Wickham Legg (ed.), *Coronation Records*, p. 80.
29 Ibid.
30 Lord Twining, *A History of the Crown Jewels of Europe* (London, 1960), p. 89; Prince of Greece, *Crown Jewels*, p. 92.
31 See R. Strong, 'Three Royal Jewels: The Three Brothers, the Mirror of Great Britain and the Feather', *BM*, 108 (1966), pp. 350–3.
32 Pietro Da Milano, 'Marguerite d'Anjou', fifteenth century, Milan, gilt bronze, Victoria & Albert Museum (A. 182–1910); F. Hepburn, 'The Queen in Exile: Representing Margaret of Anjou in Art and Literature', in L. Clark (ed.), *The Fifteenth Century: XI, Concerns and Preoccupations* (Croydon, 2012), pp. 61–90.
33 Hepburn, 'Queen in Exile', p. 62.
34 Scarisbrick, *Portrait Jewels*, p. 36.
35 Strong, *Coronation*, p. 122; See D. Hoak, 'The Iconography of the Crown Imperial', in D. Hoak (ed.), *Tudor Political Culture* (Cambridge, 2002), pp. 54–103.
36 Hepburn, 'Queen in Exile', p. 68.
37 Ibid, p. 69.
38 Ibid, p. 70.
39 See Maurer, *Margaret of Anjou*, p. 205.
40 J.A. Smith, 'Queen-Making and Queenship in Early Medieval England and Francia', unpublished PhD thesis, University of York, 1993, p. 213.
41 Cited in L. Visser-Fuchs, 'English Events in Caspar Weinreich's Danzig Chronicle, 1461–1495', *The Ricardian*, 7 (1986), p. 31.
42 F.W.D. Brie (ed.), *The Brut; or, The Chronicles of England*, EETS, orig. ser., 131, 136 (London, 1906–08), ii, p. 489.

43 J.L. Chamberlayne, 'Crowns and Virgins: Queenmaking During the Wars of the Roses', in K.J. Lewis, N.J. Menuge, and K.M. Phillips (eds), *Young Medieval Women* (Stroud, 1999), p. 60.
44 Ibid, pp. 47–68.
45 Flemish School, 'Family of Henry VII', RCT.
46 Weir, *Elizabeth of York*, p. 257; Unknown Artist, 'Rous Roll', BL, Add MS 48976, f. 7cr.
47 Chadour-Sampson and Bari, *Pearls*, p. 54; Howell, *Eleanor of Provence*, p. 256.
48 Chamberlayne, 'Crowns and Virgins', p. 57.
49 Unknown Artist, 'Margaret of Anjou', Bodleian Library.
50 Drimmer, 'Beyond Private Matter', p. 113.
51 Ibid, p. 95.
52 Unknown Artist, 'Elizabeth Wydeville', Worshipful Company of Skinners' Fraternity. Reproduced in J.J. Lambert (ed.), *Records of the Skinners of London, Edward I to James I* (London, 1933), p. 82.
53 Chamberlayne, 'Crowns and Virgins', p. 62; Unknown Artist, 'Elizabeth Wydeville', Worshipful Company of Skinners' Fraternity.
54 T.A. Heslop, 'The Virgin Mary's Regalia and Twelfth-Century English Seals', in A. Borg and A. Martindale (eds), *The Vanishing Past: Studies of Medieval Art, Liturgy and Metrology Presented to Christopher Hobler*, British Archaeological Reports, III (1981), pp. 53–6; Landergren (ed.), *Treasury*, p. 14.
55 Landergren (ed.), *Treasury*, p. 12.
56 Laynesmith, *Last Medieval Queens*, p. 33.
57 For two of the best known portraits see Unknown Artist, 'Katherine of Aragon', early eighteenth century, NPG, NPG 163 & Unknown Artist, 'Anne Boleyn', late sixteenth century, based on a work of circa 1533–6, NPG, NPG 668.
58 D. MacCulloch, *Reformation: Europe's House Divided 1490–1700* (London, 2003), pp. 186–7.
59 Scarisbrick, *Tudor and Jacobean Jewellery*, p. 51.
60 Unknown Artist, 'Henry VIII Procession', 1512, BL, Add MS 22306.
61 Unknown Artist, 'Elizabeth I', c. 1600, NPG, NPG 5175.
62 SoA, MS 129, f. 7r-8v.
63 Ibid, f. 7r.
64 E. Hall, *Chronicle*, ed. C. Whibley (London, 1904), p. 510.
65 Cherry, *Medieval Goldsmiths*, p. 61.
66 Hinton, *Medieval Jewellery*, p. 6.
67 Prince of Greece, *Crown Jewels*, p. 136.
68 Ibid.
69 BL, Egerton MS 985, f. 55v.
70 A. Hunt, *Drama of Coronation: Medieval Ceremony in Early Modern England* (Cambridge, 2008). p. 52.

71 J. Laynesmith, 'Fertility Rite or Authority Ritual? The Queen's Coronation in England 1445–87', in T. Thornton (ed.), *Social Attitudes and Political Structures in the Fifteenth Century* (Stroud, 2000), p. 61.
72 SoA, MS 108, f. 17v.
73 See SoA, MS 129, f. 7r-8v.
74 C. Blair (ed.), *The Crown Jewels: The History of the Coronation Regalia in the Jewel House of the Tower of London* (London, 1998), p. 265.
75 SoA, MS 129, f. 7v-8r.
76 BL, Egerton MS 985, f. 55v.
77 *CSPM*, i, pp. 557–8.
78 Ibid.
79 Anthony van Dyck, 'Henrietta Maria', 1632, RCT, RCIN 404430.
80 SoA, MS 129, f. 7r-8v.
81 G. Smith (ed.), *The Coronation of Elizabeth Wydeville* (London, 1935), p. 15; Sutton and Hammond (eds), *Coronation of Richard III*, p. 278; BL, Egerton MS 985, f. 18v.
82 BL, Egerton MS 985, f. 55v.
83 Wickham Legg (ed.), *Coronation Records*, p. 243.
84 Ibid, p. 123; Laynesmith, *Last Medieval Queens*, p. 105.
85 Smith (ed.), *Coronation of Elizabeth Wydeville*, p. 15.
86 Hall, *Chronicle*, p. 803; BL, Egerton MS 985, f. 55v.
87 See Laynesmith, 'Fertility Rite', p. 61.
88 SoA, MS 129, f. 7r-8v.
89 Hall, *Chronicle*, p. 803.
90 Ibid, p. 508.
91 BL, Egerton MS 985, f. 55r; Ibid, f. 58v.
92 J. Loach, 'The Function of Ceremonial in the Reign of Henry VIII', *Past and Present*, 142 (1994), pp. 43–68.
93 See Strong, *Lost Treasures*, pp. 118–25; SoA, MS 108, f. 16v.
94 Blair (ed.), *Crown Jewels*, p. 346.
95 SoA, MS 108, f. 4r-19r.
96 Ibid.
97 Ibid, f. 14r-v.
98 Ibid, f. 17v.
99 Loach, 'Function of Ceremonial', p. 68.
100 See Keay, *Crown Jewels*, p. 20.
101 Ibid.
102 Strong, *Coronation*, p. 101.
103 See Wickham Legg (ed.), *Coronation Records*, pp. 57–65; Howell, *Eleanor of Provence*; T. Rose, *The Coronation Ceremony and the Crown Jewels* (London, 1992), p. 36.
104 Earenfight, 'Persona', p. 12.
105 See Okerlund, *Elizabeth of York*, p. 75.

106 Starkey, *Six Wives*, pp. 584–616.
107 Laynesmith, *Last Medieval Queens*, p. 82.
108 Earenfight, 'Persona', pp. 11–21.
109 *L & P*, x, no. 952; *L & P*, x, no. 909.
110 *L & P*, xi, no. 528.
111 C.H. Williams (ed.), *English Historical Documents*, V (1485–1558) (London, 1967), p. 519; See also Starkey, *Six Wives*, p. 8.
112 H.S. Hurlburt, 'Public Exposure? Consorts and Ritual in Late Medieval Europe: The Example of the Entrance of the Dogaresse of Venice', in M.C. Erler and M. Kowaleski (eds), *Gendering the Master Narrative: Women and Power in the Middle Ages* (Ithaca and London, 2003), p. 185.
113 Ibid.
114 *L & P*, xv, no. 401; *L & P*, xv, no. 485.
115 Warnicke, *Marrying of Anne of Cleves*, p. 184.
116 Ibid.
117 *L & P*, xvi, no. 1183.
118 Parsons, 'Family', p. 8.
119 I.W. Archer, 'City and Court Connected: The Material Dimensions of Royal Ceremonial, ca. 1480–1625', *HLQ*, 71 (2008), p. 160.
120 Two further children, a son and a daughter, had died young prior to 1603. In May 1603 Anna also experienced a miscarriage.
121 See Rhodes, 'Wardrobe of Queen Isabella', pp. 517–21.
122 Sutton and Hammond (eds), *Coronation of Richard III*, pp. 270–82.
123 LC 9/50.
124 See Sutton and Hammond (eds), *Coronation of Richard III*, pp. 270–82; Wickham Legg (ed.), *Coronation Records*, pp. 193–7.
125 LC 9/50, f. 218r.
126 Myers, 'Household of Queen Margaret', p. 9.
127 See Maurer, *Margaret of Anjou*, pp. 25–7.
128 T. Rymer (ed.), *Rymer's Foedera*, XI (London, 1739–45), p. 81.
129 Ibid.
130 See C.L. Scofield, *The Life and Reign of Edward the Fourth*, 2 vols (London, 1923), I, p. 375.
131 C.A. Edie, 'The Public Face of Royal Ritual: Sermons, Medals, and Civic Ceremony in Later Stuart Coronations', *HLQ*, 53 (1990), pp. 311–36; Loach, 'Function of Ceremonial', p. 43.
132 R. Strong, *The Culture of Elizabeth: Elizabethan Portraiture and Pageantry* (London, 1977), p. 114.
133 E 101/425/19, pp. 1–10.
134 Earenfight, *Queenship*, p. 247.
135 Ibid, p. 84.
136 *CSPS*, iv, part 2, no. 1062.

137 Smith (ed.), *Coronation of Elizabeth Wydeville*, pp. 14–25; BL, Egerton MS 985, f. 49r-59v.
138 See Blair (ed.), *Crown Jewels*, p. 193.
139 Okerlund, *Elizabeth*, p. 61.
140 See Starkey, *Six Wives*, p. 344.
141 Hunt, *Drama of Coronation*, p. 39.
142 *Liber Regalis* in Wickham Legg (ed.), *Coronation Records*, p. 128.
143 Ibid, p. 122.
144 Rose, *Coronation Ceremony*, p. 63.
145 *Liber Regalis* in Wickham Legg (ed.), *Coronation Records*, p. 122.
146 Brie (ed.), *Brut*, ii, p. 48.
147 Sutton and Hammond (eds), *Coronation of Richard III*, p. 276; BL, Egerton MS 985, f. 17v.
148 Weir, *Elizabeth of York*, p. 255; Rhodes, 'Wardrobe of Queen Isabella', pp. 517–21.
149 Sutton and Hammond (eds), *Coronation of Richard III*, p. 214.
150 *Liber Regalis* in Wickham Legg (ed.), *Coronation Records*, p. 123.
151 Ibid.
152 Scarisbrick et al. (eds), *Brilliant Europe*, p. 30.
153 Wickham Legg (ed.), *Coronation Records*, p. 56.
154 Rymer (ed.), *Foedera*, XI, p. 122.
155 *L & P*, iii, no. 463; *L & P*, iv, no. 6789. The 1519 entry also describes the ring as being 'enamelled white'.
156 See Smith (ed.), *Coronation of Elizabeth Wydeville*, pp. 14–25.
157 Sutton and Hammond (eds), *Coronation of Richard III*, p. 239.
158 See S. Anglo, 'The Foundation of the Tudor Dynasty: The Coronation and Marriage of Henry VII', *Guildhall Miscellany*, II (1960), p. 5.
159 *Little Device* in Wickham Legg (ed.), *Coronation Records*, p. 235.
160 BL, Egerton MS 985, f. 18v.
161 *Liber Regalis* in Wickham Legg (ed.), *Coronation Records*, p. 123.
162 Rose, *Coronation Ceremony*, p. 63.
163 *Liber Regalis* in Wickham Legg (ed.), *Coronation Records*, p. 123.
164 Ibid.
165 Scarisbrick et al. (eds), *Brilliant Europe*, p. 29; Rose, *Coronation Ceremony*, p. 38.
166 Earenfight, *Queenship*, p. 11.
167 Sutton and Hammond (eds), *Coronation of Richard III*, pp. 228–9.
168 Smith (ed.), *Coronation of Elizabeth Wydeville*, p. 19.
169 Keay, *Crown Jewels*, p. 28.
170 See F. Kisby, 'The Royal Household Chapel in Early-Tudor London, 1485–1547', unpublished PhD thesis, Royal Holloway and Bedford New College, University of London, 1996, p. 146.
171 Keay, *Crown Jewels*, p. 28.

172 J. Leland, *Antiquarii De Rebvs Britannicis Collectanea*, ed. T. Hearne, iv (London, 1774), p. 235.
173 See Hans Holbein, 'Henry VIII and the Barber Surgeons', c. 1543, Worshipful Company of Barbers, Barber-Surgeons' Hall, London, for one example.
174 Kingsford, *English Historical Literature*, p. 383.
175 Hall, *Chronicle*, p. 380.
176 Phillips, *Jewelry*, p. 70; Dickson and Balfour (eds), *Accounts of the Lord High* Treasurer, II, p. 206.
177 BL, Royal 20 E. vi, f. 9v; Martial d'Auvergne, 'Marriage of Henry VI and Margaret of Anjou', Bibliothèque Nationale de France, MS Français 5054.
178 See Rymer (ed.), *Foedera*, XI, p. 122.
179 C. Wriothesley, *A Chronicle of England During the Reigns of the Tudors from 1485 to 1559*, ed. W.D. Hamilton, I (London, 1875), p. 111.
180 Unknown Maker, 'Crown of Princess Blanche', fourteenth century, gold, Munich Residenz; E. Harper, '*Pearl* in the Context of Fourteenth-Century Gift Economies', *Chaucer Review*, 44 (2010), pp. 421–39; Cherry, 'Late Fourteenth-Century Jewellery', pp. 137–40.
181 Harper, '*Pearl*', p. 421.
182 See N. Saul, 'Anne [Anne of Bohemia]', *ODNB*.
183 Harper, '*Pearl*', p. 421.
184 Unknown Maker, 'Coronet of Margaret of York', late fifteenth century, gilt, Aachen Cathedral.
185 BL, Cotton MS Nero C IX, f. 175r.
186 Twining, *Crown Jewels of Europe*, p. 611.
187 BL, Cotton MS Julius E IV, f. 22v.
188 See Unknown Artist, 'Elizabeth Woodville', RCT, RCIN 406785, for example.
189 *L & P*, v, no. 120.
190 Hume (trans.), *Chronicle of King Henry VIII*, p. 44.
191 College of Arms, MS I.ii, f. 27r-32r. See also Litten, 'The Funeral Effigy', pp. 6–7.
192 College of Arms, MS I.ii, f. 27r-32r.
193 Chamberlayne, 'Crowns and Virgins', p. 50; C. Carpenter, 'Edward, styled Earl of Warwick', *ODNB*.
194 Pronay and Cox (eds), *Crowland Chronicle*, p. 175.
195 Twining, *Crown Jewels of Europe*, p. 221.
196 Ibid, p. 613.
197 See R. Brus, *Crown Jewellery and Regalia of the World* (Amsterdam, 2011), p. 200.
198 BL, Stowe MS 559, f. 55r-68r; SoA, MS 129, f. 178r-183v.
199 Hunt, *Drama of Coronation*, p. 30.

References

Manuscript Sources

Kew, The National Archives

EXCHEQUER

E 101 King's Remembrancer, Various Accounts.

LORD CHAMBERLAIN'S DEPARTMENT

LC 9 Accounts and Miscellanea.

LONDON, THE BRITISH LIBRARY

Cotton Manuscripts	Julius E IV, Nero C IX.
Egerton Manuscripts	985.
Royal Manuscripts	20 E. vi.
Stowe Manuscripts	559.

LONDON, COLLEGE OF ARMS

MS I.ii Account of the Funeral of Elizabeth of York.

LONDON, SOCIETY OF ANTIQUARIES

MS 108 Inventory of the Crown Jewels, 1649.
MS 129 Inventory of King Henry VIII.

Portraits

Anthony van Dyck, 'Henrietta Maria', 1632, RCT, RCIN 404430.

Daniel Mytens, 'King Charles I', 1631, NPG, NPG 1246.

Flemish School, 'The Family of Henry VII with St George and the Dragon', c. 1503–9, RCT, RCIN 401228.

Hans Holbein, 'Henry VIII and the Barber Surgeons', c. 1543, Worshipful Company of Barbers, Barber-Surgeons' Hall, London.

Martial d'Auvergne, 'Marriage of Henry VI and Margaret of Anjou', Bibliothèque Nationale de France, MS Français 5054.

Unknown Artist, 'Anne Boleyn', late sixteenth century, based on a work of c. 1533–6, NPG, NPG 668.

Unknown Artist, 'Elizabeth I', c. 1600, NPG, NPG 5175.

Unknown Artist, 'Elizabeth Woodville', c. 1513–30, RCT, RCIN 406785.

Unknown Artist, 'Elizabeth Wydeville', c. 1470, Worshipful Company of Skinners' Fraternity, Guildhall Library, MS 31692, f. 32v.

Unknown Artist, 'Henry VIII Procession', 1512, BL, Add MS 22306.

Unknown Artist, 'Katherine of Aragon', early eighteenth century, NPG, NPG 163.

Unknown Artist, John Rous, 'The Rous Roll', c. 1483–84 BL, Add MS 48976, f. 7cr.

Unknown Artist, 'The Prayer Roll of Margaret of Anjou', c. 1445–55, Bodleian Library, Jesus College, MS 124.

Physical Objects

Pietro Da Milano, 'Marguerite d'Anjou', fifteenth century, Milan, gilt bronze, Victoria & Albert Museum (A. 182–1910).

Unknown Maker, 'Coronet of Margaret of York', late fifteenth century, gilt, Aachen Cathedral.

Unknown Maker, 'Crown of Princess Blanche', fourteenth century, gold, Munich Residenz.

Printed Primary Sources

Bergenroth, G.A., et al., (ed.), *Calendar of State Papers, Spain*, 13 vols (London, 1862–1954).

Brewer, J.S., (ed.), *Letters and Papers, Foreign and Domestic, of the Reign of Henry VIII, 1509–47*, 21 vols and addenda (London, 1862–1932).

Brie, F.W.D., (ed.), *The Brut; or, The Chronicles of England*, EETS, orig. ser., 131, 136 (1906–08), ii, p. 489.

Dickson, T., and Balfour Paul, J., (eds), *Accounts of the Lord High Treasurer of Scotland*, 13 vols (Edinburgh, 1877–1916).

Hall, E., *Chronicle*, ed. Whibley, C., (London, 1904).

Hinds, A.B., (ed.), *Calendar of State Papers and Manuscripts in the Archives and Collections of Milan 1385–1618*, 1 vol (London, 1912).

Hume, M.A.S. trans., *The Chronicle of King Henry VIII of England* (London, 1889).

Leland, L., *Antiquarii De Rebvs Britannicis Collectanea*, ed. Hearne, T., 6 vols (London, 1774).

Pronay, N., and Cox, J., (eds), *The Crowland Chronicle Continuations: 1459–1486* (London, 1986).

Rymer, T., (ed.), *Rymer's Foedera*, 16 vols (London, 1739–45).

Smith, G., (ed.), *The Coronation of Elizabeth Wydeville* (London, 1935).

Sutton, A.F., and Hammond, P.W. (eds), *The Coronation of Richard III: The Extant Documents* (London, 1983).

Trollope, E., (ed.), 'King Henry VIII's Jewel Book', *Associated Architectural Societies*, 17 (1883–4), pp. 155–229.

Wickham Legg, L.G., (ed.), *English Coronation Records* (Oxford, 1901).

Williams, C.H., (ed.), *English Historical Documents*, V (1485–1558) (London, 1967).

Wriothesley, C., *A Chronicle of England During the Reigns of the Tudors from 1485 to 1559*, ed. Hamilton, W.D., I (London, 1875).

Secondary Sources

Anglo, S., 'The Foundation of the Tudor Dynasty: The Coronation and Marriage of Henry VII', *Guildhall Miscellany*, II (1960).

Archer, I.W., 'City and Court Connected: The Material Dimensions of Royal Ceremonial, ca. 1480–1625', *HLQ*, 71 (2008).

Blair, C., (ed.), *The Crown Jewels: The History of the Coronation Regalia in the Jewel House of the Tower of London* (London, 1998).

Brus, R., *Crown Jewellery and Regalia of the World* (Amsterdam, 2011).

Carpenter, C., 'Edward, Styled Earl of Warwick', *ODNB*, https://doi.org/10.1093/ref:odnb/8525

Chadour-Sampson, B., and Bari, H., *Pearls* (London, 2013).

Chamberlayne, J.L., 'Crowns and Virgins: Queenmaking During the Wars of the Roses', in Lewis, K.J., Menuge, N.J., and Phillips, K.M. (eds), *Young Medieval Women* (Stroud, 1999).

Cherry, J., 'Late Fourteenth-Century Jewellery: The Inventory of November 1399', *BM*, 130 (1988).

Cherry, J., *Medieval Goldsmiths* (London, 1992).

Drimmer, S., 'Beyond Private Matter: A Prayer Roll for Queen Margaret of Anjou', *Gesta*, 53 (2014), pp. 95–120.

Earenfight, T., *Queenship in Medieval Europe* (Basingstoke, 2013).

Earenfight, T., 'Without the Persona of the Prince: Kings, Queens and the Idea of Monarchy in Late Medieval Europe', *Gender and History*, 19 (2007), pp. 1–21.

Edie, C.A., 'The Public Face of Royal Ritual: Sermons, Medals, and Civic Ceremony in Later Stuart Coronations', *HLQ*, 53 (1990), pp. 311–36.

Glanville, P., *Silver in Tudor and Stuart England* (London, 1990).

Harper, E., '*Pearl* in the Context of Fourteenth-Century Gift Economies', *Chaucer Review*, 44 (2010), pp. 421–39.

Hepburn, F., 'The Queen in Exile: Representing Margaret of Anjou in Art and Literature', in Clark, L. (ed.), *The Fifteenth Century: XI, Concerns and Preoccupations* (Croydon, 2012), pp. 61–90.

Heslop, T.A., 'The Virgin Mary's Regalia and Twelfth-Century English Seals', in Borg, A., and Martindale, A. (eds), 'The Vanishing Past: Studies of Medieval Art, Liturgy and Metrology Presented to Christopher Hobler', *British Archaeological Reports*, III (1981), pp. 53–6.

Hinton, D., *Medieval Jewellery* (Aylesbury, 1982).

Hoak, D., 'The Iconography of the Crown Imperial', in Hoak, D. (ed.), *Tudor Political Culture* (Cambridge, 2002), pp. 54–103.

Howell, M., *Eleanor of Provence: Queenship in Thirteenth Century England* (Oxford, 1998).

Hunt, A., *The Drama of Coronation: Medieval Ceremony in Early Modern England* (Cambridge, 2008).

Hurlburt, H.S., 'Public Exposure? Consorts and Ritual in Late Medieval Europe: The Example of the Entrance of the Dogaresse of Venice', in Erler, M.C., and Kowaleski, M. (eds), *Gendering the Master Narrative: Women and Power in the Middle Ages* (Ithaca and London, 2003), pp. 174–89.

Keay, A., *The Crown Jewels: The Official Illustrated History* (London, 2012).

Kingsford, C.L., *English Historical Literature in the Fifteenth Century* (Oxford, 1913).

Kisby, F., 'The Royal Household Chapel in Early-Tudor London, 1485–1547', unpublished PhD thesis, Royal Holloway and Bedford New College, University of London, 1996.

Lambert, J.J., (ed.), *Records of the Skinners of London, Edward I to James I* (London, 1933).

Landergren, U., (ed.), *The Treasury: The Regalia and Treasures of the Realm* (Stockholm, 2009).

Laynesmith, J., 'Fertility Rite or Authority Ritual? The Queen's Coronation in England 1445–87', in Thornton, T. (ed.), *Social Attitudes and Political Structures in the Fifteenth Century* (Stroud, 2000), pp. 52–68.

Laynesmith, J., *The Last Medieval Queens* (Oxford, 2004).

Litten, J., 'The Funeral Effigy: Its Function and Purpose', in Harvey, A., and Mortimer, R. (eds), *The Funeral Effigies of Westminster Abbey* (Woodbridge, 1994), pp. 3–19.

Loach, J., 'The Function of Ceremonial in the Reign of Henry VIII', *Past and Present*, (1994), pp. 43–68.

Longworth, P., 'Legitimacy and Myth in Central and Eastern Europe', in Kirschbaum, S.J. (ed.), *Historical Reflections on Central Europe: Selected Papers from the Fifth World Congress of Central and East European Studies* (Basingstoke, 1999), pp. 5–14.

MacCulloch, D., *Reformation: Europe's House Divided 1490–1700* (London, 2003).

Maurer, H.E., *Margaret of Anjou: Queenship and Power in Late Medieval England* (Woodbridge, 2003).

Morgan, E., '"Lapis Orphanus" in the Imperial Crown', *Modern Language Review*, 58 (1963), pp. 210–14.

Myers, A.R., 'The Household of Queen Margaret of Anjou, 1452–3', *BJRL*, 50 (1957–8), pp. 79–113.

Okerlund, A., *Elizabeth: England's Slandered Queen* (Stroud, 2005).

Okerlund, A., *Elizabeth of York* (Basingstoke, 2009).

Parsons, J.C., 'Family, Sex and Power: The Rhythms of Medieval Queenship', in Parsons, J.C. (ed.), *Medieval Queenship* (Stroud, 1993), pp. 1–12.

Phillips, C., *Jewelry: From Antiquity to the Present* (London, 1996).

Prince Michael of Greece, *Crown Jewels* (New York, 1983).

Rhodes, W.E., 'The Inventory of the Jewels and Wardrobe of Queen Isabella (1307–8)', *EHR*, 12 (1897), pp. 517–21.

Rose, T., *The Coronation Ceremony and the Crown Jewels* (London, 1992).

Saul, N., 'Anne [Anne of Bohemia]', *ODNB*, https://doi.org/10.1093/ref:odnb/555

Scarisbrick, D., *Diamond Jewelry: 700 Years of Glory and Glamour* (London, 2019).

Scarisbrick, D., *Portrait Jewels: Opulence and Intimacy from the Medici to the Romanovs* (London, 2011).

Scarisbrick, D., *Tudor and Jacobean Jewellery* (London, 1995).

Scarisbrick, D., Vachaudez, C., and Walgrave, J., (eds), *Brilliant Europe: Jewels from European Courts* (Brussels, 2007).

Scofield, C.L., *The Life and Reign of Edward the Fourth*, 2 vols (London, 1923).

Smith, J.A., 'Queen-making and Queenship in Early Medieval England and Francia', unpublished PhD thesis, University of York, 1993.

Stafford, P., *Queens, Concubines and Dowagers: The King's Wife in the Early Middle Ages* (London, 1983).

Starkey, D., *Six Wives: The Queens of Henry VIII* (London, 2004).

Strong, R., *Coronation: A History of Kingship and the British Monarchy* (London, 2005).

Strong, R., *Lost Treasures of Britain* (London, 1990).

Strong, R., *The Culture of Elizabeth: Elizabethan Portraiture and Pageantry* (London, 1977).

Strong, R., 'Three Royal Jewels: The Three Brothers, the Mirror of Great Britain and the Feather', *BM*, 108 (1966), pp. 350–3.

Tait, H., (ed.), *7000 Years of Jewellery* (London, 1986).

Twining, L., *A History of the Crown Jewels of Europe* (London, 1960).

Visser-Fuchs, L., 'English Events in Caspar Weinreich's Danzig Chronicle, 1461–1495', *The Ricardian*, 7 (1986).

Warnicke, R.M., *The Marrying of Anne of Cleves: Royal Protocol in Tudor England* (Cambridge, 2004).

Weir, A., *Elizabeth of York: The First Tudor Queen* (London, 2013).

Conclusion

Henry VIII's death on 28 January 1547 brought Kateryn Parr's three-and-a-half-year reign as queen consort to an end. She was now a dowager queen, and it would not be until 1603, 56 years after Henry's death, that England would have another queen consort.[1] Thus, the end of the reign of Henry VIII also brought an end to the line of queen consorts who have been the subject of this book. Nevertheless, the 17 months following Henry's death that witnessed Kateryn Parr's transition from a consort to a dowager queen had monumental ramifications on her jewel collection. Its reference in Chapters 2 and 3 in the context of wills and inventories are therefore critical in order to aid our understanding of both Kateryn's jewels and the queens' collection as a whole. Her death on 5 September 1548 as a result of the effects of childbirth, however, provides the ideal point on which to end the book. The Stuart dynasty that followed the Tudors in 1603 brought queen consorts whose experiences differed from their fifteenth- and sixteenth-century predecessors, accompanied by both new styles of jewellery and self-fashioning.

Six years after Henry VIII's death, the country embarked on a new kind of queenship when both of Henry's daughters, Mary I and Elizabeth I, succeeded to the English throne in their own right.[2] In a similar manner to their predecessors, both queens regnant revelled in the pleasure brought by jewels and continued to add to and develop the collection. In 1554 the Venetian ambassador remarked that Mary 'makes great use of jewels', in which 'she delights greatly'.[3] Moreover, the ambassador

DOI: 10.4324/9781003202592-9

continued, 'she has a great plenty of them left her by her predecessors', testimony that Mary enjoyed and appreciated jewels in the same manner as those who had come before her.[4] An inventory made a month after her accession shows many of the same items that had once been owned by Katherine Howard and Kateryn Parr, and she also received a number of important pieces from her husband, Philip II of Spain, several of which had their own impressive heritage.[5] Elizabeth I had a similar penchant for jewels, which made a dazzling impression on her contemporaries. Just a month after her accession the Count de Feria informed Philip II that 'she was so fond of her jewels', while during her coronation procession in January 1559, the Venetian ambassador observed that 'the whole Court so sparkled with jewels and gold collars that they cleared the air'.[6] It is unsurprising, therefore, that the collection of royal jewels grew dramatically during Elizabeth's reign. This is reflected in the numerous surviving gift rolls, which note the magnificent jewelled gifts that were given to the Queen, and which provide a wealth of evidence as to the way in which her collection developed.[7] Elizabeth also obtained jewels from other sources, including as security against a loan to Don Antonio, Prior of Crato, who seized the Portuguese throne in 1580.[8] At the end of her reign Elizabeth's jewels still made enough of an impact to draw comment from her contemporaries, and in February 1603 – the month before her death – she received the Venetian secretary dripping in pieces which included:

> a coif arched round her head and an Imperial crown, and displayed a vast quantity of gems and pearls upon her person; even under her stomacher she was covered with golden jewelled girdles and single gems, carbuncles, balas-rubies, diamonds; round her wrists in place of bracelets she wore double rows of pearls of more than medium size.[9]

Cassie Auble's work has shown that, like her stepmother Kateryn Parr, Elizabeth used her gems in order to create an image of royal authority both in person and through her portraiture.[10] This was reflected in Elizabeth's appearance when she met with the Venetian secretary. Not only did her jewels assert her sovereignty, but they could also 'convey the prosperity and stability of England and her monarch'.[11] In contrast to their predecessors, as queen regnants – a concept that was almost unprecedented in England – Mary and Elizabeth needed to put their jewels to different uses in order to exude sovereign power, and the need to impress both their subjects and visitors to the English court was more explicit as the ambassadors' reports bear testimony to.[12]

This book has emphasised that Mary and Elizabeth's love of jewels was neither new nor unique. By investing in and showcasing their jewellery, the two regnant queens were continuing a trend that had been enjoyed and capitalised upon by their predecessors – both male monarchs and queen consorts – for many centuries. Both women had been given the opportunity to observe first hand and learn from the way in which their father's wives had used their gems. They were thus provided with a platform from which to continue and heighten the opulence communicated by jewels. Observations have been made about the potential influence that Kateryn Parr had on Elizabeth in terms of a woman's ability to rule a country, with Susan James stating that the 'pattern of queenship that Elizabeth learned was the pattern of queenship that Catherine Parr provided'.[13] The effect that Kateryn is likely to have had on Elizabeth in terms of using jewels as tools to aid and emphasise power, however, has yet to be recognised. It is hoped that this book may provide a starting point for exploring this important aspect of Kateryn's influence.

Unlike Kateryn Parr and any of her predecessors, however, both Mary and Elizabeth were regnant queens with different roles and responsibilities. This meant that it was necessary for them to employ jewels as a way of emulating sovereign power, rather than that of consorts. Given her comparatively longer reign it was Elizabeth, rather than Mary, who fully exploited this, the results of which can be seen in many of her surviving portraits.[14] Many of these provide tangible evidence of the ways in which she used her jewels to convey power and send important messages to those who viewed her image: the use of the phoenix jewel in her portrait of the same name, for example, was symbolic not only of rebirth and chastity but also of Elizabeth's unique identity.[15] By using her jewels in such a way, Elizabeth crafted the persona of Gloriana or the Virgin Queen that has endured to this day.[16]

Tracking the jewels of the queens of England from 1445 to 1548 has shown that these queens had access to an impressive amount of material wealth, much of which was inherited from their predecessors. Many chose to alter and add to their jewel collection through their patronage of goldsmiths, although in the case of the late medieval queens Laynesmith has underlined that the nature of their financial resources strongly influenced each queen's role, which therefore impacted their ability to buy jewels.[17] This, in turn, is reflected in the wills of both Margaret of Anjou and Elizabeth Wydeville.[18] Likewise, it was possible for queens to acquire jewels in other ways than through their patronage of goldsmiths, and some of the methods, such as ordering directly from overseas merchants, run beyond the scope of this book.

The material wealth of queens also served a greater purpose. Jewels provided queens with physical tools that enabled them to use this wealth in a manner that expressed their own power and regality, whether through portraiture or display. Sydney Anglo emphasised that 'Magnificence was obligatory for effective kingship', yet until now the importance of this concept in the context of queenship has been neglected.[19] The prominence of this should not be underestimated, for splendour was an essential aspect of queenship that was more critical during this period than any that had come before. This was because, as highlighted in the introduction, the experiences of queenship in fifteenth- and sixteenth-century England were both turbulent and unprecedented: what is more, time has revealed that they were also completely unique. As such, it was both imperative and necessary during periods of political turbulence and dynastic change for queens to assert their legitimate right to rule as consorts alongside their husbands: jewels were a vital material element in this spectacle of royalty. For queens who had gained their position through their husband's unorthodox rise to power, such as Anne Neville as the wife of the 'usurper' Richard III or their own unusual accession as in the manner of Anne Boleyn, whose marriage and coronation were facilitated by Henry VIII's break with Rome in order to end his marriage to Catherine of Aragon, using jewels – particularly the coronation regalia – underlined their status as the legitimate queen. These jewels were at the very centre of a queen's life and were a pivotal part of her identity.[20]

Examining the way in which queens used jewels in a variety of contexts has revealed not only the interest that these women took in crafting their own personas but also how they were able to use jewels as a way of acquiring and demonstrating power in a male-dominated world. In an era in which women – even queens – were expected to be fully subservient to their husbands, jewels provided a way of expanding and enhancing their networks, while remaining within the boundaries of contemporary expectations of them as consorts. Circumstances, however, forced Margaret of Anjou to push these boundaries, and in so doing blackened her reputation as a consort. Despite this, Maurer's conclusion that with few exceptions, 'she represented herself throughout the reign in terms and images that conveyed acceptable notions of queenship', is accurate.[21]

Scholars studying queenship have long been interested in many areas of the queen's role: the relationship between a queen and her husband, image creation, patronage, networking and gift giving.[22] Yet when these elements are analysed in a different context through the medium of jewellery, it becomes apparent that the jewel collections of the queens of England underpinned all of these in a number of ways. The splendour that surrounded these queens not only underlined their power and authority but that of their husbands and the realm itself, confirming Stafford's assertion that 'Queens appeared loaded with gems and finery, displaying their husband's wealth'.[23] Ultimately, therefore, the jewel collections of the queens of England represented the power and majesty of the dynasty of which they were a part, thus validating that 'the queen personifies the household's need for treasure, for its management and its display'.[24] Within this framework, jewels gave queens a freedom through which to express themselves as individuals and as consorts, for they 'acted as metaphors for a variety of societal messages and cultural concepts'.[25] In so doing, jewels provided queens with the tools to craft their personas as consorts and were an indispensable part of their identity as well as the practice and authority of queenship.

Notes

1 See M.M. Meikle and H. Payne, 'Anne [Anna, Anne of Denmark]', *ODNB*.
2 See A. Hunt and A. Whitelock (eds), *Tudor Queenship: The Reigns of Mary and Elizabeth* (Basingstoke, 2010).
3 *CSPV*, x, no. 934.
4 Ibid.
5 BL, Harley MS 7376, f. 1r-42v; Scarisbrick, *Diamonds*, p. 46.
6 *CSPS*, i, p. 10; *CSPV*, vii, no. 10.
7 For examples see BL, Add MS 4827, BL Add MS 8159. See also Lawson (ed.), *Gift Exchanges*.
8 Scarisbrick, *Diamonds*, p. 48.
9 *CSPV*, ix, no. 1135.
10 C. Auble, 'Bejeweled Majesty: Queen Elizabeth I, Precious Stones, and Statecraft', in D. Barrett-Graves (ed.), *The Emblematic Queen: Extra-Literary Representations of Early Modern Queenship* (Basingstoke, 2013), p. 37.
11 Ibid, p. 48.
12 The only brief attempts of female rule in England came from the Empress Matilda in the twelfth century and Lady Jane Grey in the summer of 1553. Both were unsuccessful.
13 James, *Catherine Parr*, p. 154.
14 James, *Feminine Dynamic*, pp. 187–228.
15 Nicholas Hilliard, 'Queen Elizabeth I', c. 1575, NPG, NPG 190; Bolland and Cooper, *Real Tudors*, p. 144.
16 See Howey, 'Dressing a Virgin Queen', pp. 201–8; J.N. King, 'Queen Elizabeth I: Representations of the Virgin Queen', *Renaissance Quarterly*, 43 (1990), pp. 30–74.
17 Laynesmith, *Last Medieval Queens*, p. 234.
18 See Bagley, *Margaret of Anjou*, p. 240; PROB 11/9/207.
19 Anglo, *Tudor Kingship*, p. 8. See also R. Barber, *Magnificence and Princely Splendour in the Middle Ages* (Woodbridge, 2020).
20 See James, *Feminine Dynamic*, p. 101.
21 Maurer, *Margaret of Anjou*, p. 210.
22 See Benz, *Three Medieval Queens*; Laynesmith, *Last Medieval Queens*; Campbell Orr (ed.), *Queenship in Britain*.
23 Stafford, *Queens*, p. 108.
24 Ibid, p. 109.
25 James, *Feminine Dynamic*, p. 3.

References

Manuscript Sources

Kew, National Archives

PREROGATIVE COURT OF CANTERBURY

PROB 11 Registered Copy Wills.

LONDON, BRITISH LIBRARY

Additional Manuscripts 4827, 8159.
Harley Manuscripts 7376.

Portraits

Nicholas Hilliard, 'Queen Elizabeth I', c. 1575, NPG, NPG 190.

Printed Primary Sources

Bergenroth, G.A., et al., (ed.), *Calendar of State Papers, Spain*, 13 vols (London, 1862–1954).

Brown, R., et al., (ed.), *Calendar of State Papers, Venice*, 38 vols (London, 1864–1947).

Lawson, J., (ed.), *The Elizabethan New Year's Gift Exchanges 1559–1603* (Oxford, 2013).

Secondary Sources

Anglo, S., *Images of Tudor Kingship* (London, 1992).

Auble, C., 'Bejeweled Majesty: Queen Elizabeth I, Precious Stones, and Statecraft', in Barrett-Graves, D. (ed.), *The Emblematic Queen: Extra-Literary Representations of Early Modern Queenship* (Basingstoke, 2013), pp. 35–51.

Bagley, J.J., *Margaret of Anjou* (London, 1948).

Barber, *Magnificence and Princely Splendour in the Middle Ages* (Woodbridge, 2020).

Benz St John, L., *Three Medieval Queens: Queenship and the Crown in Fourteenth-Century England* (Basingstoke, 2012).

Bolland, C., and Cooper, T., *The Real Tudors: Kings and Queens Rediscovered* (London, 2014).

Campbell Orr, C., (ed.), *Queenship in Britain, 1660–1837: Royal Patronage, Court Culture, and Dynastic Politics* (Manchester, 2002).

Howey, C.L., 'Dressing a Virgin Queen: Court Women, Dress, and Fashioning the Image of England's Queen Elizabeth I', *Early Modern Women*, 4 (2009), pp. 201–8.

Hunt, A., and Whitelock, A., (eds), *Tudor Queenship: The Reigns of Mary and Elizabeth* (Basingstoke, 2010).

James, S.E., *Catherine Parr: Henry VIII's Last Love* (Stroud, 2008).

James, S.E., *The Feminine Dynamic in English Art, 1485–1603: Women as Consumers, Patrons and Painters* (Abingdon, 2009).

King, J.N., 'Queen Elizabeth I: Representations of the Virgin Queen', *Renaissance Quarterly*, 43 (1990), pp. 30–74.

Laynesmith, J., *The Last Medieval Queens* (Oxford, 2004).

Maurer, H.E., *Margaret of Anjou: Queenship and Power in Late Medieval England* (Woodbridge, 2003).

Meikle, M.M., and Payne, H., 'Anne [Anna, Anne of Denmark]', *ODNB*, https://doi.org/10.1093/ref:odnb/559

Scarisbrick, D., *Diamond Jewelry: 700 Years of Glory and Glamour* (London, 2019).

Stafford, P., *Queens, Concubines and Dowagers: The King's Wife in the Early Middle Ages* (London, 1983).

Appendix

Matching items that appear in both Katherine Howard and Kateryn Parr's jewel inventories: BL, Stowe MS 559, f. 55r-68r and Society of Antiquaries MS 129, f. 178r-183v. The items from Kateryn Parr's inventory are referenced with both the folio number and the item number in brackets as they appear in Starkey, (ed.), *The Inventory of King Henry VIII*.

Jesuses

Katherine Howard, f. 59v: Item a Jehus of Golde garnesshed throughoute with diamondes That is to say xxxv peces greate and small.
Kateryn Parr, f. 178v (2635): Item one Iesus furnysshed with xxxv Dyamountes.

Katherine Howard, f. 59v: Item one other Jehus of golde ennamuled conteignyng one Rubye/xxiij diamondes/and thre small Emeraldes with thre feir perles hanging at the same.
Kateryn Parr, f. 178v (2637): Item one other Iesus conteyning xxiij Dyamountes iij small Emerodes one small rubie and three pendaunt Perles.

Katherine Howard, f. 60r: Item a Jehus of golde conteignyng xxxij diamondes hauyng thre peerlles hanging at the same.
Kateryn Parr, f. 178v (2636): Item a Iesus furnysshed with xxxij Dyamountes and three perles pendaunt.

Crosses

Katherine Howard, f. 59r: Item one Crosse of golde conteignyng v diamondes whereof two be poynted/and threst squared/hauyng also a verey feir greate peerle hanging at the same.
Kateryn Parr, f. 178v (2631): Item a hedles Crosse and fyve fair dyamountes and one Perle pendaunt.

Katherine Howard, f. 59r: Item one other Crosse of Golde ennamuled conteignyng v feir Table diamondes/and one other verey feir lozenge diamond under the same v/with iiij verey feire peerlles hanging at the same in one Cluster.
Kateryn Parr, f. 178v (2633): Item a Crosse of vj fair dyamountes and four perles pendaunte.

Katherine Howard, f. 59r: Item oone other verey feir Crosse of golde conteignyng iiij verey feir large diamondes in acrosse/with thre verey feir large peerlles hanging at the same.
Kateryn Parr, f. 178v (2630): Item a Crosse of foure fair dyamountes and three perles pendaunt.

Katherine Howard, f. 59r: Item oone other ffeir Crosse of golde conteignyng xij verey feir diamondes without any other addition.
Kateryn Parr, f. 178v (2632): Item one Crosse of xij dyamountes onelye.

Ouches

Katherine Howard, f. 59r: Item one other ooche of golde wherin is averey ffeir diamond holden by two antiquez personz with averey ffeir peerle hangyng at the same.
Kateryn Parr, f. 178r (2619): Firste one ouche or flower conteyning a fair Diamount tabled holden by Antyques with a large pendaunt perle.

Katherine Howard, f. 58v: Item an Ooche of Golde wherin is a feir poynted diamonde and a verey feir ruby/with averey feir peerle hangyng at the same.

Kateryn Parr, f.178r (2621): Item one Ouche or flower with a poynted Dyamounte A Rubye and a perle pendant.

Katherine Howard, f. 58v: Item oone other ooche of golde ennamuled white and red conteignyng two Emeraldes/and a feyer perle hangyng at the same.

Kateryn Parr, f. 178r (2622): Item one Ouche or flower with twoo emerodes and a pendaunte Perle.

Katherine Howard, f. 58v: Item one other ooche of Golde ennamuled conteignyng one rubye, one Emeralde, and one diamond all verey ffeir, with a verey feir perle hangyng at the same.

Kateryn Parr, f. 178r (2624): Item ouche or Flower with a dyamounte a Ruby an Emerode and a perle pendaunt.

Katherine Howard, f. 58v: Item oone other ooche of golde conteignyng two verey ffeir rubyes/and a verey feir Emeralds with averey feir perle hangyng at the same.

Kateryn Parr, f. 178r (2625): Item one Ouche or Flower with twoo rubies an Emerode and a perle pendaunt.

Habillements

Katherine Howard, f. 55v: Item a nether habulyment conteyning Cxij peerlles set lyke True loves with liiij beades of golde black ennamuled.

Kateryn Parr, f. 181v (2697): Item a nether habillement conteyning Cxij perles by Trewloues.

Chains

Katherine Howard, f. 66r: Item oone Cheyne conteignyng xiiij peces of goldesmyhes wercke wherin are sett xiiij diamondes and xiiij rubyes and xxvij other peces of goldesmythes worcke longe and ennamuled with blacke/tying to euery of them oone peerle. that is so say xiiij peerlles in the same Cheyne.

Kateryn Parr, f. 180r (2667): Item a Cheyne conteyning xiiij peces of goldesmythes worke set with xiiij dyamountes and xiiij Rubies and xxvij other peces of goldsmythes worke long enameled black tyeng to euery of them one perle Videlicet xiiij perles in the same Cheyne.

Katherine Howard, f. 66r: Item oone othe Cheyne conteiging xix peces of golde smythesworcke rounde ennamuled black/and xviij Clusters of peerlles set in golde that is to say v peerlles in every Cluster.

Kateryn Parr, f.180v (2674): Item a Cheyne conteyning xix peces of goldsmythes worke rounde enameled blacke and xviij Clusters of perle set in golde that is to saie v perles in euery Cluster.

Katherine Howard, f. 66r: Item oone Cheyne of golde conteignyng x pillors of golde being in every pillor thre rubyes/ xx peces of golde lyke longe peares ennamuled blewe and blacke/and x peces of golde lyke a Salte being upon every of them thre peerlles conteigning in the whole xxx peerlles.

Kateryn Parr, f. 180r (2668): Item a Cheyne of golde conteyning x pillers hauing in euery of them iij Rubies xx peces of golde pere fasshion enameled blewe and black and x peces of golde salt fasshion hauing in euery of them iij perles conteyning in thole xxx perles.

Katherine Howard (4): Item oone other Cheyne of golde conteignyng x pillors of golde being in every pillor thre diamondes/xx peces of goldes lyke longe peares ennamuled blacke/and x peces of golde lyke a Salte being upon every of them thre peerlles conteignyng in the whole xxx peerlles.

Kateryn Parr, f. 80v (2669): Item a Cheyne of golde conteyning x pillers in euery of thesame iij dyamountes xx peces of golde longe pere fasshion enameled blacke and tenne peces salt fasshion in euery of them iij perles.

Katherine Howard, f. 66r: Item oone other Cheyne of golde conteignyng xxiiij peces of golde/In xij peces of whereof is set in every pece thre small table diamondes in the whole xxxvj diamondes/and in euery of thother xij peces of golde is set thre rubyes/in the whole xxxvij rubyes/and betwixt every of the same peces of golde so garnesshed with diamondes and rubyes is set affeir peerle in a lynke of golde in the whole in peerlles xxiij/There was oone loost before the charge given in custody to Mrs herbert/or else there shulde haue been written her xxiiij peerlles.

Kateryn Parr, f. 180v (2670): Item a Cheyne conteyning xxiiij peces of golde wherof xij set with three small table dyamountes in euery of them and thother xij set likewise euery of them with iij small Rubies hauing set betwixt euery of all thesaid peces a fair perle in a lynke of golde conteyning xxiij perles.

Katherine Howard, f. 66v: Item oone other Cheyne of golde conteignyng x peces of oone fasshoon wherin are x diamondes tabled and x rubyes/and xx pillors of gold ennamuled grene blue and white with also xx peerlles betwixt every peerle one litle pece of goldesmytheswerwerck.

Kateryn Parr, f. 180v (2671): Item a Cheyne <of gold> conteyning x peces of one fasshion set with x Dyamountes tabled and x rubies and xx pillers golde enameled with sundrie collours and likewise xx perles set betwixt euery perle a small pece of goldsmythes worke.

Ships

Katherine Howard, f. 59v: Item a Ship of golde saylyng conteignyng one feir rubye in two ffysshes mouthes/and xxix diamondes greate and small in the same Ship with affeir peerle hanging at the same.

Kateryn Parr, f. 178v (2638): Item a Shipp garnysshed fullie with Dyamountes lacking ij small Dyamountes and set with one Rubie and a perle pendaunt.

Tablets

Katherine Howard, f. 68r: Item one Tablet of Golde on thonesyde thereof conteigneth the passon of our Lorde/and on thothersyde the resurrection both being of white agathe conteigning upon the same xxiiij rubyes and two diamondes with thre peerlles hanging in a cluster/and one litle rubye amongst the said peerlles.

Kateryn Parr, f. 179r (2650): Item a Tablet enameled black garnysshed with rubies and twoo small dyamountes and thistorie of the passion on thone side and the Resurreccion on thother both of Agathe.

Katherine Howard, f. 68r: Item one Tablet of Golde conteignyng on thonesyde a goodly diamonde lozenged with divers other small rubyes and diamondes two naked boyes and a litle boy with a crosse in his hand and divers other persones one with a sawe/and scripture under the said diamonde/and on thothersyde a ffeyer Ballas and the pycture of the busshopp of Rome comyng awey lamentyng/ and divers other persones one settyng his sole upon the busshop ouerthowen.

Kateryn Parr, f. 179r (2649): Item a Tablet hauing on thone side a large Table Dyamounte and garnysshed with small Rubies and Dyamountes and on thother side a ballays.

Girdles

Katherine Howard, f. 61r: Item one other Gurdell of golde conteignyng xj pillors in euery pillor ix peerlles/and lx lynkes of golde ennamuled black furnesshed with rubyes/ that is to say one lynke hauyng two rubyes/and another iiij rubyes and at eche ende of the same Gurdell is two other pillors square one with a whooke/in which two pillors is vij rubyes/hauyng also a bell of golde full furnesshed with rubyes/That is to say xviij Rubyes/with a great peerle upon the Top of the same/and divers ffeir peerlles hanging in the bottome.

Kateryn Parr, f. 182v (2718): Item a girdell conteyning xj pillers of golde hauing in euery of them ix perles and lx lynkes golde enameled black furnysshed with Rubies videlicet one linke hauing twoo rubies and an other foure rubies and at thende of thesame girdell is twoo other pillers square one with a hooke in which twoo pillers is vij Rubies hauing also a bell of golde furnysshed with small rubies and a lardge perle vpon the toppe of the same and dyuers other perles hanging in the bottome.

Katherine Howard, f. 61v: Item oone Gurdell of golde conteignyng xii peces of one sorte and euery of the sames peces is vj Turquezes in the whole – lxxij Turquezes/and in euery of the same peces is thre Rubyes in the whole – xxxvj rubyes/and xxiiij peces of another fashon in euery pece being xv peerless small in the whole – iijclx perles/ with a buttone of golde wherein is two antiquemen and one woman white the same garnesshed with xiiij rocke rubyes and xv Turquezes/hauyng also divers Tasselles of Peerll and small cheynes of golde.

Kateryn Parr, f. 182v (2719): Item a Girdell conteyning xij peces of one sorte and in euery of them vj Turkeis and three Rubies and xxiiij other peces of an other fasshion hauing in euery of them xv small perles with a button of golde garnysshed with xiiij rock rubies and v Turkais hauing also dyuerse Tasselles of perle and small Cheynes of golde.

Glossary

Agate: A mineral of the Quartz family.

Aglette: Metal tags, often ornamented or jewelled, that could be attached to a garment or used in pairs attached to a ribbon, as a fastening or purely decorative.

Agnus Dei: A religious pendant, often featuring the lamb of God.

Ballas Ruby: A mineral often associated with rubies in their source rock.

Billiment/Habillement: Ornamental part of a woman's dress often relating to the decorative border of gold and jewels used to edge the upper and lower curves of a French hood.

Cameo: A gem, hardstone or shell, usually having two or more layers of contrasting colours, of which the upper section(s) are carved in relief, the lower serving as a ground.

Carcenet: Heavy necklace, resembling a collar, and decorated with jewels and gold.

Chape: The metal point of a scabbard or a buckle.

Chopin: A type of platform shoe.

Coffer: A box or chest in which valuables are stored.

Girdle: A narrow band, chain or cord worn at the waist to encircle, or 'gird'. Usually decorative, and used to support items such as a small book, fan or pendant.

Intaglio: A design which is engraved into a material.

Lozenge: A diamond shape in which diamonds are often cut, or in which jewels are fashioned.

Muffler: Part of a female dress.

Ouche: A brooch, pendant or clasp set with jewels.

Partlet: Decorative female garment filling the neck and upper part of the chest for modesty or warmth.

Pointed Diamond: A diamond cut in a pyramid shape.

Pomander: The term applies both to a mixture of aromatic substances and to their openwork, enamelled and jewelled containers, intended to scent the air. Jewels in themselves, pomanders were suspended from chains at the neck or the waist.

Reliquary: A container for storing relics.

Spangle: Ornaments made of gold, silver or silver gilt that were stitched on to dresses and costumes.

Square: The band of jewels outlining the square neckline of a woman's gown.

Table Cut Diamond: A diamond cut so that the top appears flat, like a table.

Tablet: A type of pendant that could be worn around the neck, or more commonly attached to a girdle or belt.

Tau Cross: A cross in the shape of the letter 'T'.

Bibliography

I. Manuscript Sources

Kew, The National Archives

EXCHEQUER

E 23	Treasury of Receipt, Royal Wills.
E 36	Treasury of Receipt, Miscellaneous Books.
E 101	King's Remembrancer, Various Accounts.
E 314	Court of Augmentations, Miscellaneous Books.
E 315	Court of Augmentations and Predecessors, Miscellaneous Books.
E 404	Warrants for Issue.

LORD CHAMBERLAIN'S DEPARTMENT

LC 9 Accounts and Miscellanea.

PREROGATIVE COURT OF CANTERBURY

PROB 11 Registered Copy Wills.

SPECIAL COLLECTIONS

SC 8/26/1295 Ancient Petitions.

STATE PAPERS

SP State Papers.

LONDON, BRITISH LIBRARY

Additional Manuscripts	4827, 7099, 8159, 11301, 18985, 21481, 28199, 30367, 46348, 48976, 59899.
Cotton Manuscripts	Appendix LXV, Caligula D VI, Julius E IV, Nero C IX, Otho C X, Titus B I.
Egerton Manuscripts	985.
Loan Manuscripts	90.
Royal Manuscripts	Appendix 68, Appendix 89, B XXVIII, 7 C XVI, 20 E VI.
RP	294.
Stowe Manuscripts	555, 556, 559, 1047.

LONDON, COLLEGE OF ARMS

MS I. ii Account of the Funeral of Elizabeth of York.

LONDON, GOLDSMITHS' COMPANY

MS 1520	Minute Book A, 1444–1516.
MS 1521	Minute Book B, 1492–7.

LONDON, WESTMINSTER ABBEY MUNIMENTS

6643 Holland Inventory, 1447, Plate and jewels of John Holland, late Duke of Exeter, taken 8 September 1447.

LONDON, SOCIETY OF ANTIQUARIES

MS 108 Inventory of the Crown Jewels, 1649.
MS 129 Inventory of King Henry VIII.

EDINBURGH, NATIONAL LIBRARY OF SCOTLAND

MS 31.1.10 Anna of Denmark's Jewel Inventory.

II. Portraits

After Hans Holbein the Younger, 'Henry VIII', probably 17th century based on a work of 1536, NPG, NPG 157.

After Hans Holbein the Younger, 'Thomas Cromwell, Earl of Essex', early 17th century, based on a work of 1532–3, NPG, NPG 1727.

After Hans Holbein the Younger, 'Unknown woman, formerly known as Catherine Howard', late seventeenth century, NPG, NPG 1119.
After Master John, 'Queen Catherine Parr (1512–1548)', 1600–1770, Seaton Delaval Hall, Northumberland, National Trust, NT 1276906.
Anthony van Dyck, 'Henrietta Maria', before 1632, RCT, RCIN 404430.
Daniel Mytens, 'King Charles I', 1631, NPG, NPG 1246.
Flemish School, 'The Family of Henry VII with St George and the Dragon', c. 1503–9, RCT, RCIN 401228.
Hans Holbein, 'Anne of Cleves', 1538, Louvre Museum, Paris, Inv. 1348.
Hans Holbein, 'Box in the form of a rose, with a miniature portrait of Anne of Cleves', c. 1539, Victoria & Albert Museum, P. 153:1, 2–1910.
Hans Holbein, 'Christina of Denmark, Duchess of Milan', 1538, National Gallery, NG2475.
Hans Holbein, 'Design for a pendant', c. 1536–7, British Museum, SL,5308.117.
Hans Holbein, 'Drawing', c. 1532–43, British Museum, SL, 5308.37.
Hans Holbein, 'Henry VIII and the Barber Surgeons', c. 1543, Worshipful Company of Barbers, Barber-Surgeons' Hall, London.
Hans Holbein, 'Jane Seymour', 1536–7, Kunsthistorisches Museum, Vienna, Inv. No. 881.
Hans Holbein, 'Jane Seymour's Cup', c. 1536, Ashmolean Museum, Oxford, WA1863.424.
Hans Holbein, 'King Henry VIII: King Henry VII', 1536–7, NPG, NPG 4027.
Hans Holbein, 'Oval pendant', c. 1532–43, British Museum, SL,5308.107.
Hans Holbein, 'Portrait of a Lady, perhaps Katherine Howard', c. 1540, RCT, RCIN 422293.
Hans Holbein, 'Queen Jane Seymour', c. 1536, RCT, RCIN 912267.
Hans Holbein, 'Ring with crest', c. 1532–43, British Museum, SL,5308.78.
Hans Holbein, 'Table fountain design for Anne Boleyn', 1533–4, Öffentliche Kunstsammlung, Basel, 1662.165.89.
Jean Clouet, 'Portrait of François I, King of France (1494–1547)', c. 1530, Louvre Museum, Paris, Inv. 3256.
Levina Teerlinc, 'Katherine Parr', c. 1544–5, Sudeley Castle.

Lucas Horenbout, 'Henry VIII', c. 1526–7, RCT, RCIN 420010.
Lucas Horenbout, 'Katherine of Aragon', c. 1525, NPG, NPG 4682.
Lucas Horenbout, 'Katherine of Aragon', c. 1525–6, NPG, NPG L244.
Lucas Horenbout, 'Queen Mary I', c. 1525, NPG, NPG 6453.
Martial d'Auvergne, 'Marriage of Henry VI & Margaret of Anjou', *Vigiles de Charles VII*, c. 1475–1500, Bibliothèque Nationale de France, MS Français 5054.
Master John, 'Katherine Parr', c. 1544–5, NPG, NPG 4451.
Michel Sittow, 'Mary Rose Tudor', c. 1514, Kunsthistorisches Museum, Vienna, Inv. No. 5612.
Nicholas Hilliard, 'Queen Elizabeth I', c. 1575, NPG, NPG 190.
Possibly Lucas Horenbout, 'Jane Seymour', sixteenth century, Sudeley Castle.
Remigius van Leemput, 'Henry VII, Elizabeth of York, Henry VIII and Jane Seymour', 1667, RCT, RCIN 405750.
Tiziano Vecelli (Titian), 'The Empress Isabel of Portugal', 1548, Museo del Prado, Madrid.
Unknown Artist, 'Anne Boleyn', late sixteenth century, based on a work of c. 1533–6, NPG, NPG 668.
Unknown Artist, 'Anne Boleyn', sixteenth century, Hever Castle.
Unknown Artist, 'Anne Boleyn', sixteenth century, Nidd Hall.
Unknown Artist, 'Anne Boleyn', sixteenth century, NPG, NPG 4980(15).
Unknown Artist, 'Edward IV, with Elizabeth Woodville, Edward V and Richard, Duke of Gloucester', c. 1477, Lambeth Palace Library, MS 265, f. 6v.
Unknown Artist, 'Elizabeth I', c. 1600, oil on panel, NPG, NPG 5175.
Unknown Artist, 'Elizabeth of York', late sixteenth century, based on a work of c. 1500, NPG, NPG 311.
Unknown Artist, 'Elizabeth of York', sixteenth century, RCT, RCIN 403447.
Unknown Artist, 'Elizabeth Woodville', c. 1513–30, RCT, RCIN 406785.
Unknown Artist, 'Elizabeth Woodville', late sixteenth century, RCT, RCIN 404744.
Unknown Artist, 'Elizabeth Woodville', sixteenth century, Queen's College, Cambridge, portrait 88.
Unknown Artist, 'Elizabeth Wydeville', c. 1470, Worshipful Company of Skinners' Fraternity, Guildhall Library, MS 31692, f. 32v.
Unknown Artist, 'Henry VII', c. 1520–40, SoA, LDSAL 332.

Unknown Artist, 'Henry VIII Procession', 1512, BL, Add MS 22306.

Unknown Artist, 'Jane Seymour', c. 1536–40s, Weiss Gallery, London.

Unknown Artist, 'Katherine of Aragon', c. 1520, NPG, NPG L246.

Unknown Artist, 'Katherine of Aragon', early eighteenth century, NPG, NPG 163.

Unknown Artist, 'Margaret of Anjou', c. 1475, Worshipful Company of Skinners' Fraternity, Guildhall Library, MS 31692, f. 34v.

Unknown Artist, 'Richard II', c. 1390, Westminster Abbey.

Unknown Artist, 'Rous Roll', BL, Add MS 48976

Unknown Artist, 'Talbot Shrewsbury Book', 1445, BL, Royal MS 15 E. vi, f. 2v.

Unknown Artist, 'The Battle of Neville's Cross' in Jean Froissart, *Chroniques*, fourteenth century, Bibliothèque municipale de Besançon, Besançon, MS 864, f. 145v.

Unknown Artist, 'The Family of Henry VIII', c. 1545, RCT. RCIN 405796.

Unknown Artist, 'The Prayer Roll of Margaret of Anjou', c. 1445–55, Bodleian Library, Jesus College, MS 124.

Unknown Artist, 'The Salisbury Roll', 1483–5, BL, Loan MS 90, f. 154r.

William Scrots, 'Katherine Parr', late sixteenth century, NPG, NPG 4618.

III. Physical Objects

Pietro Da Milano, 'Marguerite d'Anjou', fifteenth century, Milan, gilt bronze, Victoria & Albert Museum (A. 182–1910).

Unknown Maker, 'Boleyn Cup', 1535–6, silver-gilt, Church of St John the Baptist, Cirencester.

Unknown Maker, 'Chequers Ring', sixteenth century, mother of pearl, gold, rubies, Chequers, Buckinghamshire.

Unknown Maker, 'Clare Reliquary', early fifteenth century, gold, pearls, wood, RCT, RCIN 69738.

Unknown Maker, 'Coronet of Margaret of York', late fifteenth century, gilt, Aachen Cathedral.

Unknown Maker, 'Crown of Princess Blanche', fourteenth century, gold, pearls, sapphires, rubies, emeralds, diamonds, Munich Residenz.

Unknown Maker, 'Dunstable Swan Jewel', fifteenth century, gold and enamel, British Museum, 1966,0703.1.

Unknown Maker, 'Lead medal', 1534, lead, British Museum, M.9010.

Unknown Maker, 'Lennox Jewel', c. 1571–78, gold, enamel, rubies, emerald, RCT, RCIN 28181.

Unknown Maker, 'Livery Badge', late fifteenth century, silver gilt, British Museum, 2003,0505.1.

Unknown Maker, 'Middleham Jewel', fifteenth century, gold and sapphire, Yorkshire Museum, YORYM: 1991.43.

Unknown Maker, 'Miniature Whistle Pendant', 1525–1530, gold, Victoria & Albert Museum, LOAN:MET ANON.1–1984.

Unknown Maker, 'Pendant reliquary cross', c. 1450–1475, silver, silver gilt, ruby, sapphire, garnet, pearl, Victoria & Albert Museum, 4561–1858.

Unknown Maker, 'Ring of Mary of Burgundy', c. 1477, gold and diamond, Kunsthistorisches Museum, Vienna, Inv: P 1 131

IV. Printed Primary Sources

Arnold, J., (ed.), *Queen Elizabeth's Wardrobe Unlock'd* (Leeds, 1988).

Astle, T., (ed.), *The Will of Henry VII* (London, 1775).

Bacon, F., *The History of the Reign of King Henry VII*, ed. Vickers, B. (Cambridge, 1998).

Bentley, S., (ed.), *Excerpta Historica: Or, Illustrations of English History* (London, 1831).

Brie, F.W.D., (ed.), *The Brut; or, the Chronicles of England*, EETS, orig. ser., 131, 136 (London, 1906–08).

Byrne, M.C., *The Lisle Letters*, 6 vols (Chicago, 1981).

Campbell, W., (ed.), *Materials for a History of the Reign of Henry VII from Original Documents Preserved in the Public Record Office*, 2 vols (London, 1873).

Cavendish, G., *The Life and Death of Cardinal Wolsey*, ed. Sylvester, R.S. (London and New York, 1959).

Collins, A.J., (ed.), *Jewels and Plate of Queen Elizabeth I: The Inventory of 1574* (London, 1955).

Crawford, A., (ed.), *Letters of the Queens of England 1100–1547* (Stroud, 1994).

Cremades, F.C., (ed.), *Los inventarios de Carlos V y la familia imperial*, iii (Madrid, 2010).

Davis, N., (ed.), *The Paston Letters* (Oxford, 1983).

De Cessolis, J., *The Game and Playe of the Chesse*, ed. Adams, J. (Kalamazoo, 2009).

Dickson, T., and Balfour Paul, J., (eds), *Accounts of the Lord High Treasurer of Scotland*, 13 vols (Edinburgh, 1877–1916).

Douet-D'Arcq, L., (ed.), 'Inventaire des meubles de la reine Jeanne de Boulogne, 1360', *Bibliotheque de 'Ecole des Chartes*, XL (1879).

Douet-D'Arcq, L., (ed.), *Nouveau recueil de comptes de l'argenterie des rois de France* (Paris, 1874).
Ellis, H., (ed.), *Three Books of Polydore Vergil's English History* (London, 1844).
Gardiner, J., (ed.), *The Historical Collections of a Citizen of London in the Fifteenth Century* (London, 1876).
Hall, E., *Chronicle*, ed. Whibley, C. (London, 1904).
Hayward, M. (ed.), *The Great Wardrobe Accounts of Henry VII and Henry VIII* (London Record Society XLVII, 2012).
Hayward, M., (ed.), *The 1542 Inventory of Whitehall* (London, 2004).
Hayward, M., and Ward, P., (eds), *The Inventory of King Henry VIII: Textiles and Dress* (London, 2012).
Historical Manuscripts Commission, *Calendar of the Manuscripts of the Most Honourable the Marquess of Salisbury*, I (London, 1883).
Hume, M.A.S. trans., *The Chronicle of King Henry VIII of England* (London, 1889).
Kingsford, C.L., (ed.), *Chronicles of London* (London, 1905).
Kipling, G., (ed.), *The Receyt of the Ladie Kateryne* (London, 1990).
Knighton, C.S., (ed.), *Calendar of State Papers Domestic Series of the Reign of Edward VI 1547–1553* (London, 1992).
Lawson, J., (ed.), *The Elizabethan New Year's Gift Exchanges 1559–1603* (Oxford, 2013).
Leland, L., *Antiquarii De Rebvs Britannicis Collectanea*, ed. Hearne, T., 6 vols (London, 1774).
Madden, F., (ed.), 'Narrative of the Visit of the Duke of Najera', *Archaeologica*, XXIII (1831), pp. 344–57.
Madden, F., (ed.), *Privy Purse Expenses of the Princess Mary* (London, 1831).
Mancini, D., *Usurpation of Richard III*, ed. and trans. Armstrong, C.A.J. (Sutton, 1984).
Monro, C., (ed.), *Letters of Queen Margaret of Anjou* (London, 1863–4).
Mueller, J., (ed.), *Katherine Parr: Complete Works and Correspondence* (Chicago, 2011).
Myers, A.R., (ed.), *The Household of Edward IV: The Black Book and the Ordinance of 1478* (Manchester, 1959).
Nichols, J.G., (ed.), *A Collection of All the Wills, Now Known to Be Extant, of the Kings and Queens of England* (London, 1780).
Nichols, J.G., (ed.), *Chronicle of the Grey Friars of London* (London, 1852).
Nichols, J.G., (ed.), *Inventories of the Wardrobe, Plate, Chapel Stuff, Etc. of Henry Fitzroy, Duke of Richmond, and of the Wardrobe Stuff at Baynard's Castle of Katherine, Princess Dowager* (London, 1855).

Nichols, J.G., (ed.), *Society of Antiquaries, A Collection of Ordinances and Regulations for the Government of the Royal Household, Made in Divers Reigns: From King Edward III to King William and Queen Mary, Also Receipts in Ancient Cookery* (London, 1790).

Nichols, J.G., and Bruce, J., (eds), *Wills from Doctors' Commons: A Selection from the Wills of Eminent Persons Proved in the Prerogative Court of Canterbury, 1495–1695* (London, 1863).

Nicolas, N.H., (ed.), *Privy Purse Expenses of Elizabeth of York* (London, 1830).

Nicolas, N.H., (ed.), *Privy Purse Expenses of King Henry the Eighth from 1529–1532* (London, 1827).

Palgrave, F., (ed.), *The Antient Calendars and Inventories of the Treasury of His Majesty's Exchequer*, I (London, 1836).

Pronay, N., and Cox, J., (eds), *The Crowland Chronicle Continuations: 1459–1486* (London, 1986).

Rymer, T., (ed.), *Rymer's Foedera*, 16 vols (London, 1739–45).

Sander, N., *Rise and Growth of the Anglican Schism* (London, 1573).

Searle, W.G., (ed.), *The Narrative of the Marriage of Richard, Duke of York with Anne of Norfolk, 1477* (Cambridge, 1867).

Shakespeare, W., *Henry VI, Part One*, ed. Taylor, M. (Oxford, 2003).

Shakespeare, W., *Henry VI, Part Three*, ed. Martin, R. (Oxford, 2001).

Shakespeare, W., *Henry VI, Part Two*, ed. Warren, R. (Oxford, 2002).

Smith, G., (ed.), *The Coronation of Elizabeth Wydeville* (London, 1935).

Starkey, D. (ed.), *The Inventory of King Henry VIII: The Transcript*, trans. Ward, P. (London, 1998).

Stow, J., *The Annals of England*, ed. Kingsford, C.L., 2 vols (Oxford, 1908).

Stratford, J., (ed.), *Richard II and the English Royal Treasure* (Woodbridge, 2012).

Stratford, J., (ed.), *The Bedford Inventories: The Wordly Goods of John, Duke of Bedford, Regent of France (1389–1435)* (London, 1993).

Sutton, A.F., and Hammond, P.W., (eds), *The Coronation of Richard III: The Extant Documents* (London, 1983).

Thomas, A.H., and Thornley, I.D., (eds), *The Great Chronicle of London* (London, 1983).

Thomson, T., (ed.), *A Collection of Inventories and Other Records of the Royal Wardrobe and Jewelhouse; and of the Artillery and Munition in Some of the Royal Castles* (Edinburgh, 1815).

Trollope, E., (ed.), 'King Henry VIII's Jewel Book', *Associated Architectural Societies*, 17 (1883–4), pp. 155–229.

Tuetey, P.A., (ed.), *Inventaire des biens de Charlotte de Savoie, reine de France, (1483)* (Paris, 1865).

Turnbull, W.B.D.D., (ed.), *Account of the Monastic Treasures confiscated at the Dissolution of the Various Houses in England* (Edinburgh, 1836).

Ullmann, W., (ed.), *Liber Regie Capelle* (London, 1961).

Wickham Legg, L.G., (ed.), *English Coronation Records* (Oxford, 1901).

Williams, C.H., (ed.), *English Historical Documents*, V (1485–1558) (London, 1967).

Wingfield, R., *Vita Mariae Reginae*, trans. MacCulloch, D., Camden Miscellany XXVIII, 4th series, 29 (London, 1984).

Wood, M.A.E., (ed.), *Letters of Royal and Illustrious Ladies of Great Britain*, 3 vols (London, 1846).

Wriothesley, C., *A Chronicle of England During the Reigns of the Tudors from 1485 to 1559*, ed. Hamilton, W.D., I (London, 1875).

V. Secondary Sources

Anderson Black, J., *A History of Jewels* (London, 1974).

Anglo, S., 'Ill of the Dead: The Posthumous Reputation of Henry VII', *Renaissance Studies*, 1 (1987), pp. 27–47.

Anglo, S., *Images of Tudor Kingship* (London, 1992).

Anglo, S., 'The Foundation of the Tudor Dynasty: The Coronation and Marriage of Henry VII', *Guildhall Miscellany*, II (1960), pp. 3–11.

Anglo, S., *The Great Tournament Roll of Westminster: Historical Introduction* (Oxford, 1968).

Anglo, S., 'The London Pageants for the Reception of Katherine of Aragon: November 1501', *Journal of the Warburg and Courtauld Institutes*, 26 (1963), pp. 53–89.

Archer, I.W., 'City and Court Connected: The Material Dimensions of Royal Ceremonial, ca. 1480–1625', *HLQ*, 71 (2008), pp. 157–79.

Arthurson, I., 'The King of Spain's Daughter Came to Visit Me: Marriage, Princes and Politics', in Gunn, S., and Monckton, L. (eds), *Arthur Tudor, Prince of Wales: Life, Death and Commemoration* (Woodbridge, 2009), pp. 20–30.

Auble, C., 'Bejeweled Majesty: Queen Elizabeth I, Precious Stones, and Statecraft', in Barrett-Graves, D. (ed.), *The Emblematic Queen: Extra-Literary Representations of Early Modern Queenship* (Basingstoke, 2013), pp. 35–51.

Auerbach, E., *Tudor Artists* (London, 1954).

Auwers, M., 'The Gift of Rubens: Rethinking the Concept of Gift-Giving in Early Modern Diplomacy', *European History Quarterly*, 43 (2013), pp. 421–41.

Awais-Dean, N., *Bejewelled: Men and Jewellery in Tudor and Jacobean England* (London, 2017).

Bagley, J.J., *Margaret of Anjou* (London, 1948).

Bak, J.M., (ed.), *Coronations: Medieval and Early Modern Monarchic Ritual* (Oxford, 1990).

Baldwin, D., *Elizabeth Woodville: Mother of the Princes in the Tower* (Stroud, 2002).

Barber, R., *Magnificence and Princely Splendour in the Middle Ages* (Woodbridge, 2020).

Becker, L.M., *Death and the Early Modern Englishwoman* (Aldershot, 2003).

Beem, C., and Taylor, M., (eds), *The Man Behind the Queen: Male Consorts in History* (Basingstoke, 2014).

Beer, M.L., 'Between Kings and Emperors: Catherine of Aragon as Counsellor and Mediator', in Matheson-Pollock, H., Paul, J., and Fletcher, C. (eds), *Queenship and Counsel in Early Modern Europe* (Basingstoke, 2018), pp. 35–58.

Beer, M.L., *Queenship at the Renaissance Courts of Britain: Catherine of Aragon and Margaret Tudor, 1503–1533* (Fakenham, 2018).

Ben-Amos, I.K., *The Culture of Giving: Informal Support and Gift-Exchange in Early Modern England* (Cambridge, 2008).

Benz St John, L., *Three Medieval Queens: Queenship and the Crown in Fourteenth-Century England* (Basingstoke, 2012).

Bernard, G.W., *Anne Boleyn: Fatal Attraction* (London, 2010).

Bernard, G.W., 'Anne Boleyn's Religion', *Historical Journal*, 36 (1993), pp. 1–20.

Bernard, G.W., 'The Dissolution of the Monasteries', *History*, 96 (2011), pp. 390–409.

Bernard, G.W., 'The Fall of Anne Boleyn', *EHR*, 106 (1991), pp. 584–610.

Bernard, G.W., 'The Fall of Anne Boleyn: A Rejoinder', *EHR*, 107 (1992), pp. 665–74.

Biedermann, Z., Gerritsen, A., and Riello, G., (eds), *Global Gifts: The Material Culture of Diplomacy in Early Modern Eurasia* (New York, 2017).

Blair, C., (ed.), *The Crown Jewels: The History of the Coronation Regalia in the Jewel House of the Tower of London* (London, 1998).

Bolland, C., and Cooper, T., *The Real Tudors: Kings and Queens Rediscovered* (London, 2014).

Broomhall, S., (ed.), *Women and Power at the French Court, 1483–1563* (Amsterdam, 2018).

Brotton, J., *The Sale of the Late King's Goods: Charles I and His Art Collection* (London, 2006).

Brown, M.C., 'The "Three Kings of Cologne" and Plantagenet Political Theology', *Mediaevistik*, 30 (2017), pp. 61–85.

Brus, R., *Crown Jewellery and Regalia of the World* (Amsterdam, 2011).

Buettner, B., 'Past Presents: New Year's Gifts at the Valois Court, ca. 1400', *Art Bulletin*, 83 (2001), pp. 598–625.

Bunt, C.G.E., *The Goldsmiths of Italy: Some Account of their Guilds, Statutes, and Work* (London, 1926).

Burnett, C.J., and Tabraham, C.J., *The Honours of Scotland: The Story of the Scottish Crown Jewels* (Edinburgh, 1993).

Bury, S., *Rings* (London, 1984).

Campbell, L., *Renaissance Portraits: European Portrait-Painting in the 14th, 15th and 16th Centuries* (New Haven and London, 1990).

Campbell, M., 'Gold, Silver and Precious Stones', in Blair, J., and Ramsey, N. (eds), *English Medieval Industries* (London and New York, 1991), pp. 107–66.

Campbell, M., *Medieval Jewellery* (London, 2009).

Campbell Orr, C., (ed.), *Queenship in Britain, 1660–1837: Royal Patronage, Court Culture, and Dynastic Politics* (Manchester, 2002).

Campbell Orr, C., (ed.), *Queenship in Europe 1660–1815: The Role of the Consort* (Cambridge, 2004).

Carley, J.P., *The Books of King Henry VIII and His Wives* (London, 2004).

Chadour-Sampson, B., and Bari, H., *Pearls* (London, 2013).

Chamberlayne, J.L., 'Crowns and Virgins: Queenmaking During the Wars of the Roses', in Lewis, K.J., Menuge, N.J., and Phillips, K.M. (eds), *Young Medieval Women* (Stroud, 1999), pp. 47–68.

Cherry, J., 'Healing Through Faith: The Continuation of Medieval Attitudes to Jewellery into the Renaissance', *Renaissance Studies*, 15 (2001), pp. 154–71.

Cherry, J., 'Late Fourteenth-Century Jewellery: The Inventory of November 1399', *BM*, 130 (1988), pp. 137–40.

Cherry, J., *Medieval Goldsmiths* (London, 1992).

Cherry, J., 'The Dunstable Swan Jewel', *Journal of the British Archaeological Association*, 32 (1969), pp. 38–53.

Cherry, J., *The Middleham Jewel and Ring* (York, 1994).

Cole, A., *Art of the Italian Renaissance Courts* (London, 1995).

Conway, A., *Henry VII's Relations with Scotland and Ireland 1485–98* (Cambridge, 1932).

Coombs, K., *The Portrait Miniature in England* (London, 1995).

Cooper, J.K.D., 'An Assessment of Tudor Plate Design, 1530–1560', *BM*, 121 (1979), pp. 342, 346, 358, 360–4.

Cooper, T., *A Guide to Tudor and Jacobean Portraits* (London, 2008).

Cooper, T., 'Making Art in Tudor Britain: New Research on Paintings in the National Portrait Gallery', *British Art Journal*, 9 (2009), pp. 3–11.

Cox-Rearick, J., 'Power-Dressing at the Courts of Cosimo de'Medici and François I: The "moda alla spagnola" of Spanish Consorts Eléonore d'Autriche and Eleanora di Toledo', *Artibus et Historiae*, 30:60 (2009), pp. 39–69.

Crawford, A., 'The King's Burden?: The Consequences of Royal Marriage in Fifteenth-century England', in Griffiths, R.A. (ed.), *Patronage, the Crown and the Provinces: In Later Medieval England* (Gloucester, 1981), pp. 33–56.

Crawford, A., 'The Piety of Late Medieval English Queens', in Barron, C.M., and Harper-Bill, C. (eds), *The Church in Pre-Reformation Society: Essays in Honour of F.R.H Du Boulay* (Woodbridge, 1985), pp. 48–57.

Crawford, A., 'The Queen's Council in the Middle Ages', *EHR*, 116 (2001), pp. 1193–1211.

Cressy, D., *Birth, Marriage and Death: Ritual, Religion and the Life-Cycle in Tudor and Stuart England* (Oxford, 1997).

Cust, L., 'A Portrait of Queen Catherine Howard, by Hans Holbein the Younger', *BM*, 17 (1910), pp. 192–5, 199.

Cust, L., 'John of Antwerp, Goldsmith, and Hans Holbein', *BM*, 8 (1906), pp. 356, 359–60.

Davies, W., and Fouracre, P., (eds), *The Language of Gift in the Early Middle Ages* (Cambridge, 2010).

DeMolen, R.L., 'The Birth of Edward VI and the Death of Queen Jane: The Arguments for and against Caesarean Section', *Renaissance Studies*, 4 (1990), pp. 359–91.

Denny, J., *Anne Boleyn: A New Life of England's Tragic Queen* (London, 2004).

Denny, J., *Katherine Howard: A Tudor Conspiracy* (London, 2005).

Dewhurst, J., 'The Alleged Miscarriages of Catherine of Aragon and Anne Boleyn', *Medical History*, 28 (1984), pp. 49–56.

Dickinson, J.C., *The Shrine of Our Lady of Walsingham* (Cambridge, 1956).

Dmitrieva, O., and Murdoch, T. (eds), *Treasures of the Royal Courts: Tudors, Stuarts and the Russian Tsars* (London, 2013).

Dodge Pattee, E., 'The Miniaturist's Art', *American Magazine of Art*, 16 (1925), pp. 517–22.

Dolman, B., 'Reading the Portraits of Henry VIII's Queens', in Lipscomb, S., and Betteridge, T. (eds), *Henry VIII and the Court: Art, Politics and Performance* (Farnham, 2013), pp. 115–30.

Downie, F., *She Is But a Woman: Queenship in Scotland 1424–1463* (Edinburgh, 2006).

Drimmer, S., 'Beyond Private Matter: A Prayer Roll for Queen Margaret of Anjou', *Gesta*, 53 (2014), pp. 95–120.

Duffy, M., *Royal Tombs of Medieval England* (Stroud, 2011).

Dunn, D., 'Margaret of Anjou, Queen Consort of Henry VI: A Reassessment of Her Role, 1445–53', in Archer, R. (ed.), *Crown, Government and People in the Fifteenth Century* (New York, 1995), pp. 107–43.

Dunn, D., 'The Queen at War: The Role of Margaret of Anjou in the Wars of the Roses', in Dunn, D. (ed.), *War and Society in Medieval and Early Modern Britain* (Liverpool, 2000), pp. 141–61.

Eales, J., *Women in Early Modern England, 1500–1700* (London, 1998).

Earenfight, T.M., 'A Precarious Household: Catherine of Aragon in England, 1501–1504', in Earenfight, T. (ed.), *Royal and Elite Households in Medieval and Early Modern Europe* (Leiden, 2018), pp. 338–56.

Earenfight, T.M., *Catherine of Aragon: Infanta of Spain, Queen of England* (Pennsylvania, 2021).

Earenfight, T.M., 'Highly Visible, Often Obscured: The Difficulty of Seeing Queens and Noble Women', *Medieval Feminist Forum: A Journal of Gender and Sexuality*, 44 (2008), pp. 86–90.

Earenfight, T.M., *Queenship in Medieval Europe* (Basingstoke, 2013).

Earenfight, T.M., 'Raising *Infanta* Catalina de Aragón to be Catherine, Queen of England', *Anuario de estudios medievales*, 46 (2016), pp. 417–43.

Earenfight, T.M., 'Regarding Catherine of Aragon', in Levin, C., and Stewart-Nuñez, C. (eds), *Scholars and Poets Talk about Queens* (New York, 2015), pp. 137–57.

Earenfight, T.M., 'Without the Persona of the Prince: Kings, Queens and the Idea of Monarchy in Late Medieval Europe', *Gender and History*, 19 (2007), pp. 1–21.

Edie, C.A., 'The Public Face of Royal Ritual: Sermons, Medals, and Civic Ceremony in Later Stuart Coronations', *HLQ*, 53 (1990), pp. 311–36.

Eichberger, D., 'A Courtly Phenomenon from a Female Perspective', in Eichberger, D. (ed.), *Women of Distinction* (Leuven, 2005), pp. 286–95.

Erler, M.C., and Kowaleski, M., (eds), *Gendering the Master Narrative: Women and Power in the Middle Ages* (Ithaca and London, 2003).

Evans, J., *A History of Jewellery 1100–1870* (New York, 1953).

Evans, J., *English Jewellery: From the Fifth Century A.D. to 1800* (London, 1921).

Evans, J., *Magical Jewels of the Middle Ages and the Renaissance* (New York, 1976).

Facinger, M.F., 'A Study of Medieval Queenship: Capetian France, 987–1237', *Studies in Medieval and Renaissance History*, 5 (1968), pp. 3–47.

Fahy, C., 'The Marriage of Edward IV and Elizabeth Woodville: A New Italian Source', *EHR*, 76 (1961), pp. 660–72.

Fenno Hoffman, C., 'Catherine Parr as a Woman of Letters', *HLQ*, 23 (1960), pp. 349–67.

Ferguson, J., *English Diplomacy: 1422–1461* (Oxford, 1972).

Fisher, N.R.R., 'The Quenes Courte in Her Councell Chamber at Westminster', *EHR*, 108 (1993), pp. 314–37.

Fisher, S., '"Margaret R": Lady Margaret Beaufort's Self-fashioning and Female Ambition', in Fleiner, C., and Woodacre, E. (eds), *Virtuous or Villainess? The Image of the Royal Mother from the Early Medieval to the Early Modern Era* (Basingstoke, 2016), pp. 151–72.

Fletcher, J., 'Tree Ring Dates for Some Panel Paintings in England', *BM*, 116 (1974), pp. 250–8.

Foister, S., *Holbein and England* (New Haven and London, 2004).

Foister, S., 'Paintings and Other Works of Art in Sixteenth-Century English Inventories', *BM*, 123 (1981), pp. 273–82.

Forsyth, H., 'An Inscribed Sixteenth-Century English Silver-Gilt Chape', *BM*, 138 (1996), pp. 392–3.

Forsyth, H., *The Cheapside Hoard: London's Lost Jewels* (London, 2013).

Fradenburg, L.O., *City, Marriage, Tournament: Arts of Rule in Late Medieval Scotland* (Madison, 1991).

Fraser, A., *The Six Wives of Henry VIII* (London, 1992).

Fremantle, R., 'Goldsmiths in Florence', *BM*, 119 (1977), pp. 524, 527.

Frinta, M., 'Observation on Michel Sittow', *Artibus et Historiae*, 30 (2009), pp. 147–51.

Ganz, P., 'Henry VIII and His Court Painter, Hans Holbein', *BM*, 63 (1933), pp. 144, 146, 148–51, 154–5.

Ganz, P., 'Holbein and Henry VIII', *BM*, 83 (1943), pp. 269–73.

Ganz, P., 'Two Unpublished Portraits by Hans Holbein', *BM*, 20 (1911), pp. 31–3.

Gentilini, G., and Mozzatti, T., '"142 Life-size Figures . . . with the King on Horseback": Baccio Bandinelli's Mausoleum for Henry VIII', in Sicca, C.M., and Waldman, L.A. (eds), *The Anglo-Florentine Renaissance: Art for the Early Tudors* (New Haven, 2012), pp. 203–34.

Gibbons, R., 'Medieval Queenship: An Overview', *Reading Medieval Studies*, 21 (1995), pp. 97–107.

Gittings, C., *Death, Burial and the Individual in Early Modern England* (London, 1984).

Glanville, P., 'Cardinal Wolsey and the Goldsmiths', in Gunn, S.J., and Lindley, P.G. (eds), *Cardinal Wolsey: Church, State and Art* (Cambridge, 1991), pp. 131–48.

Glanville, P., *Silver in Tudor and Stuart England* (London, 1990).

Greenblatt, S., *Renaissance Self-Fashioning: From More to Shakespeare* (Chicago, 1980).

Griffey, E., (ed.), *Sartorial Politics in Early Modern Europe: Fashioning Women* (Amsterdam, 2019).

Gunn, S., *Henry VII's New Men and the Making of Tudor England* (Oxford, 2016).

Hackenbroch, Y., *Renaissance Jewellery* (London, 1979).

Hacker, P., and Kuhl, C., 'A Portrait of Anne of Cleves', *BM*, 134 (1992), pp. 172–5.

Hamilton, D.L., 'The Learned Councils of the Tudor Queens Consort', in Carlton, C., Woods, R.L., Robertson, M.L., and Block, J.S. (eds), *State, Sovereigns and Society in Early Modern England: Essays in Honour of A.J. Slavin* (Stroud, 1998), pp. 87–101.

Hamling, T., and Richardson, C., (eds), *Everyday Objects: Medieval and Early Modern Material Culture and Its Meanings* (Farnham, 2010).

Harper, E., '*Pearl* in the Context of Fourteenth-Century Gift Economies', *Chaucer Review*, 44 (2010), pp. 421–39.

Harper, S.P., 'Royal Servants and City Fathers: The Double Lives of London Goldsmiths at the Court of Henry VII', in Allen, M., and Davies, M. (eds), *Medieval Merchants and Money: Essays in Honour of James L Bolton* (London, 2016), pp. 177–93.

Harris, B.J., *English Aristocratic Women 1450–1550: Marriage and Family, Property and Careers* (Oxford, 2002).

Harris, B.J., 'The View from My Lady's Chamber: New Perspectives on the Early Tudor Monarchy', *HLQ*, 60 (1997), pp. 215–47.

Harris, C., *Queenship and Revolution in Early Modern Europe: Henrietta Maria and Marie Antoinette* (Basingstoke, 2015).

Haugaard, W.P., 'Katherine Parr: The Religious Convictions of a Renaissance Queen', *Renaissance Quarterly*, 22 (1969), pp. 346–59.

Hayward, J.F., *Virtuoso Goldsmiths and the Triumph of Mannerism, 1540–1620* (London, 1976).

Hayward, M., *Dress at the Court of King Henry VIII* (Leeds, 2007).

Hayward, M., 'Fashion, Finance, Foreign Politics and the Wardrobe of Henry VIII', in Richardson, C. (ed.), *Clothing Culture, 1350–1650* (Aldershot, 2004), pp. 165–78.

Hayward, M., 'Gift Giving at the Court of Henry VIII: The 1539 New Year's Gift Roll in Context', *Antiquaries Journal*, 85 (2005), pp. 125–75.

Hayward, M., *Rich Apparel: Clothing and the Law in Henry VIII's England* (Farnham, 2009).

Hayward, M., 'Rich Pickings: Henry VIII's Use of Confiscation and Its Significance for the Development of the Royal Collection', in Lipscomb, S., and Betteridge, T. (eds), *Henry VIII and the Court: Art, Politics and Performance* (Farnham, 2013), pp. 29–46.

Heal, F., *The Power of Gifts: Gift-Exchange in Early Modern England* (Oxford, 2014).

Hepburn, F., *Portraits of the Later Plantagenets* (Woodbridge, 1986).

Hepburn, F., 'The Portraiture of Prince Arthur and Katherine of Aragon', in Gunn, S., and Monckton, L. (eds), *Arthur Tudor, Prince of Wales: Life, Death and Commemoration* (Woodbridge, 2009), pp. 31–49.

Hepburn, F., 'The Queen in Exile: Representing Margaret of Anjou in Art and Literature', in Clark, L. (ed.), *The Fifteenth Century: XI, Concerns and Preoccupations* (Croydon, 2012), pp. 61–90.

Heslop, T.A., 'The Virgin Mary's Regalia and Twelfth-Century English Seals', in Borg, A., and Martindale, A. (eds), 'The Vanishing Past: Studies of Medieval Art, Liturgy and Metrology Presented to Christopher Hobler', *British Archaeological Reports*, III (1981), pp. 53–6.

Hicks, M., *Anne Neville: Queen to Richard III* (Stroud, 2007).

Hicks, M., 'The Changing Role of the Wydevilles in Yorkist Politics to 1483', in Ross, C. (ed.), *Patronage, Pedigree, and Power in Later Medieval England* (Gloucester: 1979), pp. 60–86.

Hinton, D., *Medieval Jewellery* (Aylesbury, 1982).

Hoak, D., 'The Iconography of the Crown Imperial', in Hoak, D. (ed.), *Tudor Political Culture* (Cambridge, 2002), pp. 54–103.

Hollis, J., (ed.), *Princely Magnificence: Court Jewels of the Renaissance, 1500–1630* (London, 1980).

Horrox, M., 'Financial Memoranda of the Reign of Edward V', *Camden Miscellany XXIX*, 34 (Camden Fourth Series, 1987), pp. 200–44.

Howard, M., *The Tudor Image* (London, 1995).

Howarth, D., *Images of Rule* (Basingstoke, 1997).

Howell, M., *Eleanor of Provence: Queenship in Thirteenth Century England* (Oxford, 1998).

Howey, C.L., 'Dressing a Virgin Queen: Court Women, Dress, and Fashioning the Image of England's Queen Elizabeth I', *Early Modern Women*, 4 (2009), pp. 201–8.

Howgrave-Graham, R.P., 'Royal Portraits in Effigy: Some New Discoveries in Westminster Abbey', *Journal of the Royal Society of Arts*, 101 (1953), pp. 465–74.

Hughes, G., *A Pictorial History of Gems and Jewellery* (Oxford, 1978).

Huneycutt, L.L., *Matilda of Scotland: A Study in Medieval Queenship* (London, 2003).

Huneycutt, L.L., 'Medieval Queenship', *History Today*, 39 (1989), pp. 16–22.

Hunt, A., *The Drama of Coronation: Medieval Ceremony in Early Modern England* (Cambridge, 2008).

Hunt, A., and Whitelock, A., (eds), *Tudor Queenship: The Reigns of Mary and Elizabeth* (Basingstoke, 2010).

Hurlburt, H.S., 'Public Exposure? Consorts and Ritual in Late Medieval Europe: The Example of the Entrance of the Dogaresse of Venice', in Erler, M.C., and Kowaleski, M. (eds), *Gendering the Master Narrative: Women and Power in the Middle Ages* (Ithaca and London, 2003), pp. 174–89.

Inglis, E., 'Expertise, Artifacts, and Time in the 1534 Inventory of the St-Denis Treasury', *Art Bulletin*, 98 (2016), pp. 14–42.

Ives, E.W., 'Anne Boleyn and the Early Reformation in England: The Contemporary Evidence', *Historical Journal*, 37 (1994), pp. 389–400.

Ives, E.W., 'Anne Boleyn on Trial Again', *Journal of Ecclesiastical History*, 62 (2011), pp. 763–77.

Ives, E.W., 'Faction at the Court of Henry VIII: The Fall of Anne Boleyn', *History*, 57 (1972), pp. 169–88.

Ives, E.W., 'The Fall of Anne Boleyn Reconsidered', *EHR*, 107 (1992), pp. 651–64.

Ives, E.W., *The Life and Death of Anne Boleyn* (Oxford, 2004).

Ives, E.W., 'The Queen and the Painters: Anne Boleyn, Holbein and Tudor Royal Portraits', *Apollo*, 140 (1984), pp. 49–56.

Jackson, C.J., *English Goldsmiths and Their Marks: A History of the Goldsmiths and Plate Workers of England, Scotland and Ireland* (London, 1949).

James, S.E., *Catherine Parr: Henry VIII's Last Love* (Stroud, 2008).

James, S.E., 'Lady Jane Grey or Queen Kateryn Parr?' *BM*, 138 (1996), pp. 20–4.

James, S.E., *The Feminine Dynamic in English Art, 1485–1603: Women as Consumers, Patrons and Painters* (Abingdon, 2009).

James, S.E., *Women's Voices in Tudor Wills, 1485–1603: Authority, Influence and Material Culture* (Farnham, 2015).

Jansen, S.L., *The Monstrous Regiment of Women: Female Rulers in Early Modern Europe* (Basingstoke, 2002).

Jenkinson, A.V., 'The Jewels Lost in the Wash', *History*, 8 (1923), pp. 161–8.

Johnson, J., 'Elizabeth of York: Mother of the Tudor Dynasty', in Oakley-Brown, L., and Wilkinson, L.J. (eds), *The Rituals and Rhetoric of Queenship* (Dublin, 2009), pp. 47–58.

Johnston, H., 'Catherine of Aragon's Pomegranate, Revisited', *Transactions of the Cambridge Bibliographical Society*, 13 (2005), pp. 153–73.

Jones, A.R., and Stallybrass, P., *Renaissance Clothing and the Materials of Memory* (Cambridge, 2000).

Jones, M., and Underwood, M.G., *The King's Mother: Lady Margaret Beaufort Countess of Richmond and Derby* (Cambridge, 1992).

Keay, A., *The Crown Jewels: The Official Illustrated History* (London, 2012).

King, J.N., 'Queen Elizabeth I: Representations of the Virgin Queen', *Renaissance Quarterly*, 43 (1990), pp. 30–74.

Kingsford, C.L., *English Historical Literature in the Fifteenth Century* (Oxford, 1913).

Kisby, F., '"When the King Goeth a Procession": Chapel Ceremonies and Services, the Ritual Year, and Religious Reforms at the Early Tudor Court, 1485–1547', *Journal of British Studies*, 40 (2001), pp. 44–75.

Kleineke, H., and Steer, C. (eds), *The Yorkist Age* (Donington, 2013).

Kujawa-Holbrook, S.A., 'Katherine Parr and Reformed Religion', *Anglican and Episcopal History*, 72 (2003), pp. 55–78.

Labarge Wade, M., *Women in Medieval Life: A Small Sound of the Trumpet* (London, 1986).

Lachaud, F., 'Dress and Social Status in England Before the Sumptuary Laws', in Coss, P., and Keen, M. (eds), *Heraldry, Pageantry and Social Display in Medieval England* (Woodbridge, 2002), pp. 105–23.

Lambert, J.J., *Records of the Skinners of London: Edward I to James I* (London, 1933).

Lander, J.R., 'Marriage and Politics in the Fifteenth Century: The Nevilles and the Wydevilles', in *Crown and Nobility 1450–1509* (Montreal, 1976), pp. 94–126.

Landergren, U., (ed.), *The Treasury: The Regalia and Treasures of the Realm* (Stockholm, 2009).

Laynesmith, J.L., *Cecily Duchess of York* (London, 2017).

Laynesmith, J.L., 'Fertility Rite or Authority Ritual? The Queen's Coronation in England 1445–87', in Thornton, T. (ed.), *Social Attitudes and Political Structures in the Fifteenth Century* (Stroud, 2000), pp. 52–68.

Laynesmith, J.L., *The Last Medieval Queens* (Oxford, 2004).

Lee, P.A., 'Reflections of Power: Margaret of Anjou and the Dark Side of Queenship', *Renaissance Quarterly*, 39 (1986), pp. 183–217.

Levin, C., Barrett-Graves, D., and Eldridge Carney, J., (eds) *High and Mighty Queens of Early Modern England* (Basingstoke, 2003).

Levin, C., and Bucholz, R. (eds), *Queens and Power in Medieval and Early Modern England* (Lincoln NE, 2009).

Leyser, H., *Medieval Women: A Social History of Women in England 450–1500* (London, 1995).

Lightbown, R.W., *Mediaeval European Jewellery* (London, 1992).

Lipscomb, S., and Betteridge, T., (eds), *Henry VIII and the Court: Art, Politics and Performance* (Farnham, 2013).

Litten, J., 'The Funeral Effigy: Its Function and Purpose', in Harvey, A., and Mortimer, R. (eds), *The Funeral Effigies of Westminster Abbey* (Woodbridge, 1994), pp. 3–19.

Lloyd, C., *The Royal Collection* (London, 1992).

Loach, J., 'The Function of Ceremonial in the Reign of Henry VIII', *Past and Present*, (1994), pp. 43–68.

Logan, S., 'Margaret and the Ban: Resistances to Sovereign Authority in Henry VI 1, 2, & 3 and Richard III', in Logan, S. (ed.), *Shakespeare's Foreign Queens: Drama, Politics and the Enemy Within* (Basingstoke, 2018), pp. 209–60.

Longworth, P., 'Legitimacy and Myth in Central and Eastern Europe', in Kirschbaum, S.J. (ed.), *Historical Reflections on Central Europe: Selected Papers from the Fifth World Congress of Central and East European Studies* (Basingstoke, 1999), pp. 5–14.

Lutkin, J., 'Luxury and Display in Silver and Gold at the Court of Henry IV', in Clark, L. (ed.), *The Fifteenth Century IX* (2010), pp. 155–78.
Lynn, E., *Tudor Fashion* (London, 2017).
MacCulloch, D., *Reformation: Europe's House Divided 1490–1700* (London, 2003).
MacGibbon, D., *Elizabeth Woodville: A Life* (London, 1938).
Mack, P., 'Women and Gender in Early Modern England', *Journal of Modern History*, 73 (2001), pp. 379–92.
Mansfield, L., 'Portraits of Eleanor of Austria: From Invisible to Inimitable French Queen Consort', in Broomhall, S. (ed.), *Women and Power at the French Court, 1483–1563* (Amsterdam, 2018), pp. 173–205.
Mattingly, G., *Catherine of Aragon* (London, 1942).
Mattingly, G., *Renaissance Diplomacy* (London, 1955).
Maurer, H.E., *Margaret of Anjou: Queenship and Power in Late Medieval England* (Woodbridge, 2003).
McGlynn, S., and Woodacre, E., (eds), *The Image and Perception of Monarchy in Medieval and Early Modern Europe* (Cambridge, 2014).
Mears, K., *The Crown Jewels* (London, 1986).
Mears, N., 'Courts, Courtiers, and Culture in Tudor England', *Historical Journal*, 46 (2003), pp. 703–22.
Mellen, P., *Jean Clouet: Complete Edition of the Drawings, Miniatures and Paintings* (London, 1971).
Miller, E.H., 'New Year's Day Gift Books in the Sixteenth Century', *Studies in Bibliography*, 15 (1962), pp. 233–41.
Milliken, W.M., 'The Art of the Goldsmith', *Journal of Aesthetics and Art Criticism*, 6 (1948), pp. 311–22.
Mitchell, L.E., *Women in Medieval Western European Culture* (London, 1999).
Monter, W., *The Rise of Female Kings in Europe, 1300–1800* (New Haven and London, 2012).
Morgan, E., '"Lapis Orphanus" in the Imperial Crown', *Modern Language Review*, 58 (1963), pp. 210–14.
Mudan, K., '"So Mutable Is That Sexe": Queen Elizabeth Woodville in Polydore Vergil's *Anglica historia* and Sir Thomas More's *History of King Richard III*, in Oakley-Brown, L., and Wilkinson, L.J. (eds), *The Rituals and Rhetoric of Queenship: Medieval to Early Modern* (Dublin, 2009), pp. 104–17.
Mudan Finn, K., *The Last Plantagenet Consorts* (Basingstoke, 2012).
Mueller, J., 'Devotion as Difference: Intertextuality in Queen Katherine Parr's "Prayers or Meditations" (1545)', *HLQ*, 53 (1990), pp. 171–97.

Munby, L.M., *All My Worldly Goods: An Insight into Family Life from Wills and Inventories 1447–1742* (St Albans, 1991).

Munn, G.C., *The Triumph of Love: Jewelry 1530–1930* (London, 1993).

Myers, A.R., 'The Captivity of a Royal Witch: The Household Accounts of Queen Joan of Navarre, 1419–21', *BJRL*, 24 (1940), pp. 263–84.

Myers, A.R., 'The Household of Queen Elizabeth Woodville, 1466–7', *BJRL*, 50 (1967–8), pp. 207–15.

Myers, A.R., 'The Household of Queen Margaret of Anjou, 1452–3', *BJRL*, 50 (1957–8), pp. 79–113.

Myers, A.R., 'The Jewels of Queen Margaret of Anjou', *BJRL*, 42 (1959), pp. 113–31.

Nelson, J.L., 'Medieval Queenship', in Mitchell, L.E. (ed.), *Women in Medieval Western European Culture* (London, 1999), pp. 179–207.

Noppen, J.G., 'More Goldsmiths of the Time of Henry III', *BM*, 55 (1929), pp. 16, 21–4.

Nuttall, P., *From Flanders to Florence: The Impact of Netherlandish Painting, 1400–1500* (New Haven and London, 2004).

Okerlund, A., *Elizabeth: England's Slandered Queen* (Stroud, 2005).

Okerlund, A., *Elizabeth of York* (Basingstoke, 2009).

Parsons, J.C., *Eleanor of Castile: Queen and Society in Thirteenth-Century England* (London, 1995).

Parsons, J.C., 'Family, Sex and Power: The Rhythms of Medieval Queenship', in Parsons, J.C. (ed.), *Medieval Queenship* (Stroud, 1993), pp. 1–12.

Parsons, J.C., (ed.), *Medieval Queenship* (Stroud, 1993).

Parsons, J.C., ' "Never Was a Body Buried in England with Such Solemnity and Honour": The Burials and Posthumous Commemorations of English Queens to 1500', in Duggan, A. (ed.), *Queens and Queenship in Medieval Europe: Proceedings of a Conference Held at King's College London, April 1995* (Woodbridge, 1997), pp. 317–37.

Parsons, J.C., (ed.), *Medieval Queenship* (Stroud, 1993).

Phillips, C., 'Mothers, Daughters, Marriage, Power: Some Plantagenet Evidence, 1150–1500', in J.C. Parsons (ed.), *Medieval Queenship*, pp. 63–78.

Phillips, C., *Jewelry: From Antiquity to the Present* (London, 1996).

Phillips, C., *Jewels and Jewellery* (London, 2000).

Phipps Darr, A., 'Pietro Torrigiani and His Sculpture in Henrician England: Sources and Influences', in Sicca, C.M., and Waldman, L.A. (eds), *The Anglo-Florentine Renaissance: Art for the Early Tudors* (New Haven, 2012), pp. 49–80.

Piacenti, K., and Boardman, J., *Ancient and Modern Gems and Jewels in the Collection of Her Majesty the Queen* (London, 2008).

Pollard, A.F., 'New Year's Day and Leap Year in English History, *EHR*, 55 (1940), pp. 177–93.

Pollard, A.F., 'The Smethon Letter, St Penket and the Tablet of Gold', in Aston, M., and Horrox, R. (eds), *Much Heaving and Shoving: Late-Medieval Gentry and Their Concerns, Essays for Colin Richmond* (London, 2005), pp. 138–44.

Pope-Hennessy, J., *The Portrait in the Renaissance* (London, 1966).

Popham, A.E., 'Hans Holbein's Italian Contemporaries in England', *BM*, 84 (1944), pp. 12–17.

Porter, L., *Katherine the Queen: The Remarkable Life of Katherine Parr* (London, 2011).

Prince Michael of Greece, *Crown Jewels* (New York, 1983).

Proctor-Tiffany, M., *Portrait of a Medieval Patron: The Inventory and Gift Giving of Clemence of Hungary* (Providence, 2007).

Reddaway, T.F., *The Early History of The Goldsmiths' Company: 1327–1509* (London, 1975).

Reddaway, T.F., 'The London Goldsmiths Circa 1500', *Transactions of the Royal Historical Society*, 12 (1962), pp. 49–62.

Reynolds, A., *In Fine Style: The Art of Tudor and Stuart Fashion* (London, 2013).

Reynolds, G., *The Sixteenth and Seventeenth Century Miniatures in the Collection of Her Majesty the Queen* (London, 1999).

Rhodes, W.E., 'The Inventory of the Jewels and Wardrobe of Queen Isabella (1307–8)', *EHR*, 12 (1897), pp. 517–21.

Richards, J.M., 'Mary Tudor as 'Sole Quene?': Gendering Tudor Monarchy', *Historical Journal*, 40 (1997), pp. 895–924.

Richards, J.M., '"To Promote a Woman to Beare Rule": Talking of Queens in Mid-Tudor England', *Sixteenth Century Journal*, 28 (1997), pp. 101–21.

Richardson, G., '"As Presence Did Present Them": Personal Gift-giving at the Field of Cloth of Gold', in Lipscomb, S., and Betteridge, T. (eds), *Henry VIII and the Court* (Farnham, 2013), pp. 47–64.

Richardson, G., 'Entertainments for the French Ambassadors at the Court of Henry VIII', *Renaissance Studies*, 9 (1995), pp. 404–15.

Roberts, J., (ed.), *Treasures: The Royal Collection* (London, 2008).

Rose, T., *The Coronation Ceremony and the Crown Jewels* (London, 1992).

Rosenthal, J.T., *The Purchase of Paradise: Gift Giving and the Aristocracy, 1307–1485* (London, 1972).

Ross, C., *Edward IV* (London, 1974).

Rowlands, J., *Holbein: The Paintings of Hans Holbein the Younger* (Oxford, 1985).

Rowlands, J., and Starkey, D., 'An Old Tradition Reasserted: Holbein's Portrait of Queen Anne Boleyn', *BM*, 125 (1983), pp. 88–92.

Rush, S., 'French Fashion in Sixteenth-Century Scotland: The 1539 Inventory of James V's Wardrobe', *Furniture History*, 42 (2006), pp. 1–25.

Russell, G., *Young and Damned and Fair: The Life and Tragedy of Catherine Howard at the Court of Henry VIII* (London, 2017).

Sandford, F., *A Genealogical History of the Kings and Queens of England, and Monarchs of Great Britain, &c. from the Conquest, Anno 1066, to the Year 1677* (London, 1677).

Scarisbrick, D., 'Anne of Denmark's Jewellery Inventory', *Archaeologica*, CIX (1991), pp. 193–237.

Scarisbrick, D., *Diamond Jewelry: 700 Years of Glory and Glamour* (London, 2019).

Scarisbrick, D., *Historic Rings: Four Thousand Years of Craftsmanship* (Tokyo, 2004).

Scarisbrick, D., *Jewellery in Britain 1066–1837* (Norwich, 1994).

Scarisbrick, D., *Portrait Jewels: Opulence and Intimacy from the Medici to the Romanovs* (London, 2011).

Scarisbrick, D., *Rings: Jewelry of Power, Love and Loyalty* (London, 2007).

Scarisbrick, D., *Tudor and Jacobean Jewellery* (London, 1995).

Scarisbrick, D., and Henig, M., *Finger Rings* (Oxford, 2003).

Scarisbrick, D., Vachaudez, C., and Walgrave, J., (eds), *Brilliant Europe: Jewels from European Courts* (Brussels, 2007).

Schama, S., 'The Domestication of Majesty: Royal Family Portraiture, 1500–1850', *Journal of Interdisciplinary History*, 17 (1986), pp. 155–83.

Schaus, M.C., (ed.), *Women and Gender in Medieval Europe: An Encyclopedia* (London, 2006).

Schroder, T., *'A Marvel to Behold': Gold and Silver at the Court of Henry VIII* (Woodbridge, 2020).

Schroder, T., 'A Royal Tudor Rock-Crystal and Silver-Gilt Vase', *BM*, 137 (1995), pp. 356–66.

Scofield, C.L., *The Life and Reign of Edward the Fourth*, 2 vols (London, 1923).

Scott, J., 'Painting from life? Comments on the Date and Function of the Early Portraits of *Elizabeth Woodville* and *Elizabeth of York* in the Royal Collection', in Kleineke, H., and Steer, C. (eds), *The Yorkist Age* (Donington, 2013), pp. 18–26.

Scott, J., *The Royal Portrait: Image and Impact* (London, 2010).

Sharpe, K., *Selling the Tudor Monarchy: Authority and Image in Sixteenth-Century England* (London, 2009).

Shaw, W.A., 'The Early English School of Portraiture', *BM*, 65 (1934), pp. 171–84.

Shephard, R., 'Court Factions in Early Modern England', *Journal of Modern History*, 64 (1992), pp. 721–45.

Sicca, C.M., 'Pawns of International Finance and Politics: Florentine Sculptors at the Court of Henry VIII', *Renaissance Studies*, 20 (2006).

Sicca, C.M., and Waldman, L.A., (eds), *The Anglo-Florentine Renaissance: Art for the Early Tudors* (New Haven and London, 2012).

Silber, I.F., 'Gift-Giving in the Great Traditions: The Case of Donations to Monasteries in the Medieval West', *European Journal of Sociology*, 36 (1995), pp. 209–43.

Sinclair, A., (ed.), *The Beauchamp Pageant* (Donington, 2003).

Smith, J.A., 'The Earliest Queen-Making Rites', *Church History*, 66 (1997), pp. 18–35.

Somers Cocks, A., *An Introduction to Courtly Jewellery* (London, 1980).

Sowerby, T., and Hennings, J., (eds), *Practices of Diplomacy in the Early Modern World c. 1410–1800* (Abingdon, 2017).

Stafford, P., *Queens, Concubines and Dowagers: The King's Wife in the Early Middle Ages* (London, 1983).

Stafford, P., 'The Portrayal of Royal Women in England, Mid-Tenth to Mid-Twelfth Centuries', in Parsons, J.C. (ed.), *Medieval Queenship* (Stroud, 1993), pp. 143–67.

Stapleton, M.L., '"I of Old Contemptes Complayne": Margaret of Anjou and English Seneca, *Comparative Literature Studies*, 43 (2000), pp. 100–33.

Starkey, D., *Elizabeth* (London, 2000).

Starkey, D., 'Intimacy and Innovation: The Rise of the Privy Chamber, 1485–1547', in Starkey, D., Morgan, D.A.L., Murphy, J., Wright, P., Cuddy, N., and Sharpe, K. (eds), *The English Court: From the Wars of the Roses to the Civil War* (London and New York, 1987), pp. 71–118.

Starkey, D., *Six Wives: The Queens of Henry VIII* (London, 2004).

Steward, W.A., 'Goldsmiths' and Silversmiths' Work – Past and Present', *Journal of the Royal Society of Arts*, 81 (1933), pp. 865–76.

St John's College Quatercentenary Publication, *Collegium Divi Johannis Evangelistae, 1511–1911* (Cambridge, 1911).

Strickland, A., *Lives of the Queens of England* (London, 1842).

Strong, R., *And When Did You Last See Your Father? The Victorian Painter and British History* (London, 1978).

Strong, R., *Artists of the Tudor Court: The Portrait Miniature Rediscovered 1520–1620* (London, 1983).
Strong, R., *Coronation: A History of Kingship and the British Monarchy* (London, 2005).
Strong, R., 'Hans Eworth Reconsidered', *BM*, 108 (1966), pp. 222, 225–31, 233.
Strong, R., 'Holbein in England-I and II', *BM*, 83 (1967), pp. 276–81.
Strong, R., 'Holbein in England-III to IV', *BM*, 109 (1967), pp. 698–703.
Strong, R., *Lost Treasures of Britain* (London, 1990).
Strong, R., 'More Tudor Artists', *BM*, 108 (1966), pp. 83–5.
Strong, R., *The Culture of Elizabeth: Elizabethan Portraiture and Pageantry* (London, 1977).
Strong, R., *The English Renaissance Miniature* (London, 1983).
Strong, R., 'Three Royal Jewels: The Three Brothers, the Mirror of Great Britain and the Feather', *BM*, 108 (1966), pp. 350–3.
Strong, R., *Tudor and Jacobean Portraits*, 2 vols (London, 1969).
Sutton, A., and Visser-Fuchs, L., 'A *'Most Benevolent Queen'*: Queen Elizabeth Woodville's Reputation, Her Piety and Her Books', *The Ricardian*, 10 (1995), pp. 214–45.
Sydney, F., 'The Arms and Badges of the Wives of Henry VIII', *BM*, 41 (1922), pp. 108–10.
Tait, H., (ed.), *7000 Years of Jewellery* (London, 1986).
Tillander, H., *Diamond Cuts in Historic Jewellery 1381–1910* (London, 1995).
Tinagli, P., *Women in Italian Renaissance Art* (Manchester, 1997).
Tittler, R., *Portraits, Painters, and Publics in Provincial England, 1540–1640* (Oxford, 2012).
Travitsky, B., 'Reprinting Tudor History: The Case of Catherine of Aragon', *Renaissance Quarterly*, 50 (1997), pp. 164–74.
Twining, L., *A History of the Crown Jewels of Europe* (London, 1960).
Visser-Fuchs, L., 'English Events in Caspar Weinreich's Danzig Chronicle, 1461–1495', *The Ricardian*, 7 (1986).
Walker, G., 'Rethinking the Fall of Anne Boleyn', *Historical Journal*, 45 (2002), pp. 1–29.
Walsh, W.S., *Curiosities of Popular Customs and of Rites, Ceremonies, Observances, and Miscellaneous Antiquities* (London, 1898).
Wardropper, I., 'Between Art and Nature: Jewelry in the Renaissance', *Art Institute of Chicago Museum Studies*, xxv (2000), pp. 6–15, 104.
Warnicke, R.M., 'Anne Boleyn Revisited', *Historical Journal*, 34 (1991), pp. 953–4.
Warnicke, R.M., 'Anne Boleyn's Childhood and Adolescence', *Historical Journal*, 28 (1985), pp. 939–52.

Warnicke, R.M., *Elizabeth of York and Her Six Daughters-in-Law* (Basingstoke, 2017).

Warnicke, R.M., 'Henry VIII's Greeting of Anne of Cleves and Early Modern Court Protocol', *Albion*, 28 (1996), pp. 565–85.

Warnicke, R.M., 'Integrating Gender Analysis in Tudor Queenship Studies', *Sixteenth Century Journal*, 40 (2009), pp. 277–8.

Warnicke, R.M., 'Queenship: Politics and Gender in Tudor England', *History Compass*, 4 (2006), pp. 203–27.

Warnicke, R.M., 'The Eternal Triangle and Court Politics: Henry VIII: Anne Boleyn, and Sir Thomas Wyatt', *Albion*, 18 (1986), pp. 565–79.

Warnicke, R.M., 'The Fall of Anne Boleyn: A Reassessment', *History*, 70 (1985), pp. 1–15.

Warnicke, R.M., 'The Fall of Anne Boleyn Revisited', *EHR*, 108 (1993), pp. 653–65.

Warnicke, R.M., *The Marrying of Anne of Cleves: Royal Protocol in Tudor England* (Cambridge, 2004).

Warnicke, R.M., *The Rise and Fall of Anne Boleyn* (Cambridge, 1989).

Warnicke, R.M., *Wicked Women of Tudor England: Queens, Aristocrats, Commoners* (New York, 2012).

Weightman, C., *Margaret of York: The Diabolical Duchess* (Stroud, 2009).

Weir, A., *Elizabeth of York: The First Tudor Queen* (London, 2013).

Weiss, M., *Tudor and Stuart Portraits* (London, 2012).

Weissberger, B.F., *Isabel Rules: Constructing Queenship, Wielding Power* (London, 2004).

Welch, E., *Fashioning the Early Modern: Dress, Textiles, and Innovation in Europe 1500–1800* (Oxford, 2017).

Whinney, M., *Early Flemish Painting* (London, 1968).

Whitelock, A., *Mary Tudor: England's First Queen* (London, 2009).

Wild, B.L., 'A Gift Inventory from the Reign of Henry III', *EHR*, 125 (2010), pp. 529–69.

Wilkinson, J., *Katherine Howard: The Tragic Story of Henry VIII's Fifth Queen* (London, 2015).

Williams, M., and Echols, A., *Between Pit and Pedestal: Women in the Middle Ages* (Princeton, 1994).

Wilson, H.A., 'The English Coronation Orders', *Journal of Theological Studies*, 2 (1901), pp. 481–504.

Winter, C., 'Holbein's Miniatures', *BM*, 83 (1943), pp. 266–9.

Woodacre, E., 'Introduction', in Woodacre, E., and Fleiner, C. (eds), *Royal Mothers and Their Ruling Children: Wielding Political Authority from Antiquity to the Early Modern Era* (Basingstoke, 2015), pp. 1–7.

Woodacre, E., *Queens and Queenship* (Leeds, 2021).

Woodacre, E., (ed.), *Queenship in the Mediterranean: Negotiating the Role of the Queen in the Medieval and Early Modern Eras* (Basingstoke, 2016).

Woodacre, E., *The Queens Regnant of Navarre: Succession, Politics, and Partnership, 1274–1512* (Basingstoke, 2013).

Woodacre, E., and Fleiner, C., (eds), *Royal Mothers and Their Ruling Children: Wielding Political Authority from Antiquity to the Early Modern Era* (Basingstoke, 2015).

Woodacre, E., and Fleiner, C., (eds), *Virtuous or Villainess? The Image of the Royal Mother from the Early Medieval to the Early Modern Era* (Basingstoke, 2016).

Worsley, L., and Souden, D., *Hampton Court Palace: The Official Illustrated History* (London, 2005).

Wright, N.E., Ferguson, M.W., and Buck, A.R. (eds), *Women, Property, and the Letters of the Law in Early Modern England* (Toronto, 2004).

Younger Dickinson, J., *The Book of Diamonds: Their History and Romance from Ancient India to Modern Times* (London, 1965).

Zemon Davis, N., *The Gift in Sixteenth-Century France* (Oxford, 2000).

Zollner, F., *Michelangelo: The Complete Paintings, Sculptures and Arch* (Berlin, 2017).

VI. Unpublished PhD Theses

Barrett, E.G., 'Art and the Construction of Early Medieval Queenship: The Iconography of the Join Royal/Imperial Portrait and the Visual Representation of the Ruler's Consort', unpublished PhD thesis, Courtauld Institute of Art, University of London, 1997.

Beer, M.L., 'Practices and Performances of Queenship: Catherine of Aragon and Margaret Tudor, 1503–1533', unpublished PhD thesis, University of Illinois, 2014.

Benz, L., 'Queen Consort, Queen Mother: The Power and Authority of Fourteenth Century Plantagenet Queens', unpublished PhD thesis, University of York, 2009.

Chamberlayne, J., 'English Queenship 1445–1503', unpublished PhD thesis, University of York, 1999.

Hamilton, D.L., 'The Household of Queen Katherine Parr', unpublished PhD thesis, University of Oxford, 1992.

Harper, S.P., 'London and the Crown in the Reign of Henry VII', unpublished PhD thesis, University of London, 2015.

Hayward, M., 'The Possessions of Henry VIII: A Study of Inventories', unpublished PhD thesis, London School of Economics and Political Science, University of London, 1998.

Johnson, J.J., 'Elysabeth ye Quene: Understanding Representations of Elysabeth of York in the Tudor Period 1485–1603', unpublished PhD thesis, Queen Mary, University of London, 2010.

Kisby, F., 'The Royal Household Chapel in Early-Tudor London, 1485–1547', unpublished PhD thesis, Royal Holloway and Bedford New College, University of London, 1996.

Mayhew, M.J., 'Skewed Intimacies and Subcultural Identities: Anne Boleyn and the Expression of Fealty in a Social Media Forum', unpublished PhD thesis, London South Bank University, 2018.

Smith, J.A., 'Queen-making and Queenship in Early Medieval England and Francia', unpublished PhD thesis, University of York, 1993.

VII. Online Resources

British Museum, www.britishmuseum.org

Institute of Historical Research, 'Philippa of Hainault (1310/15–1369) and Richard II', https://archives.history.ac.uk/richardII/philippa.html

Royal Collection Trust, royalcollection.org.uk

The Oxford Dictionary of National Biography, www.oxforddnb.com

Victoria and Albert Museum, www.vam.ac.uk

Index

Note: page numbers in italic type refer to Figures; those in bold type refer to Tables.
The format and spelling of personal names follows the system set out in the Explanatory Notes on page xvii.

9781032065021